BORDERLINE JAPAN

This book offers a radical reinterpretation of postwar Japan's policies towards immigrants and foreign residents. Drawing on a wealth of historical material, Tessa Morris-Suzuki shows how the Cold War played a decisive role in shaping Japan's migration controls. She explores the little-known world of the thousands of Korean 'boat people' who entered Japan in the immediate postwar period, focuses attention on the US military service-people and their families and employees, and also takes readers behind the walls of Japan's notorious Ōmura Migrant Detention Centre, and into the lives of Koreans who opted to leave Japan in search of a better future in Communist North Korea. This book offers a fascinating contrast to traditional images of postwar Japan and sheds new light on the origins and the dilemmas of migration policy in twenty-first-century Japan.

TESSA MORRIS-SUZUKI is Professor of Japanese History at the Australian National University. She is a Fellow of the Australian Academy of the Humanities and a former president of the Asian Studies Association of Australia. Her research covers issues of historical conflict and reconciliation in Northeast Asia and her work has been translated into Japanese, Korean, Chinese, Spanish and Dutch. Her previous publications include *The Technological Transformation of Japan* (1994), *Reinventing Japan: Time, Space, Nation* (1998) and *Exodus to North Korea: Shadows from Japan's Cold War* (2007).

BORDERLINE JAPAN

*Foreigners and Frontier Controls
in the Postwar Era*

TESSA MORRIS-SUZUKI

CAMBRIDGE
UNIVERSITY PRESS

CAMBRIDGE UNIVERSITY PRESS
Cambridge, New York, Melbourne, Madrid, Cape Town,
Singapore, São Paulo, Delhi, Tokyo, Mexico City

Cambridge University Press
The Edinburgh Building, Cambridge CB2 8RU, UK

Published in the United States of America by Cambridge University Press, New York

www.cambridge.org
Information on this title: www.cambridge.org/9780521683104

© Tessa Morris-Suzuki 2010

First published 2010
First paperback edition 2011

A catalogue record for this publication is available from the British Library

ISBN 978-0-521-68310-4 Hardback
ISBN 978-0-521-86460-2 Paperback

The past, that ghostly traveler, is liable to forge his papers. We must be wary of the trap.

(Victor Hugo, Les Misérables)

Contents

List of illustrations   *page* viii
List of maps and figures   x
Acknowledgements   xi

1   Border politics: rethinking Japan's migration controls   1

2   Drawing the line: from empire to Cold War   28

3   Crossing the line: 'unauthorized arrivals' in
occupied Japan   52

4   Guarding the line: the Cold War and the Immigration
Bureau   90

5   Worlds apart I: the armed archipelago   123

6   Worlds apart II: the liminal space of Ōmura   147

7   Special permission to stay: 'hidden lives' in
postwar Japan   172

8   A point of no return: repatriation to China and
North Korea   194

9   Beyond the postwar system: what changed; what stayed
the same   229

References   252
Index   264

Illustrations

Image 2.1. Monument to wartime labour. The view across this
giant reservoir in Hokkaido, which was constructed
between 1939 and 1943 by thousands of workers,
including labour conscripts from Korea, is dominated
by a monument to the workers who 'gave their lives' to
the building of the dam (author's photograph).   *page* 40

Image 3.1. Korean repatriates about to embark, Senzaki, 1946.
(Photographer unknown. Reproduced courtesy of the
War History Collection, Alexander Turnbull Library,
Wellington, NZ, ref. no. J-0158.)   57

Image 3.2. Repatriation centre, Senzaki. A very disappointed
Korean. Artwork by Australian war artist Reginald
Rowed, 1946. The notes accompanying this picture state,
'Koreans are only allowed to retain 1000 yen before
being sent back to their homeland. This one has just
been relieved of a large sum and is a little upset. A New
Zealand soldier gently pushes him on his way.'
(Reproduced courtesy of the Australian War Memorial,
Canberra, ref. no. ART26738.)   66

Image 3.3. New Zealand soldiers apprehend Korean boat people,
1946. (Photographer unknown. Reproduced courtesy
of the War History Collection, Alexander Turnbull
Library, Wellington, NZ, ref. no. J-0433.)   70

Image 5.1. A Japanese clerk selects from the eight thousand records
held in the library of Iwakuni Military Base (c.1947–8).
(Photographer unknown. Reproduced courtesy of the
Australian War Memorial, Canberra, ref. no. JK 0013.)   129

Image 5.2. Practising bowling at Yokohama Engineering Depot, 1956. (Photographer Donald Albert (Tim) Meldrum; reproduced courtesy of the Australian War Memorial, Canberra, ref. no. MELJ1259.)   133

Image 6.1. Ōmura Detention Centre in the mid-1950s. (Reproduced courtesy of the International Committee of the Red Cross, Geneva, ref. no. v-p-kpkr-e-00002.)   155

Image 6.2. The women and children's section of Ōmura Detention Centre, mid-1950s. (Reproduced courtesy of the International Committee of the Red Cross, Geneva, ref. no. v-p-kpkr-e-00017.)   158

Image 6.3. ICRC representative Harry Angst distributes aid to Ōmura detainees, 1958. (Reproduced courtesy of the International Committee of the Red Cross, Geneva, ref. no. v-p-kpkr-n-00037.)   162

Image 6.4. Ōmura Immigration Reception Centre, 2005. (Author's photograph.)   165

Image 8.1. Inside the Red Cross Centre, Niigata: returnees to North Korea prepare their luggage for the journey. (Reproduced courtesy of the International Committee of the Red Cross, Geneva, ref. no. v-p-kpkr-n-00039.)   211

Image 8.2. The smiling face of repatriation: commemorative stamp issued by the DPRK in 1960 to celebrate the return of the Korean compatriots from Japan. (Author's collection.)   215

Maps and figures

Maps

Map 2.1. The MacArthur, Clark and Rhee Lines.   *page* 30

Map 2.2. Sources of Korean migration to Japan, 1937.
(The figures in each province show the estimated
number of Koreans in Japan originating from that
province. Source: Tsuboe Senji, *Zai-Nihon Chōsenjin
no Gaikyo* (Tokyo: Gannandō Shoten, 1965), p. 14.)   35

Figures

Figure 5.1. US troop deployments, Japan (including Okinawa)
1950–2005. (Source: Tim Kane, 'Global US Troop
Deployment, 1950–2003', http://www.heritage.org/
research/nationalsecurity/cda04–11.cfm. Note,
despite this document's title, Kane's data in fact
extend to 2005.)   125

Acknowledgements

Very many people have contributed to the making of this book – so many that I cannot possibly thank them all. However, special thanks are due to the interviewees who kindly agreed to share their remarkable stories with me, and to Jen Badstuebner, Hyun Moo-Am, Iyotani Toshio, Kang Sang-Jung, Amarjit Kaur, Koh Sun-Hui, Nishinaka Seiichirō, Shiobara Yoshikazu, Song Ahn-Jong, Yi Yang-Soo and Yoshimi Shunya. I also owe a large debt of gratitude to Fabrizio Bensi and Daniel Palmieri of the Archives of the International Committee of the Red Cross, Geneva; to Toshio Takagi of the Menzies Library, Australian National University; and to Shinozaki Mayumi of the National Library of Australia. Anthony Bright kindly assisted with map making, and Helen Gruber with preparing the manuscript for submission.

An earlier draft of a section of Chapter One was published in the Japan Center for Area Studies (JCAS) Symposium Series No. 22, *Motion in Place/Place in Motion* (ed. T. Iyotani and M. Ishii, 2005), and an earlier draft of a section of Chapter Four (in Japanese) in the journal *Zenya* (3, Spring 2005). My thanks go to JCAS and *Zenya*, and to the Australian Research Council for the grant which supported this research.

CHAPTER I

Border politics

Rethinking Japan's migration controls

THE CRIME OF MR KOH

One day in the summer of 1949, 'Mr Koh'[1] went back to his birthplace to look after his mother, who was critically ill. In November of the same year she died, and after the funeral, Mr Koh returned home to the small wooden house in a Japanese provincial town where he lived and worked. There, in his absence, his wife and children had been looking after the family second-hand goods business, supplementing its income in the summer months by making and selling ice creams.

This is a very ordinary story: one of those moments of crisis which besets the lives of most families at some time or another. But in this case, the seemingly ordinary train of events had extraordinary consequences: the arrest and imprisonment of Mr Koh. These events in turn generated a petition to the prefectural governor and a flurry of correspondence between Japanese officials and the General Headquarters of the Supreme Commander Allied Powers (GHQ/SCAP), the body responsible for the postwar occupation of Japan.

How is it that such normal human behaviour attracted so much bureaucratic intervention and displeasure? The problem was this: although Mr Koh and his wife had lived in Japan since the 1920s, both originally came from Korea, where other members of their family still lived, and (as we shall see), in the late 1940s and early 1950s there was no way in which Mr Koh, or the other 600,000 or so Koreans in Japan, could legally cross the border between Japan and Korea, even to visit a dying parent. Besides, in 1947 the Japanese government had introduced an Alien Registration Law which required 'foreigners' like Mr Koh and his family to carry registration cards at all times. Early attempts at registration had proved ineffective, and in January 1950 – while Mr Koh was trying to find a boat to take him back from Korea to Japan – a new registration had been conducted, and a new set of cards issued.

Even though Mr. Koh managed to slip back into Japan undetected, he had missed the deadline for re-registration; and without one of the new cards, he could now live only an outlaw existence in Japan. Hoping to resolve the problem, three days after his return, he presented himself to the local police station and tried to explain the special circumstances that had forced him to leave and re-enter Japan. His story, however, met with scant sympathy. The police chief seems to have suspected ulterior motives for the trip to Korea, and Mr Koh was promptly arrested for illegal entry to Japan and violation of the Alien Registration Law, crimes punishable by a sentence of up to two years' hard labour followed by deportation.

Mr Koh's story is not unique. Many other people suffered similar fates in Japan in the late 1940s and 1950s, and we shall encounter some of their stories later in this book. What is unusual is that the Koh family possessed a modicum of property (the authorities meticulously calculated their assets, including the ice cream-making machine, at 800,000 yen), and they also had a strong network of friends and neighbours in the Japanese country town where they lived. Mrs Koh and the couple's eldest son, who was studying at a university in Tokyo, embarked on an energetic campaign to have Mr Koh released from prison, and to secure his right to remain in Japan.

They succeeded in collecting supportive statements from members of their local community – the shoemaker, the watch-mender and the local postmaster – and gathered more than 1,800 signatures on a petition to the prefectural governor. Mr Koh's imprisonment therefore generated a substantial amount of documentation. The papers on the case in the GHQ/SCAP files run to over one hundred pages, and speak eloquently of the anguish of a man facing the probable loss of the business he had built up over twenty years, the break-up of his family and deportation to Korea – a country by then in the process of being torn apart by civil war. Reading them, I am reminded of a comment made by Peruvian economist Hernando de Soto in a different context: 'migrants do not so much break the law as the law breaks them'.[2]

Amongst the letters on the file are appeals from the eldest four of the family's five children: Mr Koh's nine-year-old daughter Keiko, for example, addressed herself to General Douglas MacArthur, Supreme Commander Allied Powers, in pencil as follows:

Your Highness,
    Please use your power as a General to send Father home. I pray to God that he will come home any day now. My mother and big brother can't sleep at night for worrying about Father. If Father is forced to return to Korea, I won't be able

to go to school any more. Do send him back to us quickly. It's lonely at home without Father. Please.

There were letters of testimony from the mayor (who assured the Allied occupation authorities that Mr Koh had no 'dangerous thoughts') and even from the prefectural governor himself. In his desperation, Mr Koh also tried to invoke help from much further afield. As he wrote in an appeal addressed to General Douglas MacArthur, sometime around the end of the war he had befriended a group of British prisoners of war, who had been working as forced labourers in a nearby Japanese coal mine. Apparently they had come to trust Mr Koh after realizing that, as a Korean, he was regarded with hostility by the Japanese police. In his letter, he painstakingly spells out their unfamiliar names and addresses: Mr C. R. Loveday from Norwich, Edward George Parnell from Mansfield, and a W. Jones, who has jokingly given his address as 'Tin Pan Alley, Blighty, England'. Attached to the letter is a little photo which one of the prisoners of war had left behind as a token of friendship – a faint and incongruous image of a young English couple gliding across a skating rink adorned with fairy lights.

'Upon their departure from this country', wrote Mr Koh to General MacArthur (who doubtless never read his letter)

they told us that they would never forget my friendship and were pleased to be of service to us whenever I met difficulties. I am now in a very difficult situation. I pray for assistance of these friends of mine who are now in Europe, far away from this jail, and I wish them to become petitioners for me.[3]

THE BALLOT BOX AND THE BORDER POST

Stories like that of Mr Koh impel me to write this book. For the disaster that overtook him vividly illustrates the impact which migration and border controls have on individual lives. His story is also just part of a much larger but little-known history of undocumented crossings of the border between Japan and its Asian neighbours in the postwar decades. Without understanding this history, it is impossible to understand the issues of migration in modern Japan.

This book is an attempt to explore the creation of Japan's contemporary migration and border control system, and to discover how it has affected both the destiny of individuals and the nature of Japanese society itself. I began this study as part of a collaborative project with my colleague Amarjit Kaur, looking at border controls in four countries: Malaysia,

Indonesia, Australia and Japan. At the time when we started our research, soon after the 9/11 attacks in the United States, border security was an issue of impassioned political debate in many parts of the world. In Australia, the Howard government was introducing what many saw as draconian policies to curtail the arrival of boat people on the nation's shores; Southeast Asian countries such as Malaysia, Thailand and the Philippines were moving to close the long-porous borders between their nations; and in Europe, the opening of frontiers between members of the European Union (EU) was accompanied by growing fears of an influx of non-European 'others'.

In some ways, Japan appeared the odd one out in the group of nations we had chosen to study – a nation with relatively little linguistic or ethnic diversity, and one which had long maintained tight controls on entry to the nation. Yet Japan was not immune from the waves of anxiety over border security that swept the world in the first decade of the twenty-first century. There, too, newspapers ran lurid headlines about illegal immigrants, people smugglers and so-called 'foreigner crime' (*gaikokujin hanzai*).

In framing our study, we deliberately chose to focus not on 'immigration policy', but rather on 'migration and border controls'. The distinction may seem small, but it is significant. Discussion of 'immigration policy' tends to direct the eye to the laws and statements of central governments, to nationwide statistics and to debates about the contribution or otherwise of migrants to national prosperity and power. As Iyotani Toshio has observed, studies of immigration policy often implicitly define their *raison d'être* in terms of their contribution to national policy making, and tend to view migrants as 'subjects in need of management'.[4] We were more interested in exploring what happens on the ground, when migrants (legal or otherwise) arrive at the frontier. Who inspects their papers, and decides to accept or reject them? How are illegal migrants treated once they are detected, and how do they respond to that treatment? To put it another way, we wanted to reverse the normal angle of vision described by Iyotani. Movement across the areas which were to be divided by the modern borders between Japan, Korea, China, Taiwan and Russia had continued for centuries before the borders themselves were drawn. Rather than asking what impact migrants have on the economy and society of the nation state, then, we tried to confront the question, what impact do nation states and national borders have on the people who move around?[5]

Thinking about these questions prompted a comparison between two very different places where individuals encounter the presence of the nation state: the ballot box and the border post. In most theories of modern democracy, the crucial encounter between the individual and the state takes place at the polling booth – in that all-important sanctum of democracy where citizens, having listened to the debates of the election campaign, cast their secret ballots for the candidates of their choice. For many people (a growing number), however, the crucial encounter with the state occurs not in the polling booth but at the border post: in that little booth at which one's right to cross the frontier is decided, or in the immigration offices where residence documents are issued, visas renewed and suspected 'illegal immigrants' investigated. Here, the relationship between individual and state is radically different from the relationship which is established in the polling booth.

Within the polling booth, the state and the individual are bound together, in theory at least, by a contract governed by rules set out in the constitution. The constitution promises the people the right to choose those who will govern them, and the people in turn agree to abide by the laws instituted by their rulers. Though the practice of democracy seldom fully accords with the contractual ideals set out in most constitutions, the ideal of the contract remains a powerful force in contemporary society.

At the border post or immigration office, however, the encounter is inverted. Here it is not the people who choose the government, but the state which chooses people – selecting those who will be allowed to enter its territory, and determining the terms of entry. This relationship is almost entirely non-contractual. Nation states generally have laws defining, in rather broad terms, which categories of people may or may not cross the border, but the way in which the laws are applied to each individual is determined by the officials on the spot. Even in the most democratic of societies, the power of these officials is generally arbitrary and almost absolute. There is no need for them to justify their decisions. The ways in which they exercise their power are not open to public scrutiny and can seldom be challenged. The circumstances of Cold War East Asia, as we shall see, meant that a particularly large proportion of border crossers in postwar Japan were governed by bureaucratic discretion rather than by clear laws. As a result, many found themselves in a situation where they had almost no legally enshrined rights of residence.

Robert Miles, writing in the British context, has shown how airports, which are 'sites of migration control and therefore of state power', provide an 'excellent opportunity to observe the practice and consequences of the institutional organization of social differentiation and exclusion'.[6] In the modern nation, encounters between migrants and the state take place not just at the physical boundaries of national territory, but also at a variety of specialized places which mark the presence of the 'frontiers within'. These places include refugee and repatriation camps and migrant detention centres. In the course of this research, I have found myself focusing on particular confined spaces in which the encounter between foreigners and the boundary-drawing power of the Japanese state was distilled: Senzaki and Hario repatriation camps in the late 1940s, Ōmura Migrant Detention Centre throughout the postwar decades, Niigata Red Cross Centre in the 1960s, and (in a different way) the US military bases scattered across Japanese soil. By looking closely at the architecture and daily life of these special points of contact, we can, I think, open up new ways of looking at the nature of cross-border movement.

Exploring the formation of Japan's modern border controls was, to me, eye-opening. Aspects of Japan which had been wholly invisible when I read national government reports and statistical overviews of migration suddenly came into view. To my particular surprise, I discovered that the story of the creation of Japan's modern migration controls had unexpected connections to my home country, Australia. The Australian National Archives in my home town, Canberra (which I visited for the first time in search of information on the Australian section of our comparative project), proved to be a mine of information on 'illegal entry to Japan'.

The material I found there forced me to rethink my image of immigration and the migrant experience in modern Japan, and especially to focus on a period of Japanese history which I had always assumed to be a hiatus in movement into and out of Japan – the period from Japan's surrender to the Allies in 1945 to the late 1970s. Far from being a blank in Japan's migration history, it soon became clear that this was a time of crucial (though often forgotten) cross-border movement. It was also the formative period in the creation of a migration control system that remains largely intact to the present day, and has had a profound effect on the nature of Japanese society for the past half-century and more.

The wealth of historical documents on this topic, which exist not only in Japanese archives but also in the United States, Korea, Australia and (as I later discovered) New Zealand, Switzerland and elsewhere, was a reminder of the international dimensions of border controls. Border politics are neither national nor international politics, but always both at once. Borders have two sides, and what happens at the frontier post is influenced by forces from both sides, though in some times and places the power on one side may be far greater than the power on the other. (Indeed, at times such as the postwar occupation of Japan and Korea, the same power may have primary control over events on both sides of the border.) Most importantly, borders are part of an international system, and that system has an important effect on the border controls imposed by individual nations. As Malcolm Anderson points out, 'there is no compelling reason why the state should be the sole arbiter of immigration, and some matters may be regulated by international organization'.7

The international dimensions of border politics are often obscured by the tendency of scholars to look at migration history from within the framework of the nation state. In the case of Japan, for example, many accounts of migration history treat Japan's policies towards border crossers as though they were almost entirely and autonomously determined by the Japanese state. As we shall see in the chapters that follow, however, these policies have been shaped by Japan's shifting political relations with its neighbours, and crucially by its postwar relationship with the United States. As we gain a clearer picture of the global forces which have helped to mould Japan's migration control system, so we can more clearly appreciate the need for future visions of migration to be created through negotiations and dialogues that cross national boundaries.

MIGRANTS AND NATIONAL BORDERS: THE MODERN DILEMMA

The concept of the nation assumes that clear distinguishing lines can be drawn between some people ('nationals') and others ('aliens'). The nation is static. It occupies a clearly bounded block of territory on the map; its people are a group whose origins and destinies lie firmly within those boundaries. But in this, from the very start, there was a paradox. For modern nations came into being as parts of a global system, and that system itself was created by human mobility – by the Renaissance voyages of exploration, and by the mass migrations which created that quintessential modern nation state, the United States of America.

Nation states, therefore, need both movement and stasis, both boundaries and boundary crossings. On the one hand, to compete successfully in the global system, nations need trade, diplomacy and the cross-border movement of labour. In economic terms, border crossers are a necessary resource: a source of new knowledge, international economic connections or cheap labour. But in political terms they are non-citizens – destabilizing the tidy boundaries of the national political community. For that reason, the rules and institutions created to guard borders and to distinguish 'nationals' from 'aliens' have become some of the most contentious aspects of state policy in the modern world.

This tension has become particularly fraught in recent decades, as globalization has increased cross-border flows of communication, ideas and people.[8] In a time of rapid technological change, nations contend to import workers with scarce skills, or those willing to perform the low-paid tasks which the state's own citizens find unattractive. The result is both an acceleration of migration flows and increasing differentiation between different groups of migrants.[9] Meanwhile, concerns over national security had begun to be reflected in heightened border control measures even before the 9/11 attacks,[10] and concerns over border security have been further intensified in the context of the 'global war on terror'.

Global population trends add a further twist to the story, and one that has particular importance for Japan. By the first decade of the twenty-first century, Japan had become the most rapidly ageing society in the world. A combination of high life expectancy, dramatically falling birth rates and a rise in the age of marriage meant that Japanese demographic growth dropped precipitously, and since 2006 the population appears to have entered a phase of decline.[11] Sober predictions suggested that the population of 127 million will shrink to about 100 million by 2050, and that by the end of the century it may be no more than 64 million. Some scholars project an even more alarming decline to around 46 million by 2100.[12]

The spectre of 'vanishing Japanese' prompted nationwide schemes like a 1992 Welcome Baby Campaign, and when these failed to yield results, policy makers increasingly turned to the idea of migration as a solution to a growing imbalance between the dwindling workforce and the burgeoning aged population. A far-reaching Vision of Japan in the Twenty-First Century, produced by a government-appointed think tank in 2000, called for the creation of a new immigration policy. The report's authors argued that

in order to adjust to globalization and to maintain Japan's vitality, it will be essential in the twenty-first century to create a general environment in which many foreigners can live normally and comfortably in Japan ... Increasing ethnic diversity has the potential to expand the scope of Japan's intellectual creativity and to raise the level of social dynamism and international competitiveness.[13]

Others have presented the argument in starker terms. The former head of the Tokyo Immigration Bureau (Nyūkoku Kanrikyoku), Sakanaka Hidenori (of whom more hereafter), published a book soon after his retirement in 2005, in which he presented a personal view on the challenges facing Japan. Dramatically entitled *A Migration Control War Diary* (Nyūkan Senki) Sakanaka's book depicts the nation as faced with the choice between becoming a weak, stagnant 'small Japan' with high taxes and a shrinking economy, or a vibrant 'big Japan' with a major role to play on the world stage. To achieve 'big Japan' status, he argues, the country needs dramatically to change its attitude to migration, opening its doors to an annual inflow of 500,000 immigrants a year. His utopian image of the 'big Japan' of 2050 envisages a total Japanese population of 120 million (little changed from today), but with an immigrant population of 20 million, ten times today's figure of registered foreign residents.[14]

The existing system, however, is deeply entrenched, and resistance to change remains profound. Many of Sakanaka's former colleagues appear wary of grand plans for an opening of borders. Recent official statements from the Immigration Bureau urge caution. They acknowledge that some changes to migration restrictions may be needed to address the problem of an ageing population, and recognize the need to 'develop an environment where foreign nationals can live comfortably'. But they also express alarm at the level of immigration which would be necessary to offset future population decline. It is, the Bureau insists, 'not appropriate to simply supplement the declining birthrate by accepting foreign nationals alone'.[15]

So the Bureau's response to current challenges has been a series of relatively minor changes to migration categories and procedures, all of which have left fundamentally intact a migration control system first established more than half a century ago. To understand how this system has become so enduring, and how it has influenced not simply levels of immigration, but even popular visions of Japanese national identity itself, we need to examine how the system was established. And to do this, we need first to take a closer look at some of the existing narratives of Japanese society and its encounters with immigrants.

THE 'CLOSED COUNTRY' NARRATIVE

One of the most influential of these narratives presents Japan's restrictive policy towards foreigners as a natural outcome of the nation's historical and cultural peculiarities. Japan, we are told, is an ethnically homogeneous country which, in the course of its history, experienced many centuries of closure to the outside world. Tight restrictions on migration in modern Japan, both pre-war and postwar, are seen as a natural extension of this history.

This perception of Japan as inherently hostile to migrants is one frequently evoked by the Japanese government itself. The Immigration Bureau's cautious attitude towards a loosening of migration controls, for example, is reinforced with an appeal to tradition and culture: 'If you trace back the history of Japanese society and give thought to the Japanese people's perception of society, culture and their sensitivity, it would not be realistic to suddenly introduce a large amount of foreign labour.'[16]

Others who take a more critical approach to Japan's migration policies also emphasize the central importance of culture in determining these policies. As one account puts it,

The Japanese have long believed themselves to be a pure race. This has extended to ideas of uniqueness and superiority. Certainly it is indisputable that they are a highly homogeneous people, in the order of 99 per cent. Foreigners on Japan's soil present a threat to that homogeneity, that purity, that self-assured superiority, that uniqueness … They represent, then, an interconnected mix of negatives – the outside, the unknown, the threatening, the disruptive, the impure. In short they are best avoided.[17]

Japan's systems of citizenship and migration control are sometimes seen as an inevitable outcome of this deep-rooted 'closed country' (*sakoku*) mind-set: 'Japanese nationality law is, first and foremost, a by-product of the *sakoku* mentality'; 'no other legislation more vividly embodies the *sakoku* mentality than the immigration and labour laws'.[18]

Criticisms of widespread xenophobia in Japanese society are well founded (though Japan is not unique in this respect, and the figure of '99 per cent' homogeneity raises profound questions about the measurement of homogeneity itself). There is also no denying that insularity and myths of ethnic homogeneity have helped to shape public and official attitudes to immigration. But the origins and impact of that xenophobia are complex. As Oguma Eiji has argued, the myth of Japanese homogeneity itself seems to have been less pervasive in the first half of the twentieth century, when Japanese efforts to construct a multiethnic empire in fact generated widespread debate about the role of migrants in Japanese history and pre-history.[19] In the 1930s and 1940s, the multiethnic origins of the Japanese were sometimes even vaunted as the source of Japanese national superiority.[20] It was in the immediate postwar decades that the notion of Japan as a self-contained, unique and ethnically 'pure' nation acquired its greatest power over the public imagination.

Most significantly, though, the framework of laws and institutions which restricts immigration to Japan today was actually created during the postwar Allied occupation of Japan in the mid-twentieth century. This framework, moreover, was not simply determined by the Japanese government, but was designed through close collaboration between the Allied occupation authorities (SCAP) and the Japanese state. In other words, it is very much part of what John Dower has called the 'SCAPanese model' of postwar democracy.[21] The new laws and institutions introduced in the wake of the Pacific War to strengthen the power of the ballot box went hand in hand with measures strengthening the discretionary power of the officials who manned the border posts. As we shall see, the new border control practices built on pre-war and wartime precedents, but for the first time coordinated the regionalized and often confused pre-war and wartime system into a single centralized national migration control system.

The restrictive policies introduced in the occupation period helped not only to keep out potential migrants, but also to obscure the presence of migrants who did enter the country. In this way, they contributed to the dominance of the myth of Japanese ethnic homogeneity. Meanwhile, the myth of homogeneity itself offered a useful ideological justification for immigration restrictions which were not always easily defensible on other political or moral grounds: a fact which helps to explain why it was so frequently reiterated in public statements on border controls and migration policy.

The 'closed country' narrative is a narrative of Japanese exceptionalism: it suggests that Japan's experience was fundamentally different from that of most 'normal' countries. The account I shall give in this book, by contrast, is not intended to mark Japan out as 'unique'. In a literal sense, of course, every country's past is by definition unique. Particular conjunctions of domestic and international events certainly shaped Japan's postwar migration. However, the main features of this history – undocumented migration despite relatively tight border controls, discretionary policies towards migrants, systemic discrimination towards certain ethnic minorities – can be found in one form or another in almost every corner of the world.[22] Some aspects of Japan's postwar experience (for example, the long-term detention of undocumented migrants in Ōmura) indeed foreshadowed phenomena which were to become increasingly widespread elsewhere as the century progressed. Rather than emphasizing uniqueness, I hope to show how the history of the borderline sheds new light on the nature of postwar Japanese society, and how the history of postwar Japan can shed new light on the twentieth- and twenty-first-century migrant experience.

THE 'TWO WAVES OF MIGRATION' NARRATIVE

The image of an inherently closed and homogeneous Japan has, to be sure, been widely challenged in the last few decades, and since the 1980s there has been a wealth of research and writing on immigration and ethnic minorities in Japan. The indigenous Ainu people of northern Japan, Okinawans and Korean and other foreign communities in Japan have all been the subject of many books and articles both in Japanese and in other languages.[23] Yet, while the mid-twentieth-century image of homogeneity has lost some of its power, it has often been replaced by an alternative narrative which also, I think, obscures some important aspects of Japan's past and present.

According to this narrative, Japan has a long history of immigration, but it is a history marked by radical discontinuity. In the modern era, migration is seen as occurring in two quite distinct waves. Prewar colonialism generated large-scale movements of people, including mass emigration of Japanese to other parts of Asia, and the forced and voluntary entry of Korean and other colonial subjects to Japan. As a result, there were over 2 million Koreans in Japan at the end of the Pacific War. Of these, however, almost three-quarters returned to Korea soon after the war, and their places in the Japanese workforce were filled by the repatriation of more than 6 million Japanese from all over the former empire, and by rural–urban migration within Japan itself.

Though some writers draw attention to the small outflow of Japanese (and particularly Okinawan) emigrants to Latin America, generally speaking postwar Japan is seen as characterized by its lack of international migration. Japan, it is repeatedly emphasized, achieved high economic growth in the postwar decades without immigration. It is therefore only since the 1980s that Japan has had to adapt once more to the unfamiliar phenomenon of inflows of foreign workers, with all the social and cultural challenges which these inflows entail.

Versions of this story form a refrain which runs through many accounts of migration and ethnic diversity in Japan. For example, migration researcher Kuwahara Yasuo writes, 'Until the beginning of the 1980s Japan had never considered itself to be a host to immigrants with the exception of the Korean and Chinese who were brought to Japan as forced labourers before and during the Second World War'.[24] In the same vein, Stephen Spencer notes the presence of 'Koreans and Chinese who were brought to Japan as forced labourers before and during World War II', but argues that, with this exception, 'up until the 1980s, comparatively few foreigners have actually gone to live and work in Japan'.[25]

Yamawaki Keizō has rightly criticized Spencer for ignoring the fact that Koreans and Chinese also migrated to Japan voluntarily in the 1920s and 1930s,[26] but even those who acknowledge the complexity of prewar immigration to Japan often imply that this inflow of people was quite distinct from the new, post-1980 inflow, and was separated from it by a hiatus during the 1950s and 1960s.[27] Mike Douglass and Glenda Roberts's otherwise excellent overview of migration in contemporary Japan, for example, states that 'Japan has had a number of waves of immigration over the past century', and divides this history into 'migration up to the early post Second World War years' and 'the 1970s and 1980s', leaving the 1950s and 1960s as the empty trough between the waves.[28] One of the very few works to refer to immigration in the immediate postwar decades is Komai Hiroshi's *Foreign Migrants in Contemporary Japan*, which states that, as a result of restrictive postwar migration controls, 'there was no large-scale influx of foreigners, including workers, into Japan until the late 1970s', but in passing qualifies this with the words 'the exception to this rule were an estimated 150,000 people who were smuggled into the country from the Korean Peninsula, as well as a significant number of foreign workers who entered the country in the late 1960s under the pretext of training'.[29] The most vivid and detailed accounts of the postwar migrant experience, in fact, come not from general analyses of migration to Japan but from the personal accounts and fictionalized writings of Koreans in Japan, including the literary works of well-known novelists such as Kim Seok-Beom and Yi Hoe-Seong.[30]

Part of the problem lies in the vexed issue of the terminology that surrounds any debate about migration in Japan. One difficulty is the fact that debates about 'migrants', 'migrant workers' and 'foreign residents' in Japan often become inextricably intertwined, so that the categories often elide into one another. But in fact the seemingly self-explanatory terms beg many questions, for those who (in Spencer's words) 'go to live and work in Japan' include many who do not fit the generally accepted notion of a 'migrant worker'.[31] Which 'foreigners in Japan' are 'migrants'? Which 'migrants' are 'migrant workers'? To add to the complexity, the Japanese word *imin*, which is generally translated as 'migrant', has distinctive nuances: it suggests a conscious decision to settle permanently in a foreign country. For this reason, Japanese writings on recent arrivals in Japan tend to use the term *zainichi gaikokujin* ('foreigners living in Japan') or *gaikokujin rōdōsha* ('foreign workers'), rather than *imin rōdōsha* (migrant workers). The problem of language helps to explain much-quoted cases where Japanese officials have denied to foreigners that Japan has any immigrants at all.[32] All of these considerations become important when we look at cross-border movement in the neglected decades from 1945 to the late 1970s.

COLD WAR AND UNCOUNTED FOREIGNERS I

In this book I shall argue that the Cold War order had a profound effect on the nature of borders and border controls in Northeast Asia. It resulted not only in the creation of almost impassable barriers between 'communist' and 'capitalist' spheres, but also in the barricading of boundaries between the nations within both spheres, including the creation of tightly controlled borders between Japan and South Korea and between Okinawa and Taiwan. As a result, from the late 1940s to the 1970s the region came to be divided by a maze of fissures which hampered human movement and interaction between one nation state and the next. The consequences of this fragmentation for social interaction between the countries of Northeast Asia continue to be felt to the present day.

But the Cold War also stimulated waves of cross-border movement which have generally been neglected in writings on the history of foreign communities in Japan. In particular, it helped create two important groups of foreigners whose presence (for very different reasons) was never recorded in Japan's official figures for 'foreign residents'. Placing these two categories of 'uncounted' foreign entrants back into the picture forces us to revise commonly held perceptions of Japanese history.

The first and most visible group were the Allied military forces themselves. At the start of the occupation some 430,000 US troops arrived in Japan, and in the spring of 1946 they were supplemented by troops of the British Commonwealth Occupation Force (BCOF), whose numbers at their peak exceeded 40,000. As it quickly became obvious that the Allied occupation would encounter no armed resistance in Japan, the size of the US force was cut, but the outbreak of the Korean War led to a renewed boost in numbers.[33] Amidst the rapidly rising tensions of the Cold War, Japanese security came to be seen as crucial to the defence of Asia from communism and, under the US–Japan Security Treaty signed in 1951, large numbers of US troops remained stationed in Japan after the end of the occupation.

In the early part of the occupation (as we shall see) US and British Commonwealth troops played a direct and central part in controlling Japan's borders and apprehending undocumented migrants. These powers were gradually transferred to a newly created Japanese immigration service. However, the system created during the occupation exempted Allied troops and their civilian employees themselves from the Japanese state's immigration procedures. After the end of the occupation, too, the quarter of a million or more US service-people and foreign civilian employees who remained on military bases throughout Japan were excluded from Japanese migration control procedures such as the process of obtaining the alien registration cards which other foreigners in Japan were required to carry. As a result, they were never included in Japanese government statistics of 'foreign residents' – a situation that continues to the present day.

The US bases in Japan therefore constituted an archipelago of spaces in, but not of, Japan. Like the foreign concessions of the nineteenth century, they were beyond the reach of Japanese law. Yet their presence had a huge influence on postwar Japanese culture, and particularly on the culture of the communities which adjoined the bases. Just as nineteenth-century Yokohama was irrevocably shaped by the architecture, dress, food and habits of Western and Chinese merchants, so the culture of base towns such as Yokosuka, Sunagawa, Iwakuni and a host of other Japanese cities was permeated by big-band jazz, the PX packaged foods and the second-hand uniforms that filtered out from the bases in their midst. As Yoshimi Shunya points out, the character of areas like the Tokyo district of Roppongi is even today powerfully coloured by the lingering impact of the long-vanished US base which once stood at its centre.[34]

Because the inhabitants of the military bases were neither migrants (in the normal sense of the word) nor counted in the figures of foreign residents, their presence often disappears from accounts of cross-border migration in Japanese history. While the inhabitants of the nineteenth-century foreign settlements generally at least rate a mention in histories of foreigners in Japan, the inhabitants of US bases tend to appear fleetingly if at all.

This silence can be very misleading. If, for example, we take the official figures of 'registered foreign residents' at face value, as a literal representation of the number of foreigners in Japan, it seems as though the size of the foreign community more than doubled between 1955 and 1995.[35] But in fact, the growth of other foreign communities coincided with a reduction in the size of the US military presence, particularly on the islands of Honshu and Kyushu, so trends in the actual foreign presence in Japan are more complex than these figures suggest. In Chapter Five, we will see how these 'uncounted foreigners' occupied a landscape whose borders were governed by a quite distinctive set of border controls. We will also consider some of the ways in which their presence shaped the culture and identity of postwar Japan.

A second important group of foreigners in postwar Japan – also excluded from the statistics and therefore often forgotten – were undocumented migrants: mostly people who arrived without passports or papers on small boats from Korea, and who lived in Japan without registering their presence. Undocumented migrants are, by their very nature, often invisible to the official eye. They are also therefore often invisible to academic researchers who, all too readily, rely on official records in interpreting the events of the past and present. In the Japanese case particularly, trust in the 'official version' is encouraged by the presence of a powerful bureaucracy with a penchant for producing reports adorned with impressive-looking statistical charts and tables. The seemingly precise figures presented in these reports obscure a fact which is worth emphasizing: at no time in Japan's modern history has the Japanese government ever possessed a precise figure for the number of foreigners living in Japan.

It is impossible to tell how many people crossed the borders between Japan and neighbouring countries without official permission between the end of the war and the 1980s, though the numbers (as we shall see) were certainly in the tens of thousands, and are likely to have been in the hundreds of thousands. Among these were many people like Mr Koh, who had in fact already lived in Japan for decades, and crossed back and forth 'illegally' to visit family. But there was also a wide range of other undocumented entrants. Many were people fleeing the Korean War or the political turmoil and repression that characterized Cold War Korea. Others came in search of work or educational opportunities, or to rejoin family members who had migrated to Japan in earlier decades. Often the motives for becoming a 'stowaway' were multiple and mixed.

In global terms, and in relation to the size of the Japanese population, these were not very large migratory flows. Existing accounts are right in suggesting that immigration did not have a noticeable impact on Japanese economic growth in the 'miracle' decades of the 1950s and 1960s, though it did have a significant effect on the development of particular industries in particular localities. Cross-border flows in the postwar decades are nonetheless important for several reasons.

First, the lives of tens of thousands of people were transformed in complex ways by the experience of migration. Second, the immigration and border-control systems which exist in present day Japan have been shaped by experiences of, and responses to, immigration in the late 1940s, 1950s and 1960s. These systems, created to stem the subversive effects of an inflow of migrants, have had lasting effects on Japan's relations with its nearest Asian neighbours. By restricting legal entry and forcing most border crossers to become 'illegal migrants', strict border controls reinforced the social isolation of Japan from other countries of the East Asian region: an isolation which continues to have repercussions for Japan's place in the region today. Third, those undocumented entrants who were detected and arrested were incarcerated in Ōmura Detention Centre, near Nagasaki: a place which (as we shall see in Chapter Six) became both a potent symbol of the discrimination and divisions which beset the Korean community in Japan during the Cold War years, and a source of ongoing friction between the Japanese and South Korean governments.

The problems of undocumented migration and Ōmura were also related to a significant mass emigration from Japan which, until recently, has seldom been mentioned in accounts of migration to and from Japan. This was the mass relocation of some 87,000 Korean residents, together with over 6,000 Japanese spouses and dependents, from Japan to North Korea between the end of the 1950s and 1984. The history of this migration was for long relatively neglected even in Japan itself, and it is only recently, as growing numbers of these migrants and their descendants have attempted to escape from North Korea and return to Japan, that the memory of their story has begun to attract greater public attention.[36] In Chapter Eight we shall see how this cross-border movement, too, was a product both of Japan's postwar border control system and of the complex international politics of the Cold War era.

THE POWER AND THE PERILS OF CLASSIFICATION

Like other forms of politics, the politics of the border have changed over time. Despite much recent debate about 'migrants' rights', though, the main change over the past century or so has not been a 'democratizing' of border controls. The power relationship between state and migrant seems to remain as unequal as ever. Rather, particularly from the middle of the twentieth century onward, the main development has been the emergence of an increasingly complex multiplicity of categories which sift border crossers into hierarchies of different groups, each with its own distinct sets of rights determined by visa status: business migrants, tourists, those on student visas, guest workers, refugees and so on. These categories, in turn, come to assume a life of their own. We begin to take them for granted, and as they become part of the accepted vocabulary of public debate, they frame the way in which migrants themselves are perceived. The 'business migrant', for example, tends to be seen purely as a source of investment and entrepreneurship, the 'guest worker' merely as a labouring body, not as a person with family ties, political beliefs, enthusiasms for music or movies or sports and so on.

While creating and refining these hierarchies of migrant groups, most governments nonetheless also carefully preserve the realms of bureaucratic discretion: the right to make exceptions to their own regulations. Critic of democracy Carl Schmitt once famously observed that the essence of political power lies in the ability to make exceptions to the rule: 'the sovereign is whoever decides what constitutes an exception'.[37] If this is so, immigration and border control are surely the areas of government action where sovereign power is most conspicuously on display, and (as we shall see) this is nowhere more true than in the treatment of undocumented migrants.

The fundamental shift which occurred in the 1980s was not that, after a hiatus of some forty years, Japan once again began to be a host to immigrants. Migration levels may have risen in the 'economic bubble' years from the late 1970s onwards, but (largely undocumented) immigration at some level had been occurring ever since the occupation period. Rather, the key change in the 1980s was that the government began to develop new policies to recognize, regularize and control immigrants. The status of Korean residents in Japan became clearer and more stable; the Japanese government ratified the International Convention on the Status of Refugees, and started to accept asylum seekers (though only in extremely small numbers); new provisions were created to allow the entry of the descendants of Japanese emigrants to Brazil, Peru and elsewhere.

The greater public acknowledgement of cross-border flows in the 1980s, and the changes of terminology which accompanied the shift in official attitudes, made it easier for the state to acknowledge and document the presence of foreign residents, and easier for migration researchers to fit events in Japan into a 'globally standardized' set of notions about immigration, in fact mostly derived from the European and US experience. To put it in rather stark terms, then, we might say that, rather than the onset of immigration in the 1980s posing challenges to the policies of the Japanese government, it was a shift in government policies which made the already existing inflow of immigrants a little more visible.

This shift in perspective clarifies two points. On the one hand, classification helped erase postwar undocumented border crossers from public consciousness. On the other, a closer examination of the experiences of postwar undocumented migrants in Japan forces us to look critically at the present-day labels which we often so easily and unthinkingly apply to the migrant experience.

Every migrant's story is unique; every border crossing is different from all others. In this sense, there is not one history of undocumented migration in postwar Japan, but tens of thousands of histories. The story of 'Pak Young-Sik', however, may serve to illustrate some of the problems which emerge from efforts to name, classify and reconstruct the story of journeys across borders between Japan and its neighbours in the postwar decades, and to comprehend the response of the state to those journeys.

Pak Young-Sik was fourteen when he was arrested on a tiny islet just off the coast of Tsushima, the Japanese island nearest to Korea, on 26 June 1951. With a small group of other people, he had left the Korean port of Busan in a small fishing craft on 13 June, and had been hiding on the islet for several days. According to the local newspaper, which obtained its account from the police, Pak Young-Sik had been born in Osaka and lived there until the age of six. During the Pacific War, however, he had accompanied his mother when she returned to Korea, leaving an elder brother, who was sixteen years older than Young-Sik, behind in Osaka. Mother and son settled in Seoul, where Young-Sik completed his primary education and entered junior high school just before the outbreak of the Korean War.

However, according to the Japanese newspaper account, 'he left junior high school after two years, and the following year he fled the wartime destruction of Keijo [Seoul] for Pusan [Busan]'. Reading the words of this terse account, I find myself remembering the pictures of Seoul in the Korean War that I have seen in history books and documentary films: the massive death and destruction wrought by the unexpected forward surge of the North Korean army, the long columns of refugees clogging the roads south. Presumably Pak Young-Sik and his mother were in one of those columns. Once in Busan, Pak told the police, he started work in a cotton-spinning factory but, keen to complete his education, also attended night school after work.

Soon after, however, his mother died, in circumstances which the newspaper article does not explain. With war still continuing in Korea, Pak Young-Sik turned to an uncle for help, and the uncle advised him to go and live with his elder brother in Osaka, where it was hoped that he might be able to re-enter school full time. The uncle lent him 120,000 won, of which 80,000 won was paid to a 'people smuggler' for a place on the boat to Tsushima.[38] At this point the story ends. I know nothing else about Pak Young-Sik, but it seems most likely that (like almost all others in his situation), after being arrested and questioned he was sent to the newly established Ōmura Migrant Detention Centre near Nagasaki, detained there and later deported back to Korea. If he is still alive today (as he may well be) he would be in his late sixties; and – as with all such unfinished stories – I wonder about the life he lived and the person he became.

Pak Young-Sik's story illustrates the dilemmas raised by efforts to write about undocumented migration. Some of these dilemmas concern the nature of the historical record, an issue which I shall turn to later. Here, however, I want to focus on the question of the language we use to describe people who cross borders. Scholars of migration tend to follow the lead of governments and bureaucracies in adopting increasingly intricate hierarchies of status into which migrants are categorized. But the stories of Pak Young-Sik, and of very many others, refuse to slot neatly into one of the accepted categories. Was he a 'refugee' fleeing war? Was he coming to Japan for 'family reunion' purposes? Was he an 'educational migrant', expecting to return to his own country after he had completed study in Japan? Or was he a potential 'migrant labourer' who would in fact (if he had evaded the Japanese police) have ended up in a low-paid job in some Osaka factory? Most probably, he was all these things. Like most undocumented migrants, his decision to make the hazardous journey to Japan can surely not be understood simply in terms of a singular motivation such as 'economic rationality', 'family ties' or 'a justified fear of persecution'. Rather, it was the product of many circumstances, and was almost certainly also the product of much anxious weighing of the pros and cons.

In a society with a more clearly defined immigration policy, creating a hierarchy of distinct gateways for entry, Pak Young-Sik might have chosen to tell his story in a different way, focusing on one aspect alone (his desire to study in Japan, or his experiences during the Korean War, for example) in order to fit his life to the categories of migration defined by the state. But in 1951 the new law governing entry to Japan, which was just being put in place when Young-Sik made his perilous journey to Japan, was characterized by a curious disjuncture from reality. As we shall see in Chapter Four, this consigned almost all the groups of people most likely to seek entry to the country to the undifferentiated ranks of 'illegal entrants' (*fuhō nyūkokusha*) or 'stowaways' (*mikkōsha*).

Because of this blanket official denial of the migrant experience, the only way for historians to reconstruct the story of postwar immigrants is by sifting through the surviving fragmentary stories of people like Mr Koh and Pak Young-Sik. And this process itself forces us to confront the way in which the individual stories always overflow the limits of the simple categories into which migration policy sorts border crossers.

AN UNFINISHED JOURNEY

This book, then, is a preliminary step towards re-examining the history of the border control system and unearthing forgotten aspects of the migrant experience in postwar Japan. It is, inevitably, an incomplete and fragmentary account. Any effort to reconstruct this story is limited by the nature of the historical record itself. The official documents which I have explored offer fleeting and often tantalizing glimpses of the processes by which Japan's postwar border control systems were created. At some points, the decisions of particular officials or committees are recorded in some detail. Official memos, or (even more importantly) the pencilled jottings between the lines of memos offer sudden insights into the ideas which shaped the structures of border politics. But often the documentation simply ceases, leaving the historian to speculate on the actions which filled those long official silences.

The difficulty of reconstructing the migrants' experience of border politics is even greater. Only very rarely can one find accounts written by migrants themselves long after the event.[39] The great majority of the evidence left in the written record comes from the authorities who arrested or questioned 'stowaways', or from journalists who obtained their information from the same authorities. Such evidence is fragmentary and heavily shaped by the interests and biases of the police and other border control authorities. At times, indeed, it is coloured by the disturbingly palpable emotions of fear and racism which the authorities and the media directed at 'stowaways'. Meanwhile, undocumented migrants themselves, if arrested and questioned, were obviously eager to present their stories in a way which they hoped might arouse the sympathy of listeners, and even possibly win them the opportunity to stay in Japan. There is therefore no reason to assume that they offered 'the whole truth and nothing but the truth' to their questioners.

Most of the historical evidence is generated from the vastly unequal encounter between border crossers and state officialdom. And a further unequal power relationship comes into play when the historian enters the picture. The relationship between the stories obtained by officials from border crossers, and the historian who treats the stories as 'raw material' from which to construct a scholarly analysis of the past, is itself inevitably complex and difficult. Sitting in air-conditioned libraries and archives, I suddenly find myself, as it were, looking over the shoulder of police officers, immigration officials or government censors as they probe the lives of 'illegal immigrants'. Quite often, the desperation of the people they were observing shines through even the most dry and bureaucratic prose. Here are people fleeing war and torture, people longing to be reunited with their parents or children, people who see poverty and hopelessness all around them and are determined that they and their families are going to find the path to a better future.

The records contain personal details that were divulged unwillingly, information obtained from people without their knowledge or consent. In the files of the Allied occupation censors I find an intercepted letter, apparently written by a Japanese woman to her Korean partner who had fled the house just hours before the police arrived to arrest him. 'It is hopeless this time', she writes.

Your sword and straw sandals have been found by the authorities; they know I have burnt the trousers and other articles. They have searched our house for the evidence … We cannot live together any longer. So I want you to go back to your native country by all means … For your safety, you should not write to me for the time being, until I contact you, or you take a ship at Nagasaki for your country. Once again, I pray you will go back there as quickly as possible.

An anonymous official censor has read and translated the letter before resealing it and sending it on to its destination, knowing that it would help to lure the recipient into the hands of the police. Elsewhere, a man writes to his wife in Korea, 'My dear darling, after I parted from you on 20 Jul 49, I arrived safely in Japan a few days ago.' This letter has also been intercepted, the name and address of the sender recorded, and its message of affection neatly labeled 'Travel: Illegal Entry of Korean into Japan Revealed'.

I cannot be an impartial observer, viewing these pasts with the godlike omniscience of the twenty-first century. The past recorded here still echoes in the present day, resonating with the experiences of those arrested at the borders of the US, the EU, Australia and Japan, and of those interned in detention centres without prospect of release, even as I write.

Sometimes I am uncertain which material should or should not be used. How should I balance the dangers of intruding on the privacy of people

I shall never meet – people who may or may not still be alive – against hope of rescuing a part of history from oblivion, the hope of casting a little new light on the system of borders which still shapes the lives of so many people? How can I avoid a naive and absolute identification with the stories of the border crossers, while respecting their human integrity and acknowledging the reality of their pain? How best to convey the quality of that pain without presenting the border crosser merely as the passive victim of circumstances?

The same difficulties beset the use of interview data. In the course of this research I have had the privilege of talking to a small number of people who are willing to share their memories of life in Japan as an undocumented migrant. Listening to hours of recorded material in which these border crossers describe their extraordinary lives, the task of picking out a few sentences for quotation seems almost impossible. How can I select without distorting or even doing violence to these complex personal narratives?

There are no simple answers to any of these questions. My only answer has been to try to feel my way cautiously through the stories as I have encountered them. In deciding which material to quote and which to leave private, I have sought to ensure that I quote nothing that is likely to cause damage to undocumented migrants who may be still living, or to their families. I have also tried to look at material written from as many different perspectives as possible: police records, censored letters, petitions from arrested 'illegal migrants' seeking release, literary and oral accounts written by those who have been undocumented migrants. From these I have attempted to piece together some broad patterns in the migrant experience, while still attending as far as possible to the uniqueness of each story.

At the same time, I am also interested in trying to explore the feelings and experiences of those on the other side of the story: the police, immigration officials, detention centre guards and others who play such a central role in the implementation of border politics. It would be dishonest to imagine that this story could be told with moral and ideological detachment – without any sense of sadness at the pain that people inflict on each other, or any sense of anger at the political actions taken by specific officials, advisers and others. At the same time, this is a story in which the actions of individuals do not take place in a vacuum, but always both shape and are shaped by pre-existing institutions and power systems. Exploring the endless interplay between personal action and the historical world in which each person acts can, I hope, provide some insights into the ways in which personal and social action may shape migration policies and border controls in the present day.

NOTES

1. Except where otherwise stated, the names of undocumented migrants given in this book (including those of the Koh family) are pseudonyms. Since the people concerned may still be alive and may not wish their stories to be widely publicized, I use real names only where those concerned have given express permission for their names to be used, or have chosen to publish an account of their story under their own name. When quoting from government records or newspaper reports in which the original source gave the migrant's real name, I have replaced this with a pseudonym.
2. H. do Soto, *The Mystery of Capital: Why Capitalism Triumphs in the West and Fails Everywhere Else* (London: Black Swan Books, 2000), p. 23.
3. The story of 'Mr Koh' is derived from documents of GHQ/SCAP Civil Affairs Section C, 'Petition for Release', Microfiche CAS (C) – 01670–01671, held in the National Diet Library, Tokyo. I have revised the translations provided by the GHQ/SCAP translators.
4. T. Iyotani, 'Migration as Method', in T. Iyotani and M. Ishii, *Motion in Place/Place in Motion: 21st Century Migration* (Osaka: Japan Center for Area Studies/National Museum of Ethnography, 2005) pp. 3–16, quotation from p. 4.
5. See J. Scott, 'The State and People Who Move Around: How Valleys Make the Hills in Southeast Asia' (IIAS Annual Lecture 1998), *IIAS Newsletter*, 19 (1999), www.iias.nl/iiasn/19/general/1.html (accessed 15 January 2008).
6. R. Miles, 'Analysing the Political Economy of Migration: The Airport as an "Effective" Institution of Control', in A. Brah, M. J. Hickman and M. Mac an Ghaill (eds.), *Global Futures: Migration, Environment and Globalization* (London: Macmillan, 1999), pp. 161–84, quotations from pp. 161–2.
7. M. Anderson, *Frontiers: Territory and State Formation in the Modern World* (Cambridge: Polity Press, 1996), p. 128.
8. See A. Appadurai, 'Disjuncture and Difference in the Global Cultural Economy', in M. Featherstone (ed.), *Global Culture: Nationalism, Globalization and Modernity* (London: Sage, 1990), pp. 295–310.
9. S. Castles and M. J. Miller, *The Age of Migration: International Population Movements in the Modern World* (Basingstoke: Macmillan, 1998).
10. See, for example, M. Anderson and E. Bort (eds.), *The Frontiers of Europe* (London: Pinter, 1998).
11. M. Rebich and A. Takenaka, 'Introduction: The Changing Japanese Family', in M. Rebich and A. Takenaka (eds.), *The Changing Japanese Family* (London: Routledge, 2006), pp. 3–16, citation from p. 3.
12. L. MacKellar, T. Ermolieva, D. Horlacher and L. Mayhew, *The Economic Impacts of Population Ageing in Japan* (Cheltenham: Edward Elgar, 2004), p. 39.

13. '21-Seiki Nihon no Kōsō' Kondankai, *Nihon no Furontia wa Nihon no Naka ni aru,* (Tokyo: 21-Seiki Nihon no Kōsō Kondankai, 2000), www.kantei. go.jp/jp/21century/houkokusyo/1s.html (accessed 1 September 2001).
14. Sakanaka Hidenori, *Nyūkan Senki: 'Zainichi' Sabetsu, 'Nikkeijin' Mondai, Gaikokujin Sabetsu to Nihon no Kinmirai* (Tokyo: Kōdansha, 2005), chs. 9 and 10.
15. Immigration Bureau of Japan, *Basic Plan for Immigration Control,* 3rd edition, 2005, section 3, Tokyo, Ministry of Justice, www.moj.go.jp/ENGLISH/ information/bpic3rd-03.html#3–1 (accessed 30 November 2007).
16. Immigration Control Bureau, Ministry of Justice, Japan, *Basic Plan for Immigration Control,* 2nd edition, 2000, www.moj.go.jp/ENGLISH/ information/bpic2nd-01.html (accessed 30 November 2007).
17. K. G. Henshall, *Dimensions of Japanese Society: Gender, Margins and Mainstream* (London: Macmillan, 1999), p. 78. The view of Japan as wholly hostile to outsiders is reflected in the work of some international authorities on border controls and migration. For example, Malcolm Anderson describes the Japanese as having believed that 'the requirement of preserving a culture is the total exclusion of persons belonging to other ethnic groups'. See Anderson, *Frontiers,* p. 128.
18. M. Itoh, *Globalization of Japan: Japanese Sakoku Mentality and US Efforts to Open Japan* (New York: St Martin's Press, 1998), p. 109.
19. Oguma Eiji, *Tan'itsu Minzoku Shinwa no Kigen* (Tokyo: Shinyōsha, 1995).
20. One interesting example of this idea can be found in the work of the feminist nationalist Takamure Itsue. See ibid., p. 201.
21. J. Dower, *Embracing Defeat: Japan in the Wake of World War II* (New York: W. W. Norton, 1999), pp. 558 and 560.
22. On the complexities of discrimination see F. Anthias and N. Yuval-Davis, *Racialized Boundaries: Race, Nations, Gender, Colour and Class and the Anti-racist Struggle* (London: Routledge, 1992); R. Takaki, *Strangers from a Different Shore: A History of Asian Americans* (New York: Penguin Books, 1989); G. Hage, *White Nation* (Sydney: Pluto Press, 1998); E. Balibar and I. Wallerstein, *Race, Nation, Class: Ambiguous Identities* (London: Routledge, 1991).
23. For example, Hatsusei Ryūhei, 'Nihon no Kokusaika to Tabunkashugi', in Hatsusei Ryūhei (ed.), *Esunishiti to Tabunkashugi* (Tokyo: Dōbunkan, 1996), pp. 205–30; Komai Hiroshi (ed.), *Nihon no Esunikku Shakai* (Tokyo: Akashi Shoten, 1996); Kurihara Akira (ed.), *Kyōsei no Kanata e* (Tokyo: Kōbundō, 1997); M. Weiner, *Race and Migration in Imperial Japan* (London: Routledge, 1994); R. Siddle, *Race, Resistance and the Ainu of Japan* (London: Routledge, 1996); D. Denoon, M. Hudson, G. McCormack and T. Morris-Suzuki (eds.), *Multicultural Japan: Palaeolithic to Postmodern* (Cambridge: Cambridge University Press, 1996); M. Weiner (ed.), *Japan's Minorities: The Illusion of Homogeneity* (London and New York: Routledge, 1997); S. Ryang (ed.), *Koreans in Japan: Critical Voices from the Margin* (London: Routledge, 2000); J. Lie, *Multiethnic Japan* (Cambridge, MA: Harvard University Press, 2001); David Blake Willis and Stephen

Murphy-Shigematsu (eds.), *Transcultural Japan: At the Boundaries of Race, Gender, and Identity* (London: Routledge, 2008).

24. Y. Kuwahara, 'Japan's Dilemma: Can International Migration be Controlled?', in M. Weiner and T. Hanami (eds.), *Temporary Workers or Future Citizens? Japanese and US Migration Policies* (New York: New York University Press, 1998), pp. 355–83, quotation from p. 355.

25. S. A. Spencer, 'Illegal Migrant Labourers in Japan', *International Migration Review*, 26, 3 (1992), pp. 754–86, quotation from p. 754.

26. K. Yamawaki, 'Foreign Workers in Japan: A Historical Perspective', in M. Douglass and G. A. Roberts (eds.), *Japan and Global Migration: Foreign Workers and the Advent of Multicultural Society* (Honolulu: University of Hawaii Press, 2000), pp. 38–51, citation from p. 50.

27. For example, M. Weiner, 'Japan in the Age of Migration', in Douglass and Roberts, *Japan and Global Migration*, pp. 52–69, citation from p. 58.

28. M. Douglass and G. S. Roberts, 'Japan in an Age of Global Migration', in ibid., pp. 3–37, quotations from pp. 5, 8 and 11.

29. H. Komai (trans. Jens Wilkinson), *Foreign Migrants in Contemporary Japan* (Melbourne: Trans Pacific Press, 2001), p. 15.

30. For example, Kim Seok-Beom, 'Mangetsu', in Kim Seok-Beom, *Kim Seok-Beom Sakuhinshū*, Vol. II (Tokyo: Heibonsha, 2005) pp. 475–594 (first published 2001); Yi Hoe-Seong, *Hyakunen no Tabibitotachi* (Tokyo: Shinchō Bunko, 1994).

31. Iyotani Toshio and Kajita Toshimichi (eds.), *Gaikokujin Rōdōsha Ron: Genjō kara Riron e* (Tokyo: Kōbundō, 1992).

32. For example, P. Brimelow, *Alien Nation: Common Sense about America's Immigration Disaster* (New York: Random House, 1995), p. 169; see also J. Miles, 'The Coming Immigration Debate', *Atlantic Monthly (Online Edition)*, April 1995, www.theatlantic.com/politics/immigrat/miles2f.htm (accessed 3 May 2008).

33. E. Takemae (trans. Robert Ricketts and Sebastian Swann), *Inside GHQ: The Allied Occupation of Japan and Its Legacy* (London: Continuum, 2002), pp. 126–31.

34. Yoshimi Shunya, *Shinbei to Hanbei: Sengo Nihon no Seijiteki Muishiki* (Tokyo: Iwanami Shinsho, 2007). For further discussion, see Chapter Five below.

35. Immigration Bureau, Ministy of Justice, Japan, *Immigration Control Report 2006, Part 1: Immigration Control in Recent Years*, Tokyo, Ministry of Justice. www.moj.go.jp/NYUKAN/nyukan54–2.pdf (accessed 20 November 2007).

36. See T. Morris-Suzuki, *Exodus to North Korea: Shadows from Japan's Cold War* (Lanham, MD and New York: Rowman and Littlefield, 2007); S. Ryang, *North Koreans in Japan: Language, Ideology and Identity* (Boulder, CO: Westview Press, 1997), pp. 113–15; S. Ryang, 'The North Korean Homeland of Koreans in Japan', in Sonia Ryang (ed.), *Koreans in Japan: Critical Voices from the Margin* (London: Routledge, 2000); see also Okonogi Masao (ed.), *Zainichi Chōsenjin wa naze Kikoku shita no ka?*

(Tokyo: Gendai Jinbunsha, 2004); Kang Sang-Jung, *Nicchō Kankei no Kokufuku* (Tokyo: Shūeisha Shinsho, 2003), pp. 70–9; Takasaki Sōji and Pak Jeong-Jin (eds.), *Kikoku Undō to ha Nan data no ka* (Tokyo: Heibonsha, 2005). For a harrowing, lightly fictionalized account of the fate of the 'returnees', written by a participant in the repatriation, see Han Sok-Gyu, *Nihon kara 'Kita' ni Kaetta Hito no Monogatari* (Tokyo: Shinkansha, 2007).

37. C. Schmitt (trans. E. Kennedy), *The Crisis of Parliamentary Democracy* (Cambridge, MA: MIT Press, 1988), p. 43.
38. The story of 'Pak Young-Sik' is derived from the *Tsushima Shinbun*, 30 June 1951.
39. Yoon Hak-Jun, 'Waga Mikkōki', *Chōsen Kenkyū*, 190 (June 1979), pp. 5–15; Koh Sun-Hui, *20 Seiki no Tainichi Chejudōjin: Sono Seikatsu Katei to Ishiki* (Tokyo: Akashi Shoten, 1998).

CHAPTER 2

Drawing the line

From empire to Cold War

At the time of Japan's defeat in the Asia–Pacific War, a series of lines were drawn across the map of Northeast Asia, dividing up the territorial expanse of the Japanese empire. In surrendering to the Allies, Japan had accepted the terms of the Potsdam Declaration of 26 July 1945, which restricted Japanese sovereignty to 'the islands of Honshu, Hokkaido, Kyushu and Shikoku and such minor islands as we [the Allied powers] determine'. But determining control of the 'minor islands', and of the great expanses of sea that surrounded them, was to prove a major headache for the occupiers.[1] In the meanwhile, lines were drawn in haste, with the rough-and-ready pencil strokes of people forced to make urgent decisions. All these decisions, in the end, were to have a profound influence on the region's destiny.[2]

One of these bold lines quickly became known as the 'MacArthur Line', after the Supreme Commander of the Allied occupation forces in Japan, General Douglas MacArthur. Given MacArthur's power and personality – the almost imperial aura which surrounded his presence in Japan – the name seems an appropriate one, and although MacArthur himself did not explicitly endorse this title, neither did he repudiate it.[3]

The MacArthur Line had a very specific and limited purpose. It was supposed to mark the boundaries of the sea in which Japanese boats were allowed to fish. In the first months of the Allied occupation, the most pressing task for the occupiers was to establish control over the defeated nation, and so they initially prohibited Japanese boats from leaving port at all. On 14 September 1945, almost a month after Japan's surrender, this prohibition was lifted to allow wooden fishing vessels to fish within a twelve-mile limit; two weeks later the fishing zone was expanded and the MacArthur Line was officially established as its outer limit.

The line ran between the northernmost Japanese island of Hokkaido and the island of Sakhalin (Karafuto), whose southern half had been a Japanese colony, but had now been surrendered to the USSR. It then turned south, taking a course roughly equidistant between the Japanese coast and the coast of Japan's erstwhile colony, Korea, before inscribing a right angle which cut through the South China Sea.

Practical necessity, however, quickly forced the revision of the line. By the middle of 1946, the Allied occupiers were firmly in control of Japan, and were less concerned with curtailing the movement of Japanese seafarers than they were with avoiding 'the necessity of the United States sending into Japan a vast quantity of food paid for by the American taxpayer'.[4] As a result, in June 1946 the MacArthur Line was redrawn much further out to the south and east, more than doubling the expanse of Pacific Ocean and East China Sea open to Japanese fishermen.[5] After another extension in September 1949, the line became a rectangle which extended from 24° to 40° north and from 125° to 180° east.

But it was in the west (where it ran between Japan and Korea) and in the north (where it ran between Japan and the Soviet Union) that the line was most contentious. To the west of Japan lay a constellation of 'minor islands' which had formed stepping stones in millennia of cultural contact, and these islands stubbornly refused to follow the tidy geometry of the boundary drawers. Korea claimed the historical right to the small inhabited archipelago of Ulleungdo which lay close to the MacArthur Line, as well as to the tiny uninhabited islet of Dokdo (known in Japanese as Takeshima). The Allies (in a decree issued in January 1946) excluded Ulleungdo and Dokdo,[6] as well as the large Korean island of Jeju,[7] from Japanese territory, and special instructions were issued by the occupiers forbidding Japanese fishermen to go within twelve miles of Dokdo (though the decree said nothing about the ultimate sovereignty of these rocks and islets).[8]

On the other hand, the island of Tsushima, which the Allies included in its definition of Japan, was much nearer to the Korean mainland than it was to any of the major Japanese islands. For the first year of the occupation, the MacArthur Line ran right along the west coast of Tsushima, and the island's unfortunate inhabitants found themselves prohibited from fishing off their own western shores. The 1946 redrawing of the line allowed them a narrow fishing corridor to the west, but also brought the MacArthur Line deep into the rich fishing grounds surrounding Jeju.[9]

None of this would have mattered quite so much if the line had remained, as it was supposed to be, no more than the boundary of a

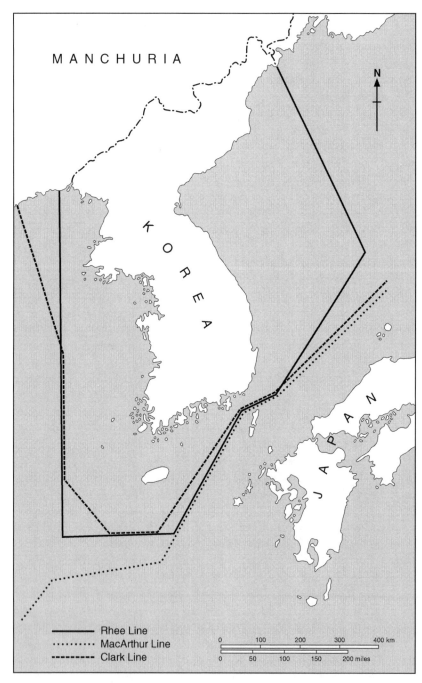

Map 2.1. The MacArthur, Clark and Rhee Lines.

fishing zone. But the US military authorities who ruled the southern part of the Korean peninsula from 1945 to 1948 soon came to treat the MacArthur Line as defining the limit of Korea's territorial waters, and Japanese fishing boats which crossed the line were frequently captured by Korean coastguards.[10] The line therefore was quickly invested with a significance that went far beyond its practical impact. It became a symbol of the boundary of nationhood and sovereignty, a point of friction where all the painful memories of conflict and colonialism were repeatedly rubbed raw.

In 1949, rumours of a plan to move the MacArthur Line closer to the Korean coastline provoked a furore of protest in Korea. Three years later, in 1952, with the end of the Allied occupation of Japan, the line was abolished, to be briefly replaced by a United Nations Sea Defence Line (the 'Clark Line') around Korea (itself rescinded in August 1953). Meanwhile, however, South Korean president Yi Seung-Man (Syngman Rhee) had unilaterally adopted the MacArthur Line as the limits of South Korea's territorial waters, in places extending it outwards to a distance of two hundred miles from the Korean coastline. This new boundary (known in Korea as the 'Peace Line' and in Japan as the 'Rhee Line') was to become the source of many years of contention, and although a settlement of sorts was achieved in the 1960s, echoes of these disputes can still be heard in the twenty-first century, in ongoing conflicts over control of Dokdo/Takeshima.

To the south, meanwhile, the Allied occupiers drew a frontier separating the main islands of Japan from the Nansei (South-West) Islands of Amami and the Ryukyu archipelago (Okinawa), which were placed under the direct control of a separate US military government. Of all the postwar lines, this proved the most unworkable. The Amami Islands had deep historical and social ties to the southern Japanese island of Kyushu: islanders sent their children to high school in Kyushu and travelled there for hospital treatment. Suddenly, these mundane activities became impossible, and in recognition of the disruption caused by the border, in 1953 the US military authorities moved the line southward, reincorporating Amami into Japan, though they retained control of Okinawa until 1972.[11]

These multiple lines together defined the contours of postwar Japan. But it was the western border, between Japan and the Korean peninsula, that became the focus of postwar migration control efforts; and that line is the one that figures most prominently in this book.

There was also one more line whose presence cannot be escaped: the line drawn along the 38th parallel, dividing the Korean peninsula between north and south. For this was to become the most volatile and dangerous of all the boundary lines in Northeast Asia.

Korea had been a Japanese colony for thirty-five years, and colonial rule had been bitterly resented by most Koreans. For a country which had preserved its autonomy within the Chinese world order for centuries, it was a humiliating experience to be ruled by the upstart empire to the east. Though (as in all empires) some of the colonized collaborated with the colonial rulers – reluctantly or opportunistically, with enthusiasm or with quiet resignation – other Koreans fought on for independence, some fleeing across their country's northern border to join partisan movements in Manchuria or Siberia.

The United States, however, was anxious at the prospect of political instability in a newly liberated Korea, and as early as 1943 President Franklin D. Roosevelt proposed a plan by which, once Japan was defeated, the Korean peninsula would be placed under the 'trusteeship' of the victorious allies until it was judged to be 'ready' for full independence. His plan appears to have envisaged a Korea jointly controlled by the USA and the Soviet Union, at that time still wary allies. But in the first frost of the Cold War, which crystallized even before Japan's surrender, the plan cracked apart: Korea was subjected to the separate military occupation of the two hostile superpowers.

The line along the 38th parallel, separating the Soviet and US zones of occupation, was sketched in haste by a couple of US junior officers on the night after the atomic bombing of Nagasaki. No Koreans were consulted, and the officers did not even have a detailed map of the Korean peninsula on which to draw their line.[12] No one could have imagined that it was to become an impassable militarized frontier which would last for more than six decades. Its influence was to extend far beyond the bounds of Korea itself. The line created a mass of subsidiary fissures through the politics of Northeast Asia; and some of these fissures (as we shall see) extended deep into the politics and society of the former colonial power, Japan.

SPACES OF MOVEMENT

Maps depict the static physical presence of seas and oceans, islands and continents. This inert space can be endlessly divided and redivided. But society is never static; people are always on the move, and the lines that are drawn on the map determine which paths of movement are possible and which impossible, which journeys are legal and which illegal.

The Japanese Empire had created a new space of movement in Northeast Asia and beyond. In one direction, a mass of people from poorer agricultural regions of Japan sought new opportunities overseas – many of them migrating to the colonies of Taiwan, Korea and Karafuto or later to the quasi-colony of Manchukuo (north-eastern China), while others went even further afield, to work on plantations in Brazil, Peru and elsewhere. It is estimated that over 750,000 Japanese emigrated between 1868 and 1941.[13] Meanwhile, some colonial subjects sought work or education in the imperial metropolis, or migrated from one colonized territory to another. The empire was not, of course, a space of *free* movement. A maze of colonial regulations determined who could go where, and on what conditions. Sometimes migration was constrained or prohibited, as during the economic depression of the late 1920s, when restrictions were placed on the entry of Korean colonial subjects to Japan. At other times mobility was encouraged or coerced, as when poor Japanese farmers were urged to migrate to Manchuria, or Korean and Chinese labourers were conscripted to work in wartime Japan.

The movement through empire, however, had woven webs of social connection linking northern Japan to Manchuria, southern Korea to Osaka, Okinawa to Taiwan and Micronesia, and so on. Now, with the drawing of new boundaries, millions of people were turned (in that most evocative of postwar terms) into 'displaced persons', stranded on the wrong side of the line. To understand the impact of these new borderlines, we need first to know something of the space of movement through which they cut.

Movement across the sea between the Korean peninsula and Japan (known in Korea as the 'East Sea' and in Japan as the 'Sea of Japan') has a history many millennia old. The history of modern migration across this sea, however, goes back to the late nineteenth century. In the 1880s and 1890s, as Korea's Yi dynasty struggled to come to terms with a rapidly transforming East Asia, Meiji Japan – under the rule of an energetically modernizing group of former samurai – underwent rapid industrialization and military expansion. The Sino-Japanese War of 1894–5 (much of which was actually fought on the Korean peninsula) gave Japan substantial political influence over Korea, and, a decade later, Japan was able to take on its other main rival for regional power, Tsarist Russia. Victory in the Russo-Japanese War of 1904–5 (part of which was also fought out on Korean soil) in turn enabled Japan to extend its influence further, reducing the Korean kingdom to a protectorate. In 1910, the last of the Yi kings was forced to abdicate, and full-scale Japanese colonial rule of Korea began: it was to continue until Japan's defeat in war in 1945.

Even before colonial rule was established, Japanese traders, settlers and adventurers had begun to make their presence felt in Korean society, and by 1907, three years before Korea formally became a Japanese colony, over 125,000 Japanese people were already living on the Korean peninsula.[14] Meanwhile, some Koreans were migrating to Japan in search of educational opportunities, while others were already being recruited by labour-hungry Japanese firms. Yamawaki Keizō, for example, points out that over two hundred Korean workers were recruited by a Kyushu coal mine as early as the 1890s.[15] In 1915, the number of Koreans in Japan was probably less than four thousand, but during and after the First World War this number soared, reaching (according to official figures) 136,709 in 1925, 735,689 in 1937, and more than 2 million by 1945.[16]

Most came from the south and east of the Korean peninsula – the areas closest to Japan. Those from the north and west of the peninsula were more likely to cross the border into Manchuria and northern China. Japanese officials estimated that about 83 per cent of the Koreans living in Japan in 1937 came from the three southernmost provinces of South Gyeongsang, North Gyeongsang and South Jeolla.[17]

One particularly dense flow of movement occurred between the island of Jeju, off the southern coast of Korea, and the Japanese city of Osaka (which was in fact much nearer to Jeju than the Korean capital of Keijo – today's Seoul). Because Jeju Island was not a separate province, but was at that time administered by South Jeolla Province, it is difficult to find precise figures for the number of Jeju islanders in Japan, but estimates put the number at just under 50,000 in 1935, and at around 150,000 by 1940.[18] The total population of Jeju island in 1935 was about 200,000,[19] so this means that the share of the Jeju islander population living in Japan rose from around 20 per cent to as much as 40 per cent in the second half of the 1930s. In other words, by the time of the Asia–Pacific War almost every Jeju family had at least one member living in Japan.[20]

Many Jeju migrants to Japan travelled on the *Kimigayo II*, a converted Russian warship which had been bought by a Japanese shipping firm, was renamed after the Japanese national anthem and, from 1925 onwards, made regular journeys around their island, stopping at ports along the way to pick up workers bound for the factories of Osaka.[21] The ferry, with a normal capacity of 365 passengers, had been given special permission to carry up to 685 people on the route from Jeju to Japan. Photos from the 1930s show its decks crammed with the white-clad figures of migrants, staring anxiously and expectantly towards the horizon, beyond which lay the smoke-stacks of Daeban (the Korean name for Osaka).[22]

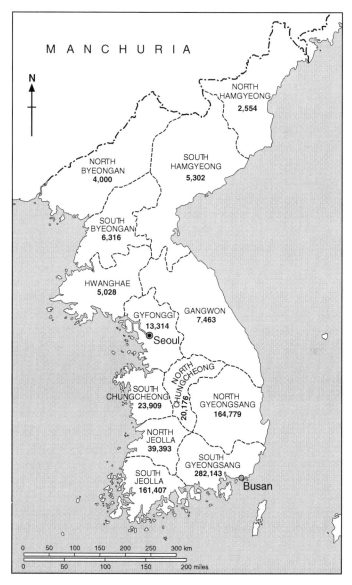

Map 2.2. Sources of Korean migration to Japan, 1937. (The figures in each province show the estimated number of Koreans in Japan originating from that province.)

The migrants who packed the decks of the *Kimigayo II* in the 1920s and 1930s were mostly young men and women – the women heading for jobs in the textile mills; the men hoping to pick up work in Osaka's metal-working or rubber factories. Among them, here and there, were diving women, travelling to seasonal work in Japan. Jeju is famous for its women divers (*haenyo* – 'women of the sea' – more traditionally known in Korean as *chamsu*), who perform extraordinary physical feats to gather abalone and other prized shellfish from the sea floor, diving to depths of up to twenty metres without breathing gear.[23] The arrival of large, relatively mechanized Japanese fishing boats in the waters around Jeju from the later nineteenth century onwards had put great pressure on the delicate balance of the island's marine resources. Once-abundant shellfish had become scarce, and by 1932 more than half the island's diving women had begun to leave the island for seasonal work – most heading to other parts of Korea or Japan, but some as far afield as Dalian (Dairen) and Vladivostok.[24]

Other migrants from Korea to Japan responded to similar colonial pressures. In recent years, historians have passionately debated whether Japanese colonization brought economic growth or exploitation to Korea. But of course the two are not mutually exclusive. Colonial investment, the building of roads and railways and the introduction of new agricultural methods and industrial technologies certainly increased the size of the Korean economy. In the countryside, colonial officials surveyed the land, imposed modern legal forms of land-ownership, and introduced new methods to increase the output of rice (much of which was exported to Japan and other parts of the empire). Markets, money and commercialization penetrated even remote rural areas, where farm life had been relatively self-sufficient. But these changes themselves brought new pressures, particularly to tenant farmers. Rising prices and a growing population forced farmers to grow more cash crops, while the quality of the food they themselves ate often deteriorated. At least throughout the 1920s, the Korean countryside experienced (in Gi-Wook Shin's words) 'growth without development'.[25]

New taxes also placed a burden on communities which had few sources of cash income. In 1931 and 1932 diving women in north-eastern Jeju staged mass demonstrations against their colonial rulers, protesting about the heavy taxes imposed on them (including the high cost they were required to pay for licences to travel outside the island).[26] Their protests were forcibly suppressed and over a hundred demonstrators were arrested by the colonial authorities.[27] As commercialization increased and prices and taxes rose, employment in Japan became a vital means for many families to earn money, and remittances sent back by family members in Osaka became a crucial part of the economy of Jeju Island.

It was a pattern repeated across the southern regions of the Korean peninsula. People from villages around the city of Busan travelled to the Japanese island of Tsushima (the part of Japan nearest to Korea) to earn money fishing, diving or making charcoal in kilns which they set up on the mountain slopes. Others from the surrounding regions of South and North Gyeongsang responded to recruiters who came looking for labour for Japanese coal mines and construction sites. Many migrants, after reaching Japan, travelled from one city to another in search of any work on offer. The son of one such migrant recalls,

My father had come to Japan in the early 1930s, at the time of the Manchurian Incident. He was fifteen at the time, and came to Japan by himself, with just the clothes on his back. My father was the eldest son of a typical poor ten-ant farming family from Namsan Village, Gyangwon District in the South Korean province of Southern Gyeongsang … [His] youth in Japan was so unsettled that I don't know how many times he shifted from one place and one job to another. Finally he moved to Tokyo, where he got a job in a muni-tions factory. By this time, the national mobilization system had been imposed on Korea as well, and forced labour was being recruited. Under the slogan 'integrating Japan and Korea' [*naisen ittai*], forced assimilation was proceeding apace, and finally the door was opened to the enlistment of colonial subjects in the Japanese army.[28]

COLONIAL MIGRATION: FREE AND FORCED

Who went freely, and who was forced? The issue of *kyōsei renkō* – the forced recruitment of Koreans and Chinese to work in Japan and other parts of the empire – is one of the most controversial and least-understood aspects of migration to Japan in the first half of the twentieth century. It is an issue whose legacy still casts long shadows on the postwar relationship between Japan and its neighbours, and is surrounded (in public discourse at least) by much myth and misinformation. Some writings imply that all Koreans in postwar Japan were forced labourers or their descendants;[29] some revisionists, on the contrary, deny that forced labour ever existed.[30] Both views are deeply misleading.

Part of the problem lies in the distinction between 'forced' and 'free' migration itself. This dichotomy implies that there is some simple way to separate the voluntary migrant from the slave, the victim of people-trafficking or the persecuted refugee. But in real life (as we shall also see in the postwar years) the dividing line between freedom and compulsion can be complex.[31] Coercion comes in many forms and degrees, and a wide range of pressures and attractions provide the motive force behind migrations.

A small proportion of migrants from pre-war Korea to Japan were well-to-do people seeking new opportunities as university students or entrepreneurs in the colonial power. Their migration stands at the most unequivocally 'free' end of the spectrum. Others left their homes with varying mixtures of hope and reluctance: dreaming of a better life, but also impelled by the need to escape a grinding poverty which was (in many cases) aggravated by the policies of the colonial state. Others again – those at the most unequivocally 'forced' end of the spectrum – were lured away from home by the promises of unscrupulous brokers, coerced into labour schemes by threats from local police, or marched away at gunpoint to an uncertain fate.[32]

Labour recruitment of many sorts took place throughout the empire, in Japan itself as well as in the colonies. In Jeju Island, for example, local people were conscripted to build a maze of tunnels through the basalt rock of the island, in preparation for an expected Allied assault. (Though the assault never took place, the tunnels survive to this day.) The Japanese poor, meanwhile, sometimes found themselves recruited into mines and construction projects where they worked alongside Korean and Chinese forced labourers in equally harsh conditions (though usually for somewhat better pay). However, there remains an important distinction between the experiences of those recruited to work in or near their own home area, and those who were sent overseas to utterly unfamiliar places, with no certainty when or if they would return.

The issue of forced labour is also clouded by the fact that measures to recruit workers in the colonies were complex, confusing and carried out in varying ways by a multiplicity of authorities. Recruitment of labour was enforced in three stages. In 1939, Japan's National Labour Mobilization Law was applied to Korea and Taiwan, and plans were drawn up to recruit hundreds of thousands of workers for strategic industries from the colonies, as well as within Japan itself. Contracts were supposed to be voluntary and limited to two years.

By 1942, however, it was clear that the existing scheme was not delivering labour to Japanese industry on the scale required, and in February of that year the more overtly coercive 'official mediation' (*kan assen*) scheme was introduced. In September 1944 this in turn was replaced by a new and yet more coercive scheme for the mass conscription of labour from colonial Korea.[33] For, as a postwar Japanese intelligence report noted,

During the final stages of the war, few people responded with enthusiasm to recruitment for work in Japan, which was experiencing terrible bombing raids. There were continuous efforts to avoid the labour draft, and the ordinary people expressed great resentment towards the colonial, provincial and country officials who were on the front line [of the recruitment process]. The mobilization of labour under this [1944] conscription ordinance was, along with the requisitioning of rice and other grains, one of the two most hated policies introduced by the colonial government.[34]

In addition to schemes directed at recruiting male workers, the *teishintai* system was used to recruit women, some of whom were used as factory workers, but many of whom ended up in military brothels, enduring the most terrible forms of institutionalized sexual abuse.[35]

Wartime recruitment shifted rapidly from the voluntary to the forcible end of the spectrum, but the line between voluntary migration and coercion was blurred even before 1942. Under the 1939 recruitment system, migrants were often induced to volunteer for work in Japan by offers of two-year contracts with wages which seemed tempting to underemployed Korean peasant farmers. On arrival in Japan, however, many found themselves incarcerated in remote mines or construction sites working in backbreaking conditions. At the end of the two years, it was common for contracts to be unilaterally renewed by employers.[36]

Throughout, the measures used to implement the three labour recruitment laws were variable and inconsistent. Local agents (often police or village headmen in the colonies) were given recruitment targets to fulfil: how they met the targets was largely left to their own discretion, and might include anything from persuasion, to threats, to outright violence. Sometimes (as in the case of labour recruitment from north China) quotas were met, in part at least, by shipping prisoners of war to Japan.[37] In this sense, Japanese wartime labour recruitment closely resembled the forced labour system of Nazi Germany, which has been described as one of 'shifting, contradictory policies and unpredictable turns, of volunteerism and wage offers as well as threats and beatings'.[38]

The most widely cited figure for Korean civilians conscripted to work for private companies in Japan from 1939 is around 660,000. This, however, underestimates the number of female recruits and those conscripted to work for the military.[39] One report compiled by the Japanese Red Cross in 1956, and approved by Japanese government officials, states that a quarter of a million Korean labourers entered Japan 'by enlistment', and

Image 2.1. Monument to wartime labour. The view across this giant reservoir in
Hokkaido, which was constructed between 1939 and 1943 by thousands of workers,
including labour conscripts from Korea, is dominated by a monument to the workers
who 'gave their lives' to the building of the dam.

that there were also a further 365,263 Koreans who had been drafted as
servicemen or auxiliaries by the Japanese armed forces: 'it is presumed
that many of them were in this country at the end of the war'. In addition,
520,000 had been sent to Japan 'under contract', between 1942 and 1945.[40]
Taken together, the figures suggest that rather over one-third of the estimated 2.1 million Koreans living in Japan at the end of the Asia–Pacific
War had been brought there under one or other of the official labour
recruitment schemes.

The complex ways in which forced and voluntary migration were intertwined in individual lives is illustrated by story of one migrant from Jeju
to Osaka: Pu Song-Gyu.[41] Pu first migrated to Japan to look for work in
the spring of 1929, when he was just thirteen years old. He settled in an
area of Osaka where other people from his Jeju village were already living,
and moved from one low-paid casual job to another – everything from
serving customers in a tailor's shop to labouring at a blacksmith's forge.

Pu's story illustrates both the possibilities and the perils which awaited
Korean migrants in their journeys through the empire. Because he was
little more than a child when he arrived in Japan, his Japanese became
fluent enough for him to pass for a native, and he invented a plausible
resumé as a recent Japanese school leaver, which enabled him to win a
place as a trainee in a photographic processing firm. His boss was evidently

a benevolent employer, for even when Pu belatedly 'confessed' to being an immigrant from Korea, the boss continued to employ him, and even helped him to go to Tokyo to train as a professional photographer.

Armed with this new skill, Pu married a fellow migrant from Jeju, and in his early twenties moved to Manchuria to open his own photographic studio. It was here, however, that he was caught up in the widening net of labour mobilization – he was conscripted and sent to Tinian Island in the Pacific, where he was probably among the 1,300 other Korean workers recruited to level airfields out of the coral rock of the island. He was fortunate to survive the experience: most of the island's Japanese defenders and the Korean workers were killed in the US assault on Tinian in July 1944. From Tinian, Pu returned to Japan, where he set up a tiny restaurant and earned extra income taking photos of his fellow Koreans in his spare time, until he had saved the resources to re-establish a studio of his own, this time in the Ōkubo district of Tokyo.

By now, Pu and his wife had five children, and their lives might seem a model tale of a migrant's triumph over adversity. But (as he told a Japanese newspaper in the 1950s) Pu was haunted by the wartime deaths of those close to him and troubled by experiences of discrimination in Japan. He 'longed to have his own homeland', and so in 1959 he became one of the first people to volunteer for repatriation – not to his home island of Jeju, but to North Korea.

That, however, is another story, to which we shall return in Chapter Eight. In order to understand why Jeju islander Pu Song-Gyu and his family wanted to 'go home' to North Korea, we first need to learn more about the profound effect which the drawing of boundaries had upon lives and identities of migrants in postwar Japan.

SYSTEMS OF CONTROL IN PRE-WAR AND WARTIME JAPAN

Japan is generally seen, by its own citizens as well as by foreigners, as a country with tightly controlled borders and an efficient and powerful bureaucracy. It is therefore rather surprising to realize that until the middle of the twentieth century Japan had no centralized migration control service. Control of immigrants was in the hands of local government officials and local police, and the laws governing entry to the country were multilayered, complex and often very confused.

In modern states there are two sets of laws that determine the right of people to cross borders. The first are nationality laws, which define who

is and who is not a member of the national community; the second are
migration controls, defining which groups of foreigners are allowed to
enter the country, and on what terms. Japan's first Nationality Law and
its first significant migration control ordinance – Imperial Ordinance No.
352 – were both introduced in the same year, 1899, at a time when Japan
was in the midst of rapid modernization and industrialization and had
recently acquired its first formal colony, Taiwan. Both the Nationality
Law (Kokuseki Hō) and the migration ordinance appeared to impose
clear and tight restrictions on the boundaries of the Japanese nation, but
in practice both proved to be filled with contradictions.

The 1899 Nationality Law created a legal framework for 'Japaneseness'
which centred on a patriarchal version of the principle of *ius sanguinis* –
law of bloodline. In other words, Japanese nationality was passed on from
father to children. Children of foreigners born on Japanese soil did not
acquire a right to become Japanese; nor did children of Japanese mothers and foreign fathers. The law did include provision for foreigners to
become naturalized Japanese, but the process was cumbersome, and was
in fact little used until after the introduction of a new Nationality Law
following Japan's defeat in the Asia–Pacific War.

But it is also important to remember that Japan had already acquired
the colony of Taiwan before the formal legal framework of nationality was established. When the 1899 Nationality Law was introduced, a
local version was quickly extended to Taiwan. So the 'bloodline' which
legally defined people as Japanese nationals from the start included
'Taiwanese blood', and soon after various other categories of blood also
came to be legally redefined as 'Japanese'. In Korea the inhabitants were
deemed – automatically and without choice – to have become Japanese
subjects, even though (for complex reasons of political strategy) a local
version of the Nationality Law was never introduced. Despite the law's
apparent emphasis on 'ethnic purity', then, the boundaries of nationality that it established were elastic, susceptible both to expansion and to
contraction.

The fact that colonial subjects were legally Japanese did not, of course,
mean that they enjoyed the same civic rights as the people of the colo-
nizing power, nor that they were accepted as 'Japanese' by their coloniz-
ing fellow subjects. While nationality united colonizers and colonized,
another legal framework divided them. This second framework was the
'family registration' (*koseki*) system, which has been described as creating
'states within a state'.[42] Family registers had been introduced in the 1870s
as a means of social control and a basis for measures such as military

conscription. All people in Japan, soon after birth, are entered into a register which becomes a continuous record of each household's journey through time – births, marriages, divorces, deaths, movements of primary place of residence, and so on.

As Japan's empire expanded, each colony acquired its own family registration system, and people were not free to move their registration between one colony and another, or between the 'external territories' (*gaichi*) and 'Japan proper' (*naichi*). In other words, while colonial peoples possessed 'Japanese nationality' in terms of international law, they also had what might be termed a 'local nationality' in terms of their family registration. The family registration system did not automatically prevent the movement of people between different parts of the empire, but it did ensure that colonial migrants to Japan were always distinguishable from the metropolitan population in terms of legal status.[43] This in turn at times made it possible for various Japanese authorities to impose restrictions on the migration of people who possessed Korean or Taiwanese registration.

For example, in 1919, following a major failed independence movement in Korea, the colonial government imposed travel restrictions which required Koreans to obtain official permission to leave their place of residence. Though the requirement for permits was abolished in 1922, further restrictions were briefly introduced in the wake of the Great Kantō Earthquake of 1923, and thereafter various Japanese local governments introduced their own sets of regulations.[44] During the late 1920s and early 1930s, a bewildering variety of measures were used by various authorities in an effort to maintain some control over the flows of people from Korea and Taiwan to Japan. These generally required migrants to provide letters of authorization from their local police stations and evidence that they had enough money to support themselves on their immediate arrival in Japan. The controls, however, changed frequently, varied from place to place, and do not always seem to have been effectively enforced.[45]

The family registration system had important implications which carried on into the postwar period. As the empire fell apart, Japanese settlers overseas (even those who had been born in the colonies) could readily be distinguished from the colonized because they possessed *naichi* family registration, while Koreans and Taiwanese in Japan could be distinguished from other Japanese nationals by their *gaichi* registration.

Meanwhile, just three months after the 1899 Nationality Law came into force, the Japanese government had issued Imperial Ordinance No. 352, which provided a basis for the control of foreign (ie. non-colonial) migration to Japan. This prohibited foreign entrants to Japan from working in a wide range of 'low-skilled' labouring occupations. A detailed directive from the Ministry of the Interior (Directive No. 42 of 1899) specified these occupations as including 'farming, fishing, mining, construction, building, manufacturing, transport, hauling, longshore work and other miscellaneous trades'. On the other hand, foreign immigrants were allowed to work as cloth merchants, tailors, cooks, household servants and knife grinders, and in various other specified occupations.[46]

The motives behind these measures are made disconcertingly clear in a postwar government report on Japan's migration policies:

At this time [i.e. in the 1890s], Chinese people were causing problems by migrating as cheap labour to countries all over the world, and America, Australia, Canada etc. had already taken measures to prohibit the entry of Chinese labourers. By taking these measures at a time when cheap labour was in demand, our country, which was then in the phase of the rise of capitalism, can be said to have forestalled the problem of Chinese labour migration.[47]

In other words, rather like Australia's White Australia policy (introduced not long after), the measure was designed to prevent the entry of Chinese migrant labourers at a time of large-scale emigration from China.

The implementation of these controls was in the hands of local government and local police forces, however, and they seem to have applied the rules with a good deal of variability, in the light of what they saw as their own region's economic and social interests. At the height of the First World War boom, for example, Yamaguchi Prefecture managed to bring in some three thousand Chinese labourers to construct dockyards, and the 1919–20 *Japan Year Book* acknowledged that 'it is believed that pretty large numbers of Chinese labourers must be employed in factories in the Kwansai [Kansai] district including Osaka and Kobe'.[48]

Japan, like many other countries, did not legally require arriving foreigners to have passports and visas until the time of the First World War.[49] Growing fear of the entry of 'enemy aliens' led to the implementation in 1918 of an ordinance forbidding the entry of foreigners who lacked a 'passport or documentary evidence of citizenship' (*ryoken mata wa kokuseki shōmeisho*) or were suspected of subversion.[50] Even then, passport-free travel continued to be permitted between China and Japan: a situation which, remarkably enough, continued until 1939, two years after the outbreak of full-scale war between the two countries. In general, foreigners other than Chinese found it relatively easy to enter Japan until the late 1930s, when rising nationalist sentiments led to heightened scrutiny of foreigners entering Japan. As an Australian official stationed in Japan reported, by 1936 every arriving foreigner was being interviewed by police at ports, and passengers were often

given the impression that they are objects of suspicion. This is particularly the case at one or two of the ports, but it also applies in varying degrees at other places; some arrivals are unruffled enough, others very far from it – it depends upon the individual officers who examine the passengers.[51]

As the war in China and global diplomatic tensions intensified, in 1939 the Ministry of the Interior introduced new measures giving local police enhanced powers to control the entry and movement of foreigners in their areas. The new system distinguished between stays of up to fifteen days (which were treated as 'transit') and longer stays. Foreigners who intended to stay for more than a month were required to register with the police within ten days of their arrival in Japan. Hotels were also instructed to provide detailed information on all foreign guests. The new ordinance for the first time also made provision for travellers arriving in Japan on that newfangled mode of transport, the aeroplane (although in fact the vast majority still arrived by ship, most through the ports of Kobe and Yokohama).[52] Even then, though, enforcement remained a matter for local authorities, though some of the new measures provided prototypes for features to be included in the centralized immigration controls introduced by the Allied occupation authorities after Japan's defeat in the Asia–Pacific War.

LINES IN THE MIND: THE DUAL SPACE OF MOVEMENT
IN POSTWAR NORTHEAST ASIA

To draw a borderline is both a political and a cognitive act. The frontiers drawn on maps generally come to influence not only government and diplomacy, but also the way that societies, cultures and histories are studied and understood. So the carving up of the space of empire into nation states further divided by Cold War barriers profoundly affected interpretations of postwar Northeast Asia itself. The postwar world was, pre-eminently, a world of nation states, in which colonial empires were subdivided into independent countries, each with their own, supposedly autonomous, systems of border control. But in practice, the orderly patchwork of nation states was complicated by the fact of the Cold War, which created new geographical blocs and new power hierarchies which generated their own logic of cross-border movement.

There are many excellent scholarly studies of the postwar Allied occupation of Japan, and some (though fewer) of the occupation of Korea and Okinawa.[53] Until recently, however, there has been little recognition of the way in which all these separate realms were interconnected.[54] Yet each of these occupations was part of a larger system, so that none can be fully understood without considering the region-wide set of Allied (in practice, largely US) control in which it nested. The 'divided occupation' had profound implications for Northeast Asia as a whole.[55] In some senses, it connected the various occupied areas, while in others it created deep divisions between them. Or, to put it another way, we may argue that it created two coexisting but very different spaces of movement, inhabited by different groups of people.

Japan, Okinawa and Korea were occupied for differing periods of time, and each was controlled by a separate administering power. Japan was administered from 1945 to 1952 by the General Headquarters of the Supreme Commander for the Allied Powers (GHQ/SCAP), which operated in conjunction with an elected Japanese government. South Korea, from 1945 to 1948, was controlled by the United States of America Military Government in Korea (USAMGIK), which then handed most of its powers to a South Korean government elected in controversial and contested circumstances. Even after 1948, however, operational control of the South Korean police and military remained in US hands. Meanwhile Okinawa, which was regarded by the United States as central to its Pacific strategy, was separated from the rest of Japan and placed under the control of the Military Government of the Ryukyu Islands. (A similar US military government, in this case run by the Navy, controlled the small Ogasawara or Bonin Island group to the east of Japan.)

The policies adopted in these separate spheres of occupation carved deep rifts through the fabric of Northeast Asian society. Above all, as we shall see, tight restrictions on the movement of people between the various occupation zones made social and cultural interaction between Japanese, Koreans and Taiwanese extremely difficult, intensifying the inward-looking nationalisms which still hamper attempts at regional integration to this day. In this sense, the postwar destiny of Northeast Asia was profoundly different from that of Western Europe, where the postwar order (sustained by the US Marshall Plan) encouraged cross-border interaction throughout the area to the west of the 'Iron Curtain'.

And yet the carefully separated zones were parts of a single occupation strategy for Northeast Asia. All were administratively connected, since the line of military command passed from Washington to Okinawa and South Korea via the Supreme Commander Allied Powers in Tokyo. Occupation policies for Japan were devised in the context of this larger regional framework, and the policies introduced in Okinawa and Korea were always shaped with an eye to their impact on Japan. Occupation officials often moved from one zone to another. The hundreds of thousands of US troops who served in Northeast Asia in the late 1940s, the 1950s and the early 1960s also moved through an interconnected network of bases spanning the territories of Japan, South Korea and Okinawa, and extending to Guam, the Philippines and beyond, their movement being controlled (as we shall see) by a system quite separate from the one which governed the cross-border movement of most Japanese, Koreans and Taiwanese.

The curious two-layer human geography that characterized movement in the region during the immediate postwar decades has created legacies which last to the present day. From the 1970s onward, as the scale of the US military presence in Northeast Asia diminished and conditions for foreign residents in Japan gradually improved, new spatial geographies, both domestic and international, began to redefine the relationship between 'the national' and 'the foreign' in Japan. In the final sections of this book we shall look more closely at these changes, and consider how far they have transformed the nature of Japan's border politics, and how far the system created in the wake of wartime defeat still shapes the human borderlines of Japan today. But first let us focus on occupied Japan itself: beginning with one particular small town in occupied Japan where the social realities of the border were most sharply exposed.

NOTES

1. SCAP Directive 677 of 29 January 1946 provided greater detail, specifically including in Japanese territory 'the Tsushima Islands and the Ryukyu (Nansei) Islands North of 30 degrees North Latitude (excluding Kuchinoshima Island)' and specifically excluding '(a) Utsuryo (Ullung) Island, Liancourt Rocks (Take Island) and Quelpart (Saishu or Cheju) Island, (b) the Ryukyu (Nansei) Islands south of 30 degrees North Latitude (including Kuchinoshima Island), he Izu, Nanpo, Bonin (Ogasawara) and Volcano (Kazan or Iwo) Island Groups and all other outerlying Pacific Islands'; see Government Section, Supreme Commander Allied Power, *Political Reorientation of Japan, September 1945 to September 1948* (Washington, DC: US Government Printing Office, 1949), p. 477.
2. See Hara Kimie, 'Cold War Frontiers in the Asia–Pacific: The Troubling Legacy of the San Francisco Treaty', *Japan Focus*, 4 September 2006, http://japanfocus.org/ (accessed 10 June 2007).

3. Top Secret Memorandum for Commander-in-Chief, GHQ, from Military Intelligence Section, General Staff, 29 October 1951, 'Seizure and Confiscation of Japanese Fishing Vessels', in GHQ/SCAP Records, National Diet Library, Tokyo, microfiche no. TS-00327; see also K. Yun, *Die Rolle der Friedeslinie (Rhee Line) im Normalisierungsprozess der Beziehungen zwischen Korea und Japan in der Nachkriegsära* (Frankfurt-am-Main and Bern: Peter Lang, 1983), pp. 54–5.

4. Government Section, Supreme Commander for the Allied Powers, *History of the Non-military Activities of the Occupation of Japan, 1945 through 1950*, Vol. 14, *Natural Resources, Part B* (facsimile reprint), (Tokyo: Nihon Tosho Sentā, 1990), p. 20.

5. Ibid.; see also S. Cheong, *The Politics of Anti-Japanese Sentiment in Korea: Japanese–South Korean Relations under American Occupation, 1945–1952* (New York and Westport, CT: Greenwood Press, 1991), p. 22.

6. Also referred to in English as the Liancourt Rocks.

7. Also known in Japanese as Saishutō, and in English sometimes referred to as Quelpart Island.

8. SCAPIN 677, 'Governmental and Administrative Separation of Certain Outlying Islands from Japan', 29 January 1946, reproduced in Government Section, *Political Reorientation*, p. 477; see also Cheong, *Politics of Anti-Japanese Sentiment*, pp. 23 and 37.

9. Cheong, *Politics of Anti-Japanese Sentiment*, pp. 22–3; see also GHQ/SCAP, *History of the Non-military Activities*, p. 19.

10. Cheong, *Politics of Anti-Japanese Sentiment*, p. 24.

11. On the problems of the border for the Amami Islanders, see Satake Kyōko, *Gunseika Amami no Mikkō, Mitsu Bōeki* (Tokyo: Nampō Shinsha, 2003).

12. B. Cummings, *Korea's Place in the Sun: A Modern History* (New York and London: W. W. Norton and Co., 1997), pp. 185–8.

13. Y. Sellek, '*Nikkeijin*: The Phenomenon of Return Migration', in M. Weiner (ed.), *Japan's Minorities: The Illusion of Homogeneity* (London: Routledge, 1997) pp. 178–210, quotation from p. 187.

14. P. Duus, *The Abacus and the Sword: The Japanese Penetration of Korea 1895–1910* (Berkeley: University of California Press, 1995) p. 335.

15. K. Yamawaki, 'Foreign Workers in Japan: A Historical Perspective', in M. Douglass and G. A. Roberts (eds.), *Japan and Global Migration: Foreign Workers and the Advent of Multicultural Society* (Honolulu: University of Hawaii Press, 2000) pp. 38–51, quotation from p. 43.

16. M. Weiner, *Race and Migration in Imperial Japan* (London and New York: Routledge, 1994) p. 53; Tsuboe Senji, *Zai-Nihon Chōsenjin no Gaikyo* (Tokyo: Gannandō Shoten, 1965) (original report composed in 1953), p. 14.

17. Tsuboe, *Zai-Nihon Chōsenjin*, p. 14.

18. Sugihara Tōru, *Ekkyō suru Tami: Kindai Ōsaka no Chōsenjinshi Kenkyū* (Tokyo: Shinkansha, 1998) p. 84; D. J. Nemeth, *The Architecture of Ideology: Neo-Confucian Imprinting on Cheju Island, Korea* (Berkeley and Los Angeles: University of California Press, 1987) pp. 148 and 150.

19. Sugihara, *Ekkyō suru Tami*, p. 84, gives a figure of 197,543; Nemeth, *Architecture of Ideology*, p. 149, cites a figure of 207,217.
20. Yang Hang-Won, '"Saishūtō Yon-San Jiken" no Hakei ni Kansuru Kenkyū', in Saishū tō Yonsan Jiken Yonjisshū nen Tsuitō Kinen Kōenshū Kankō Iinkai *Saishūtō 'Yon-San Jiken' to wa Nani ka* (Tokyo: Shinkansha, 1988), pp. 92–3.
21. Sugihara, *Ekkyō suru Tami*, pp. 109–11. The *Kimigayo II* was the successor to an earlier *Kimigayo* which had plied the Jeju–Osaka route from 1923, but foundered in a typhoon in 1925.
22. This is a scene also made familiar to many cinema-goers by the opening scene of Sai Yōichi's 2004 feature film *Chi to Hone* (Blood and Bone), which is based on novelist Yang Sok-Gil's memoirs of his father, a pre-war migrant from Jeju to Osaka.
23. Haenyo Museum (ed.), *Mothers of the Sea: The Jeju Haenyo* (Jeju City: Jeju Communication, 2007), p. 14; see also Kim Yeong and Yang Jungja, *Umi o Watatta Chōsenjin Ama* (Tokyo: Shinjuku Shobō, 1988).
24. Kim and Yang, *Umi o Watatta Chōsenjin Ama*, p. 226.
25. G. Shin, *Peasant Protest and Social Change in Colonial Korea* (Seattle and London: University of Washington Press, 1996), pp. 43–6.
26. Information from displays in the Haenyo Museum, Hado Village, Jeju.
27. Kim and Yang, *Umi o Watatta Chōsenjin Ama*, p. 234.
28. Kang Sang-Jung, *Zainichi* (Tokyo: Kōdansha, 2004), pp. 27–8; see also Kang Sang-Jung (trans. R. Fletcher), 'Memories of a *Zainichi* Korean Childhood', *Japanese Studies*, 26, 3 (December 2006), pp. 269–70.
29. A good example of this perception can be found in 'Contemporary Japan: Culture and Society', part of the 'Asia for Educators' website hosted by Columbia University, which states, 'Another major ethnic group in Japan is the Korean Japanese population – in Japanese sometimes called *zai-nichi kankokujin*, "Koreans-resident-in-Japan" – who are a large population estimated in the hundreds of thousands, perhaps in the low millions, of descendants of Koreans who were brought to Japan as forced laborers by the Japanese, from the beginning of the Japanese colonial period in Korea, which started in 1910 when Korea was annexed by Japan.' See http://afe.easia.columbia.edu/at_japan_soc/common/all.htm (accessed 12 May 2008).
30. One of these is Tokyo University professor Fujioka Nobukatsu. See W. Underwood, 'Names, Bones and Unpaid Wages (1): Reparations for Korean Forced Labor in Japan', *Japan Focus*, September 2006, www.japanfocus.org/products/topdf/2219 (accessed 10 September 2007).
31. For a discussion of this problem see D. Eltis (ed.), *Coerced and Free Migration: Global Perspectives* (Stanford: Stanford University Press, 2002).
32. Some examples of these recruitment practices can be found in Oguma Eiji and Kang Sang-Jung (eds.), *Zainichi Issei no Kioku* (Tokyo: Shūeisha Shinsho, 2008). For example, Song Ju-Pal, who was living in Keijo (Seoul) at the time, recalls being summoned to a police station, where he was told that the authorities were looking for people to work for two to three months on

Borderline Japan

a railway construction project in Osaka. Song was considering volunteering for this work, but when he went back to the police station to ask for further information, he found himself forced onto a train with a group of some eighty others, and taken to Hokkaido, where he was put to work in the coal mines until the end of the war.

33. Underwood, 'Names, Bones and Unpaid Wages (1)'; Utsumi Aiko, 'Teikoku no Naka no Rōmu Dōin', in Kurasawa Aiko, Sugihara Tōru, Narita Ryūichi, Tessa Morris-Suzuki, Yui Daizaburō and Yoshida Yutaka (eds.), *Iwanami Kōza Taiheiyō Sensō 4: Teikoku no Sensō Keiken* (Tokyo: Iwanami Shoten, 2006), pp. 91–118.
34. Tsuboe, *Zai-Nihon Chōsenjin no Gaikyō*, pp. 18–19.
35. See Y. Yoshimi, *Comfort Women: Sexual Slavery in the Japanese Military during World War II* (New York: Columbia University Press, 2000).
36. Tsubouchi Hirokiyo, *'Bōshū' to iu na no kyōsei renkō: Kikikaki aru Zainichi issei no shōgen* (Tokyo: Sairyūsha, 1998).
37. Sugihara Tōru, *Chūgokujin Kyōsei Renkō* (Tokyo: Iwanami Shoten, 2002).
38. M. Wyman, *DP: Europe's Displaced Persons, 1945–1951* (Philadelphia: Balch Institute Press, 1989), p. 22.
39. Underwood, 'Names, Bones and Unpaid Wages (1)', p. 13.
40. Japan Red Cross Society, *Repatriation Problem of Certain Koreans Residing in Japan* (Tokyo: Japan Red Cross Society, 1956), p. 2 (copy held in the Archives of the International Committee of the Red Cross, Geneva, File B AG 232 105–027, *Documentation concernant le rapatriement des Coréens et les pêcheurs japonais détenues à Pusan*. 10.10.1956–04.03.1959).
41. 'Sokoku Mochitai Isshin', *Asahi Shinbun*, 14 December 1959.
42. Tashirō Aritsugu, *Kosekihō chikujō kaisetsu* (Tokyo: Yuzankaku, 1974), p. 795.
43. Tanaka Hiroshi, 'Shokuminchi tōchi o sasaeta kokuseki', in Doi Takako (ed.), *'Kokuseki' o kangaeru* (Tokyo: Jiji Tsūshinsha, 1984), pp. 155–76.
44. Sugihara, *Ekkyō suru Tami*, pp. 86 and 92.
45. Weiner, *Race and Migration*, pp. 120–1.
46. Niki Fumiko, *Saigaika no Chūgokujin gyakusatsu: Chugokujin rōdōsha to wa naze gyakusatsu sareta ka* (Tokyo: Aoki Shoten, 1993), p. 133.
47. Hōmushō Nyūkoku Kanrikyoku, *Shutsunyūkoku kanri to sono jittai* (Tokyo: Ōkurashō Insatsukyoku, 1964), p. 8.
48. Quoted in letter of Sir C. Elliot to the Marquess Curzon of Kedlestone, 1921, held in the National Archives of Australia file *Aliens in Japan*. Series no. A11804; control symbol 1922/185, Canberra; see also Niki, *Saigaika no Chūgokujin gyakusatsu*; also A. Vasishth, 'A Model Minority: The Chinese Community in Japan', in M. Weiner (ed.), *Japan's Minorities*, pp. 108–39.
49. On the First World War and the introduction of passport controls see J. Torpey, *The Invention of the Passport: Surveillance, Citizenship and the State* (Cambridge: Cambridge University Press, 2000).
50. Hōmushō Nyūkoku Kanrikyoku, *Shutsunyūkoku kanri to sono jittai*, p. 8; Naimushō Keibōkyoku, *Gaiji keisatsu reiki shū* (facsimile) (Tokyo: Ryūkei Shosha, 1979), pp. 1–2.

51. Longfield Lloyd, 'Report from Longfield Lloyd, Australian Trade Commissioner in Japan, to Secretary, Prime Minister's Department, Canberra', 1936, typescript held in Australian National Archives, Canberra, File A1667/2, Control Symbol 194/A/15, Part 1, 'Japan – Economic Conditions – Immigration and Rights of Aliens'.

52. Hōmushō Nyūkoku Kanrikyoku, *Shutsunyūkoku Kanri no Kaikō to Tenbō: Nyūkan Hasoku 30-Shūnen o Kinen shite* (Tokyo: Hōmushō Nyūkoku Kanrikyoku, 1980), p. 69; see also 'Guidelines of the Ministry of Interior Concerning Entry, Stay and Exit of Aliens' (unofficial translation), attached to informal memo from A. C. Oppler to Maj. Gen. Robert E. Beightler, Deputy Governor, US Civil Administration, Ryukyu Islands, 'Japanese Immigration System and Laws', January 1951, in GHQ/SCAP Archives, Box 2189, *Immigration*, Feb. 1950–March 1952, held in National Diet Library, Tokyo, microfiche no. GS(B) 01603.

53. On the occupation of Japan see E. Takemae (trans. Robert Ricketts and Sebastian Swann), *Inside GHQ: The Allied Occupation of Japan and Its Legacy* (London: Continuum, 2002); J. Dower, *Embracing Defeat: Japan in the Wake of World War II* (New York: W. W. Norton, 1999); Nakamura Masanori, *Sengo Nihon: Senryō to Sengo Kaikaku* (Tokyo: Iwanami Shoten 1995); on Korea see B. B. C. Oh (ed.), *Korea under the American Military Government, 1945–1948* (Westport, CT and London: Praeger, 2002); on Korea see Monna Naoki, *Amerika Senryō Jidai Okinawa Genron Tōseishi: Genron no Jiyū e no Toi* (Tokyo: Yūzankaku, 1996).

54. One of the recent works which specifically emphasizes the connections between the various East Asian occupations is Nakano Toshio (ed.), *Okinawa no Senryō to Nihon no Fukkō: Shokuminchishugi wa ika ni Keizokushita ka* (Tokyo: Seikyūsha, 2006).

55. For further discussion of the 'divided occupation' see Takemae, *Inside GHQ*, pp. 120–5.

CHAPTER 3

Crossing the line

'Unauthorized arrivals' in occupied Japan

LIBERTY SHIPS

It was the last day of July, almost a year after Japan had surrendered to the Allies at the end of the Asia–Pacific War. The humid heat of midsummer hung over the calm waters of Senzaki Bay, where the liberty ship *Gilbert M. Hitchcock* lay at anchor. On either side of the sheltered inlet, mountain slopes dropped sheer to the water's edge. The mountains were thickly forested except for bare patches where pine trees had been cut for fuel, or their roots dug out to extract the oil that was used as a substitute for petrol in the last desperate days of war. Only on the innermost shore of the bay was the land flat enough for building; and along that shore stood a straggle of newly constructed wooden sheds, their roofs covered with tarpaulin to keep out the rain.

In the damp summer weather, the unpaved spaces between the sheds were churned to mud, which was tramped into the wooden boards of the jetty by the thousands of feet of those who thronged there, waiting for lighters to ferry them the short distance to the waiting ship. The *Gilbert M. Hitchcock*'s log for 31 July 1946 begins in the dry, business-like tones of all such documents:

1330 – Party less 1 NCO & 4 men (detailed as guard to assist the Japanese Police to bring Koreans from Shimonoseki and Kogushi to Senzaki by train) left 'C' Coy Chofu in two 3 ton trucks for Senzaki with 3 weeks rations ...
1530 – Tps [troops] and stores aboard. Koreans beginning to come aboard ...
1910 – Last boatload of Koreans for today aboard. Total 1322.[1]

But, hour by hour, as the log continues, the events of that voyage begin to strain and tear at the tight military syntax of the logbook. Even in the very first days, there are signs that something is amiss:

2300 – 3 Koreans (2 sick and suspected cholera cases; 1 to act as attendant) were taken off by a Japanese party from the quarantine hospital. Total 1319.

52

The Koreans appear to be very docile and though they tend to crowd around the alleyways on either side of the ship on 'C' deck, they move back when so ordered by the guard …
1 Aug. 1946
1610 – Last Korean on board Total 2506.

And as the voyage of the *Gilbert M. Hitchcock* unfolds, a note of sadness suffuses the commanding lieutenant's account of a seemingly routine assignment. The journey becomes one of the long-forgotten but still disquieting tragedies of the Allied occupation of Japan. Somehow, liberty for Koreans in Japan was not turning out quite as planned.

The *Gilbert M. Hitchcock* was one of last of the 2,751 liberty ships to be built by the US as wartime cargo vessels. Assembled a breakneck speed, the liberty ships were great ugly vessels, designed for function and capacity, not style or comfort. Publicity leaflets boasted that each vessel could carry 440 light tanks, 156,000 boxes of ammunition, or enough 'D' rations to feed 16,464,000 men for one day.[2] But the liberty ships which plied the waters between Japanese towns like Senzaki, Maizuru, Hakata and Sasebo and ports all over Asia carried people: mostly frightened, confused people.

In the words of US historian John Dower, describing the massive repatriation operation that became one the principle achievements of the first year of the Allied occupation of Japan, 'between October 1, 1945, and December 31, 1946, over 5.1 million Japanese returned to their homeland on around two hundred Liberty Ships and LSTs [landing ships, tank] loaned by the American military, as well as on the battered remnants of their own once-proud fleet'.[3] The incoming passengers were defeated Japanese soldiers from China, Southeast Asia and the Pacific, and colonial settlers who had fled Manchuria, Korea and Taiwan and other parts of Asia and the Pacific in the chaos that followed Japan's surrender, often suffering harrowing experiences on their journey.

On their outward voyages, the ships carried Koreans and Chinese, many of them people who had been brought to Japan as conscript labourers during the war. Between the Japanese surrender on 15 August 1945 and the end of that year, around 1.3 million out of the 2 million Koreans in Japan left, often by finding a place on any fishing vessel willing to ferry them across the waters to their home, and from February to December 1946 a further 82,900 returned to Korea under the official repatriation programme.[4]

SENZAKI

Senzaki was a little fishing port on the southwestern coast of the main Japanese island of Honshu: a place so remote that the most common comment from those who heard about its repatriation centre was, 'Senzaki? Where's that?' To which the usual reply was, 'Somewhere over the other side of Yamaguchi Prefecture.'[5] But Senzaki had a deep, sheltered harbour and was a convenient landing point for ships crossing to and fro between Japan and Korea. So it became one of the seven ports chosen to handle the official repatriation, and was specifically identified together with the port of Hakata (Fukuoka) as one of the two the main embarkation points for those being repatriated to Korea.[6]

Throughout the peak of the repatriations, Senzaki was controlled by New Zealand members of the British Commonwealth Occupation Force (BCOF), a body which has been described as 'a multinational and multiethnic force made up of Englishmen, Scots, Welshmen, Australians, Maori and Pakeha New Zealanders, Bengalis, Gurkhas, Hazarwals, Jats, Madrassis, Mahrattas, Musselmans, Rajputs and Sikhs serving under a common flag in "the last gasp of an Empire that would never be seen again"'.[7] In controlling the movement of people between Japan and its lost colonial empire, this vestige of the British Empire had a particularly important practical role to play. Its troops were responsible for the occupation of south-western regions of Honshu (including Tottori, Shimane and Yamaguchi Prefectures) and on the island of Shikoku – areas facing the Asian mainland where many of the arrivals from the continent made landfall, and where many of those departing for China or Korea spent their last days in Japan. Ironically, indeed, the Indian troops, who were stationed in Tottori and Shimane, spent much of their time in Japan seeking to control the activities of Japan's former colonial subjects at the very time when conflicts over India's impending independence were causing rising tensions between Indian forces and other sections of BCOF.[8]

Homecoming Japanese who arrived in Senzaki, mostly from Korea and Manchuria, were given medical inspections, had their luggage examined and were liberally sprayed with DDT before being transported to nearby stations to catch trains to their home towns. For many it was an anxious and disheartening homecoming. Occupation newsreel films show dejected Japanese soldiers depositing their military insignias in collection bins before being handed over to the hygiene officials, who seem to take a ruthless pleasure in spraying disinfectant on the repatriates' hair and down the backs of their trousers. Japanese repatriates were not accommodated in the camp. Those who were unable to find places on the overcrowded trains were supplied with food and given a space to sleep in nearby temples until transport could be arranged.[9]

Outgoing Korean and Chinese repatriates, on the other hand, were housed in the sheds along the waterfront, which provided basic accommodation for those waiting for their ship to arrive. Early reports from the repatriation centre convey a confident image of a mission on target. In March 1946, shipping was plentiful. There was 'ample food' to cater for the families who crowded the centre awaiting departure, and even a small stall where 'repatriates are able to buy such things as oranges for the children which are not supplied with the meals'.[10]

Already, though, unexpected problems had arisen. On the one hand, the number of Koreans signing up for the official repatriation programme was lower than expected. Repatriation from Japan to Korea and China was voluntary (although US occupation forces in southern Korea sometimes complained that the Japanese authorities were pressuring or even forcing Koreans they regarded as 'undesirable' to return home[11]). However, it had generally been assumed that almost all former colonial subjects would take the opportunity to go back to their place of origin. But in fact many hesitated, and in the early months of 1946 some of the repatriation ships from Senzaki and other ports were leaving half empty. Meanwhile, however, another even more unexpected phenomenon was appearing: Japanese police were beginning to detain large numbers of boats smuggling Koreans in the *opposite* direction – back into Japan.[12] By late May, many hundreds of 'Korean smugglers' were being shipped to Senzaki, which had become the main centre for handling their detention and deportation back to Korea.

The problem was compounded by language. Unauthorized entrants arriving by boat on Japan's shores were referred to in Japanese as *mikkōsha*, literally meaning 'people who travel in secret by ship' – stowaways, in other words. However, the term is closely related to the Japanese word *mitsuyū* – 'secret trade', or smuggling. A minority of those who arrived in small boats in 1946 were indeed engaged in illicit trade, though most (as we shall see) were simply trying to re-enter Japan, where they had lived until recently. But the Occupation Forces routinely used the word 'smuggler' as a translation for *mikkōsha*. This dissolved the distinction between smugglers of goods, people smugglers, and the boat people who were themselves being smuggled, and produced the strange phenomenon of children as young as one or two being arrested and deported for 'smuggling'. Indeed, this single but potent noun seems to have influenced the whole way in which the border crossers were perceived and dealt with during the occupation.

Throughout the early summer of 1946, new buildings were hastily being erected along edge of Senzaki Bay to house the 'smugglers' awaiting deportation, and to separate them from the regular Korean repatriates who were still passing through the camp in large numbers. 'Pens', these new buildings were generally called, though other words such as 'cage' were also used. An official report of events in Senzaki for the week ending 4 July 1946 notes that 'the "POW" cage has been completed and is now occupied by the smugglers on hand'.[13] Perhaps '"POW" cage' was not such a bad description. The compound was guarded both by occupation troops and Japanese police, and one soldier who served at Senzaki found it to be 'a veritable rabbit warren of tunnels in true P.O.W. style',[14] as inmates made desperate bids for freedom.

By the start of July 1946, 491 Koreans were being held in Senzaki. Ten days later, the extra accommodation needed to bring 'the total capacity of the camp to 400' was yet to be completed, but meanwhile the number of Koreans held there had risen to 719.[15] By mid-July it was obvious that 'even when completed the accommodation will still not be adequate at the present rate of arrivals'. On 16 July, the camp held 1,223 Koreans, of whom 1,125 'smugglers' were being held on landing ships (LSTs) moored in Senzaki harbour. By 30 July the number of 'smugglers' detained in Senzaki had reached 3,400.[16]

That was when the cholera epidemic began; and it was at this point that the *Gilbert M. Hitchcock* was commissioned to remove over 2,500 Koreans from Senzaki and deport them to Korea.

The troubles of the voyage began even before the ship weighed anchor with its complement of 2,506 'smugglers', a Japanese crew and a guard squadron of nineteen New Zealanders plus interpreter, when one of the many children on board died of suspected cholera. Within thirty-five minutes of the ship's departure from Senzaki another seven-month-old infant had died of malnutrition. The following morning at 6 a.m., the infant was buried at sea: 'The ship's siren sounded thrice, and the ship circled the spot once'.[17]

By the time they reached Busan at 7 a.m. on 3 August, the birth of a baby had increased the number of the ship's passengers by one, but on the afternoon of that same day, another two-year-old child died of malnutrition. Meanwhile, the US military, who controlled South Korea, had ordered that, because the ship was suspected of being a cholera carrier, its passengers were not to be allowed onto Korean soil. For four days, the ship lay at anchor in the midsummer heat just outside the port of Busan. 'As yet,' the commanding officer notes in his log, with an air of mild surprise, 'the Koreans have shown neither us nor the crew any hostility.' However, two of the ship's passengers did attempt to escape by leaping

Image 3.1. Korean repatriates about to embark, Senzaki, 1946.

into the sea, and three more were caught trying to slide down the ship's anchor chain. 'As there is no place in which to confine them [they] were tied up in full view of their compatriots, which hurt them keenly, according to my interpreter.'[18]

By now, two more of the passengers were showing symptoms of cholera, and one of the New Zealand guards was also suffering from something that was diagnosed as dysentery. The guard squadron was in such a state of nervous tension that when a fishing vessel came 'suspiciously' close to their anchored ship, they chased it off with a burst of machine-gun fire. Eventually, the two cholera cases were taken to quarantine ashore in Busan, but all others on the ship were denied the right to land, and the *Gilbert M. Hitchcock* was ordered instead to return to Senzaki. Halfway through the journey, this order was countermanded, and the ship's commander was told to change course and head instead for the repatriation centre at Hario, near Nagasaki, which was run by the US military. In the course of that journey a further two people – a fifty-year-old woman and a six-year-old child – died, four others were diagnosed as suffering from cholera, another New Zealand guard became ill and two more Koreans leapt into the sea and were caught attempting to swim ashore. 'Their reason for leaving ship was: insufficient food and fear of contracting cholera. I had them tied up in full view of the other Koreans.'[19]

When they finally reached Hario, more than a week after leaving Senzaki, the Koreans were kept in quarantine on board the ship. What happened to them thereafter, and how many more died, is not documented, but it appears that the survivors were later repatriated to Korea by a different route. The New Zealand crew returned to their barracks and presented themselves to their medical officer, 'who decided that quarantine would not be necessary'.[20]

Meanwhile, though the overcrowding in Senzaki had been reduced, the problems of the camp were far from being resolved. A week after the departure of the *Gilbert M. Hitchcock*, a senior New Zealand medical officer, C. R. Burns, visited Senzaki, and was taken out to see the landing vessel, which was still being used as a quarantine station for 'smugglers':

I was given to understand that there were about 500 people on board of all ages. About half of these were lying on the iron deck, and the rest below decks in the sleeping compartment. Many of the children looked very wasted, but there were no obviously sick cases among them. The latrine and ablution arrangements seemed to me rather crude and insufficient for so many people who were likely to be in the ship for several weeks.[21]

Conditions were not much better in the local hospital, where fifteen Korean cholera sufferers and twenty-nine carriers were being treated. Burns's scathing report on Senzaki notes,

The Chief Medical Officer was not present when I visited this hospital. His assistants appear to know very little about the cases and referred all questions to the nursing staff for answers …
Patients lay in bed fully dressed, and, in some cases, a mother and three children seemed to occupy the one bed. There appeared to be no adequate nursing facilities and no system in the hospital and no order. The staff seemed more interested in the records they could produce than in the patients themselves.[22]

Worst of all, conditions on the landing vessel were encouraging the spread of disease amongst those quarantined there, and also perhaps to the wider population, since waste from the quarantine ship flowed into Senzaki Bay, and there had already been a report in the town of a local person contracting cholera from fish caught in the bay. 'The Commander 2NZEF (JAPAN)', Dr Burns noted, 'is only concerned about the welfare of New Zealand troops stationed there'.[23]

These New Zealand troops, many of them young men fresh from the war, were not heartless, and their discomfort at the unenviable task they had been given resonates throughout the records they have left. As one soldier stationed at Senzaki noted in his diary,

Men women & children [are] herded into one heap & there are over 300 in one shed & they are locked in there ... The stink in those places nearly knocks you out & it is cruel to see the way they have to sleep. When a ship comes in they are put on to it like sardines in a tin & then they have to stay there until the doctors say it is free from diseases. The Idea of keeping them so long is to prevent diseases from spreading. This place is one of the worst in Japan for diseases but we are well looked after we are DDT'ed every time we leave the place & while on guard we wash our hands in lysol every half an hour ...[24]

OCCUPIERS, OCCUPIED AND 'LIBERATED PEOPLE'

If Senzaki had in fact been a POW camp, its conditions would have given cause for concern about possible breaches of the Geneva Conventions on the treatment of prisoners of war. But the people held at Senzaki were not prisoners of war; they were, to use the official terminology of occupation regulations, 'liberated people'. How, then, do we explain the event that unfolded in the camp in the summer of 1946?

To answer this question, we need to look not at the actions of the individual soldiers who served in Senzaki, but at the higher levels of occupation decision making, for Senzaki was a microcosm of the problems that beset occupation policy towards former colonial subjects in Japan and towards the whole issue of controlling Japan's borders.

The framework of policy for occupied Japan was determined in Washington, DC, in part by the Far Eastern Commission – a body consisting of representatives of the various leading Allied powers – but in practice often by the US Joint Chiefs of Staff and Department of State. Basic instructions on the conduct of the occupation, sent from Washington to the Supreme Commander Allied Powers (SCAP) in Tokyo, divided 'non-Japanese' into five groups: United Nations nationals, neutrals, enemy nationals, nationals of countries whose status had changed as a result of the war, and 'Koreans and Formosans'. About the last group, the occupation forces in Japan were instructed,

You will treat Formosan-Chinese and Koreans as liberated people in so far as military security permits. They are not included in the term 'Japanese' ... but they have been Japanese subjects and may be treated by you, in case of necessity, as enemy nationals. They may be repatriated, if they so desire, under such regulations as you may establish. However, priority will be given to the repatriation of nationals of the United Nations.[25]

The impenetrable prose of this instruction reflects underlying ambiguities in the occupation authority's view of former colonial subjects in

Japan. Essentially, they were low on the list of the occupation's priorities, and in any case were seen as a temporary problem, since it was assumed that they would all go home soon. Meanwhile, as SCAP's legal office pointed out, though Japan's surrender had involved the loss of its former colonies, this in itself did not 'assign new nationalities to persons affected by these territorial decisions'. So 'every person who on the day before [Japan's surrender] had been a Japanese national remained a Japanese national, until by some overt step he manifested an intention to adopt another nationality'.[26] To reinforce this message, in November 1946 SCAP issued a public announcement stating that

Koreans in Japan who refuse return to their homeland under the SCAP repatriation program will be considered as retaining their Japanese nationality until such time as a duly established Korean Government accords them recognition as Korean nationals.[27]

Defining Koreans and Taiwanese in Japan as 'Japanese nationals' suited SCAP's interests rather well. If they had been defined as 'aliens', they would not have been subject to Japanese taxes or court proceedings – a situation which would have reduced government revenue and made the task of maintaining law and order more onerous.[28] However, matters were complicated by the fact that, unlike defeated Germany, Japan was not directly governed by the occupiers, but was ruled indirectly, with SCAP issuing instructions to an elected Japanese government, which put them into effect. The Japanese government had no intention of treating former colonial subjects as Japanese with access to the expanded civil rights being introduced by SCAP's democratization programme.

This was made very clear as early as December 1945, when a new election law was introduced, dramatically expanding the franchise to give Japanese women the vote for the first time. The law, a widely proclaimed step towards the democratization of Japan, was implemented in a manner which received less publicity. Until 1945, adult male colonial subjects living in Japan had the right to vote in Japanese elections, but the new law was interpreted as limiting the franchise to people whose families were registered in 'Japan proper' (*naichi*), thus stripping the right to vote from Koreans and Taiwanese. As SCAP legal officer Jules Bassin put it, 'Koreans were now being treated as Japanese nationals and not as Japanese citizens, a relation comparable to that of Guamanians to American citizens'.[29] In other words, the 'liberated people' were being treated as colonial subjects.

There were three main groups of former colonial subjects in occupied Japan, and differences between the status of each group added a further layer of complication to an already murky situation. First, there were Okinawans – generally referred to as 'Ryukyuans' in occupation-period documents. As we have seen, on Japan's defeat Okinawa had been separated from the rest of the country, and placed under direct US military rule. 'Ryukyuans' were not allowed to enter or leave the rest of Japan unless they had special permission from the Supreme Commander Allied Powers, and, like Taiwanese and Koreans, they were sometimes arrested and deported as 'smugglers' during the occupation period.

In the first phases of the occupation, General Douglas MacArthur argued strongly for the permanent separation of Okinawa from Japan, and US occupation policy aimed at cutting the political, social and cultural ties between the archipelago and other Japanese islands.[30] However, in 1951 a secret bilateral agreement gave the US continuing control over Okinawa for twenty years after the end of the occupation of Japan, while acknowledging Japan's 'residual sovereignty' over the archipelago.[31] This implied that Okinawans were seen in terms of Japanese law as Japanese nationals temporarily under foreign rule. The separate occupation of Okinawa also meant that the immigration regulations devised in Tokyo during the occupation were not applied to Okinawa until 1972, when the archipelago was returned to Japan.

Taiwanese and Koreans in Japan, on the other hand, were former colonial subjects whose homelands had been irrevocably severed from Japanese rule. But there was one significant factor which divided the destiny of these two groups. The Chinese Nationalist government had been an ally of the US and Britain in the Pacific War, and was therefore entitled to a seat at the victors' table, and to participate in the deliberations of the Far Eastern Commission and of the San Francisco peace negotiations of 1951. Even after the Communist revolution of 1949 and the flight of the Nationalist government to Taiwan, Chiang Kai-shek's Nationalist regime continued to be recognized by the US and Japan as the only legitimate government of China. So Taiwanese in Japan, at least in theory, had a government to speak on their behalf in allied debates about repatriation, citizenship and other matters (though the Chinese Nationalist government, which had other things on its mind at this time, did not always pay much attention to the problems of its citizens in Japan).

Meanwhile, Korea was under the direct occupation of the US in the south and the Soviet Union in the north until 1948, when separate Korean regimes were established in both halves of the peninsula. Even after the creation of the Republic of Korea in the south, the new government was not placed on an equal footing with the Allied powers, and was not given a place at the negotiating table in San Francisco. This left the Korean community in Japan in a particularly vulnerable position, with no government to take up its cause in international forums. In response to the power vacuum, various Korean community groups quickly appeared in Japan. The largest and most powerful of these, the League of Korean Residents in Japan (Jaeil Joseonin Ryeonmaeng in Korean; Zainichi Chōsenjin Renmei in Japanese; referred to below as the Korean League), established immediately after Japan's surrender in August 1945, sought to act as a kind of 'provisional government' for Koreans in Japan, keeping order within the Korean community while representing its interests to the wider world. During the early stages of the occupation, the Korean League often cooperated with the occupation forces, even assisting them in crime prevention. But as time went on, the increasingly left-wing political stance of the League led to growing conflict with SCAP, as well as alienating some more conservative members of the Korean community.

THROUGH THE EYES OF THE OCCUPIER

For ordinary Allied servicemen, given the task of enforcing an ill-defined occupation policy on the streets, the ambivalent attitude of SCAP towards the 'liberated people' had a predictable result: they interpreted policy on the run, in whatever way best enabled them to tackle the problem of the moment. These realities are vividly illustrated by the memoirs of an Australian BCOF soldier, Alan Clifton, who was stationed at Ujina in western Japan – another major centre for repatriation to and from the Asian mainland.

Clifton had studied Japanese before the war, and found himself assigned as an interpreter to work with the local police. He was probably unaware of SCAP legal officers' musings about the national status of 'liberated people', and made his own common-sense judgements on the dilemmas of nationality that confronted him. On one occasion, Clifton recalls, he was called in to deal with a group of Taiwanese awaiting repatriation, who were supplementing their meagre food supply by stealing sugar from a local depot and selling it on the black market.

A single policeman demanded that they should surrender the sugar and themselves to his custody, but they replied that they were no longer Japanese citizens and not answerable to him ...

The policeman made a discreet withdrawal and came to us for advice.

We decided that the law should be upheld, and gave him permission to take them.[32]

Alan Clifton's memories of his time in Japan also shed a revealing and discomforting light on the occupiers' perceptions of Japan's former colonial subjects. His story of the occupation is, on the whole, a humane and sometimes humorous one. He soon came to feel a strong sense of sympathy towards the sufferings of the defeated Japanese civilians, and a revulsion towards the racism and arrogance displayed by some of his BCOF colleagues. Courageously, he exposed cases of rape of Japanese women by Allied servicemen in occupied Japan – an honesty which earned him criticism and even death threats in his home country, Australia.

But his accounts of his encounters with Taiwanese and Koreans in Japan are written in a rather different tone. Describing one visit to an office of the Korean League in Ujina, Clifton recalls,

The tram took me across numerous bridges and rivers, through streets of hovels that had existed long before the bomb made such buildings highly-desirable habitations …

The place was packed with young men and women, all with revolutionary zeal shining on their faces. The men were by physique and clothing indistinguishable from the Japanese, but the women wore the Korean billowing skirt of raw silk. They eyed me with some suspicion, and a long discussion in Korean followed, of which, of course, I understood not a word. Then a man who would have been picked out as their leader by anyone, addressed me in a curious kind of Japanese, all hard 'js', 'ds', and 'bs' softened to 'ch', 't' and 'p'.

Many Australian prisoners of war, had they heard it, would have remembered it as the accent common to some of the more brutal guards in the camps of south-east Asia.[33]

Interpreters like Clifton spoke Japanese, not Korean. This did not prevent them from communicating with Koreans in Japan, since almost all of Japan's former colonial subjects spoke some Japanese, but it meant that they communicated in the language of the colonizer. Most of the occupying forces, even people like Alan Clifton, who had an unusually expert knowledge of Japan, knew very little of Korean and Taiwanese history and culture. The only places where substantial numbers of Allied troops had previously encountered Koreans and Taiwanese were Japanese prisoner of war camps, where colonial subjects had been recruited to perform the most menial and undesirable guard duties. Having often been subject to violent recruitment and training themselves, Korean and Taiwanese guards became notorious amongst Allied POWs for their harsh treatment of camp inmates, and were disproportionately represented amongst those punished for war crimes in the trials held in formerly occupied areas of Asia. Allied forces, in other words, knew Japan's colonial subjects in their role as collaborators with some of the uglier aspects of Japanese military expansionism, but not in the role (which some, of course, had played) of impassioned resisters against colonialism.

The problem was aggravated by the fact that intermediaries like Clifton usually entered Korean and Taiwanese communities in the company of Japanese police, who were the occupation forces' main source of information about the 'liberated people'. Not surprisingly, they soon picked up some of the entrenched prejudices which Japanese police held towards former colonials. Clifton's chapter on the Koreans in Japan is entitled 'Fifth Column'. He begins by extolling the Japanese virtue of loyalty, which he found to have survived the defeat. In this context, Korean efforts to provide information to occupying forces are presented less as praiseworthy acts of cooperation with the liberators than as the vengeful actions of a sneak. The chapter concludes with Clifton, after an unsuccessful arms raid based on confused messages from a Korean informant, 'reviling all Koreans'.[34] This throwaway line is probably not meant to be taken seriously. All the same, it is a disturbing indicator of the ease with which sweeping prejudices reminiscent of the colonial era could colour the liberators' dealings with the liberated.

These individual experiences were reflected and sometimes magnified at the higher levels of the Allied command. As Mark Caprio points out,

United States images of the Korean people had historically mirrored the prejudicial attitudes held by the Japanese. By the end of the nineteenth century the US government, under the presidency of Theodore Roosevelt, had all but written off the Koreans' ability to govern themselves. This negative attitude prevailed as the United States prepared to occupy the Korean peninsula following the war's end.[35]

The same attitude, indeed, continued to prevail in many quarters throughout the occupation. A 1948 BCOF intelligence report on the 'Korean Minority Problem in Japan', compiled on the basis of information from US intelligence agencies, provides a particularly vivid image of the way in which the rhetoric of liberation was overwhelmed by stereotypes of former colonial subjects as a 'security problem'. The report begins with the words: 'Some 600,000 Koreans, a turbulent and disrupting minority, notorious for lawlessness, live in Japan'.[36] Although it acknowledges that 'Japanese police have at times, with natural prejudice, been too quick to act on the assumption that Koreans have been guilty', it enthusiastically elaborates the image of the Korean community as unruly, criminal and subversive. 'Korean illegal entry, resulting in a shifting element prone to disorder and lawlessness,' the report continues, 'has proved one of the most serious problems confronting the Japanese and the Occupation authorities in Japan.'[37] The conclusions are stark:

As long as there is a sizeable Korean minority in Japan it will be a menace to law and order. There are no indications that the size of this minority can be reduced in the near future. The problem, rather, is to maintain it at its present numbers through more adequate guard against illegal entry and firmer police control.[38]

Not all those involved in the occupation of Japan, however, shared this view of the Korean community. The copy of the BCOF intelligence report which I read in the Australian National Archives has been carefully annotated here and there in black ink. In the passage (cited above) which contains the phrase 'natural prejudice', for example, the adjective 'natural' has been underlined, and a large question mark placed beside it. The author of the question mark appears to have been Patrick Shaw, the head of the Australian diplomatic mission in Tokyo, who forwarded his copy of the document to Canberra with the terse assessment that it 'has no lasting value to this Mission'. Commenting on the report's contents, he says,

The past history of the Koreans is such that it is only to be expected that they might be involved in more infringements of the law than the Japanese. However, I cannot but feel that the failing of xenophobia which is strongly rooted in the Japanese often attributes to the Koreans crimes which they have not committed. It is certain that an incident in which a Korean is involved receives publicity out of all proportion to its importance.[39]

RECROSSING THE WATERS

Shaw, who had served on the Far Eastern Commission and was later to be a member of the United Nations Temporary Commission on Korea, was a careful and informed observer, and his Tokyo mission collected much useful information on the issue of Koreans and Taiwanese in Japan. One of the documents which he forwarded to Canberra – an article by journalist and member of SCAP's Information Section David Conde – sheds important light on the causes of the influx of Korean boat people which was aggravating the overcrowding of the Senzaki 'pens'. The 'seemingly strange migration of people back to the land of their oppressors', Conde argued, had its origins mainly in the design of SCAP's repatriation programme, which (as a measure to protect the war-devastated Japanese economy) allowed departing Koreans and other former colonial

Image 3.2. Repatriation centre, Senzaki. A very disappointed Korean. Artwork by
Australian war artist Reginald Rowed, 1946. The notes accompanying this picture state,
'Koreans are only allowed to retain 1000 yen before being sent back to their homeland.
This one has just been relieved of a large sum and is a little upset. A New Zealand
soldier gently pushes him on his way.'

subjects 'to take only one thousand yen (twenty packs of cigarettes at current prices) when they departed from Japan and compelled them to leave
their possessions, gained though labor under their recent exploiters'. This,
he noted, 'caused much anguish. That no jobs, houses or furniture were
available to those returning to Korea seemed not to be considered.' The
result was that many chose to 'risk their lives and at great risk re-cross the
narrow waters to Japan'.[40]

Conde's observations are borne out by a study commissioned by SCAP
itself. As unease about uncontrolled cross-border movement mounted,
the occupation forces dispatched a Korean resident in Japan, Cho Rin-
Sik, to Hario repatriation centre to examine the reasons for the influx

of 'smugglers' from Korea. Cho – who was the leader of a Kyushu-based Korean residents' group, and was described by SCAP as 'known to this headquarters' – visited the camp in the first half of August 1946, just after the *Gilbert M. Hitchcock* arrived there at the end of its abortive voyage to Korea. On 30 July, he noted, about two thousand Korean boat people (whom he calls 'stowaways' rather than 'smugglers') had been detained at Hario, 1,440 of them in cholera quarantine, but on 9 August (which was the day when the *Gilbert M. Hitchcock* arrived) the number had reached four thousand.[41]

Through questioning the detainees, Cho was able to gain a clear picture of their reasons for trying to enter (or rather re-enter) Japan. He reported that 'these stowaways are all former residents of Japan', and that 80 per cent had come to Japan 'on account of hard living and for the procuration of daily food'. The crucial problem, Cho emphasized, was the tight restriction on the amount of goods and money that repatriated Koreans could take with them on their departure from Japan. Many had lived in Japan for years and managed to scrape together enough savings to buy furniture, or even to start a small business. If they chose to return home to Korea, all this had to be abandoned. To make matters worse, if they took Bank of Japan notes with them, they found that these were not accepted in Korea. When they arrived in Korea, there were no jobs waiting for them. The treasury was so depleted (Cho pointed out) that even Koreans lucky enough to have official positions had generally not been paid for months.[42]

About 10 per cent of the stowaways, Cho estimated, came intending to trade on the black market, but most of these people too seem to have been driven by desperation. He noted that many had sold their own belongings to raise money for a place on a boat to Japan, and that some were malnourished and hungry by the time they arrived on the Japanese shore. A further 10 per cent or so were driven by what Cho calls 'impelling circumstances'. They were mostly people who had become separated from their husbands, wives or children, and were trying to rejoin them.[43] Cho does not provide any detailed description of the internment section of Hario, but his final sentence, despite its slightly clumsy English, speaks volumes about conditions there: 'the present heat may cause the total death of those who are placed in camps'.[44]

Some occupation officials themselves acknowledged the problems created by the thousand-yen limit on the repatriation of assets. A detailed 'Staff Study Concerning Koreans in Japan', compiled by SCAP's Diplomatic Section in 1948, proposed (amongst other things) that the limit be raised to 100,000 yen, but the recommendations of the study were not implemented.[45] Cho's report also failed to produce any easing of the restrictive repatriation rules. Instead it coincided with an intensified effort to patrol Japan's coastline in search of 'smugglers'. The process had begun as early as March 1946, when SCAP informed the Japanese government that non-Japanese who were repatriated to their homelands would not be allowed back into Japan without the permission of the Supreme Commander for the Allied Powers.[46] By the following month, there were rising fears of a return flow of small boats across the sea from Korea to Japan, and by the middle of the year, as the cholera epidemic in Korea spread, these fears were verging on panic.

On 11 June 1946, the Japanese government, with the blessing of the Allied occupation authorities, issued 'Imperial Ordinance 311', a sweeping decree which imposed a possible punishment of up to ten years' imprisonment on anyone found guilty of 'acts prejudicial to the objectives of the Occupation Forces'. The category of crimes covered by the decree was astonishingly broad, including any 'acts contravening the aims of directives from the Supreme Allied Commander to the Japanese Imperial Government' as well as 'acts contravening the aims of orders issued by Army, Corps or Divisional Commanders of the Allied Occupation Forces in enforcing such directives, and such acts as contravene enactments issued by the Japanese Imperial Government in executing such directives'.[47]

The ostensible reason for this vague but draconian measure was an upsurge of trade union activity following May Day demonstrations in Tokyo, which had aroused fears of social unrest amongst Japanese and occupation officials alike. But it was very quickly applied to a quite different problem. The day after Imperial Ordinance 311 was issued, on 12 June 1946, SCAP announced that:

Cholera has broken out in Korea and is rapidly reaching epidemic proportions. In view of the grave danger of the introduction of this disease into Japan by carriers transported from Korea to Japan on unauthorized shipping, positive steps must be taken to detect and apprehend ships illegally entering Japanese ports.[48]

The Japanese authorities were given orders to apprehend all ships entering Japanese ports without permission, and to arrest their crews and passengers and send them to Senzaki, Sasebo (Hario) or Maizuru for deportation.[49] Some of the recommended 'positive steps' seem rather alarming. Japanese fishing boats were given confidential instructions to fly specific flags by day and show lights at night so that they would not be mistaken for people-smuggling vessels. 'Unless they provided their ships with adequate day and night signals', they were warned, '"accidents" would probably happen for which the Occupation Forces would not be responsible', since 'any unidentified vessel which fails to halt is liable to be fired on'.[50] This points to the disturbing possibility that unauthorized vessels carrying boat people from Korea to Japan may actually have been sunk by occupation forces. I have found no records of such incidents, but the hazards of the voyages made by border crossers were greatly increased by fears of possible attack. Crossings were generally made in small fishing boats which left and entered port under cover of darkness, and there are intermittent reports of wrecks in the occupation archives, though many accidents probably went unreported.[51]

Meanwhile in May 1946, the headquarters of the US 8th Army had advised British Commonwealth troops engaged in border patrol duties that 'illegal entry of repatriated Koreans is considered an act prejudicial to the Occupation Forces and Provost Courts may take jurisdiction'. BCOF forces were also reminded that 'deportation may be awarded as an additional punishment'.[52] This measure had little immediate effect, perhaps not surprisingly, since it seldom seems to have been communicated to the border crossers themselves: several months later, occupation force reports were still noting 'interrogation of Koreans apprehended while attempting to re-enter Japan has disclosed that many were not aware that re-entry was illegal'.[53]

Figures collected by the Japanese police and passed on to SCAP show that the number of Korean illegal entrants arrested soared from about 800 in May 1946 to 8,037 in June, before falling back slightly to 6,916 in July of the same year. After that, the numbers moved through a regular seasonal cycle, dropping sharply in the winter months, when rough seas made crossings perilous if not impossible, and rising again in the summer. The summer peaks never again reached the levels of 1946, but over a thousand boat people were arrested in August 1947 and in August 1949.[54] In all, between April 1946 and the end of 1951, a total of 48,076 'illegal entrants' (45,960 from Korea, 1,704 from the 'Nansei Islands' (Okinawa and Amami), 410 from China and two from elsewhere) were arrested.[55] The authorities were also well aware that many of those who arrived in small boats escaped arrest. Estimates of the numbers varied wildly. According to a secret US 8th Army memo of 1949, 'statistical studies indicate that approximately 50 per cent of the illegal entrants are not apprehended, and only 25 per cent of the ships involved in this traffic are captured'.[56] But another document of the same year, setting out the Japanese government's views on the subject,

Image 3.3. New Zealand soldiers apprehend Korean boat people, 1946.

made claims about the levels of illegal entry which were even more alarmist: 'those not arrested are considered several times as many as those arrested and are estimated to amount to 200,000 to 300,000 in total'.[57]

FIRE ON THE MOUNTAIN

The fears of cholera in 1946 were perfectly genuine. But with hindsight it seems clear that, not for the first or the last time, epidemic disease was used as an occasion to introduce stringent border controls which served much wider political purposes. After all, the cholera epidemic did not prevent the occupation authorities from continuing to repatriate Japanese from Korea, China and Manchuria, and (to judge by conditions at Senzaki) the steps taken to detain Korean boat people may have done as much to spread contagion as to control it. Besides, the stringent restrictions on cross-border movement between Japan and the Asian mainland continued long after the cholera epidemic was over. As time went on, it became obvious that fears of the spread of disease from the continent had become inseparably intertwined with fears of another sort of infection – contagion by the virus of communism.

The source of these fears, and the force that propelled the continuing flow of boat people across the sea from Korea to Japan, can best be understood by looking at migration from the opposite angle: from the vantage point (for example) of an occupation-period stowaway from the Korean island of Jeju.

'Mr Yang' was sixty-seven years old and had been living in Osaka for more than forty years when he shared his memories of migration to Japan with researcher Koh Sun-Hui. Yang came from an impoverished farm family, and was born and brought up in a village on the slopes of Jeju Island's soaring volcano, Mount Halla. After four years at school, followed by military training under the Japanese, he was recruited into the colonial armed forces just before Japan's surrender in 1945. As Yang remembers the moment of liberation in August 1945:

We didn't know what was happening. You see, in those days there was no radio or anything in Jeju villages. Old man S., he knew something was going on, because he was a village official – one of the local bosses – so he heard something, and that was where the first information came from. There was no other way of getting news, because we didn't have newspapers or radio. When the announcement came to the village from the authorities, then we knew, and we were delighted. It meant we'd been liberated. The army was going away, and we were free from Japanese rule.[58]

In that same year of liberation, Yang married a woman from the neighbouring village. It would, he later reflected,

have been good if I could have just lived my adult life like that. But in those days there was this thing called the South Korean Workers' Party. They made an organization to reclaim our country and to prepare it for building independence and all that, and I got involved in this without really knowing what it was all about.

The troubles that beset Jeju Island in the late 1940s were partly a result of the island's long history of migration to Japan. In the year following Japan's surrender some 60,000 people were repatriated from Japan to Jeju, many with nothing but the regulation thousand yen and the goods they could carry on their backs. While the allied occupation authorities in Japan were eagerly encouraging Koreans to go home, the US Military Government in Korea was doing little to prepare for their arrival.[59] The influx of repatriated Koreans from Japan immediately followed the return of evacuees to the island in the final stages of the war to escape the bombing raids on Osaka and other cities. Within a couple of years, Jeju's population had grown by around 25 per cent. Former emigrants to Japan, who for years had regularly sent money home to their families in Jeju, helping to sustain the island's economy, had now returned to become an impoverished burden on their communities.[60] Because of its deep incorporation into the migration networks of the Japanese Empire, then, Jeju suffered particularly severely from a problem which beset the entire Korean peninsula as some 4 million overseas Koreans (including around 1.4 million from Japan) headed home.[61]

On Jeju, the slide into all-out violence began more than three years before the start of the Korean War, on 1 March 1947, when a mass of islanders gathered in the centre of Jeju City to celebrate the anniversary of the 1919 anti-colonial uprising which is generally seen as marking the birth of Korea's independence movement. As Koreans became aware that the division of their country was going to be more than a passing temporary phase, the prospect of the creation of a separate government in the south aroused fierce opposition. In Jeju, anger towards the policies of the occupiers was intensified by a crop requisition scheme, introduced by the US Military Government to deal with the chronic food shortages in 1946 and 1947, but (to local farmers) horribly reminiscent of hated wartime Japanese policies. The left-wing South Korean Workers' Party (Nam Joseon Nodongdang, or Namnodang for short) played an active role in organizing protests, but the participants came from a wide spectrum of Jeju society.

The crowd which gathered to commemorate the 1 March rising, then, was a crowd with grievances to express, and was much larger than anyone had expected. It is estimated that as many as 30,000 people – about one-tenth of the island's total population – marched through the city and into the square in front of the old government building where the police headquarters were located. Tension had been rising in the days leading up to 1 March, and a large contingent of police was waiting to confront the marchers. According to some accounts, trouble began when a child in the crowd was knocked down by a police horse.[62] Some of those who witnessed the incident began to throw stones at the police, and at that point the police panicked and fired into the crowd, killing six people whom even the authorities subsequently identified as 'innocent persons'.[63] One was a fifteen-year-old schoolboy, another a woman carrying a small baby in her arms (the baby survived).

The response to these killings was a massive island-wide strike, in which bank clerks and government officials, as well as factory workers, farmers, students, teachers and others, took part.[64] The strikers demanded an enquiry into the shootings, and the dismissal of those responsible. The US Military Government conducted an investigation, and expressed 'regret' at the incident, but also portrayed it as the result of communist agitation by the South Korean Workers' Party. Further police reinforcements were brought into the island, along with a detachment of the much-feared North-West Youth League – an anti-communist vigilante organization formed from those who had fled south from the Soviet-occupied northern half of Korea.

Large numbers of suspected 'subversives' were arrested, and some were tortured and killed.[65] Mr Yang, who had become involved in handing out protest leaflets in his village, was among those arrested. He was sent for trial to a neighbouring town and sentenced to six months' imprisonment, but after villagers rallied to his support and collected money on his behalf, he was ultimately let off with a fine. From that point on, however, he and his family became suspects, closely watched by the police. It was then that Yang (who, like many islanders, had relatives still living in Japan) decided to flee to Japan:

Even though I'd decided to leave, we were under police surveillance, so my father worked out a clever scheme to get me out of the village. My sister and I were to say we were going to a memorial ceremony for our grandfather. We even carried the ritual vessels and liquor and baskets for the ceremony with us when we set off. The departure place for the smuggling boat was five villages away. The people from our village had collected money to pay the people smuggler: seven thousand won, it cost ... I had a friend from my village who was one year older than me. He had got involved in the same movement ... He wanted to leave with me, but he couldn't get the money together, so he didn't go. After I left for Japan, he was shot dead. The police shot him ...

The place where I landed in Japan was Misaki in Kanagawa Prefecture. The boat was a fifty-ton cargo boat. It took three days, or maybe four. It was a good boat – Japanese, it was. We landed round about 3 o'clock in the morning, and when it started to grow light, I caught a train to Chiba where my relatives live. No, wait a minute, that's wrong. I went to Osaka. That's it. I was with my cousin, and we went to the station together. On the way there was this police box, and we were afraid of leaving footprints, so we took our shoes off and walked barefoot to the railway station, and when we got there we caught the train to Osaka.[66]

Yang left behind a society caught in a cycle of escalating violence. In response to the fierce police crackdown, some prominent local members of the South Korean Workers' Party decided to strike back at the authorities. A group of several hundred activists withdrew into the forests of Mount Halla in the centre of Jeju Island, where they set up base camps from which, on 3 April 1948, they issued a call to arms to their fellow islanders, and launched an attack on police stations and the homes of prominent right-wing officials, killing twelve people. The date was to become enshrined in Korean history: the uprising on Jeju, and the massacres which followed, are known today as the '4.3 Incident' (*Sa-Sam Sageon*).

The historical evidence suggests that the 4.3 Incident had begun as a largely spontaneous uprising emerging from the spiral of violence between local activists and heavy-handed security forces. As the uprising turned into a prolonged guerilla campaign, however, leading insurgents developed closer links with fellow communists in North Korea.[67] The American military (who retained overall command of the South Korean security forces throughout) interpreted the events in Jeju as being, from start to finish, part of an international communist conspiracy orchestrated from Moscow and Pyongyang, and their fears were intensified in the autumn of 1948, when the insurrection spread to the Korean mainland. In September, troops in the towns of Yeosu and Suncheon who had been ordered to go to Jeju to take part in the suppression of the uprising there mutinied in support of the Jeju insurgents – a gesture of solidarity which was put down with great ferocity. Significantly, the US military in Korea believed that 'there is also connection with the Japanese Communist Party through the intermediary of agents who ply between Masan and Pusan and unknown Japanese ports'.[68] Although there is little evidence of significant assistance from the Japanese Communist Party to the Jeju insurgents, these beliefs help to explain the extreme alarm with which occupation authorities in both Korea and Japan viewed the movement of small boats across the sea between the two countries.

By the time South Korea's first election was held on 10 May 1948, then, Jeju Island was already in a state of civil war. As in all civil wars, terrible things were done on both sides, though the unequal balance of power between the US-backed South Korean authorities and the Jeju rebels meant that the largest share of the killing was performed by those acting on the orders of the authorities. Following the official establishment of the Republic of Korea under the presidency of Yi Seung-Man (Syngman Rhee) on 15 August 1948, reinforcements of police and security forces were sent to Jeju, and draconian restrictions on the movement of islanders were imposed as the government prepared for a major offensive. In October 1948, government and military officials on Jeju ordered a scorched-earth policy, which aimed to trap the insurgents in their hideouts on the upper slopes of Mount Halla, separating them from access to coastal villages.

Under the terms of this order, all villages on the middle slopes of Mount Halla – 130 in all – were to be evacuated and burnt to the ground.

As Mr Yang recalls,

After I came to Japan there was the 4.3 Incident … After I left home, they did that to the village. The people came down from the mountain. Our house was set on fire too …

They did it to repress [the rising], and then the other side retaliated, and things just got more and more extreme. In the end they brought these people [militias] over from the Mainland. People who couldn't read or write came carrying official documents and they killed the wrong people. You know, they mistakenly hit children on the head with stones and killed them, and they cut off people's heads with Japanese swords. They used swords and things that the Japanese [military] had left behind as weapons …

There are people around here [in Osaka], lots of people, who fled to Japan at the time of the 4.3 Incident. After all, whichever side you're on, people run away to avoid being killed, don't they? And then, after that, there was the Disturbance [the Korean War]. Quite a lot of people came over from Jeju at that time too.[69]

The precise number of Jeju islanders killed in the aftermath of the 3 April rising is still unknown, but is estimated at between 20,000 and 30,000. Some were police and other officials killed by the insurgents; many more were insurgents killed by the police and vigilante groups; but most of all were those caught in the middle of the government's scorched-earth policy, which by the middle of 1949 had utterly transformed the human geography of the island. The number of people from Jeju who sought refuge by fleeing to Japan is also unknown, but (as Yang's testimony suggests) was considerable.

Knowledge of the massacres was suppressed within South Korea for almost half a century, and much of the outside world's knowledge of the subject indeed came initially from Jeju islanders living in Japan. The eminent poet Kim Shi-Jong was among those who fled the fighting in Jeju in 1949, arriving by people-smuggling boat in Kobe, and spending the rest of his life in Japan.[70] Though Kim Shi-Jong found it difficult to put his experiences into words, and only began to recount his involvement in the uprising many years later, others in the Jeju Island community in Japan started to publish writings on the subject in the 1960s. Among them was Osaka-born novelist Kim Seok-Beom, whose parents came from Jeju and who had returned briefly to Korea immediately after the war. His epic work *Kazantō* (*Volcano Island* – a multivolume novel published over a thirty-year span from 1967 to 1997) remains one of the most powerful evocations of the events of that time. These had consequences for Jeju which lasted for many decades.[71] But meanwhile, these events had come to be overshadowed by the even greater conflict that overwhelmed the rest of the peninsula in 1950.

THE BORDERS OF REFUGEE PROTECTION

On 25 June 1950, after repeated minor clashes along the 38th parallel, North Korean troops with Soviet support swept across the line and moved south with astonishing speed. By late August, they were less than fifty kilometres from Busan, and almost all of the Korean peninsula was under the control of Communist forces. But in the latter part of the year, following the landing by American and other UN forces at Incheon, the tide of war turned, and the US and their allies moved north, capturing Pyongyang in November of that year and almost reaching the northernmost border of Korea before the entry of China into the conflict pushed them south again.

The Korean War created enormous numbers of casualties on both sides: around three million Koreans, half a million Chinese and tens of thousands of United Nations troops are believed to have died in the war. The fighting also caused massive homelessness and dislocation. In February 1951, it was estimated that there were around 3.5 million internally displaced refugees in South Korea, of whom over 1.1 million were in need of immediate assistance.[72] During the early months of the war, hundreds of thousands of refugees fled before the North Korean forces' southward advance, flooding into the overflowing alleyways of Busan, escaping both the fighting and the arrests and executions which the northern forces often meted out to those they identified as political enemies. When South Korean and United Nations forces moved north, many of those who attempted to return home found their houses and villages in ruins. Meanwhile, South Korean forces carried out mass killings of those believed to have collaborated with the Communist enemy.[73] The violent suppression of suspected 'imperialist lackeys' in the North and suspected 'Reds' in the South continued long after the end of the war. The head of the Truth and Reconciliation Commission established by the South Korean government has estimated that some 100,000 South Koreans civilians were executed for political reasons by their own government and military during the early phases of the Korean War.[74]

While the fighting in Korea was at its height, on the other side of the world in Geneva representatives of 25 countries were meeting to hammer out a United Nations Convention on the Status of Refugees. The Geneva Convention of 1951 was to have a profound effect in improving the protection of some of the world's most vulnerable people. But the convention was made in, and focused on, Europe. The only Asian country represented at the Geneva Conference was Iraq, and several participants (including France, Australia, New Zealand, Canada and the US) were eager to ensure that they would not be required to accept non-European refugees. The coverage of the first draft of the Convention, drawn up before the outbreak of the Korean War, was limited to 'events occurring in Europe before 1 January 1951', but in the General Assembly of the United Nations a number of countries had objected to the inclusion of the words 'in Europe', and had them removed.[75] This alarmed governments like Australia's: as one Australian official put it, 'the omission of the words "in Europe" … made the Convention quite unacceptable to us from the point of view of restricted migration and the White Australia policy since it opened the door to refugees from Communist China, India, Pakistan and Indonesia'.[76] This sticking point was one of several which almost caused the collapse of the negotiations.

Somewhat ironically, Patrick Shaw – the diplomat who had shown considerable sensitivity to the situation of Koreans in Japan – was the person entrusted with the task of arguing Australia's position in Geneva. There appears to have been relief in Canberra, Washington, Wellington and elsewhere when the French delegate proposed the reinsertion of the words 'in Europe'. His proposal was promptly accepted, and the final text of the Convention on the Status of Refugees was adopted unanimously by the twenty-four countries represented in Geneva on 25 July 1951.[77] The clause limiting the convention's scope to 'events occurring in Europe before 1 January 1951' was to remain until 1967, when a new Protocol Relating to the Status of Refugees extended the coverage both temporally and geographically.[78]

The limits of the Geneva Convention left refugees from Korea, China and other parts of Asia without international legal protection throughout the 1950s and early 1960s. It did not, however, prevent governments, on their own discretion, from granting protection to those who sought asylum. In 1949, for example, two Koreans who had been prominent collaborators with the Japanese during the colonial period (one a former senior colonial police officer and the other an entrepreneur who had been active in pro-imperial political associations) fled to Japan and sought protection from the authorities. The two arrived on a people-smuggling boat, but immediately handed themselves in to Japanese police and asked for asylum, on the grounds that they feared arrest in South Korea under that country's newly created Traitors' Punishment Law. The case was sent to SCAP's Government Section, which expressed some sympathy. SCAP, in fact, had recently issued a press release recalling that 'it had been the historical practice of the United States, for over a century, to afford unqualified refuge and safe haven to foreign nationals who are compelled by reasons of political, moral or social convictions to abandon their country'.[79] The suggestion seemed to be that something similar was planned for Japan. Occupation officials recommended that the two asylum seekers 'be given an opportunity to request permission of SCAP to remain in the country, and to submit evidence from which the merits of such request may be determined'. Provided that they were not found to be 'undesirable', they were to be granted refuge in Japan.[80]

But less than a year later, when SCAP found itself facing a refugee issue of an altogether different magnitude, the response was very different. As North Korean forces swept south towards Busan, the occupation authorities in Japan realized that there was likely to be 'a considerable influx of Korean refugees into this country'. After all, Japan's westernmost island of Tsushima is visible on a clear day from the hills above Busan, and within the first weeks of the war a flotilla of small boats landed on the island's shores, and at other points along the west coast of Japan. SCAP's Government Section noted that, although the boat people were, strictly speaking, illegal immigrants who should be deported as soon as possible, there were ethical issues involved in sending people into the middle of a war zone: 'from the point of view of humanity and in view of the internal public peace of Japan it will be necessary that these refugees should be placed under protective concentration at some proper installation until such time as they can be sent back to their home country'.[81]

By now, Senzaki repatriation centre had been closed, and its inmates transferred to Hario. The regular repatriation programme between Japan and Korea had ceased with the outbreak of the Korean War, and Hario's only function in the second half of 1950 was as a place of detention and deportation for illegal immigrants and other 'undesirables'. The centre, now referred to in SCAP documents as 'Hario Concentration Camp' or sometimes 'Hario Concentration Home', had the capacity to accommodate just eight hundred detainees in summer and a thousand in winter. To cope with the expected inflow, it was suggested that a new refugee or internment camp should be set up under the supervision of Japan's Ministry of Health and Welfare.[82] There seems to have been little consideration given to the idea of allowing refugees to apply for permanent asylum in Japan. In exceptional circumstances, however, individual appeals to be allowed to stay in Japan were considered by the Japanese Ministry of Justice, which passed these on to the SCAP for a final ruling (up to March 1951, when the Japanese government took over full control of the proceedings).[83]

One of the lucky few granted the right to stay was 'Mr Koh', whose story we encountered at the beginning of this book. In August 1950, after he had spent several months in custody, SCAP officials concluded that 'all the statements in his petition are true and that the illegal entrant is capable of supporting himself and his family ... on at least a middle-class level since his business is currently yielding 20,000 yen a month and he owns property valued at 800,000'.[84] But such life-and-death recommendations were discretionary, arbitrary and rare. They were based not on any clear standard of international humanitarian law, but merely on the personal judgement – the human feelings and political instincts – of the officials on whose desks the appeal for mercy happened to land. Each order of the release of a detainee ended with a firm reminder that 'permission for subject individual to remain in Japan is not to be considered as a precedent, but as an exception to established policy based on the facts of this particular case'.[85]

For most – even those in situations much like Mr Koh's – there was no reprieve. Some six months after the outbreak of the 4.3 Incident in Jeju, for example, over 290 undocumented entrants, all but four of them from Jeju Island, were arrested after arriving in small boats on the Sada peninsula in Ehime Prefecture on the island of Shikoku over a two-week period. The police who questioned these boat people found that 78 per cent of them had previously lived in Japan, and 24 per cent had lived in Japan for more than fifteen years.[86] Around 40 per cent were trying to rejoin relatives who were still living in Osaka or other Japanese cities, and a number of them spoke of the terrors of life in strife-torn Jeju. As one of those arrested put it, 'the people are caught between two fires – if they take the side of the police against the Communists or of the Communists against the police, they are oppressed by the opposing side'.[87]

Among those arrested was a farmer whose wife and children lived in Tokyo, a nineteen-year-old whose parents lived in Kobe, twenty-nine women whose husbands lived in Japan, and a sewing-machine dealer who lived in Osaka but (like Mr Koh) had returned to Jeju to see his critically ill mother.[88] The police report meticulously notes that 34 per cent had no school education at all, and 42 per cent had only attended primary school. Many, in other words, would have been illiterate or semi-literate, and have had little chance of making a special case to the authorities. Apart from nine crew members of the people-smuggling boats, who were sent for trial, the rest were all dispatched to Hario, from where it seems that they were deported.[89]

And despite the recommendations of SCAP's Government Section, the deportations continued even at the height of the Korean War. By late 1950, Hario concentration camp had been placed under the control of the Japanese Ministry of Justice, and contained 963 'Korean smugglers'. On 12 December 1950, the inmates were presented with an order from the Supreme Commander for the Allied Powers confirming their deportation to Korea. Just 18 of the 963 were given special permission to remain in Japan. When they heard that they were about to be shipped to Korea, about 150 of the detainees rushed to the camp's guard post protesting that 'the deportation was too sudden to let their kith and kin know and it was not the humanitarian way'.[90] However, two days later, with 70 police in attendance, the 945 who had been denied the right to remain in Japan were escorted onto a waiting ship and 'the deportation of them was completed without trouble'.

What happened to the deportees at the other end is not recorded. Even before the outbreak of the Korean War, the reception given to deportees from Japan by the Korean authorities had been far from cordial. One New Zealand soldier who accompanied a ship-load of Korean deportees from Senzaki to Busan noted,

Prior to disembarkation at Fusan [Busan] a Korean Army officer addressed the Koreans in a domineering tone stating that they were deserters from Korea and should help to hold up the now independent state. He requested the Koreans to sing the Korean National Anthem.[91]

For those suspected of links to communism the fate that awaited them was very much worse.

The policy of excluding and deporting refugees from the fighting in Korea had blessing from the highest levels. The following month, Chang Myun (also known as John Chang), who was then serving as the Republic of Korea's ambassador in Washington, sought permission to bring his family out of war-torn Korea to safety in Japan. The issue was referred to General Douglas MacArthur, whose response, conveyed by telegram to the US State Department, was blunt. Allowing Korean refugees into Japan, MacArthur believed, 'might well enrage Japanese people because of past relationship between them and Korean race' and because of 'Japan's own pressing problems with Korean minority already in Japan'. MacArthur also expressed fears that entangling Japan in issues connected to the war in Korea might draw Japan itself into the conflict, providing an 'excuse for invasion'.[92] In the end, no rights to refuge or asylum were granted to those fleeing war or persecution in Korea.

Meanwhile, many others continued to evade the border guards and enter Japan. Among them was Yoon Hak-Joon (1933–2003), who later became a lecturer at Tokyo's Hōsei University, and was one of the few people to publish a written non-fictional account of his unauthorized entry into Japan.

Yoon was a law student in the South Korean town of Daegu at the time when the Korean War broke out. He had relatively left-wing political views, and, when the North Korean forces swept south in their first offensive of the war, found himself living in an area controlled by the North Korean People's Army. After the tide of war turned, this fact alone would have made him a suspect 'collaborator with the Reds'. As the anti-Communist purge in South Korea gathered momentum in 1953, Yoon Hak-Joon boarded a people-smuggling boat to seek refuge in Japan, where his uncle and aunt were living:

The smuggling boat left from the little fishing village of Dadaepo, close to Busan. Dadaepo was well known, not so much for being a fishing village as for being a base for people-smuggling boats going to Japan. So before our departure, the boat's captain and other people with experience of these things gave us various 'lectures', envisaging the conditions we would encounter when we landed in Japan, and explaining how we should prepare mentally to be ready for them. For example, when the boat reached the shore, there would be no jetty, so we would have to jump into the shallows. We'd be soaked, so we should each take one change of clothes with us in a plastic bag. We'd probably have to climb rocks and mountains, so we should wear sports shoes … If we had to ask the way, we should try to ask a schoolgirl. We were told all sorts of things like that.[93]

The boat which Yoon Hak-Joon boarded was much smaller than the one that had taken Mr Yang from Jeju to Japan six years earlier, and the journey was cramped and terrifying.

It was only a four- or five-ton fishing boat, and it was crammed with thirty-five or thirty-six 'pigs'. The 'pigs' were us, the passengers – this was the code word for stowaways. We were piled one on top of the other in the hold of the boat … About twenty hours after leaving port, we were arrested by the [Japanese] coastguard.[94]

Yoon's boat was apprehended by the Japanese Maritime Security Agency off the coast of Kyushu, apparently following a tip-off from the

Korean authorities, and Yoon and his fellow 'pigs' were taken to the Agency's headquarters in the town of Karatsu for questioning. While they were being processed, Yoon was told to sit next to a second-floor window, out of which he could see a garden and the road beyond:

I thought about what would happen to me if I were deported. For a moment, everything seemed to grow dark before my eyes. My heart was hammering and my whole body was shaking. The window was the kind that opens if you push it outward, and I just had to turn the lever to open it. I made the decision. When I looked around the room, the guard was in the process of taking the person next to me into an adjoining annex. *Now*, I decided. I grabbed the lever, opened the window and jumped out.[95]

Yoon landed in the garden and, pursued by shots from the coastguards' pistols, fled across the road and through neighbouring fields. When he returned to the road after walking a safe distance across country, he found himself in a remote rural lane, with little idea where he was. A taxi appeared, so (although he had been warned against this before his departure) Yoon hailed it and asked the driver, in broken Japanese, to take him to the nearest station.

Though prejudice against Koreans was all too evident in the Japanese media and official documents of the times, not all ordinary Japanese people were hostile to Korean migrants and (as we saw in the case of Mr Koh) some actively supported movements to protect the rights of immigrants to Japan. Reading Yoon's account, one can only assume that he was very fortunate in his choice of taxi driver. For, despite being hailed in the middle of the night near the Coastguard headquarters by a Korean who spoke little Japanese and who asked to be taken to the station at a time when no trains were running, the taxi driver did not hand his passenger over to the nearest police station. Instead he dropped Yoon at the entrance to a house which, his grateful passenger soon discovered, belonged to a leading left-wing member of the Korean community in Japan, who welcomed the fugitive and gave him shelter until he could make contact with his relatives.

But the long and troubled story of Yoon Hak-Joon's life as an undocumented migrant was only just beginning. For by now the rather haphazard border control measures introduced by SCAP in the first year of the occupation had been replaced by a much more far-reaching nationwide system run by Japan's newly established Migration Control Agency. And this system had been designed in a way that made existence very difficult even for those who had entered Japan legally, let alone for the tens of thousands who (like Yoon Hak-Joon) had slipped across the border unobserved.

NOTES

1. 'Guard Report: being a log kept of the tripoon [*sic*] the Liberty Ship 'Gilbert M. Hitchcock' of the journey from Senzaki to Fusan (Korea) and thence to Sasebo', in New Zealand National Archives, Wellington, File WA-J 17F10 8/1/10, '22 NZ Inf. War Diary Aug. 46'.

2. Boston Port of Embarkation, *One Liberty Ship* (leaflet), (Boston, MA: Boston Port of Embarkation, 1943), see www.usmm.net/capacity.html (accessed 12 February 2008).

3. J. Dower, *Embracing Defeat: Japan in the Wake of World War II* (New York: W. W. Norton, 1999) p. 54.

4. E. Takemae (trans. Robert Ricketts and Sebastian Swann), *Inside GHQ: The Allied Occupation of Japan and Its Legacy* (London: Continuum, 2002), p. 448.

5. Kōseishō Hikiage Engo Chō, *Hikiage Engo no Kiroku*, Vol. I (reprint) (Tokyo: Kōseishō Shuppan, 2000), p. 66.

6. Ibid., p. 60.

7. G. Davis, *The Occupation of Japan: The Rhetoric and Reality of Anglo-Australian Relations, 1939–1952* (Brisbane: University of Queensland Press, 2001), pp. 299–300; the cited words on the 'last gasp of empire' quoted from historian Peter Bates; see also Takemae, *Inside GHQ*, p. 136. As Iwane Shibuya points out, the diversity of the force was even greater than this suggests, since the Australian and New Zealand contingents also included people of Asian ancestry, Aboriginal Australians and others.

8. *History of the Indian Contingent in Japan, 1945–1947*, typescript copy held in the Australian War Memorial, AWM 114, 417/20/218; H. Evans, *Thimayya of India: A Soldier's Life* (New York: Harcourt, Brace and Co., 1960).

9. 22 NZ Bn., Senzaki Repatriation Centre, Weekly Report Week Ending 30 Mar 1946, in New Zealand National Archives, Wellington, File WA-J 17/5, 8/1/5.

10. Ibid.

11. Lt Gen. John R. Hodge, the commander of US troops in Korea, wrote to SCAP in August 1947 to complain that the Japanese government had 'in many cases … exercised undue licence' in interpreting the repatriation regulations, 'using the authority delegated as a device to deport those Korean nationals considered undesirable by them. As a result, the Korean repatriation program, in effect, has ceased to be of a voluntary nature'. Memo from Hodge to Supreme Commander, Allied Powers, 'Repatriation of Koreans from Japan', 27 August 1947, in GHQ/SCAP Records, Box 385, Folder 4, '014: Civil Matters, Binder #1, 2 January 1946 thru 19 January 1948 (Japan, Korea, Miscellaneous)', March 1946–January 1948.

12. Ibid.

13. 2 NZEF (Japan) Operational Report no. 13, 29 May 1946, in New Zealand National Archives, Wellington, WA-J 68/5, 65/2; Operations Report for Week Ending 4 July 1946, in New Zealand National Archives, Wellington, WA-J 17/9, 8/1/9 '22 NZ War Diary 1–21 July 1946'.

14. Quoted in L. Brocklebank, *Jayforce: New Zealand and the Military Occupation of Japan 1945–1948* (Auckland: Oxford University Press, 1997), p. 135.
15. Operations Report for Week Ending 4 July; 22 NZ War Diary 1–21 July 1946, Operations Report for Week Ending 11 July 1946, in New Zealand National Archives, Wellington, WA-J 17/9, 8/1/9.
16. Operations Report for Week Ending 18 July 1946, in New Zealand National Archives, Wellington, WA-J 17/9, 8/1/9, '22 NZ War Diary 1–21 July 1946'; letter from G. H. Clifton (for Commander in Chief, British Commonwealth Occupation Force) to Eighth US Army, 'Further Report on Illegal Entry of Koreans', 29 July 1946, in Australian War Memorial, Canberra, AWM 114 417/1/27, 'Illegal Entry of Koreans in Japan'.
17. 'Guard Report', p. 3.
18. Ibid., pp. 5–6.
19. Ibid. p. 8.
20. Ibid., p. 9.
21. Letter from C. R. Burns, SMO NZEF to DDMS HQ BCOF, 'Cholera in Senzaki', 8 August 1946, in New Zealand National Archives, Wellington, WA-J 68/F26/G38, '2 NZEF – Illegal Immigration'.
22. Ibid.
23. Ibid.
24. Quoted in Brocklebank, *Jayforce*, p. 135. (Punctuation as in the original.)
25. Joint Chiefs of Staff, 'Basic Initial Post-Surrender Directive to Supreme Commander for the Allied Powers for the Occupation and Control of Japan', 3 November 1945, in Government Section, Supreme Commander for the Allied Powers, *Political Reorientation of Japan* (Washington, DC: US Government Printing Office, 1949), pp. 429–41, quotation from p. 432.
26. 'Joint Opinion of Legal Section, GHQ, SCAP, and Judge Advocate, GHQ, FEC, on Position of Koreans in Japan in Relation to Deportation of Undesirable Aliens', pp. 2–3 in GHQ/SCAP Records, Box LS-1, Folder 3, 'Top Secret File no. 3', microfilm held in National Diet Library, Tokyo, fiche no. TS 00327.
27. Quoted in ibid., p. 4.
28. See Takemae, *Inside GHQ*, p. 449.
29. Diplomatic Section, SCAP, 'DS Staff Study on Status and Treatment of Koreans in Japan', 23 May 1949, p. 1, in GHQ/SCAP Records, held in National Diet Library, Tokyo, microfiche no. LS 24687.
30. Takemae, *Inside GHQ*, p. 443.
31. Ibid., p. 444.
32. Allan S. Clifton, *Time of Fallen Blossoms* (London: Cassell, 1950), p. 129.
33. Ibid., p. 134.
34. Ibid., p. 140.
35. M. E. Caprio, 'The Forging of Alien Status of Koreans in American Occupied Japan', *Japan Focus*, January 2008, www.japanfocus.org/ (accessed 10 March 2008).

36. 'Korean Minority Problem in Japan', *BCOF Japan Quarterly Occupation Intelligence Review*, no. 2, 30 June 1948, pp. 7–13, quotation from p. 7, in Australian National Archives, Canberra, series no. 1838/283, control symbol 481/1/6, 'Intelligence Reports, Quarterly Occupation Intelligence Review'.

37. Ibid., p. 10.

38. Ibid., p. 13.

39. Memorandum from Patrick Shaw, Head of Mission, Australian Mission in Tokyo, to the Secretary, Department of External Affairs, Canberra, 'BCOF Intelligence Review' 1 September 1948, in Australian National Archives, Canberra, series no. 1838/283, control symbol 481/1/6, 'Intelligence Reports, Quarterly Occupation Intelligence Review'.

40. D. Conde, 'The Korean Minority in Japan', *Far Eastern Survey*, 16, 4 (February 1947), typescript version held in Australian National Archives, pp. 4–5.

41. 'Report on Stowaways', p. 1, attached to the memo 'Korean Stowaways in Japan' from Lt Col. Rue S. Link, Kyushu Military Government Headquarters, Fukuoka, to Commanding General, I Corps, APO 301, 19 August 1946, in GHQ/SCAP Records, Box 385, Folder 4, '014: Civil Matters, Binder #1, 2 January 1946 thru 19 January 1948 (Japan, Korea, Miscellaneous)', March 1946–January 1948. Cho refers to the repatriation camp by its formal address: 'Uragashira, Minami-Kakezaki, Nagasaki Prefecture', but it is generally known as 'Hario' after the island just off the coast of Uragashira where repatriates were processed and deportees detained.

42. Ibid., p. 1.

43. Ibid., p. 2.

44. Ibid., p. 2.

45. See Caprio, 'The Forging of Alien Status'.

46. Kim Tae-Gi, *Sengo Nihon seiji to Zainichi Chōsenjin mondai: SCAP no tai-Zainichi Chōsenjin seisaku 1945–1952* (Tokyo: Keisō Shobō, 1997), p. 263.

47. 'CSDIC Translations BCOF – Illegal Entry into Japan 1948', held in the Australian War Memorial, Canberra, File no. AWM 144, 417/1/27, p. 46.

48. SCAPIN 1015, 'Suppression of Illegal Entry into Japan', 12 June 1946, in GHQ/SCAP Records, Box 2189, Folder 16, 'Immigration, 1950/02–1952/03', microfiche held in National Diet Library, Tokyo, fiche no. GS(B)-01603.

49. Memo from John B. Cooley to Imperial Japanese Government, 'Suppression of Illegal Entry into Japan', 12 June 1946, in GHQ/SCAP Records, Box 2198, Folder 16, 'Immigration' February 1950–March 1952, microfilm held in National Diet Library, Tokyo, fiche no. GS(B)-01603.

50. Memo from Lt Col., Military Government Liaison Section to HQ BCOF, 'Illegal Entry of Koreans into Japan', 11 July 1946, in Australian War Memorial, File AWM 114, 410/1/27, 'Illegal Entry of Koreans into Japan'.

51. For example, in October 1946, the *Hōei Maru*, which was attempting to smuggle some 150 Amami islanders back to their home from Kagoshima, foundered on a rock with a loss of about fifty lives; see Satake Kyōko,

Gunseika Amami no Mikkō, Mitsu Bōeki (Tokyo: Nampō Shinsha, 2003), pp. 15–25. Six of ten people attempting to enter Japan were also reported to have drowned in March 1948 when their boat was wrecked at the entrance to 'Shiana Una' (Shionoura?) Bay; see 'Intelligence Summary' in GHQ/SCAP Records, Box 380, Folder 13, 'Korea File no. 1, January 1 1948 to 30 September 1948', September 1945–September 1948.

52. Memo from Lt Col., Military Government Liaison Section, to HQ BCOF 29 July 1946. See also T. Morris-Suzuki, 'An Act Prejudicial to the Occupation Forces: Migration Controls and Korean Residents in Post-surrender Japan', *Japanese Studies*, 24, 1 (May 2004), pp. 4–28.

53. Brinvid Fortnightly Intelligence Review for fortnight ending 7 September 1946, held in Australian War Memorial, File AWM 114, 423/10/63.

54. See the table 'Illegal Entry of Koreans into Japan: Total Number of Persons by Month, April 1946–December 1949', in GHQ/SCAP Records, Box 291, Folder 2, 'Illegal Entry of Koreans into Japan: Total Number of Persons by Month April 1946 to December 1946 [*sic*]', January 1950.

55. Hōmushō Nyūkoku Kanrikyoku (ed.), *Shutsunyūkoku Kanri to sono Jittai – Shōwa 39-nen* (Tokyo: Ōkurashō Insatsukyoku, 1964), p. 16.

56. Memorandum for Chief of Staff, 8th Army, 'Suppression of Korean Illegal Entry', 15 May 1949, in GHQ/SCAP Records (RG 311, National Archives and Records Service), Box 380, Folder 15, Korea File 3, 1 April 1949 to 31 December 1949.

57. 'Illegal Entry into Japan', document appended to the Japanese government report, 'Deportation of Korean Criminals', no date, GHQ/SCAP Records (RG 311, National Archives and Records Service), Box 380, Folder 15, Korea File 3, 1 April 1949 to 31 December 1949, p. 1.

58. Interview recorded in Koh Sun-Hui, 'Seikatsushi no Shiryō 3: 1946-nen ikō Rainichi', unpublished appendix to Koh Sun-Hui, *20 Seiki no Tainichi Chejudōjin: Sono Seikatsu Katei to Ishiki* (Tokyo: Akashi Shoten, 1998), pp. 34–5. I am very grateful to Professor Koh for allowing me access to this material.

59. Kim Tae-Gi, *Sengo Nihon seiji*, pp. 262–3.

60. Heo Yeong-Seon, *Cheju Yonsan* (Seoul: Minjuhwa Undong Ginyeom Saobhoe, 2006), p. 28; see also Hyun Moo-Am, 'Mikkō, Ōmura shūyōjo, Saishūtō: Ōsaka to Saishūtō o Musubu "Mikkō" no Nettowāku', *Gendai Shisō*, 35 (June 2007), pp. 158–73, particularly p. 165.

61. See Moon Gyeong-Su, *Chejudō Gendaishi* (Tokyo: Shinkansha, 2005), p. 25.

62. Heo, *Jeju Yonsan*, p. 41.

63. See memo by D. W. Kermode, 'Korean "Independence Day" Disturbances – Statement by Director of Police Dpeartment to M. Kermode and Mr. Bevin (received 28th April)', 28 April 1947, in Australian National Archives, Canberra, series no. A1838, control symbol 506/1, 'Quelpart Island – Cheju Province'.

64. See memo by D. W. Kermode, 'Korean "Independence Day" Disturbances', 24 April 1947, in Australian National Archives, Canberra, series no. A1838,

control symbol 506/1, 'Quelpart Island – Cheju Province'; also Heo, *Jeju Yonsan*, pp. 45–57.

65. Heo, *Jeju Yonsan*, p. 59. Moon Gyong-Su, *Saishūtō 4.3 Jiken: 'Tamna no Kuni' no Shi to Saisei no Monogatari* (Tokyo: Heibonsha, 2008).

66. Koh, *Seikatsushi no Shiryō*, pp. 36–7.

67. See Moon, *Saishūtō 4.3 Jiken*.

68. Departmental dispatch no. 230/1948 from Australian Mission in Japan to Department of External Affairs, Canberra, 'US Intelligence Information on Korea', in Australian National Archives, Canberra, series no. A1838, control symbol 852/20/4, Part 5, 'Korean Commission', 1948.

69. Koh, *Seikatsushi no Shiryō*, pp. 49–50.

70. See Kim Seok-Beom and Kim Shi-Jong, *Naze Kakitsuzukete Kita ka, Naze Chinmoku shite Kita ka: Saishūtō 4.3 Jiken no Kioku to Bungaku* (Tokyo: Heibonsha, 2001), pp. 115–21; see also Moon, *Saishūtō 4.3 Jiken*, pp. 140–43.

71. See Moon, *Saishūtō 4.3 Jiken*, pp. 149–95.

72. Letter from A. Bullock, Australian delegate to UNTCOK, to Secretary, External Affairs, Canberra, 27 February 1951, in Australian National Archives, Canberra, 'Korea – Refugee Problem'.

73. To give just a couple of examples, on 22 May 1951, J. de Reynier, representative of the International Committee of the Red Cross in Korea, reported accounts of the killing of the inhabitants of the village of Kochang (near Pusan) by South Korean troops. The villagers had been shot because they were believed to have cooperated with the Communists. Reynier went on to observe, 'I don't know, and everyone is wondering, why such a song-and-dance is being made about this particular village, when similar events recur every day.' See letter from de Reynier to International Committee of the Red Cross, Geneva, 22 May 1951, held in ICRC Archives, B AG 231 056–001, *Corée*, 27.03.1951–29.07,1959. On 2 November of the same year, Henry Meyer, a Danish Red Cross doctor, wrote a report on his experiences in Korea to the ICRC, in which he described the 'disgusting conditions' in which civilian detainees in South Korea were being held, and noted, 'it has been brought to my knowledge that a large number of political prisoners including women and children have been executed with and without trial'. See letter from Henry Meyer to David de Traz, 'Red Cross Problems in Korea', ICRC, 2 November 1951, in ICRC Archives, B AG 225 056–003, *Guérillas en Corée*, 14.12.1951–07.12.1953.

74. See Dô Khiem and Kim Sung-Soo, 'Crimes, Concealment and South Korea's Truth and Reconciliation Commission', *Japan Focus*, August 2008, www.japanfocus.org/ (accessed 8 August 2008).

75. Memo by United Nations Section, External Affairs, Canberra, 'Draft Convention on the Status of Refugees and Stateless Persons', 23 May 1951, Australian National Archives, Canberra, series no. A1838/1, control symbol 855/11/11, Part 3. I am very grateful to Prof. Klaus Neumann for assisting me in obtaining a copy of this file.

76. Memorandum for the Secretary, Immigration Department, Canberra, 'Conference on the Status of Refugees', 11 July 1951, in Australian National Archives, series no. A1838/1, control symbol 855/11/11, Part 3.

77. Patrick Shaw (delegate) and Dighton Burbridge (adviser), 'Report of the Australian Delegation to the Conference on the Status of Refugees held at Geneva from 2nd July to 25th July 1951', in Australian National Archives, series no. A1838/1, control symbol 855/11/11, Part 3.

78. UNHCR, *Convention and Protocol Relating to the Status of Refugees* (Geneva, UNHCR Public Information Section, 1996); see also K. Neumann, *Refuge Australia: Australia's Humanitarian Record* (Sydney: University of New South Wales Press, 2004), pp. 83–4.

79. Quoted in Untitled memo from JA to Mr Adams, 11 April 1949, in GHQ/SCAP Records, Box 380, File 16, 'Korea File no. 4', April 1949–July 1950, microfilm held in National Diet Library, Tokyo, fiche no. GIII-00040.

80. Ibid.

81. Memo, 'New State of Affairs in Korea and the Treatment of Illegal Entrants', in GHQ/SCAP Records, Box 2189, 'Immigration', February 1950–March 1952, microfilm held in National Diet Library, Tokyo, fiche no. GS(B)-01601.

82. Ibid.

83. See memo from David S. Tait, chief, Japanese Liaison Section, to Ministry of Foreign Affairs, 'Processing Petitions from Illegal Entrants', 17 March 1951, in GHQ/SCAP Records, Box 2778, 'Petitions for Release of Illegal Entrants, Suspense', February 1951–April 1951, microfilm held in National Diet Library, Tokyo, fiche no. CAS(A)-04978.

84. Memo from James N. Foreman to chief, Civil Affairs Section, GHQ/SCAP, 'Petition for Stay of Deportation Proceedings', 11 August 1950, in GHQ/SCAP Records, Box 2293, Folder 4, 'Petition for Release', October 1949–March 1950, held in the National Diet Library, Tokyo, Microfiche CAS(C) – 01670–01671.

85. See orders for release contained in the same folder, and in GHQ/SCAP Records, Box. 1418, Folder 13, 'Korean', March 1950–October 1950, microfilm held in National Diet Library, Tokyo, fiche no. LS-20998.

86. 'CSDIC Translations BCOF – Illegal Entry into Japan 1948', p. 14.

87. Ibid., p. 15.

88. Ibid., pp. 23–43.

89. Ibid., p. 13.

90. Memo, 'An Information about the Deportation of Korean Illicit Entrants', 12 January 1951, in GHQ/SCAP Records, Box 2189, 'Immigration', microfilm held in National Diet Library, Tokyo, fiche no. GS(B)-01603.

91. 'Log of Operation Order no. 8, dated 20 October 46', 26 October 1946, in New Zealand National Archives, Wellington, WA J 11 17/12 DAJ 8/1/12, War Diary 22 Bn.

92. Top secret telegram from Sebald to Department of State, 8 January 1951, in GHQ/SCAP Records, Box AG 12, Folder 16, 'Entry and Departure', January

1951–March 1951, microfilm held in National Diet Library, Tokyo, fiche no. TS-00117.

93. Yoon Hak-Jun, 'Waga Mikkōki', *Chōsen Kenkyū*, 190 (June 1979), pp. 4–15, quotation from p. 5; see also Takayanagi Toshio, 'Tonichi Shoki no Yoon Hak-Joon – Mikkō, Hōsei Daigaku, Kikoku Jigyō', *Ibunka*, 5 (April 2004), pp. 1–35.
94. Ibid., p. 6.
95. Ibid., p. 7. Emphasis added to render implicit emphasis of Japanese original.

CHAPTER 4

Guarding the line

The Cold War and the Immigration Bureau

ALIEN REGISTRATION

At first they were little more than scraps of paper: flimsy handwritten documents inscribed with the bearer's name, address and place of family registration. But as time went on they became more formal. Paper gave way to card, and then to small bound passbooks. Photographs were added, and then fingerprints; and over the course of time Japan's alien registration documents became one of the most contentious aspects of the entire border control system.

The first steps towards the creation of the system were taken in 1946 at the height of the 'smuggler' scare. In that year, the city of Osaka unsuccessfully attempted to introduce a system for fingerprinting 'foreigners'.[1] Meanwhile, in September 1946, Air Vice-Marshall Francis Bladin of BCOF was writing to the US 8th Army that 'all foreign nationals, particularly Chinese and Koreans, appear to be engaged in large scale black market activities which could be detected more easily if a check could be made on their movements'.[2] To deal with the problem, Bladin suggested that

the Japanese authorities be ordered to issue an approved form of identity card to all foreign nationals within Japan. This card could show the identity, nationality and place of residence of the holder. Any foreign national not in possession of a card after the final date of issue to be laid down, would obviously be an illegal entrant.[3]

After some debate between SCAP and the Japanese authorities, the idea was put into practice. On 2 May 1947, the Japanese government issued an Ordinance for Registration of Aliens, which required all foreigners in Japan (with certain exceptions) to carry registration cards. The exceptions were members of the occupation force, their spouses and employees, and anyone in Japan on the official business of a foreign government – in other words, the great majority of Allied nationals in Japan during the occupation years. Other foreigners in Japan were required to carry alien registration certificates at all times, and those who failed to produce them for inspection when asked to do so by the police could be sentenced to a 10,000 yen fine or one year's penal servitude. People imprisoned for this offence could also be deported.[4]

Despite SCAP's earlier announcement that Koreans who did not sign up for repatriation would be considered as retaining their Japanese nationality, the Alien Registration Ordinance specifically included in its scope 'those designated by the Minister of Foreign Affairs among Formosans [Taiwanese], and Koreans'.[5] There was, however, a distinction between the two groups: three months earlier, the Chinese Nationalist government had reached an agreement with Japan which ensured that all Taiwanese who registered as Chinese with their Tokyo Mission would be treated as United Nations nationals. As a result, though Taiwanese were required to carry alien registration documents, they at least benefited from the advantages of being foreigners in an occupied country: better rations and immunity from Japanese taxes and criminal jurisdiction.[6] Koreans, however, continued to be treated as 'Japanese' in most respects (except the right to vote), while also constituting by far the largest group forced on pain of arrest to carry alien registration certificates. Understandably, this policy generated considerable resentment amongst the Korean community in Japan, aggravating the tensions between them and occupation forces.

The Alien Registration of 1947 seems to have been a rather chaotic affair. The paperwork was left to local officials, who in the early years of the occupation were overwhelmed with other problems of reconstruction and social dislocation, and had few resources to deal with this new and complex project. The consequences were vividly illustrated three years later, when social researcher Izumi Seiichi tried to carry out a study of the large community of Jeju islanders living in an area of Tokyo north of the city's Ueno Station. He began by obtaining a copy of the 1947 alien registrations for the area, which he thought would provide the best basis for his research, but quickly discovered that this was 'in total disarray'. More than half of the Korean families he encountered in his survey either were not on the register or had their details wrongly recorded.[7]

Besides, it soon became obvious that the simple registration certificates issued in 1947 could easily be forged, and fake certificates could be bought for as little as six hundred yen.[8] So in January 1950, SCAP and the Japanese government tried again. This time, registration certificates were to carry photographs of the bearer. Foreigners were required to report to their local authorities within a short two-week period, and when the time came, it was expected that many would fail to register by the official deadline. The Japanese police predicted that as many as 13,000 people would be deported for failure to register, and detailed plans were drawn up for their mass deportation.[9]

Events did not unfold as planned. The number of people registered in 1950 turned out to be some 60,000 less than the number who had been registered in 1947, but this did not reflect an exodus of foreigners or a refusal by the aliens to register. Rather, the main reason seems to have been the confused state of the first registration, in which many people had been registered twice.[10] The number registered dropped again by about another 30,000 when new registration documents, with photographs and formats which were more difficult to replicate, were issued in 1952.[11]

The alien registration system certainly made life even more difficult for 'stowaways', and life was to become harder again in 1955, when fingerprinting was introduced as part of the registration process.[12] Without registration documents, they had no way of obtaining rations, jobs or medical care, and were in constant fear of arrest and deportation. In the many thousands of letters between Japan and Korea checked by SCAP's censors, there are passages that vividly convey the impact of the system on undocumented border crossers. 'I came to Tsushima a few days ago', writes one Korean border crosser to a relative in western Japan, 'However, I am perplexed as I cannot come to your place, for I have no foreign national registration certificate with me'. 'Since my arrival in Japan I have been staying at X's', writes another, 'I have no prospect of returning for the time being. I am now in distress as I have no winter clothes, ration certificate, foreign national [i.e. alien registration] certificate. If there is any means of coping with my difficulties, please let me know.'[13]

But the pressures impelling cross-border movement were too great for this barrier to have a decisive effect. After his dramatic escape through the window of the Coastguard office in Karatsu, Yoon Hak-Joon too faced the anxieties of life in Japan without an alien registration card. As he later recalled,

According to the information we'd been given in Busan, it was difficult to get hold of an alien registration certificate, and if you didn't have one you could be arrested and immediately deported. But I was in a situation where I desperately needed to leave Korea, and I didn't have space in my head to worry about that problem. I thought, 'ah well, I'll soon get used to playing hide and seek with the cops'.[14]

'Hide and seek with the cops', however, proved an exhausting and dangerous business. In the end, it was Yoon's aunt who came to his rescue:

One day, my aunt managed to get hold of a phantom alien registration certificate. Apparently she had bought it for 30,000 yen. The certificate was in the name of one Yi Gye-Yeong, who was just a little younger than me and came from South Gyeongsang, but the photo attached to the card was of a young man in a tight-collared student uniform who didn't really look that much like me. However, the photo had been stamped right through with a seal which made it impossible to change it. My uncle made a gloomy face, as though to say it couldn't be helped. 'At least it's better than nothing', he said as I put it in my pocket.[15]

Yoon's account indicates how refinements to the registration certificate had raised the cost of obtaining forged documents. By 1953, only those whose family had some assets could afford a document like the one obtained by Yoon. He spent the next two decades living under the assumed identity of the phantom Yi Gye-Yeong, and suffering from anxiety attacks every time he was asked to produce his registration document for inspection.

Meanwhile, the process of alien registration had created a problem which at first sight seems rather trivial, but which in practice was to have an enormous impact on the destiny of Japan's Korean community. The problem was this: what word should be written on the alien registration certificate to describe the nationality of Koreans? In colonial times, the Japanese authorities had called their Korean colony *Chōsen*, the Japanese version of the Korean name *Joseon*, by which the country had been known throughout most of the Yi dynasty. This was also the name given to the country in the Communist North. However, the South Korea government established in 1948 had chosen to call the country by the name *Daehan Minguk* (Great Korean Republic), often abbreviated to *Hanguk* (in Japanese *Taikan Minkoku* or *Kankoku*), a variant on the title *Daehan Chaeguk* (Great Korean Empire), by which the country had been known from 1897 to 1910.

When the alien registration system was introduced in 1947, Japanese officials inscribed the word *Chōsen* in the space for 'nationality' on the cards of Korean residents. But when new certificates were issued in 1950, the South Korean government vigorously protested, insisting that the correct term was *Taikan Minkoku*. The South Korean regime of Yi Seung-Man claimed all Koreans as its nationals, and indeed the 1950 registration revealed that well over 90 per cent of the Koreans registered came from the southern half of Korea.[16] However, many Koreans in Japan themselves were not enthusiastic about this description of their national identity. Like the protestors in Jeju, they were opposed to division of their country, and saw the newly created South Korean government as having little legitimacy. During the second registration, therefore, Koreans in Japan were given a choice: they could fill in the space for 'nationality' with the word *Chōsen* or with the words *Taikan Minkoku* or *Kankoku*. Out of 535,236 Koreans who registered in the early part of 1950, 92 per cent used *Chōsen*: a word which identified them with a single united Korea rather than linking them specifically to the new regime in the South.[17]

From that point on, the Korean community in Japan became divided by an increasingly powerful invisible barrier separating those with '*Chōsen* registration' (*Chōsen seki*) from those with '*Kankoku* registration' (*Kankoku seki*). This distinction caused endless misunderstandings, particularly when it was mistranslated into English as 'North Korean' versus 'South Korean'. Over the course of time, the balance between the two groups shifted. By the end of the Korean War, the percentage choosing *Chōsen* registration had fallen to 76 per cent; today, they are greatly outnumbered by those with *Kankoku* registration. But the division remains, and increasingly came to be reinforced by different sets of rights and a different sense of group belonging. Amongst other things, this division was one of the factors behind the tragedy of the mass repatriation to North Korea, which we shall explore in more detail in Chapter Eight.

WATCHERS ON THE SHORE

Accounts of the Allied occupation of Japan commonly draw a line between the years from late 1945 to 1948, when the occupiers were driven by a reforming zeal which Dower has called 'both self-righteous and genuinely visionary', and the years of 'reverse course', from 1948 onward, when Cold War fears of the 'Red Menace' pushed the occupiers into more conservative policies.[18] But the chronology of 'reform' versus 'reverse course' was uneven. In some policy areas reform persisted well into the occupation; in others (including the area of border controls), signs of a 'reverse course' became apparent even before the major postwar social and political reforms had been implemented.

Among the initial instructions given to SCAP, for example, had been the decree, 'You will assure that all units of the Japanese armed forces including the Gendarmerie (Kempei) (but not the civil police), Civilian Volunteer Corps, and all para-military organizations are promptly disarmed.'[19] One of the groups targeted by this decree was the Civil Defence Corps (Keibōdan), which had been created in 1939 to assist the police and prepare local communities for air raids and other wartime threats. During the war, local Keibōdan units had also been used on several occasions to hunt down escaped forced labourers, and in the immediate post-surrender period at least one group is known to have been involved in the murder of Korean miners. Whether or not SCAP was aware of this is uncertain. However, as occupation troops struggled to deal with the unexpected surge of unauthorized arrivals in Japan in the summer of 1946, they suddenly discovered a new use for the nationwide network of Keibōdan brigades.

At the height of the 'smuggling' panic of summer 1946, occupation forces in Yamaguchi Prefecture (where many of the boat people were arriving) decided on a series of new border control measures, including a plan to 'use the old civilian defense organizations as auxiliary police'. It is clear, however, that they felt some unease about expanding the responsibilities of the Keibōdan, for the document outlining these proposals adds in brackets, 'are there any security/intelligence objections to such a measure?'[20] Evidently no objections were forthcoming. By April of the following year, police in Yamaguchi Prefecture had set in place a detailed set of procedures for collaborating with the occupation forces in arresting arriving migrants:

If any illegal entrants are captured, a check of towns and villages is made to see whether any new ration cards have been issued lately ... A special check is made of Korean communities ... In the case of a landing the police notify the nearest Occupation Force authorities. The police may call on the local 'Keibodan' to help them round up the fugitives.[21]

The following year, the Keibōdan was officially disbanded, and many of its members incorporated into new, re-organized local fire brigades. But the change of name did not put an end to the brigades' involvement in border control activities, as evident from the detailed report on the 290-odd boat people who arrived in south-western Shikoku's Ehime Prefecture at the height of the Jeju 4.3 Incident (see Chapter Three) In response to this influx of 'smugglers', following a liaison meeting between local police and occupation forces, it was decided to establish 81 coastal watching posts along the shores of the prefecture, staffed by 394 watchers, 'reliable persons ... selected and appointed from among the Fire Brigades, Youth Movements, and the Fishing Industries. Watchmen and guards from companies, factories, etc. were also used.'[22] When boats were spotted approaching shore (generally at night), members of the fire brigade were mobilized to act as police reinforcements at the spot where the boat was expected to make landfall.

Migration controls not only involved the preservation of some of the social control mechanisms of wartime Japan, but also led to the very first measure taken by SCAP to rearm the defeated nation. In the early

part of the occupation, patrols of the coast by land and sea had been
conducted by US and BCOF troops, who used spotter planes to identify
and sometimes to buzz approaching boats, and military vessels like the
HMS *Sutlej* and USS *E. F. Larson* to intercept them.[23] The central aim
of the occupation authorities at this stage was to ensure that the Japanese
military was totally disbanded and stripped of all its armaments. This
emphasis on disarmament was famously to be incorporated into Japan's
new Constitution, which came into force in May 1947. Article Nine of the
Constitution proclaimed that the Japanese people 'forever renounce war
as a sovereign right of the nation and the threat or use of force as a means
of settling international disputes', and that consequently 'land, sea, and
air forces as well as other war potential, will never be maintained'.[24]

However, a month earlier, in April 1947, SCAP had quietly handed back
to the Japanese government twenty-eight former submarine-chasing naval
vessels that it had confiscated at the end of the war. These were to serve
as the core of Japan's Maritime Safety Board (later renamed the Maritime
Safety Agency), a coastguard whose immediate mission was to keep out
illegal migrants.[25] Beyond this goal of securing the country from border
crossers, though, lay a much more sweeping vision of the nation's security needs. As one scholar of Japan's wartime and postwar naval activities
notes, 'although under the control of the Ministry of Transport (MoT),
the coast guard was deliberately constituted to serve as the nucleus of a
future navy'.[26]

Meanwhile, the rather haphazard ad hoc border control activities of the
first year of occupation were gradually being replaced by a more formal and
centralized system. In 1949, SCAP began to transfer control of legal movement into and out of the country to the Japanese authorities. The first step
was the creation in August 1949 of an Immigration Service Division within
Japan's Ministry of Foreign Affairs, whose officials stamped passports and
maintained records of the entry of foreigners other than occupation personnel.[27] In September of the following year this body was upgraded to
become a Migration Agency (Shutsunyūkoku Kanri Chō) with enhanced
powers to approve or deny entry – although the ultimate right of decision
remained in the hands of SCAP.[28] Soon the Agency was drawing up plans
to advertise for and train the first immigration officers who would become
the front line of Japan's future border controls.

For by now the People's Republic of China had been established
and Korea had been plunged into civil war. Like other periods of international tension, these early years of rising Cold War conflict generated
intense concerns about problems of border security. In the last two years

of the occupation, therefore, the development of a fully fledged Japanese immigration service became a major issue on SCAP's political agenda, and the resolution of this issue became inextricably entangled in the wider politics of the Cold War world.

In January 1951, a rotund, balding American official arrived in Tokyo on an important mission. His name was Nicholas D. Collaer, and he had been given just three months to draft a lasting framework for Japan's postwar migration controls.[29] It must have seemed a daunting task, for Collaer had no particular expertise in Japanese politics, society or culture. He had, however, recently retired from a successful career in the US Immigration and Naturalization Service (INS), and in that capacity (as we shall see) he had certainly had experience in dealing with people of Japanese ancestry. Collaer, of course, was not single-handedly responsible for Japan's postwar immigration system. His drafts of the Migration Control Law, and his proposed procedures for the detention and deportation of migrants, were produced in consultation with Japanese and SCAP officials.[30] Yet his influence was significant. Nick Collaer (as he was generally known to his colleagues) brought with him to Tokyo strong political opinions and some idiosyncratic views about Japan's place in the Asian region, all of which were to be reflected in the immigration system which he helped to forge.

The creation of a new migration and border control system was a quiet reform, carried out with much less public fanfare than SCAP's restructuring of education, land tenure and trade union systems or the revision of the Constitution. The 1951 Migration Control Ordinance (transformed into a Migration Control Law when Japan regained its independence in 1952) retained some features of pre-war policy, and has therefore often been seen simply as a natural continuation of past approaches to migration. But this view neglects important new elements of the postwar law, and obscures the extent to which it was carefully crafted by SCAP and the Japanese authorities in the context of rapidly escalating international tensions.

The collapse of colonial empires and the onset of the Cold War were accompanied by fundamental changes in global border control and migration regimes. Colonial independence movements had challenged the racial presumptions of empire, and the Holocaust had graphically exposed the horrors to which the logic of racism ultimately led. In the new postwar order, migration policies based on overtly racial classifications were rapidly being discredited. As nation states sought to rebuild their economies, new and more complex hierarchies of preference based on national origin, education, skills, language ability and so on would be used to control the flow of people across national boundaries. At the same time, the Cold War had a paradoxical effect on the migration policies of the United States and Western European countries, as well as of countries like Canada and Australia. On the one hand, refugee programmes were created to welcome people fleeing from communist countries to the 'free world'; on the other, security concerns about potentially 'subversive' migrants loomed larger than ever in the imagination of policy makers and bureaucrats.

At the start of the 1950s, then, there was widespread agreement on the need for a new approach to immigration, but heated debate about the direction which this new approach should take. How far would the old imperial notions of race continue implicitly to shape migration controls in a decolonizing world? How would the protection of refugees be balanced against pressures to protect national security from subversion? One place where these debates were fought out with passion was the US Congress. It is worth looking a little more closely at these Congressional debates on migration because they were to have a decisive influence on postwar Japan's migration and border controls. By considering events in the US and Japan in parallel, it becomes possible to discern the ways in which Cold War forces came together to shape Japan's postwar immigration system. At the same time, it becomes clear how the legacy of pre-war imperial attitudes merged with postwar ideologies in ways which deeply influenced Japan's relations with the surrounding East Asian region.

Early in 1950, the US Senate embarked on a major inquiry into the nation's immigration policies. The inquiry's report provided the basis for a law, enacted in 1952, which would define US immigration policy for the next decade or more. Debate surrounding the new Immigration and Naturalization Law took place against the background of the Korean War and of a wave of anti-communist sentiment in the US, reflected in the 1947 investigations of well-known Hollywood figures by the House Committee on Un-American Activities, and in the controversial Alger Hiss case of 1950.[31] In September 1950, the US Internal Security Law – also known as the McCarran Law, after its chief sponsor, Democrat senator Pat McCarran – was passed. This, amongst other things, banned the entry of aliens of whom 'there is reason to believe that they would be subversive to national security'.[32]

In this context, mainstream US political opinion on immigration rapidly polarized around two positions. The first, held by President Harry S. Truman and others, called for a relatively far-reaching liberalization of US immigration policy. Racially based laws which had excluded the entry of many 'Asian' immigrants and tightly restricted the entry of others should, it was argued, be abolished; plans should be made for a major increase in immigrant numbers; and some care should be taken in balancing human rights and national security. The opposing, more conservative, position accepted the need to abolish overt racial exclusions, but was much more cautious about other areas of reform. Conservatives argued that a quota system (limiting the entry of particular nationalities to a level determined by their ratio in the existing US population) needed to be retained in order to preserve the ethnic 'balance' of the US population. Above all, tight migration controls should be enforced to prevent the possible entry to the US of communists and other subversives.

The most eloquent exponent of this second view was Congressman Francis E. Walter, Chair of the House Committee on Un-American Activities, who regarded communist subversion and immigration as inseparably connected. In the confrontation between the two approaches to immigration, the conservative side was unequivocally the winner. The Senate's 1950 inquiry into immigration was chaired by Senator Pat McCarran, and (echoing McCarran's security concerns) one of the three sections of its report of over nine hundred pages was wholly devoted to the topic of 'Subversives'.[33] The 1952 Immigration and Naturalization Law (more commonly known as the McCarran-Walter Law) was an amalgam of two very similar bills introduced in the Senate and House of Representatives, the first by Senator McCarran, architect of the Internal Security Law, and the second by Francis Walter. The law retained the quota system, and although it abolished overt forms of racial exclusion, it maintained more subtly discriminatory elements.[34] The law also reaffirmed and strengthened the 1950 McCarran Law's stringent measures to exclude and deport 'subversive' aliens.

President Truman vetoed the McCarran-Walter Law, but his veto was overturned by Congress. He also established his own Commission on Immigration and Naturalization. This committee's report – published in January 1953 – was unambiguous in its assessment of the McCarran-Walter Law. The new law, it concluded,

> embodies policies and principles that are unwise and injurious to the nation.

It rests on an attitude of hostility and distrust against aliens.

It applies discriminations against human beings on the account of national origin, race, creed and color.

It ignores the needs of the United States in domestic affairs and foreign policies.

It contains unnecessary and unreasonable restrictions and penalties against individuals.

It is badly drafted, confusing and in some respects unworkable.

It should be reconsidered and revised from beginning to end.[35]

Despite this withering assessment, the McCarran-Walter Law would, with minor amendments, remain in force until 1965. Aspects of the law (which was being debated in Congress during the months when Nick Collaer was in Japan) would also provide a model for key elements of Japan's postwar immigration system.

JAPAN AND THE DEPORTATION ISSUE

While the US Congress was debating the future of the nation's immigration policies, the Japanese Diet (parliament) and media were debating the deportation of Koreans from Japan. Ever since the first year of the occupation, some Japanese newspapers and politicians had expressed hostile attitudes to the Korean community in Japan, often playing on public resentment of the fact that former colonial subjects were publicly celebrating their liberation from Japanese rule while their Japanese neighbours were mourning defeat.[36] In the words of Kang Sang-Jung, the son of Korean parents living in a provincial Japanese city in the 1950s,

local histories of Japan's prefectures, cities and villages – and of the police forces – reflect the fact that in those days, during the Allied occupation of Japan, members of the *Zainichi* Korean community [Korean community in Japan] were generally depicted as disrupting the Japanese economy by black-market and criminal activities. They were referred to as 'third-country people' [*sangoku-jin*], and were seen as destroying public order and morality. There was virtually no recognition of any positive contribution by Koreans to the Japanese economy, society or culture.[37]

By the late 1940s, rising fears of communism were becoming deeply intertwined with these post-imperial prejudices. In the aftermath of Japan's defeat and Korea's liberation, a number of associations representing Koreans in Japan had been formed throughout the country. The most active and visible of these groups, the Korean League, had become increasingly left-wing, and by 1948 was closely identified with the newly established Communist regime in North Korea. Meanwhile rival movements had been formed by Koreans wary of the League's move towards the left, and in 1948 these groups united to form the Korean Residents Union in Japan (Jaeil Taehanminguk Georyumindan in Korean, Zainichi Daikanminkoku Kyoryūmindan in Japanese, Mindan for short in both languages[38]), which supported the newly established Republic of Korea and its president, Yi Seung-Man. A substantial number of Korean residents avoided affiliation with either of these groups. However, the Korean League attracted a larger following than Mindan, partly because of its central role in various political conflicts over the rights of Koreans in Japan. It also seems likely that heavy-handed occupation policies towards the Korean community actually encouraged hostility towards the US and towards the US-backed regime in South Korea, and thus served to swell the ranks of League supporters.

A crisis point was reached in 1948, when the Korean League came into direct conflict with SCAP and the Japanese government over the issue of education for Koreans in Japan. After Japan's surrender, many Korean communities in Japan had established their own schools, which provided education in the Korean language. From October 1947 onwards, however, the Japanese Ministry of Education sought to reincorporate these schools into the Japanese system, insisting that they should provide the standard Japanese curriculum to students. This move met with fierce resistance, led by the League. Events came to a head in Kobe in April 1948, when Korean residents defied an order by the prefectural governor to vacate their schools, and were forcibly driven out by police. In response, a group of Korean protestors stormed the governor's office.

SCAP's reaction was swift and dramatic. For the only time during the occupation, it declared a state of emergency, and troops were sent to Kobe to quell the disturbance. The occupation forces also ordered the governor of Osaka to break up demonstrations by Korean residents, which took place in that city a few days later. The governor's swift compliance left nine people severely injured and one sixteen-year-old boy dead. Thousands of Koreans were arrested, though ultimately fewer than fifty were convicted of crimes, and the following year the Korean League was banned.[39]

As researcher Choi Deok-Hyo has pointed out, this drastic response reflected the fact that SCAP officials saw the Kobe school demonstrations as part of a wider political movement extending beyond the borders of Japan. The 'Kobe Incident' occurred immediately after the start of the

4.3 Incident on the Korean island of Jeju (see Chapter Three). In this context, SCAP envisaged the Kobe protests not as a specific struggle for Korean-language education, but rather as part of a security crisis extending across the whole of East Asia.[40] Some Japanese politicians shared this alarmist perspective. Speaking in a debate in the Diet's Judicial Committee in February 1951, conservative politician Oshitani Tomizō described ongoing Korean protests over the school issue as 'having strong overtones of a power struggle designed to serve as a prelude to revolution'.[41]

Such sentiments provided the basis for demands from some political and business leaders for the forcible mass deportation of 'subversive Koreans'. The occupation archives, for example, contain quotations from public speeches by the president of the Takeda Pharmaceuticals Company (one of Osaka's major manufacturing firms) and by the president of the Hanshin Electric Railway Company, supporting mass deportation. Hanshin Electric Railway's president expressed his enthusiasm for 'the deportation of all Koreans in Japan' (seditious or not) and seemed untroubled by the very real prospect that left-wing Koreans deported to South Korea might be imprisoned or even executed. Although it was not known what would happen to the deportees on arrival, he stressed the importance of 'immediately sweeping away these such seditious elements' so that 'we may feel no anxiety about the public peace'.[42]

In December 1950, Japanese newspapers published reports that the Japanese and South Korean governments had reached an agreement on the mass deportation of 'Communist and other undesirable Koreans to their home country'. The press noted, however, that 'legal technicalities necessary for the enforcement of the measure' were still to be ironed out, and the precise number of 'Communist and other undesirable Koreans' to be deported had not yet been determined.[43] Prime Minister Yoshida Shigeru, who had already unsuccessfully tried to persuade General MacArthur that the Korean minority should be removed to Korea en masse, urged that the deportations proceed as quickly as possible.[44] However, the 'legal technicalities' in fact proved rather more complex than the Japanese government had anticipated.

Reports of the deportation plan were greeted by large-scale demonstrations by Korean residents in Japan, and fears of impending deportation continued to evoke protests throughout much of 1951, forming an ongoing counterpoint to official debates about the shaping of Japan's new immigration law. In fact, the issue proved (as Japanese police noted) to be one of the few things capable of evoking a united response from Korean residents of almost every political persuasion.[45] One protestor likened the proposal for mass deportations to 'the Jewish expulsion conducted by Hitler',[46] while a group made up largely of women and children protested to the immigration authorities that forced return to a nation in the throes of civil war was tantamount to a death sentence.[47]

SCAP too voiced its concerns about the deportation plan. Although the occupation authorities supported the introduction of a law enabling the Japanese government to deport limited numbers of 'subversives' and 'disorderly elements', some SCAP officials were alarmed at the potential human rights implications of mass deportations. Deporting ex-colonial subjects who had been born and lived all their lives in Japan, SCAP warned, might be contrary to international law, and anxieties were also expressed about the prospect of pushing ahead with the expulsions 'knowing that Koreans to be deported from Japan will be executed in Korea'. The liberal overtones of this statement, though, were blunted by the next sentence, in which GHQ/SCAP expressed the view that rather than being sent to Korea to be executed, 'subversive' Korean residents 'should be given the death sentence in Japan according to the law'.[48] There was also one other further consideration which seems to have entered SCAP's deliberations on the deportation issue. By early 1951, large numbers of US servicemen had been captured in the Korean War, and were being held in North Korean prisoner-of-war camps. Discussions between Japanese and SCAP officials raised the point that 'any actions taken upon the leftist Koreans in Japan may have grave consequences for the future treatment of American POWs'.[49]

It was in the midst of these complexities that SCAP turned to Nick Collaer, late of the US Immigration and Naturalization Service, for expert advice on deportation procedures, and on the wider framing of Japan's postwar immigration controls. Specifically, Collaer's task was to help the Japanese government create 'effective' migration controls 'in agreement with generally accepted international practice'.[50]

FROM CRYSTAL CITY TO TOKYO

The skills and attitudes which Nick Collaer brought to this task had been moulded by his years in the US Immigration and Naturalization Service. Before the outbreak of the Pacific War, he had been an INS field officer in the town of El Paso, Texas – a key point in the control of migration across the US–Mexican border. He was evidently an energetic and enthusiastic official, and he won the confidence of his superiors, who entrusted him with the task of sorting out one of the most intractable 'illegal entry' problems of the time: the fate of a group of German sailors who had arrived in the US in 1940 on a merchant vessel without proper entry authority. To deal with these unwelcome arrivals, whose repatriation to Germany was made difficult by the outbreak of war in Europe, Collaer created a new specialized detention camp at Fort Stanton, Texas – the first civilian internment camp to be established in the US during the Second World War.[51]

His efforts earned him promotion, and he was placed in charge of the detention section of the Immigration and Naturalization Service, with responsibility for supervising all INS internment camps throughout the USA (by the middle of 1943 there were nine, stretching from Idaho to Texas).[52] It was in this role that Collaer came into close contact with Japanese civilians – and also became a central player in one of the more bizarre episodes of the Pacific War.

The Immigration and Naturalization Service was not officially involved in the wartime internment of Japanese-Americans living in the USA, a task which was mainly carried out by the specially established War Relocation Authority (WRA) – though at times the demarcation lines between the two agencies became blurred. The INS was, however, in charge of a scheme developed in 1942, to transfer 'subversive aliens' (particularly Japanese) from Latin American countries to the United States for detention. After Pearl Harbor, US officials became increasingly afraid of the possibility that 'saboteurs' working for the Axis powers might smuggle themselves across the border into the US from Mexico.[53] The United States pressured its Latin American neighbours to intern Axis nationals, and entered into agreements with the Peruvian and other Latin American governments to 'export' their internees to the US. Enemy internees shipped from Latin America to the United States would be defined as 'illegal immigrants', held in US detention camps and 're-exported' to Japan, Gemany or Italy in exchange for US citizens captured by enemy nations.

In this way, Peruvian residents of Japanese ancestry (some of them Peruvian citizens) became 'pawns in a triangle of hate'.[54] Fears of subversion quickly became entangled with the power relationship between the US and Peruvian governments, and with racist sentiments against Asian immigrants in Peru. An official US investigation of wartime relocation and internment notes that 'what began as a controlled, closely monitored deportation program to detain potentially dangerous diplomatic and consular officials of Axis nations and Axis businessmen grew to include enemy aliens who were teachers, small businessmen, tailors and barbers – mostly people of Japanese ancestry'.[55]

These 'imported' detainees formed a substantial proportion of the inmates of the camps supervised by Nick Collaer, particularly at Crystal City in Texas, the largest of the INS camps. Collaer's position as supervisor of multiethnic internment camps like Crystal City provided him with considerable opportunities for contact with people of Japanese origin, including the opportunity to read some of the voluminous extracts of detainees' personal mail, which were censored by camp officials and passed on to the INS and other government agencies for their perusal.[56] He must also have become aware of the troubled history of relations between Japan and Korea, since the INS made extensive use of Korean residents in the US as translators of censored mail from the camps.[57] Most importantly, Collaer's involvement in multinational efforts to prevent the infiltration of enemy aliens across US borders undoubtedly shaped his views of the problems of migration in postwar Japan: views which were remarkable even by the generally colourful standards of early 1950s Cold War rhetoric.

INVASION BY ANOTHER NAME: NICHOLAS COLLAER AND JAPANESE MIGRATION POLICY

After his arrival in Japan in January 1951, Collaer consulted widely with Japanese and SCAP officials and travelled extensively, amongst other things visiting Ōmura, the place chosen for a new Japanese-controlled detention centre to replace Hario concentration camp.[58] In the process, he quickly became conscious of the complexity of the task that confronted him, and successfully requested an extra two months to complete his mission.[59] During these final months of his stay in Japan, he came to coordinate his work particularly closely with that of a newly created and top secret body: the Committee on Counter-Measures against Communism in the Far East, created by General Mathew Ridgeway of the US 8th Army in May 1951 to promote a range of US objectives including the surveillance of communists and the development of strategies for psychological warfare.[60]

The problems of migration control, especially the question of deportation, aroused strong feelings within SCAP as well as amongst Japanese officials. In October 1950, for example, Richard Appleton of SCAP's legal section had been moved to write a detailed memo, leaving a record of his concerns about the 'excessive' and 'arbitrary' deportation powers entrusted to the newly created Japanese Immigration Agency. In particular, he emphasized that immigration officials were being given the right to detain suspected illegal migrants without judicial supervision, in contravention of the constitutional requirement that courts should be able to review such restrictions on personal liberty. He was also concerned that immigration policy was being created through the use of 'ordinances' (which were imposed by the executive rather than debated by the legislature) and argued for the introduction of an immigration law which could be properly scrutinized by parliament.[61]

Nick Collaer's approach to the issue, however, was very different. Although he accepted the need to maintain the forms of 'due process' in the deportation of undesirable aliens, Collaer was much more worried that excessive concern for constitutional niceties might make exclusion and deportation orders difficult to enforce. His enthusiasm for swift and effective ways of screening potential immigrants and deporting 'undesirables' reflected his wider vision of the nature of migration, and of Japan's place in the Asian region, and in the Cold War world.

Collaer's report on the work he had carried out during his five months in Japan to June 1951 begins forthrightly by pointing out that migration controls are of absolutely primary importance in 'safeguarding democratic countries from those who would subvert their form of government', because 'no longer can any practical distinction be drawn between invasion by infiltration and invasion by military might'. In at least one (unspecified) recent case, Collaer darkly observed, 'the infiltration of aliens into a country largely contributed to its conquest'. Japan, he had concluded, was a prime target for such conquest by alien infiltration because of its 'highly strategic location' as a 'strong outpost for democracy in the Orient'.[62]

In Collaer's mind, Koreans in Japan figured prominently in the underground activities of this 'vast international conspiracy': he claimed (without offering supporting evidence) that 'a substantial percentage of the 467,580 North Koreans and of the 82,093 South Koreans registered as of March 1951, and the upwards of 200,000 aliens estimated by Japanese officials to be unregistered, are active communist agitators or rank-and-file members of subversive organizations'.[63] But the problem, as he was quick to emphasize, was by no means limited to Koreans. In correspondence with Nickolas Cottrell of SCAP's Government Section, who worked closely with him in drafting the immigration law, Collaer wrote,

I note that you stress the danger of Korean subversives. It is almost a certainty that highly trained communist agitators from many countries will enter Japan, legally or illegally, once the occupation terminates. Doubtless some are already awaiting the opportunity to start 'mass action' when the time is propitious.

While the Koreans will provide the bulk of forces, these highly trained and fully trusted communists from other countries will be the most dangerous. The deportation of such aliens under any form of 'due process' procedures is difficult and requires a highly specialized force of investigators and hearing examiners. I understand that the Judiciary Committee of the House of Representatives, following an investigation of Commie-inspired riots late last year in Kobe, Otsu, Nagoya, Osaka and Kyoto, recommended appropriate legislation to deport Koreans for subversive activities. The point I make is that such legislation should apply to ALL persons dedicated to the 'revolutionary movement'.[64]

Foreigners were not the only potential participants in the plans for infiltration so vividly depicted by Collaer. There were also the Japanese detained at the end of the war and still held in internment camps in China, the Soviet Union and so on. Collaer warned that 'there are possibly 350,000 Japanese citizens in the hands of its enemies, a high percentage of whom are doubtless communist-indoctrinated and some of whom are being infiltrated into Japan'. Then again, there was 'the large number of disgruntled war cripples, purgees and war crimes convicts', who constituted 'a post-Occupation threat of serious political, economic and security difficulties – especially should they merge with the foreign inspired revolutionary group or join the extreme rightist elements'.[65]

Collaer's proposals for Japan's migration law were thus designed to rescue the nation from his nightmare vision of a multinational conspiracy of resident Koreans, subversive armies of migrants-to-be, Japanese returnees, 'disgruntled war cripples' and others. In the circumstances, it was not surprising that he focused nearly all of his attention on making sure that the post-Occupation Japanese state was given all the powers it would need to keep out, detect or remove alien subversives. Meanwhile, other unresolved issues, such as the residence and re-entry rights of Koreans and Taiwanese in Japan, faded quietly into obscurity.

THE MAKING OF THE POSTWAR MIGRATION LAW

The initial plan had been for Collaer to assist in drafting an ordinance for the deportation of 'undesirable aliens'. In fact, a version of this ordinance was completed in February 1951. But, as dissension about deportation continued within SCAP, the Japanese bureaucracy and the wider community, it was eventually decided that the implementation of the ordinance should be postponed, and that the question of deportation should be dealt with in the wider framework of a general migration control law.[66] Collaer, working closely with Nickolas Cottrell of the Government Section and

S. A. Reese of the Legal Section, produced an outline of stopgap deportation proceedings to be used until the new migration law was introduced, and also wrote 'a comprehensive [migration] law which might be studied and used somewhat as a guide in drafting suitable legislation'.[67] This 'guide', Collaer noted, was partly based on the work being carried out by the US Senate committee on migration, and key parts of its deportation provisions were inspired by the McCarran Bill, then being debated in Congress.[68]

Collaer's proposals for the immigration law have become separated from their covering documentation in the SCAP files, but from internal evidence it seems clear that the 'guide' in question is an undated and anonymous draft labelled 'Proposed Law for the Regulation of Immigration'.[69] Although this contains variations to deal with local circumstances, it is strikingly similar in structure to US laws, including the McCarran-Walter Act, and is quite different in design to pre-war Japanese migration ordinances, which were much briefer and less specific.

After outlining provisions for the setting up of an Immigration Agency under the control of the Ministry of Justice, the 'Proposed Law' goes on (as does the final version of the McCarran-Walter Law) to provide detailed definitions of terminology, a long list of 'classes of aliens excluded from admission', and rules for the entry of non-immigrants.

The categories of 'excluded aliens' follow those of American law very closely, with whole sections of text at times being taken verbatim from US law.[70]

Collaer's 'guide', of course, was not the end of the story. It provided the basis for negotiations between the Japanese authorities and SCAP, as both attempted to fine-tune the final version of the Migration Control Ordinance. From 1950 onward, the Japanese Prime Minister's Office, Justice Ministry and Foreign Ministry, together with the headquarters of the National Rural Police, had been deeply engaged in negotiations with the Government Section of SCAP over issues of deportation and migration control. An important coordinating role in these discussions seems to have been played by Chief Cabinet Secretary Okazaki Katsuo, who was a close confidant of Prime Minister Yoshida.[71]

In these negotiations, the sharpest dividing lines were not necessarily those between the Japanese government and SCAP. At times, groups from the two sides might form alliances to pursue a particular policy: for example, Yoshikawa Mitsusada of the Justice Ministry's Special Investigations Division, which had amassed a wealth of information on the Korean community in Japan, worked with elements in SCAP to restrain Prime Minister Yoshida's enthusiasm for mass deportations.[72] As plans for the new system took shape, the centralization of powers into the hands of a new immigration service provoked particular resistance from the police, who continued to claim that they should retain the key role in controlling illegal entry. They were partly mollified, though, by an assurance that they could still be responsible for arresting clandestine border crossers, and could 'get credit for their arrest by delivering them to the nearest immigration inspector for appropriate action'.[73]

Though some details were revised after his departure, and the final version was generally more concise than the SCAP draft, the basic structure of Collaer's 'guide' had a profound influence on Japan's postwar Immigration Control Law: a law which, with amendments, remains in force to the present day. The Immigration Control Ordinance that came into effect on 1 November 1951 embodied fundamental changes in Japan's control of movement across the nation's borders. First, it reflected a radical centralization of migration controls. The pre-war system had entrusted the task of controlling the entry of migrants to prefectural governors and local police. By contrast, the postwar system placed this power firmly in the hands of the single, centralized Migration Control Agency (which was renamed the Immigration Agency, and then in 1952 moved from Foreign Affairs to the Ministry of Justice under the new name of Immigration Bureau).[74] This centralization was one measure on which Collaer insisted. As he emphasized, citing the fruits of 'years of expensive experimentation' in the United States, '*all* [migration control] *activities must be thoroughly integrated into one agency of enforcement for maximum results*'.[75]

Second, reflecting both its origins in the deportation debate and the influence of the McCarran Bill, a large part of Japan's Migration Control Ordinance was taken up with questions of deportation. Closely mirroring both wartime Japanese migration controls and the US McCarran-Walter Law, deportable foreigners were defined as including people convicted of crimes other than minor offences; people suffering from Hansen's disease and certain other communicable diseases; those confined to mental hospitals; and anyone who 'becomes a public charge to the state or local authorities by reason of poverty, vagrancy or physical handicap'.[76] At a time when some 80 per cent of the Korean community in Japan was said to be unemployed, it was hardly surprising that that these provisions alone caused anxiety to many *Zainichi* Koreans.

The postwar Japanese law, however, went to greater length than its US counterpart in detailing groups who could be deported on political grounds. Its definition of 'subversives' (including members of parties which planned 'the violent overthrow of the Japanese constitution or of governments established thereby' and people who belonged, or 'had close links to', any group which advocated the killing or injuring of public offi-cials) was close to US anti-subversion measures. But, reflecting his Cold War fears of 'invasion by infiltration', Collaer proposed deportation rules for Japan which placed a particularly strong emphasis on 'sabotage' or the destruction of public property.[77] In the final version of Japanese law, these fears of foreign 'sabotage' were spelled out in a detailed clause (still on the Japanese statute books today) authorizing the deportation of for-eigners who belonged, had close links to, or even published information supporting, any party or group advocating protest actions which hin-dered 'the operation of the safety equipment of factories and workplaces'. To close any possible loopholes, anyone 'determined by the Minister of Justice to be performing acts injurious to the interests and public order of the Japanese nation' could also be deported.

The ordinance went on to outline a complex set of administrative pro-cedures through which those detained by the immigration authorities could appeal against deportation. Nick Collaer strongly opposed the involvement of the judiciary in the deportation system, and rejected a suggestion from Japanese officials that the courts should be responsible for issuing deportation orders. Rather than allowing appeals against deportation to the courts, the ordinance made it possible for people who were detained by immigration officials to appeal to an administrative tri-bunal, and ultimately to the minister of justice, for the right to remain in Japan. The courts could only be involved at the very final stage, when all other avenues of appeal had been exhausted, and then only to determine whether due process had been followed by the officials involved in the case.

Despite its detailed discussion of procedures, one of the most strik-ing features of Japan's Immigration Control Ordinance was the large amount of discretion which it left to the state. This again seems to reflect Collaer's views: his report noted that it was 'no simple task in a democ-racy, in this period of world history, to draft legislation which can be efficiently enforced under constitutional limitations and still accom-plish the intended purposes, i.e., while welcoming those aliens who are desirable to prevent the entry or continued residence of those who are undesirable'. The only way of ensuring that the undesirable were sepa-rated from the desirable, he suggested, was to 'extend to administrative officials considerable discretionary authority'.[78] To achieve this end, the Immigration Control Ordinance empowered the minister of justice to overturn deportation orders, even of people in 'deportable' categories, if he decided that there were 'circumstances which make it appropriate for the Minister to grant special permission to stay'. As we shall see, this discretionary 'special permission to stay' became an invisible gateway which allowed the legalization of some postwar 'illegal migrants', while at the same time giving the Japanese authorities huge power to determine the fates of individual lives.

Japan's 1951 Immigration Control Ordinance, however, was radically different from postwar US law in one crucial respect. The McCarran-Walter Act's official title was the Immigration and Nationality Act and (as this suggests) it covered not only cross-border movement but also questions of citizenship and naturalization. In the Japanese case, however, immigration policy was separated from citizenship policy, and this was to have extraordinary and profound consequences for the majority of Japan's foreign residents.

SCAP officials were well aware of the consequences of separating migration from citizenship. Nick Collaer noted himself noted that

a sound nationality act and procedures governing naturalization is [*sic*] on a par in importance with a law and appropriate regulations to govern the admission, exclusion, deportation and registration of aliens. They are closely related subjects … With nationality laws in a state of confusion the problem of immigration enforcement, of course, becomes more difficult.[79]

Why, then, did he and others choose to treat the two issues separately? The key issue was the status of Korean and Taiwanese former colonial subjects. As we have seen (p. 60), colonial subjects had possessed Japanese nationality under international law, and until the signing of the San Francisco Peace Treaty Korean and Taiwanese residents in postwar Japan retained that nationality – theoretically at least. In practice, SCAP seems increasingly to have taken the view expressed with startling frankness by Nickolas Cottrell in March 1951: 'Those who entered Japan before the end of the war, at that time, had the status of Japanese nationals. Since the Occupation, this group may still be said to retain some portion of that status, i.e. to be at least "Japanese nationals second class".'[80]

Immigration control measures, of course, were all about the entry, residence and departure of 'aliens', and did not apply at all to Japanese nationals – not even to 'Japanese nationals second class'. So the implications of immigration controls for Koreans and Taiwanese in Japan would depend crucially on the way in which the nationality issue was handled.

Like immigration policy, nationality policy is a neglected area in the study of the Allied occupation of Japan. In 1950, the Japanese Diet passed a revised Nationality Law. The postwar law changed rather little, retaining the pre-war rule that Japanese nationality was acquired by inheritance or 'bloodline' (known in legal terms as *ius sanguinis*) rather than by place of birth (*ius soli*). As a result, it is often seen as being a purely 'Japanese' law in which the occupation had no say at all. But of course, had it wished to, SCAP could have demanded more radical change of the definition of Japanese nationality. Some SCAP officials favoured this approach – one interestingly arguing that *ius soli* should be introduced so as to promote the rapid assimilation of Korean and Taiwanese residents who might otherwise become a 'source of trouble'.[81] Senior SCAP officials, however, showed no interest in intervening in this area of Japanese life, and indeed a report by SCAP's Legal Section praised the new Nationality Law as an 'exceptionally good piece of legislation'.[82]

The Nationality Law, however, made no attempt to 'touch on problems the final solution of which will be affected by the coming Peace Treaty; thus it includes no provisions on the nationality status of Koreans, Taiwanese and Ryukyuans';[83] and as the signing of the peace treaty drew nearer, this issue became a topic of growing debate in the ranks of both SCAP and the Japanese government. Both international law and overseas experience pointed to a clear solution to the problem: former colonial subjects should be offered a choice of retaining their Japanese nationality or adopting the nationality of their newly independent homeland. This was the approach taken, for example, in 1947, when areas formerly occupied by Italy, but inhabited mainly by Croats and Serbs, were transferred to the state of Yugoslavia. The 1948 United Nations Universal Declaration of Human Rights (Article 15, Clause 2) emphasized the right to such choice: 'no one', it stated, 'shall be arbitrarily deprived of his nationality nor denied the right to change his nationality'.

On this issue, as on others, opinion within the occupation authorities was divided. Some members of SCAP's Legal Section argued strongly that the Japanese government should be required to give Koreans and Taiwanese in Japan a choice of nationality, and grant full citizenship rights to those who opted for Japanese nationality. When Collaer was drawing up drafts for the Immigration Control Law in the middle of 1951, he still seems to have assumed that this choice would be offered. But meanwhile, others were expressing concerns about this approach. R. B. Finn of the Diplomatic Section, for example, warned that any move which gave *Zainichi* Koreans voting rights could be a security risk because 'many of the Koreans are leftists and thus there would be many added votes for the Communist Party'.[84] Meanwhile, the division of the Korean Peninsula had added a new layer of complexity to the question of the nationality of Koreans in Japan. As we have seen, although nearly all originated in the south of the peninsula, large numbers of *Zainichi* Koreans regarded the Yi Seung-Man regime in the South with some mistrust, and identified themselves as nationals of *Joseon* rather than of *Daehan Minguk*. While the Japanese government was eager to define all former colonial subjects as 'foreign', the newly created South Korean regime was determined to forestall a choice of nationalities by declaring all *Zainichi* Koreans to be citizens of the Republic of Korea.

So the rights of individuals to a choice of nationality came to be overshadowed by the larger strategic considerations of Cold War East Asia. As the date for the signing of the Peace Treaty approached, with no solution to the citizenship issue in place, the occupation forces quietly resolved to wash their hands of the whole contentious problem. In September 1951, Japan entered into direct negotiations with the government of the Republic of Korea (which was not represented at the San Francisco Peace Conference). As these discussions took place, the head of SCAP's Legal Section, Alva Gardiner, wrote an eloquent exposition of the problem, explaining the reasons why international law required that Koreans in Japan be given a choice of nationality. This explanation, however, was simply for the information of the US State Department. Gardiner concluded by pointing out that SCAP was intending to take no active part in the negotiations between Japan and South Korea. Therefore 'SCAP observers propose to express NO repeat NO views re these matters unless the Department should advise otherwise'.[85] The Department issued no such advice. In the event, the negotiations between Japan and South Korea broke up without agreement, and shortly before the San Francisco Peace Treaty came into force on 28 April 1952, the Japanese Ministry of Justice announced Japan's unilateral decision that from the day when the Peace Treaty came into effect, Koreans and Taiwanese in Japan would lose their Japanese nationality and become foreigners.[86]

The outcome of the complex parallel politics of immigration and citizenship was deeply ironic. Japan ended up with an Immigration Control Law which (for the first time) provided a firm legal basis for foreigners to obtain permanent residence in Japan. The processes for becoming a permanent resident were spelled out with admirable clarity – foreigners were to apply, with the appropriate documentation, to the Japanese embassy or consulate in their country of residence. But the law said absolutely nothing at all about the residence rights of people who had been 'Japanese' when they entered Japan and had been turned into foreigners by administrative fiat thereafter. They, obviously, could not apply for permanent residence at the 'Japanese embassy in their country of residence', as they were in Japan already. And if they left Japan to apply overseas it was almost certain that they would never be allowed back in again.

Instead, as the Peace Treaty came into force, the Japanese government introduced a regulation stating that Koreans and Taiwanese who had entered Japan before the start of the Allied occupation would be 'allowed to remain in Japan, even though they still had no official residence status, until such time as their residence status and period of residence has been determined'.[87] In other words, they possessed no legally defined right to live in Japan, but were merely there on the sufferance of the authorities until the government decided what to do with them.

Meanwhile, the change in legal status had other profound consequences for Koreans in Japan – for some, indeed, life-and-death consequences. Until 28 April 1952, the 'liberated people' (as residual Japanese nationals) had not been subject to the Immigration Control Ordinance. Although undocumented entrants or those who lacked proper alien registration could be deported, other Koreans and Taiwanese in Japan could not. From that day on, however, as 'aliens' they were in principle to be treated as all other foreigners in Japan, although in practice the Japanese government exercised discretion in deciding exactly which clauses of the Immigration Control Ordinance would be applied to former colonial subjects. One of those which was applied was the clause which stated that foreigners in Japan who committed serious crimes (with sentences of over one year's imprisonment) were to be deported after serving their sentences. This was to cause endless difficulties, and became the root of some of most unhappy aspects of the Japanese state's postwar relationship both with the South Korea and with Korean community in Japan (see Chapter Six).

Another seed of future conflict was the revision of the Alien Registration Ordinance which also took place on the day when the Allied occupation of Japan ended. On 28 April, the Immigration Control Bureau, which had been carefully preparing for this day, introduced a new Alien Registration Law. A particularly controversial aspect of the law was that, for the first time, it required registering foreigners to be fingerprinted. The

Bureau itself seems initially to have envisaged taking a single fingerprint from each foreigner in Japan at the legal registration age of fourteen, and thereafter once every five years, each time the card was renewed. On the insistence of the police, however, they finally decided on a system which, for Koreans in Japan, rubbed salt into the wounds of their uneasily redefined status. Under this system each foreigner was to have a full set of ten fingerprints taken each time he or she was registered.

The practical difference was small, but the symbolic significance profound. Only one fingerprint was needed for the official purpose of confirming identity. There could only be one reason for taking all ten prints: to provide a store of data against which police could match prints found at crime scenes. Taking ten prints, in other words, imprinted on the minds and bodies of foreigners in Japan the knowledge that they were viewed as potential criminals. Indeed, the measure was so strongly opposed by various Korean community groups in Japan that its implementation had to be delayed for three years.[88] However, from May 1955 fingerprinting was enforced and, like the issue of deportation, it laid the basis for decades of conflict.

In her book *Dreamworld and Catastophe,* Susan Buck-Morss writes that 'modern sovereignties harbor a blind spot, a zone in which power is above the law and thus, at least potentially, a terrain of terror. This wild zone of power, by its very structure impossible to domesticate, is intrinsic to mass-democratic regimes'.[89] At least until the re-establishment of full diplomatic relations between Japan and South Korea in 1965, Koreans in Japan found themselves in a strange vacuum: neither permanent residents nor temporary visitors; subject to the Migration Control Law, but only as and when the state saw fit. For them, the legacy of colonialism, occupation and the post-occupation settlement was a new era of life in the wild zone.

NOTES

1. Miyazaki Shigeki, *Gaikokujin Tōroku Hō to Shimon Ōnatsu* (Tokyo: 'Chōsen Mondai' Konwakai, 1986), p. 13.
2. Memo from AVM Bladin for Commander-in-Chief BCOF, to HQ Eighth US Army, 'Foreign Nationals', 19 September 1946.
3. Ibid.
4. Imperial Ordinance no. 207 of 2 May 1947, 'Ordinance for Registration of Aliens', in GHQ/SCAP Records, Box 2198, Folder 16, 'Immigration' February 1950–March 1952, microfilm held in National Diet Library, Tokyo, fiche no. GS(B)-01603.

5. Ibid.
6. E. Takemae, (trans. Robert Ricketts and S. Swann), *Inside GHQ: The Allied Occupation of Japan and Its Legacy* (London: Continuum, 2002), p. 451.
7. Izumi Seiichi, *Saishūtō* (Tokyo: Tōkyō Daigaku Shuppankai, 1966), pp. 238–9.
8. Memo 'Dislocation of Korean Minority', in GHQ/SCAP Records, Box 385, Folder 4, '014: Civil Matters, Binder #1, 2 January 1946 thru 19 January 1948 (Japan, Korea, Miscellaneous)', March 1946–January 1948.
9. See Police Guard Section, National Rural Police HQ, 'A Deportation Plan', 23 January 1950, in GHQ/SCAP Records, Box 331, Folder 61, 'Illegal Entry – Koreans – Registration of Alliens [*sic*]' December 1949–September 1950.
10. Hōmushō Nyūkoku Kanrikyoku, *Shutsunyūkoku Kanri to sono Jittai* (Tokyo: Ōkurashō Insatsukyoku, 1964), p. 17.
11. Ibid., p. 17; see also Takemae, *Inside GHQ*, p. 498.
12. Hōmushō Nyūkoku Kanrikyoku, *Shutsunyūkoku Kanri no Kaikō to Tenbō: Nyūkan Hasoku 30-Shūnen o Kinen shite* (Tokyo: Hōmushō Nyūkoku Kanrikyoku, 1980), p. 278.
13. Extracts from censored letters contained in GHQ/SCAP Records, Box 265, Folder RG 331, 'Daily Reports of Illegal Entry of Koreans', July 1950–September 1950, and Box 266, Folder 012.42c 'CCD Intercepts – Illegal Entry and Exit of Koreans (Book #3)', 2 September 1949–14 October 1949.
14. Yoon Hak-Jun, 'Waga Mikkōki', *Chōsen Kenkyū*, 190 (June 1979), p. 10.
15. Ibid., p. 11.
16. Matsumoto Kunihiko (ed.), *GHQ Nihon Senryōshi 16 – Gaikokujin no Toriatsukai* (Tokyo: Nihon Tosho Sentā, 1996), p. 128.
17. Pak Jae-Il, *Zainichi Chōsenjin ni Kansuru Sōgō Chōsa Kenkyū* (Tokyo: Shin-Kigensha, 1957), p. 40.
18. J. Dower, *Embracing Defeat: Japan in the Wake of World War II* (New York: W. W. Norton, 1999), p. 23.
19. Joint Chiefs of Staff, 'Basic Initial Post-surrender Directive to Supreme Commander for the Allied Powers for the Occupation and Control of Japan', 3 November 1945, in Government Section, Supreme Commander for the Allied Powers, *Political Reorientation of Japan* (Washington, DC: US Government Printing Office, 1949), pp. 429–41, quotation from p. 431.
20. HQ BCOF Military Government Liaison Section, 'Minute: Illegal Entry of Koreans', 15 July 1946, in Australian War Memorial, Canberra, File no. AWM 114 417/1/27, 'Illegal Entry of Koreans in Japan'.
21. Memo on 'Organization by which Japanese Implement SCAPIN 1391', from Capt. R. Tapper Mil. Govt. Liaison Officer Yamaguchi to HQ BCOF Mil. Govt. Liaison Section, Kure, 8 April 1947, in Australian War Memorial, Canberra, series 114, control symbol 417/1/27, 'Illegal Entry of Koreans in Japan', 1946–1947.
22. 'CSDIC Translations BCOF – Illegal Entry into Japan 1948', held in the Australian War Memorial, Canberra, File AWM 144, 417/1/27, p. 7.

23. Memo from BCOF Headquarters to Eighth US Army, 'Report on Illegal Entry of Korean Immigrants into Japan', 29 July 1946, in Australian War Memorial, Canberra, AWM 114 417/1/27, 'Illegal Entry of Koreans in to Japan'.
24. Constitution of Japan, in Government Section, Supreme Commander for the Allied Powers, *Political Reorientation of Japan, September 1945 to September 1948* (Washington, DC: US Government Printing Office, 1949), pp. 670–7, citation from p. 671.
25. Matsumoto, *GHQ Nihon Senryōshi 16*, p. 153.
26. E. Graham, *Japan's Sea Lane Security 1940–2004: A Matter of Life and Death?* (London: Routledge, 2005), p. 99.
27. Cabinet Order no. 299 (10 August 1949), 'Cabinet Order Concerning Immigration Surveillance', English translation contained in GHQ/SCAP Records, Box 2189, Folder 16, 'Immigration', February 1950–March 1952, microfilm held in National Diet Library, Tokyo, fiche no. GS(B)-01603.
28. Memo from Brig. Gen. K. B. Bush to Japanese Government, 'Immigration Service', 20 February 1950, in GHQ/SCAP Records, Box 2189, Folder 16, 'Immigration', February 1950–March 1952, microfilm held in National Diet Library, Tokyo, fiche no. GS(B)-01603; see also Hōmushō Nyūkoku Kanrikyoku, *Shutsunyūkoku Kanri no Kaikō to Tenbō*, 79.
29. See Informal Memorandum from Nick D. Collaer for Lt Col. R. T. Benson, 'Progress of Efforts to have Japan Implement SCAPIN No. 2065 of 20 February 1950 through Adoption of "Effective" Controls on Immigration "in Agreement with Generally Accepted International Practice"', 12 June 1951, in GHQ/SCAP Archives, Box 1447, Folder 7, 'Alien Control in Japan 1951', held in National Diet Library, Tokyo, microfiche no. LS-26003. FBI chief Edgar Hoover, who disapproved of Collaer's methods, once unkindly described him as overweight, balding and sloppily dressed; see J. J. Culley, 'A Troublesome Presence: World War II Internment of German Sailors in New Mexico', *Prologue*, 28, 4 (Winter 1996), pp. 279–95, quotation from p. 284.
30. The SCAP officials who worked most closely with Collaer in producing the draft Immigration Law were Nickolas Cottrell of the Government Section and S. A. Reese of the Legal Section; see N. D. Collaer, untitled report appended to Informal Memorandum for Lt Col. R. T. Benson from Nick D. Collaer, 12 June 1951, in GHQ/SCAP Records, Box no. 1447, Folder no. 7, 'Alien Control in Japan', June 1951, microfiche held in National Diet Library, Tokyo, LS-26003.
31. Alger Hiss was a State Department official who was accused by an acquaintance of having been a communist spy. Called before the House Committee on Un-American Activities in 1948, Hiss denied the charge under oath, and later sued his accuser for defamation. However, Hiss in turn was indicted for perjury, and in 1950 was sentenced to five years' imprisonment, of which he ultimately served just under four years. The case became one of the most famous trials in US twentieth-century history.

32. Quoted in M. T. Bennett, *American Immigration Policies: A History* (Washington, DC: Public Affairs Press, 1963), p. 81.
33. Ibid. p. 100.
34. For example, in most cases, quotas for migrant admission were based on the country of origin (and not the ethnicity) of the immigrant. However, Chinese immigrants were treated differently: all overseas Chinese, whatever their country of residence or citizenship, were defined as falling within China's very limited quota for entry. Ibid., pp. 153–4.
35. Quoted in ibid., p. 155.
36. See, for example, R. Hanks Mitchell, 'The Korean Minority in Japan 1910–1963' (unpublished Ph.D. thesis, University of Wisconsin, 1963), p. 173.
37. Kang Sang-Jung, *Zainichi* (Tokyo: Kōdansha, 2004), p. 24.
38. The Union's name was later changed to Jae-Ilbon Daehanminguk Mindan (Korean), Zai-Nihon Taikanminkoku Mindan (Japanese).
39. See H. Inokuchi, 'Korean Ethnic Schools in Occupied Japan, 1945–1952', in S. Ryang (ed.), *Koreans in Japan: Critical Voices from the Margin* (London: Routledge, 2000), pp. 140–56; Kim Tae-Gi, *Sengo Nihon Seiji to Zainichi Chōsenjin Mondai* (Tokyo: Keisō Shobō, 1997), pp. 392–9.
40. Choi Deok-Hyo, 'Wartime Mobilization and Zainichi Koreans: Focussing on the "Experiences" Surrounding the Volunteer Soldier Recruitment Movement', paper presented at the Experiences of the Korean War workshop, Tokyo University of Foreign Studies, September 2003, p. 5.
41. *Kokkai Gijiroku*, 8 February 1956; see also N. D. Collaer, untitled report appended to Informal Memorandum for Lt Col. R. T. Benson from Nick D. Collaer, 12 June 1951, p. 6.
42. Quoted in Special Investigation, Attorney General's Office, 'Reactions of Koreans residing in Japan and Other Circles to the Compulsory Deportation of Koreans', from Mitsusada Yoshikawa, Special Investigation Bureau, Attorney General's Office, to Lt Col. Jack P. Napier, Government Section, GHQ, 15 January 1951, p. 3, in GHQ/SCAP Archives, Box 2189, Folder 16, 'Immigration, February 1950–March 1952', held in National Diet Library, Tokyo, microfiche no. GS(B)-01603.
43. Jiji Press, 'Communist Koreans May be Ordered Deported', evening bulletin 24 December 1950, English translation held in GHQ/SCAP Archives, Box 2189, Folder 16, 'Immigration, February 1950–March 1952', held in National Diet Library, Tokyo, microfiche no. GS(B)-01603.
44. A senior official of the Japanese Attorney General's office, for example, is quoted as noting that Yoshida had been asking about the progress of the deportation measures, and that 'the Prime Minister was very anxious to hurry up the matter on deportation'. Memorandum for Colonel Napier, 'Deportation of Korean [*sic*] Issue', 9 March 1951, held in GHQ/SCAP Archives, Box 2189, Folder 16, 'Immigration, February 1950–March 1952', held in National Diet Library, Tokyo, microfiche no. GS(B)-01602. On

Yoshida's message to MacArthur about the mass removal of Koreans see Takemae, *Inside GHQ*, p. 497. MacArthur opposed Yoshida's suggestion, but agreed that it would be better if the Koreans did not remain permanently in Japan.

45. An official of Japan's Metropolitan Police Department noted that 'almost all of the Koreans, with no distinction between right and left faction, are inclined to launch an opposition movement boisterously and to fight against … "compulsory deportation" together'. Memo from Chief, Liaison Section, MPD, 'Re Movements of the Koreans Centering around the Enforcement of the Emigration Control Ordinance', 30 October 1951, held in GHQ/SCAP Archives, Box 353, Folder 8, 'Immigration, April 1951–October 1951'; reproduced on Korean National Library database.
46. Memo from Matsumoto Hideyuki, Liaison Chief, MPD, 'Protest against the Attorney General around the Compulsory Deportation of the Koreans', 23 October 1951, held in GHQ/SCAP Archives, Box 353, Folder no. 6, 'Deportation, October 1951–November 1951', reproduced on Korean National Library database.
47. Memo from Chief, Liaison Section, MPD, 'A Petition Movement of the Koreans to the Emigration Board [*sic*]', 22 October 1951, held in GHQ/SCAP Archives, Box 353, Folder 8, 'Immigation, April 1951–October 1951'; reproduced on Korean National Library database.
48. Untitled memo outlining GHQ/SCAP's views on deportation, initialled 'MU', held in GHQ/SCAP Archives, Box 2189, Folder 16, 'Immigration, February 1950–March 1952', held in National Diet Library, Tokyo, microfiche no. GS(B)-01603.
49. Memorandum for Colonel Napier, 'Deportation of Korean [*sic*] Issue'.
50. See Informal Memorandum from Nick D. Collaer for Lt Col. R. T. Benson, 12 June 1951.
51. Culley, 'Troublesome Presence'.
52. Ibid., p. 290.
53. US border control officers working on the Mexican border were warned by their superiors in 1952 that 'it is entirely possible that such Axis agents may endeavour to look the part of a local farmer or at night may even black their hands and face, particularly in isolated areas, to look like Negroes'. Quoted in K. L. Hernandez, 'Distant Origins: The Mexican Roots of US Border Control Practice and American Racism, 1924–1954', paper presented at the UCLA Second Annual Interdisciplinary Conference on Race, Ethnicity and Migration, Los Angeles, 28 May 2002, p. 5.
54. C. Harvey Gardiner, *Pawns in a Triangle of Hate: The Peruvian-Japanese and the United States* (Seattle: University of Washington Press, 1981).
55. Commission on Wartime Relocation and Internment of Civilians, *Personal Justice Denied: Report of the Commission on Wartime Relocation and Internment of Civilians* (Washington, DC and Seattle: Civil Liberties Public Education Fund/University of Washington Press, 1997), p. 305.

56. L. Fiset, 'Return to Sender: US Censorship of Enemy Alien Mail in World War II', *Prologue*, 33, 1 (Spring 2001), pp. 21–35, see particularly footnote 26.
57. Ibid.; see also Hyung-Ju Ahn, *Between Two Adversaries: Korean Interpreters at Japanese Alien Enemy Detention Centers During World War II* (Fullerton: California State University Oral History Program, 2002).
58. Memorandum for the record from Nickolas Cottrell, 'Immigration', 4 April 1951, in GHQ/SCAP Records, Box 2189, 'Immigration, February 1950–March 1952', held in National Diet Library, Tokyo, microfiche no GS(B)-01602.
59. Informal Memorandum from Nick D. Collaer for Lt Col. R. T. Benson, 12 June 1951.
60. Takemae, *Inside GHQ*, pp. 197, 493 and 498–9.
61. Memo for the record from Richard B. Appleton, 'Cabinet Order Establishing the Immigration Agency', 17 October 1950, in GHQ/SCAP Records, Box 1447, Folder 7, 'Alien Control in Japan 1951', held in National Diet Library, Tokyo, microfiche no. LS-26003.
62. N. D. Collaer, untitled report appended to Informal Memorandum for Lt Col. R. T. Benson from Nick D. Collaer, 12 June 1951, pp. 1 and 4.
63. Ibid., p. 5.
64. Untitled memo from NDC [Nicholas D. Collaer] to Nickolas Cottrell, 15 March 1951, in GHQ/SCAP Records, Box 2189, 'Immigration February 1950–March 1952', held in National Diet Library, Tokyo, microfiche no. GS(B)-01601 (emphasis in the original).
65. N. D. Collaer, untitled report appended to Informal Memorandum for Lt Col. R. T. Benson from Nick D. Collaer, 12 June 1951, p. 5.
66. Hōmushō Nyūkoku Kanrikyoku, *Shutsunyūkoku Kanri to sono Jittai – Shōwa 39-nen* (Tokyo: Ōkurashō Insatsukyoku, 1964), p. 20.
67. N. D. Collaer, untitled report appended to Informal Memorandum from Nick D. Collaer for Lt Col. R. T. Benson, 12 June 1951, p. 7.
68. Ibid. p. 8; see also untitled memo from NDC to Nickolas Cottrell, 15 March 1951.
69. In GHQ/SCAP Records, Box 1510, Folder 32, 'Proposed Law for the Regulation of Immigration', held in National Diet Library, Tokyo, microfiche no. LS-11808–11809.
70. One example was the clause debarring the entry of 'aliens who have been convicted of two or more offenses (other than purely political offenses), regardless of whether the conviction was in a single trial or whether the offenses arose from a single scheme of misconduct and regardless of whether the offenses involved moral turpitude, for which the aggregate possible sentence is confinement under the law for more than five years'. In the final version of the Japanese law, this was strengthened to exclude aliens who had been convicted of a crime which carried a sentence of more than one year. See 'Shutsunyūkoku Kanrirei', reprinted in the appendix to Satō Katsumi,

Zainichi Chōsenjin no Shomondai (Tokyo: Dōseidō, 1971), p. 285; Bennett, *American Immigration Policies*, p. 146.

71. 'Development or Reform of Procedures for Deporting Illegal Immigrants', undated memo, GHQ/SCAP Records, Box 2189, Folder 16, 'Immigration, February 1950–March 1952', held in National Diet Library, Tokyo, microfiche no. GS(B)-01602.

72. See Memorandum for Colonel Napier, 'Deportation of Korean [*sic*] Issue'.

73. Informal memorandum for Lt Col. R. T. Benson, 'Views of the heads of the NRP, Customs and Maritime Safety Board in regard to the proposal to fix responsibility in the Immigration Agency of Japan for all work involving alien control', 7 July 1951, in GHQ/SCAP Records, Box 2189, Folder 16, 'Immigration, February 1950–March 1952', held in National Diet Library, Tokyo, microfiche no. GS(B)-01601.

74. Hōmushō Nyūkoku Kanrikyoku, *Shutsunyūkoku Kanri no Kaikō to Tenbō*, p. 24.

75. N. D. Collaer, untitled report appended to Informal Memorandum for Lt Col. R. T. Benson from Nick D. Collaer, 12 June 1951, pp. 2 and 3 (emphasis in the original).

76. 'Shutsunyūkoku Kanrirei', in Satō, *Zainichi Chōsenjin,* pp. 294–5.

77. 'Proposed Law for the Regulation of Immigration', p. 14.

78. N. D. Collaer, untitled report appended to Informal Memorandum for Lt Col. R. T. Benson from Nick D. Collaer, 12 June 1951, p. 1.

79. Untitled memo from NDC to Nickolas Cottrell, 15 March 1951.

80. Memorandum for Colonel Napier from Nickolas Cottrell, 'Status Revision of Immigration Laws', 19 March 1951, in GHQ/SCAP Records, Box 2189, Folder 16, 'Immigration February 1950–March 1952', held in National Diet Library, Tokyo, microfiche no. GS(B)-01601.

81. Letter from David Ramsay to Commanding General, Eighth Army, 'Citizenship of Japan', 17 January 1949, in GHQ/SCAP Records, held in National Diet Library, Tokyo, microfiche no. LS-10149.

82. GHQ/SCAP Legal Section, 'Legal Comments', May 1950, in GHQ/SCAP Records, held in National Diet Library, Tokyo, microfiche no. LS-10149. See also Kim Tae-Gi, *Sengo Nihon Seiji*.

83. GHQ/SCAP Legal Section, 'Legal Comments'.

84. Memorandum of meeting on 'DS Staff Study on Status and Treatment of Koreans in Japan', in GHQ/SCAP Records, held in National Diet Library, Tokyo, microfiche no. LS 24687–24688.

85. Draft confidential telegram from UCPOLAD to Department of State, 28 October 1951, attached to report by Alva C. Gardiner, Chief, Legal Section, in GHQ/SCAP Records, held in National Diet Library, Tokyo, microfiche no. LS 24687–24688.

86. Kim Il-Hwa, 'Zainichi Chōsenjin no Hōteki Chii', in Pak Jeong-Myeong (ed.), *Zainichi Chōsenjin: Rekishi, Genjō, Tenbō* (Tokyo: Akashi Shoten, 1995), pp. 189–232, p. 205.

87. Quoted in ibid., p. 207; see also debate of the Lower House of the Japanese Diet, 28 April, 1952, in Parliament of Japan, *Kokkai Kaigiroku Kensaku Shisutemu*, http://kokkai.ndl.go.jp/ (accessed 4 January 2008).

88. Hōmushō Nyūkoku Kanrikyoku, *Shutsunyūkoku Kanri no Kaikō to Tenbō*, p. 278.

89. S. Buck-Morss, *Dreamworld and Catastrophe: The Passing of Mass Utopias in East and West* (Cambridge, MA: MIT Press, 2000), pp. 2–3.

CHAPTER 5

Worlds apart I

The armed archipelago

On 18 March 2008, a taxi driver named Takahashi Masaaki was found stabbed to death in his cab in the Japanese port town of Yokosuka. A wallet left lying on the passenger seat revealed that Takahashi's last passenger, and the chief suspect in his murder, was a twenty-two-year-old man serving with the US Navy. However, Japanese authorities had no knowledge of this young man's presence in Japan. He had not passed through Japanese immigration, nor was he registered as a foreign resident.[1]

The reason for this was simple. Under rules whose origins go back to the postwar occupation of Japan, all members of the US military serving in Japan are exempt both from normal Japanese immigration procedures and from carrying alien registration cards. Instead, the US forces in Japan conduct their own clearance procedures. The young suspect in Takahashi's murder had entered Japan on a US naval vessel but had, several weeks earlier, gone AWOL, and disappeared into the anonymous crowds of the greater Tokyo area.[2] Since the US military was not required to pass information about AWOL service-people to the Japanese authorities, the sailor had in effect slipped through a blind spot in Japan's strict immigration control system.

This situation is not unique to Japan. Similar arrangements exist in most countries where the US has maintained a significant military presence since the Second World War. The same exemption also covered the British Commonwealth forces who remained in Japan from the end of the Allied Occupation until 1957. Foreign troops stationed in Japan, as well as their dependents and foreign civilian employees, were exempt from the alien registration system too, and therefore do not appear in the official statistics of foreigners living in Japan. And this, in turn, encourages many researchers of the foreign presence in postwar Japan to treat the people of the military bases as through they 'do not count': either failing to mention them at all, or regarding them as a mere diversionary footnote to the main story. A further reason for this neglect may be the perception that most spent only a short time in Japan – postings of one or two years are common, though some people stayed much longer. The fact that foreign military forces live on fenced and guarded bases, separated from the Japanese population, also strengthens the impression that they exist in isolation from the rest of Japan.

Yet, despite this segregation, the foreign population of the US bases had a profound impact on postwar Japanese culture and society, as well as on its politics and security. In places like Scandinavia, the Benelux countries, Latin America or Australia and New Zealand, where postwar US military deployments were very small, it makes little difference whether US base personnel are or are not counted in figures for resident foreigners. But in Germany, Japan and Korea, which (until the mass influx of US troops into Vietnam in 1964–5) were home to the largest concentrations of US forces overseas, omitting the inhabitants of US bases from the account creates a very lopsided image of the foreign presence within the nation.

THE FOREIGN MILITARY PRESENCE IN POSTWAR JAPAN

The global network of US bases established in the decade following the end of the Second World War transformed the nature of the world order. But, although the strategic significance of the bases has been the subject of much study, until recently surprisingly little attention was paid to the meaning of these bases as social realities: little pieces of America scattered around the world, interacting uneasily with their surrounding local communities.[3]

As one recent study emphasizes, the phenomenon is a curious one: 'it is historically rare for one nation to base military forces on another independent nation's territory'.[4] Roosevelt and Truman had both envisaged the need to maintain a large US military presence overseas after the Second World War was over, but in the immediate aftermath of war there was strong popular demand to 'bring our boys home'. Once the occupations of Germany and Japan were secured, troop numbers fell rapidly – the number of US forces stationed in Japan dropping from some 430,000 in late 1945 to below 140,000 in 1948.[5] With the victory of Communist forces in China and rising Cold War tensions worldwide, however, the tide turned again, and the reversal was made irrevocable by the outbreak of the Korean War. In the words of one political scientist, 'the Korean War marks the most decisive change in postwar military policy', resulting in a radical upward surge in the number of US troops deployed abroad.[6]

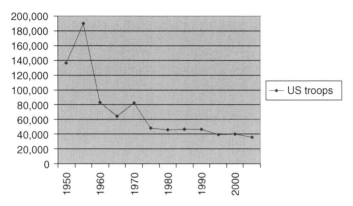

Figure 5.1. US troop deployments, Japan (including Okinawa) 1950–2005.

The effects of the Korean War were strikingly noticeable in Japan, which was, of course, still under Allied occupation when the war broke out. By April 1952, when the occupation came to an end, the number of US troops stationed in Japan had soared again to almost 200,000. Meanwhile, although the British Commonwealth Occupation Force (BCOF) was formally disbanded when the San Francisco Peace Treaty came into force, it was replaced by the British Commonwealth Forces, Korea (BCFK), made up of UK, Australian and Canadian troops, which remained in Japan until 1957. Despite its name, BCFK continued to make extensive use of bases in Japan for supply and training. After the Korean War ended, the number of US troops in Japan remained above 100,000 until 1958, and then stabilized around 80,000 until the end of the 1960s (with the exception of a sharp drop in 1965, caused by a mass redeployment of troops to Vietnam). (See Figure 5.1.) As with all such figures, though, the apparent precision of the official statistics needs to be treated with caution. The US military population in Japan was an extremely mobile one, and those on short-term deployments were not always included in the official statistics.

The prospect of long-drawn-out overseas deployments, and growing reports of low morale and criminal behaviour by troops overseas, increased the pressure for the US military to allow wives and children to join servicemen abroad.[7] Little by little, bases were transformed into 'America Towns', with 'offices, homes, shopping centers, schools, parks, fire stations, and industrial areas'.[8] While countries like South Korea were regarded as dangerous 'hardship postings' to which few soldiers brought their families, life in Japan was seen as reasonably comfortable and secure.

By 1963, there were almost 74,000 dependents of US service-people living in Japan (of whom some 24,000 were in Okinawa), and by 1970 the number had risen to over 90,000.[9]

The bases also employed foreign civilians: most from the US, but some recruited from the Philippines, Korea and elsewhere. Their numbers are particularly difficult to estimate, and only rough impressionistic figures are available for much of the period. For example, in 1952, *Pacific Stars and Stripes*, the widely read newspaper which labelled itself the 'unofficial publication of United States Forces, Japan', reported that 'the army has approximately 7,600 civil service workers in the Far East (Japan, Korea, Okinawa and the Philippines). The Air Force and Navy also augment their military staffs with civilian technicians'.[10] Civilian employees were often engineers or other technical specialists, but included people such as entertainers employed by base clubs, and American women hostesses – dozens of whom were specially recruited during the Korean War to welcome troops arriving in Japan and cheer the spirits of those evacuated to Japanese hospitals.[11]

As migration and border control functions were gradually handed over by the Allied Occupation authorities to the Japanese government, special measures were devised to ensure that control over the flow of people into and out of the bases remained firmly under US control. With the end of the occupation approaching while war still raged on the Korean peninsula, the US and Japanese governments entered into a Security Treaty which came into force on the day when the Allied occupation of Japan ended – in other words, on the day when Taiwanese and Koreans in Japan were turned into 'aliens'. This treaty allowed US troops to continue to maintain military bases on Japanese soil.[12] The Status of Forces Agreement (SOFA) attached to the treaty contained detailed rules governing the situation of foreign troops in Japan. Amongst other things, these rules stated that:

Members of the United States armed forces shall be exempt from Japanese passport and visa laws and regulations. Members of the United States armed forces, the civilian component, and their dependents shall be exempt from Japanese laws and regulations on the registration and control of aliens, but shall not be considered as acquiring any right to permanent residence or domicile in the territories of Japan.[13]

This provision was modelled on a similar agreement concluded with the North Atlantic Treaty Organization (NATO) countries in 1949. However, the agreements with Japan and with the NATO countries incorporated one significant difference which was to be a source of continuing friction between the US military and Japanese society. The NATO agreement stated that host countries had jurisdiction over crimes committed by foreign (including US) service-people on their soil.[14] By contrast, in Japan, although the Japanese police were given the right to arrest US service-people who broke the law, they had to hand them over immediately to the US military, who normally tried them in special courts on the bases.[15]

In other words, American troops in Japan were placed in a position of 'extraterritoriality', rather like the position enjoyed by nineteenth-century European and American inhabitants of the Western concessions in Japan and China. Though the Status of Forces Agreement was rewritten when the Security Treaty between Japan and the US was revised in 1960, these provisions remained more or less unchanged until the 1990s, and the exemption of US forces from normal migration controls and alien registration remains to the present day.[16]

In the context of postwar Japan, this exclusion of US service-people and their families and civilian employees has a very large impact on the way in which official statistics represent the foreign population. For example, the total number of registered foreigners in Japan in 1963 was 649,020, of whom the vast majority (571,676) were Koreans. Americans, at just 14,573, constituted the third-largest foreign group, but were far behind Chinese at 47,586. But if we add the 89,454 US troops and 73,833 US military dependents who were in Japan (including Okinawa) at that time, as well as a few thousand foreign civilians employed by the US military, the total foreign population is over 800,000, of whom more than 170,000 were American.

LITTLE AMERICA

The issue is not simply one of statistics. The American presence transformed the landscape of Japanese towns, the flavour of Japanese food and the rhythms of Japanese music. Even though they led an existence which provided only limited opportunities for contact with the local population, many Americans who lived on the bases also found their lives and attitudes deeply influenced by their time in Japan. Film-maker Donna Musil estimates that by the first decade of the twenty-first century there were some twelve million American former 'military brats' – people who had spent much of their childhood on military bases, often outside the United States.[17] Of these, hundreds of thousands had spent the formative years of their lives on bases in Japan.

The curious world inhabited by the 'military brats' – a world in, but not of, Japan – had already begun to take shape by the late 1940s, as growing numbers of family members began to join the occupation forces in Japan. At this stage, Allied military bases were widely spread across the Japanese landscape. A survey from 1954 (which excludes Okinawa) lists 131 US army bases extending from Wakkanai in northern Hokkaido to the southern tip of Kyushu, as well as numerous naval bases, airstrips and military training areas.[18] However, the largest concentrations of troops and their families were located in Sendai and Misawa (northern Honshu); Tokyo and the surrounding districts of Yokohama, Zama and Tachikawa; Nagoya; Kobe; Kyoto; Osaka; and Fukuoka and Itazuka on the island of Kyushu. As demand from troops and their families expanded, the US military began an energetic programme of construction, producing colonies of houses and apartment blocks built to standardized specifications issued from Washington. By 1949, for example, the US 8th Army was maintaining 1,821 housing units in Yokohama alone: 'the equivalent of a small city of 6,500 population'.[19]

In his remarkable study of the history and social meaning of Ōmura Immigration Detention Centre (the subject of the following chapter) social researcher Hyun Moo-Am evokes Foucault's notion of 'heterotopia': a place 'outside of all places', where 'all the other sites that are found within the culture are simultaneously represented, contested and inverted'.[20] Heterotopias are spaces apart, surrounded by a frontier separating them from the rest of the world, but also in some senses serving as a mirror of that world – places capable of juxtaposing 'several sites that are in themselves incompatible'. The notion is a far-reaching one, embracing (in Foucault's analysis of the topic) such diverse sites as prisons, brothels, libraries, museums, public gardens and saunas. The US bases, I would argue, constitute a particular form of heterotopia. They were spaces within but outside Japan, in which all the complexities and contradictions of the Japan–US relationship were expressed in concentrated form. But they also, as we shall see, formed an archipelago of *linked* 'places apart': a regional space of movement that extended far beyond Japan's borders, and that existed parallel with but largely separate from the space of movement inhabited by most of the region's people.

Base towns were designed according to blueprints and maps created for the worldwide network of US military outposts. As Mark Gillem points out, the maps produced by the military designers generally 'show no context beyond the base', so 'one could easily mistake the base for an actual island'.[21] Housing was distributed to service-people according to standardized criteria, including seniority and size of family. Eager to attract

Image 5.1. A Japanese clerk selects from the eight thousand records held
in the library of Iwakuni Military Base (c.1947–8).

new recruits, and to discourage existing members of the armed forces
from returning to the allure of civilian life, the military aimed to create
an environment which matched the suburban ideal of postwar America.
A magazine article from 1950 describes the 'dream home' at Haneda
Airbase inhabited by Air Force S/Sgt Armon Miller, his wife Grace and
their family:

Since the Millers have four children they were given a three-bedroom apartment … The kitchen is equipped with a table top electric stove, electric
refrigerator and spacious cupboard space. Since the Millers have more than
three children, they are also issued with a washing machine for their use.[22]

Like most modern frontiers, the boundary around the base embodied notions of national identity that were deeply tinged by concepts of hygiene. Base PX stores provided familiar food items (Kellogg's Variety Packs, Cheerios, V8 juice) for the inhabitants. Service families in Japan were warned that 'food items may be purchased, if desired, on the local Japanese market, but consumers must observe certain precautions concerning preparation, purification, and disinfection'.[23] As this statement itself acknowledges, however, the boundary was a porous one. US troops and their families *did* shop in Japanese markets, travel on Japanese trains and encounter Japanese people in a variety of settings: most intimately as servants in the base homes. The Miller family (relatively representative of middle-ranking US service families in Japan) employed two Japanese servants, one paid by the military, and the other by the Millers themselves. Grace Miller reported that 'the maids do all my housework with the exception of cooking and there are times when they ask me if they can prepare a meal'.[24]

In Japan, as in other overseas postings, good and cheap home help was advertised as one of the attractions of life on the base, though here, too, the hygiene frontier required regular patrols. Military families arriving in Japan were advised, 'Your servants are given regular health checks, including Kahn blood test and chest X-rays. You are responsible in part for ensuring their compliance with health regulations as a matter of your own protection.'[25]

Within the world of the base, US families sought to reconstruct a life that mirrored the ideal of 1950s middle-class American existence:

Because Mrs. Miller has little housework to do, she has a great deal of leisure time on her hands. She belongs to a women's pinochle club that meets every week. In the morning, she and other women in the neighbourhood hold informal coffee parties in their apartments.[26]

Meanwhile, the children of the US bases were also creating their own social spaces on Japanese territory. The military began establishing schools for overseas dependents just over a year after the end of the Pacific War, one of the first being Kubasaki High School in Okinawa, which was opened in September 1946. By 1950 there was a network of US military schools across Japan. For example, the Osaka area (home to the US 25th Division) had five elementary schools, two high schools and five kindergartens 'readily accessible to 797 children of military and civilian personnel of the 25th Division'.[27] Textbooks and curricula were standardized throughout the Far East command 'to fit the needs of the Far East and to prepare pupils to meet the requirements of schools and colleges on their return to the United States'.[28] It is difficult to avoid noting a small irony here. Osaka was the place where US troops had played a central role in putting down the demonstrations surrounding the closure of Korean-language schools (see p. 101). US military schools were not, of course, subject to inspection by the Japanese Ministry of Education.

Sports clubs, scout troops and other social activities burgeoned alongside the growing network of schools – many of them established by adults anxious to provide a healthy outlet for the energies of youngsters living in a foreign environment. Yokohama's Neet-Nac Canteen, for instance, set up to provide after-school entertainment for pupils from local American schools, boasted ping-pong and pool tables, a piano and a recording unit where budding musicians could cut their own discs, as well as a PX snack bar specializing in 'frosted malts, banana splits (when bananas are available), hamburgers and French fries'.[29]

The US bases in Japan, then, mirrored American political and cultural hegemony, and embodied a deep-seated fear of contamination by the viruses of the unfamiliar societies into which these corners of US suburbia had been transplanted. But they also reflected the postwar USA's benign democratizing self-image. According to this image, the bases not only kept the free world safe from communism, but also radiated friendship and goodwill to neighbouring communities. Service wives were encouraged to engage in clubs and charities, and generally (as Donna Alvah notes) to serve as 'unofficial ambassadors' for their home country. Journals like *Pacific Stars and Stripes*, in between reporting on the activities of various military units and relaying news of political events at home, exhorted its readers to learn Japanese and instructed them on topics such as Okinawan lacquer making and the history of the *bunraku* puppet theatre. Though most service-people and their dependents remained largely within the world of the base, some military wives did become actively involved in local society. Donna Alvah cites the examples of Margery Finn Brown, who wrote a column for an English-language newspaper in Japan and donated to charitable causes, and Marian Merritt (based in Okinawa in the late 1940s and early 1950s) who taught English to Okinawans and established a Maid School to improve the skills and working conditions of domestic servants.[30]

FENCES AND NEIGHBOURS

Viewed from the other side of the fence, the impact of these foreign enclaves on Japanese soil was enormous. In sheer physical terms, the bases occupied vast tracts of land in a country where inhabitable land was at a premium. In 1952, US bases in Japan covered some 262,400 acres.[31] Much of this land was used for training, munitions storage and other purposes, but even the sections of the base used for housing occupied dispropor-tionately large spaces since their population density was much lower than that of surrounding Japanese towns and villages.[32] Chitose airbase in Hokkaido, which was constructed in 1951 to house some 18,000 mem-bers of the 45th Division, was described as being 'comparable in size to Florida's capitol [*sic*] city of Tallahassee'.[33]

The bases were not only tenants but also employers: indeed, in the 1950s the United States military was one of the largest employers in Japan, with a Japanese workforce which exceeded 200,000 at the end of the Korean War, and still totalled some 152,000 in 1957.[34] Employees included inter-preters, stenographers, drivers, maids, construction workers and others, and were divided into two categories: the majority were employed by the Japanese government on behalf of the US military, while a smaller number (mostly those employed in clubs, PX stores and so on) were hired directly by the bases. In the early 1950s, some 13,000 Japanese people were also employed by the British Commonwealth forces based in Kure.[35] At a time when the economy was still recovering from the devastation of war, the employment provided by the bases was welcome. Wages, however, were generally low, with maids being paid on average around $16 to $18 a month in the early 1950s.[36] One consequence of the democratization poli-cies introduced by the Allied occupiers was a resurgence of trade union-ism in Japan, and industrial disputes on bases were not uncommon.

The economic impact of the bases, of course, went far beyond the dir-ect recruitment of workers. The US military presence, particularly dur-ing the Korean War, stimulated demand for a mass of Japanese goods and services, creating far-reaching economic ripple effects. Large military bases quickly spawned satellite towns filled with shops, restaurants, dance halls and brothels catering to US customers. In the early stages of the Allied occupation a brief attempt was made by the Japanese government to organize an official network of brothels – known as the Recreation and Amusement Association (RAA) – to serve the conquerors, thus (it was believed) protecting the chastity of other Japanese women. However, the scheme was rapidly abandoned (in part because it was accompanied by the rapid spread of venereal disease), and thereafter the task was left to private enterprise.[37]

Cultural studies scholar Yoshimi Shunya provides a vivid description of the ambiguous relationships between the bases and their surrounding

Image 5.2. Practising bowling at Yokohama Engineering Depot, 1956.

communities. For many Japanese people, the hallmarks of the postwar era were the 'jazz, Hawaiian and other popular music which flowed out from the other side of the base fence, and the permeating image of "prosperous America" in the form of films, fashion, cuisine etc.'[38] The Japanese musicians who performed for American troops in the bars, cabarets and dance halls surrounding the bases learnt tunes and rhythms which were to influence Japanese popular music for decades to come.[39] US bases brought with them new entertainments such as the dance hall and (later in the 1950s) bowling. Japanese technicians employed in the construction of military dependents' housing projects, such as the Washington Heights development in Tokyo's Harajuku district, went on to incorporate design elements copied from the base housing into the houses they built for Japanese customers.[40]

But the dream homes transplanted to Japan also brought with them less appealing aspects of 1950s US suburban life, including unofficial racial segregation. In 1960, just over 6 per cent of US service-people overseas were African-Americans. Although President Truman had declared a policy of racial equality for the military in 1948, and the desegregation of military forces had been completed by 1954, discrimination in social life surrounding the bases continued long after, interacting in complex ways with the racial prejudices of the host society.[41] At Misawa, home to one of the largest US airbases, a representative of local bar owners was reported in the mid-1960s as saying that '38 of the city's 44 bars had a policy of serving only white servicemen. He said that the policy had been followed by an informal agreement among bar operators since white soldiers would not patronize establishments that were frequented by Negroes'.[42]

While serving as representations of the alluring 'prosperous America', the bases were also tangible reminders of an unequal power relationship and of a military alliance which many Japanese people opposed. During the Korean War US bases attracted protests from left-wing Japanese and *Zainichi* Koreans, who were disturbed at the use of Japanese territory as a launching pad for a massive military intervention in Asia, and major demonstrations also erupted in 1956 over plans for base expansion at Sunagawa, west of Tokyo. Crimes committed by US servicemen, such as the shooting of a young Japanese woman by US soldier William Gerard in January 1957, provoked widespread anger, particularly because the culprit was not subject to the Japanese justice system.

The discontents that swirled around the bases helped to fuel the massive protests which erupted in 1960 against the renewal of the US–Japan Security Treaty (commonly known by the acronym *Ampo*). The *Ampo* demonstrations of 1960 mobilized millions of protestors, led to the last-minute cancellation of a planned official visit by President Eisenhower to Japan, and generated a fear in some US government quarters that Japan was on the brink of revolution. Although the demonstrations died down almost as quickly as they had erupted, they left a legacy of activism which resurfaced later in the 1960s, when protests against the Vietnam War again resulted in pitched battles between police and demonstrators outside US bases in Sasebo and elsewhere.

OGASAWARA AND OKINAWA

If American bases were heterotopias, located within Japan yet maintaining their own borders and operating according to their own rules, then Ogasawara and Okinawa were, even more, separate worlds. When the Allied occupation of Japan ended in April 1952, two parts of 'Japan proper' – Ogasawara (the Bonin Islands) and Okinawa (the Ryukyu Islands) remained under American military control. Ogasawara (which was controlled by the US navy) was ultimately returned to Japan in

1968, and Okinawa (which was initially under direct military rule and then, from 1950 onward, ruled by a US civil administration) reverted to Japanese control in 1972.

The small Ogasawara archipelago, just over a thousand kilometres south-east of Tokyo, had first been settled in the 1830s by a small group of adventurers from America, Europe and the Pacific islands. After Ogasawara was officially incorporated into Japan in 1876, Japanese migrants were encouraged to move to the islands, and by 1925 they had a population of around 5,800.[43] During the Asia–Pacific War, the civilian population of Ogasawara was evacuated to the Japanese mainland, and the US naval authorities who controlled the islands after Japan's defeat allowed only the descendants of the original non-Japanese inhabitants with their wives and families – 129 people in all – to return to live on Ogasawara.[44]

During the US interregnum, the tiny island population lived a largely American life. As ethnographer Mary Shephard observed,

Their passports gave their nationality as 'Bonin Islanders', but they were in the American orbit. Some of the girls married sailors; some boys went into the US Army and fought America's wars in Korea and Vietnam. Few trips were made to Japan and then only with special permission for such important business as finding a wife.[45]

The children attended the base school, where they learnt English, not Japanese: 'they saluted the American flag and recited the Pledge of Allegiance at school; most of their parents hoped that American citizenship ultimately could be arranged for them'.[46] In the end, however, no such arrangements were made, although a law passed in 1970 made it easier for the Bonin Islanders to migrate to the US if they chose.[47] Most remained, merging once more into the population of Japanese who flowed back to Ogasawara after the islands returned to Japanese rule in 1968.

In Okinawa, with its much larger population (around 700,000 in 1950), the US administration operated a border control and migration system entirely separate from that of the rest of Japan. In the immediate postwar years the situation was fluid, if not chaotic. During colonial times, there had been much movement to and fro between the Ryukyu Islands (particularly southern islands such as Yonaguni) and the Japanese colony of Taiwan, which was much nearer to Okinawa than Tokyo was. Considerable numbers of Koreans had also been brought to the islands as labourers and as so-called 'comfort women' to serve the sexual demands of the Japanese military. Immediately after Japan's defeat, most of these people were repatriated, but a small number remained (some of the former 'comfort women' reportedly being employed in brothels created to serve US servicemen).[48]

For the people of the southernmost islands of the archipelago, cross-border movement was part of a pattern of life which could only be severed at considerable economic cost. Okinawan historian Yakabi Osamu describes how, in colonial times, villagers from Yonaguni fished off the coast of Taiwan, taking their catch to sell in Taiwanese markets, buying goods in Taiwan with the money they earned, and then taking these goods back home with them before embarking on their next fishing trip.[49] Despite efforts by the authorities to restrain it, this unregulated movement across the border continued thoughout the immediate post-defeat years. Yakabi also describes three clandestine trade routes which connected Okinawa to the surrounding region during this period: one route extended south to Taiwan, another south-west to Hong Kong and Macao, and a third north via the Amami group to the main islands of Japan. At the height of the region's 'smuggling boom', before unauthorized border crossing was virtually stamped out by the US occupation authorities in August 1950, some seven thousand traders from Taiwan were regularly making crossings of the border back and forth from Taiwan to Yonaguni.[50]

The penal code devised for Okinawa by the US military in 1949 stated that anyone entering the islands required the written permission of the Military Government, Ryukyus or the Commander-in-Chief, Far East. Illegal entrants were liable to up to one year's imprisonment or a fine of up to 10,000 yen, or both.[51] The Korean War, however, brought with it a sudden upsurge of anxiety about the possible unauthorized entry of subversives and black-marketeers. The US military authorities were, it seems, particularly anxious that military matériel purloined from US bases might be exported from Okinawa and find its way into the hands of America's enemies in East Asia.[52] The consequence was a crackdown on movement between Taiwan and Yonaguni, followed by a new ordinance, introduced in 1952, which imposed a draconian maximum penalty of ten years' imprisonment and a 100,000-yen fine on illegal entrants.[53]

Once the Korean War was over, the penalties reverted to their more temperate original level, and a local immigration service began to be developed. Its officials had relatively little to do, since the vast majority of those entering and leaving the islands were 'occupation personnel' – a broad category encompassing not only US troops and their dependents and foreign employees, but also American Red Cross nurses and even house guests of US service-people. Occupation personnel, like the populations of US bases on the Japanese mainland, were not covered by normal migration rules, nor were they registered as foreigners or counted in the Ryukyu census. Instead, they were processed separately 'in accordance with the applicable military regulations'.[54]

In Okinawa, where a high population density and shortage of farm land had been problems since before the Asia–Pacific War, the US presence created particular tensions. In 1947, US military installations occupied about one-third of Okinawa's arable land.[55] The estimated 25,000 US military personnel and 13,000 other Americans in Okinawa in 1953 not only represented almost 5 per cent of the archipelago's population, but were also a population with a particularly heavy footprint – consuming a disproportionately large share of Okinawa's energy and water, and transforming the face of base towns such as Kōza and Kadena.[56] Crimes committed by members of the armed forces caused ongoing friction with the local population, as did environmental damage caused by the bases and rumours (which we now know were based on fact) that the US bases were home to an arsenal of nuclear weapons.[57]

Under the direction of General Douglas MacArthur, from 1947 on, a key aim of US control of the archipelago was the 'liquidation of political, social and economic ties with the [Japanese] mainland'.[58] This reflected a belief that Okinawa, 'the Keystone of the Pacific', was 'a vital link' in US defensive strategy and 'should be retained under the control of the United States for the foreseeable future'.[59] As a result 'Ryukyuans' were defined by Okinawa's US administration (though not by the Japanese government) as having a separate nationality from other Japanese. People who had lived in the archipelago since before Japan's surrender, and those with Okinawan family registration who had been officially allowed back to the islands by the US administration, were 'Ryukyuan nationals'; other Japanese living in the Ryukyu Islands were 'foreign nationals'.[60] One interesting point about this system is that, unlike the Japanese alien registration system, it does not seem to have enquired into the family origins of those who had arrived in Okinawa before 1945. One Korean woman who had been brought to Okinawa during the war recalls that she did not register as an 'alien' until after Okinawa was returned to Japanese rule.[61] She was just one of some six thousand residents of Okinawa to whom Japan's Alien Registration Law was applied for the first time in 1972.[62]

Meanwhile, to ensure the separation of Okinawans from the rest of Japan, tight restrictions were imposed on movement between the archipelago and the Japanese 'mainland' (*hondo*), and occupation educational and cultural policy sought to emphasize the difference between Okinawan and Japanese culture. Throughout the 1950s and early 1960s, Okinawans travelling to other parts of Japan had to obtain special 'Japan travel documents' issued by the US Civilian Administration's Immigration Department.

By the end of the 1950s, however, US policy was changing. One turning point was the revision of the US–Japan Security Treaty in 1960. The treaty was deeply unpopular in Japan, but regarded in the US as vital to American strategic interests in the Pacific. To sweeten the bitter pill of treaty renewal, the US began to take a more conciliatory line on Ogasawara and Okinawa, making it clear that both would be returned to Japanese rule in due course. In the latter part of the 1960s, increasingly vocal demands for reversion from within Okinawa as well as from other parts of Japan finally pushed the US to set a firm date for the return of the islands. As these shifts in US strategy occurred, travel between the Ryukyu Islands and the rest of Japan gradually became easier; and from 1967 onward, Okinawans were allowed to apply for Japanese passports rather than for 'Japan travel documents'.[63] Thus 'Ryukyu islanders' and 'Bonin islanders' again became Japanese, and by the mid-1970s both territories had been reintegrated into a single Japanese migration and border control regime.

THE 'TOKYO AIRLIFT' AND THE HUMAN GEOGRAPHY OF THE BASE

In the immediate postwar years, while efforts were made to draw firm lines separating Bonin islanders and Ryukyu islanders from other Japanese, the people of US bases occupied a quite different world, in which movement from one zone to another was smooth and frequent. Each military base did not simply exist as a single heterotopia, a single American island in the sea of Japanese society. Rather, the bases were linked into a heterotopian archipelago – a whole realm of interconnected spots on the map which constituted a distinct human geography, separate from but overlapping with the geography inhabited by other local residents.

Bases in Japan were connected by command structures, communications and transport infrastructure: the US military ran its own postal system and broadcasting service, as well as operating a telephone exchange which, in 1951, connected around 30,000 out of the total 270,000 telephones in Japan.[64] And this connecting infrastructure was not contained within Japan's borders, but extended throughout East Asia, to bases in Ogasawara, Okinawa, Guam, Korea, the Philippines and beyond. While the cross-border movement of people between Japan and its neighbours was extremely tightly restricted in the 1950s and 1960s, for US service-people the region virtually formed a single realm, through which flowed a dense traffic of people, goods and culture.

This alternative space of movement became most strikingly visible during the Korean War. Though the Berlin Airlift is remembered as a turning-point in Cold War history, few people remember the 'Tokyo Airlift', which in the autumn of 1950 saw massive US transport planes arriving every fifteen minutes at Haneda Airbase. Between the outbreak of the Korean War in June and the start of September 1950, these trans-ports had reportedly brought '12,200 passengers and 2,400,000 pounds of cargo' to Japan.[65] Most of this was then shipped onward to Korea through ports like Sasebo in southern Japan. Meanwhile, as the fighting in Korea intensified, thousands of troops made the return journey from Korea to Japan for medical treatment or for rest and recreation. Between 4 October and 18 November 1950 alone, it was reported,

A total of 9,564 wounded and sick had been evacuated by plane from combat areas to hospitals in Southern Japan … In addition, 7,626 patients have been airlifted from southern Japan to more advanced medical facilities near Osaka and Tokyo.[66]

The airlifts and sea-transports from the US to Japan and between Japan and Korea carried civilians as well as combatants. While Korean refugees from the conflict were excluded from Japan, US civilians evacuated from South Korea to escape the fighting were brought to Tokyo, and members of the Korean military were regularly brought to Japan by the US military for special training at bases such as Yokosuka.[67] Growing numbers of ser-vice wives came to Japan so that they could be near husbands fighting in Korea, and could meet their husbands during spells of leave in Japan.[68]

Meanwhile, the fighting in Korea was being coordinated from Japan. The Liaison Section of the United Nations Command, representing the sixteen countries which sent troops to support the southern side in the Korean conflict, had its headquarters in Tokyo's Dai-Ichi Building, which was also home to General Douglas MacArthur's occupation head-quarters.[69] Auxiliary agencies and humanitarian organizations (such as the International Committee of the Red Cross) responding to the Korean conflict also maintained their headquarters in Tokyo. A mass of more mundane threads, too, wove US bases in Japan into the fabric of the Korean conflict. Dozens of Japanese postal staff in Tokyo sorted mail for the troops fighting in Korea.[70] The US military's Octagon Library in Yokohama circulated books from its 250,000-volume collection to 'both those in Japan and to American forces in Korea'.[71] And in the weeks before Christmas 1950 the Tokyo Quartermasters Depot, a miniature city covering 253 acres of prime land in the Japanese capital, baked (amongst other things) 16,000 Christmas cakes for the frontline forces in Korea.[72]

THE FORGOTTEN VOLUNTEERS

Most of those who took part in this dense traffic linking Japan to mainland Asia were non-Japanese, but some Japanese people also entered into the trans-national space of movement via US military bases. Under the new and democratic Constitution, which was the centrepiece of the Allied occupation's reforms, Japan had (as we have seen) renounced 'war as a sovereign right of the nation and the threat or use of force as a means of settling international disputes'.[73] As a result, Japan officially had no military forces and could in no way be directly involved in the fighting in Korea. But in fact a small number of Japanese did die on active service in Korea. In November 1950 Japan had suffered its first overseas military casualties since the end of the Pacific War, when one member of the Japanese Coastguard was killed and eighteen were injured on a US-controlled minesweeping mission off the Korean coast. In all, a further twenty-two other Japanese sailors working on contracts for the US military were later to die in action in the Korean War.[74]

An unknown number of other Japanese were also killed in land battles. Newspaper articles from the early 1950s report the unsuccessful struggle by the father of Hiratsuka Shigeki to gain compensation for the death of his son in one of the early battles of the Korean War. The younger Hiratsuka, who had worked as a painter on a US military base, had gone with his military employers to Korea and been killed at the front, reportedly 'after he had wiped out several of the enemy'.[75] After 'several other similar cases' were brought to light, the Japanese Ministry of Foreign Affairs informally asked the US military to stop taking Japanese personnel with them into the Korean battle zone.[76] The Japanese government noted that the Japanese involved had been serving illegally in Korea, since their actions constituted 'violation of the relevant law governing entry and departure'.[77] Not all, it seems, fought on the South Korean side. There were reports that some Japanese who had remained in China after the war volunteered for service with the Communist Chinese forces fighting in North Korea.[78] Interestingly, the official figures for prisoners of war held by the United

Nations forces in South Korea in March 1952 enumerate 113,829 Koreans, 20,782 Chinese and one Japanese.[79]

Outside the Tokyo head office of the South Korean affiliated organization Mindan stands a reminder of another and larger group of participants in the Korean War whose story has largely been forgotten. It is a small stone monument to 642 Koreans in Japan who volunteered for service with the United Nations Command in the Korean War, of whom 135 were killed or went missing in action.[80] Soon after the outbreak of the war, Mindan began to conduct an energetic recruitment campaign in Japan, while North Korean affiliated groups also tried to persuade Koreans in Japan to fight on the Northern side. The 642 recruits who went to fight in South Korea, however, suffered a particularly ironic fate, for they found themselves trapped between the two conflicting spaces of movement in which postwar Japan was situated.

Their departure from Japan was largely unhindered, and their participation in the Incheon landing – one of the most significant battles of war – was welcomed by the UN forces. But when the volunteers attempted to return to Japan, they discovered that their path was barred by Japan's migration controls, for they were not formally part of the US or Allied forces in Japan, but merely Korean residents who, having left Japan, had no right of re-entry. After desperate appeals from their families in Japan and the Yi Seung-Man regime, the Japanese government finally relented– but on one condition. It would only accept back those volunteers who had valid alien registration cards. A number of the volunteers, however, were people who had crossed the border back and forth between the end of the Asia–Pacific War and the start of the Korean War, and had failed to acquire proper registration documents. In other cases, the complications of the registration process and reissuing of alien registration cards in 1950 and 1952 meant that returning volunteers had difficulty proving that they were registered. Cut off from the families whom they had left in Japan, a number of these demobilized volunteers became 'stowaways' in an effort to re-enter Japan.[81]

In many parts of the world, migration controls create not a single clearly bounded space of movement, but rather a hierarchy of spaces occupied by different sections of the population. Postwar Japan, in this sense, was not unique. What was unusual, though, was the extreme contrast which existed between the highly mobile world of the US bases, with their constant comings and goings between Japan and its regional neighbours, and the tightly controlled boundaries prohibiting the movement of ordinary people from Japan's neighbours into Japan. The contrast becomes particularly vivid if we follow the trajectories of some of the unregistered Korean volunteers who left the US bases in Korea for Busan, and from there boarded people-smuggling boats heading for southern Japan, only to find themselves in a new 'space apart': the heterotopia constituted by Japan's largest and most symbolically important migrant detention centre, Ōmura.

NOTES

1. *Yomiuri Shinbun* (Tokyo), 21 March 2008; *Asahi Shinbun*, 22 March 2008.
2. *Mainichi Shinbun*, 22 March 2008.
3. Three recent studies which do address this topic are Mark L. Gillem's *America Town: Building the Outposts of Empire* (Minneapolis and London: University of Minnesota Press, 2007); Donna Alvah's *Unofficial Ambassadors: American Military Families Overseas and the Cold War, 1946–1965* (New York and London: New York University Press, 2007); and Yoshimi Shunya's *Shinbei to Hanbei: Sengo Nihon no Seijiteki Muishiki* (Tokyo: Iwanami Shinsho, 2007).
4. K. Calder, *Embattled Garrisons: Comparative Base Politics and American Globalism* (Princeton and Oxford: Princeton University Press, 2007), p. 36.
5. E. Takemae (trans. Robert Ricketts and Sebastian Swann), *Inside GHQ: The Allied Occupation of Japan and Its Legacy* (London, Continuum, 2002) p. 126; Tim Kane, *Global US Troop Deployments, 1950–2003* (Washington, DC: Heritage Foundation, 2004), www.heritage.org/research/nationalsecurity/cda04–11.cfm (accessed 15 March 2008).
6. D. W. Tarr, 'The Military Abroad', *Annals of the American Academy of Political and Social Science*, 368 (November 1966), pp. 31–40; quotation from pp. 34–5.
7. See Alvah, *Unofficial Ambassadors*, pp. 26–9.
8. Gillem, *America Town*, p. 73.
9. Tarr, 'The Military Abroad', p. 36; United States Census of Population, 'Dependents of Armed Forces Personnel 1970', *United States Census of Population,* 1970, www2.census.gov/prod2/decennial/documents/42053794v2p10a1obch1.pdf (accessed 30 May 2008).
10. 'Soldiers in MUFTI', *Pacific Stars and Stripes*, 28 September 1952.
11. 'The Distaff Side of War', *Pacific Stars and Stripes Far East Weekly Review*, 19 August 1950.
12. Umebayashi Hiromichi, *Zainichi Beigun* (Tokyo: Iwanami Shinsho, 2002).
13. 'Administrative Agreement under Article III of the Security Treaty between the United States of America and Japan' (28 February 1952), in Australian National Archives, Canberra, series no. 1838/278, control symbol 481/1/7, 'British Commonwealth Forces in Korea – Bases in Japan, Part 1'.
14. 'Agreement between the Parties to the North Atlantic Treaty Regarding the Status of Their Forces', in Australian National Archives, Canberra, series no. A1209/23, control symbol 1957/4680, 'North Atlantic Treaty Organization: Status of Forces Agreement'.

15. 'Administrative Agreement under Article III of the Security Treaty'.
16. On the 1960s Treaty see Hōmushō Nyūkoku Kanrikyoku, *Shutsunyūkoku Kanri no Kaikō to Tenbō: Nyūkan Hasoku 30-Shūnen o Kinen shite* (Tokyo: Hōmushō Nyūkoku Kanrikyoku, 1980), p. 84.
17. See the website accompanying Musil's film *Brats: A Journey Home*, www.bratsjourneyhome.com (accessed 8 May 2008).
18. Kichi Mondai Chōsa Iinkai (ed.), *Gunkichi no Jittai to Bunseki* (Tokyo: San-Ichi Shobō, 1954).
19. 'Yokohama Home Makers', *Pacific Stars and Stripes Far East Weekly Review*, 26 November 1949, p. 4.
20. Hyun Moo-Am, 'Mikkō, Ōmura shūyōjo, Saishūtō: Ōsaka to Saishūtō o Musubu "Mikkō" no Nettowāku', *Gendai Shisō*, 35, 7 (June 2007) pp. 158–173, quotation from p. 158; see also Michel Foucault, 'Des Espaces autres', (1967), English translation by Jay Miskowiec, http://foucault.info/documents/heteroTopia/foucault.heteroTopia.en.html (accessed 10 February 2008).
21. Gillem, *America Town*, p. 129.
22. 'Dream Home', *Pacific Stars and Stripes Far East Weekly Review*, 3 June 1950, p. 4.
23. Headquarters, Far East Command, *Information for Dependents Coming to Japan* (revised edition, 1953), www.militarybrat.com/yokohama.cfm (accessed 14 April 2008).
24. 'Dream Home'.
25. Headquarters, Far East Command, *Information for Dependents*.
26. Ibid.
27. '3 "Rs" in Osaka', *Pacific Stars and Stripes Far East Weekly Review*, 29 April 1950.
28. Headquarters, Far East Command, *Information for Dependents*.
29. 'Juke Box and Coke Set', *Pacific Stars and Stripes Far East Weekly Review*, 18 February 1950, p. 7.
30. Alvah, *Unofficial Ambassadors*, pp. 103–4 and 183–9.
31. Maeda Tetsuo, *Zainichi Beigun Kichi no Shushi Kessan* (Tokyo: Chikuma Shinsho, 2000), p. 19.
32. See Gillem, *America Town*, pp. 77–9.
33. 'Chitose Shapes Up', *Pacific Stars and Stripes*, 9 October 1951.
34. Kichi Mondai Chōsa Iinkai, *Gunkichi no Jittai*, p. 175; 'Welcome to US Forces Japan', information posted on the homepage of US Forces Japan, http://www.usfj.mil/ (accessed 10 May 2008).
35. Kichi Mondai Chōsa Iinkai, *Gunkichi no Jittai*, p. 175.
36. Headquarters, Far East Command, *Information for Dependents*.
37. J. Dower, *Embracing Defeat: Japan in the Wake of World War II* (New York: W. W. Norton, 1999), pp. 123–32.
38. Yoshimi, *Shinbei to Hanbei*, p. 120.
39. Ibid., pp. 121–3.
40. Ibid., pp. 162–4.
41. Alvah, *Unofficial Ambassadors*, pp. 85 and 121.

42. Quoted in Tarr, 'The Military Abroad', p. 39.

43. Tokyo Fu, *Ogasawarato Sōran* (Tokyo: Tokyo Fu, 1929), p. 128.

44. M. Shephardson, 'Pawns of Power: The Bonin Islanders', in Raymond D. Fogelson and Richard N. Adams (eds.), *The Anthropology of Power: Ethnographic Studies from Asia, Oceania, and the New World* (New York: Academic Press, 1977), pp. 99–114, quotation from p. 109.

45. Ibid., p. 111.

46. T. E. Head and G. Daws, 'The Bonins – Isles of Contention', *American Heritage*, 29, 2 (February 1968), pp. 58–74, quotation from p. 74.

47. Shephardson, 'Pawns of Power', p. 112.

48. See Yamatani Tetsuo (ed.), *Okinawa no Harumoni* (Tokyo: Banseisha, 1979), particularly pp. 156–8.

49. Yakabi Osamu, '"Kokkyō" no Kengen: Okinawa Yonaguni no Mitsubōeki Shūsoku no Haikei', *Gendai Shisō* (September 2003), pp. 186–201, quotation from p. 188.

50. Ibid.

51. Military Ordinance no. 1, 28 June 1949, 'Codified Penal Law and Procedure', in Gekkan Okinawa Sha (ed.), *Laws and Regulations during the US Administration of Okinawa 1945–1972*, Vol. I (Naha: Ikemiya Shōkai, n.d.), p. 245.

52. Yakabi Osamu, '"Kokkyō" no Kengen'.

53. 'Control of Entry and Exit into and from the Ryukyu Islands', 2 February 1952, in Gekkan Okinawa Sha, *Laws and Regulations*, p. 284.

54. US Civilian Administration of the Ryukyu Islands, Office of the Deputy Governor, APO 719, 11 February 1954, 'Control of Entry and Exit of Individuals into and from the Ryukyu Islands', in Gekkan Okinawa Sha (ed.), *Laws and Regulations during the US Administration of Okinawa 1945–1972*, Vol. II (Naha: Ikemiya Shōkai, n.d.), pp. 2 and 200–7.

55. Takemae, *Inside GHQ*, p. 441.

56. The estimate of the US population for 1953 is cited from Alvah, *Unofficial Ambassadors*, p. 170.

57. Numerous documents refer to the presence of nuclear weapons on Okinawa before reversion. For example, J. Graham Parsons, who headed the Far Eastern Bureau of the US State Department in the late 1950s and early 1960s, refers in his unpublished memoirs to such problems in the US–Japan relationship as 'nuclear weapons on board US Navy ships, the presence of which we never confirmed or denied, or in Okinawa where they had long been stored'. See J. Graham Parsons, 'The Far Eastern Bureau – March 8 1958–March 31 1961', typescript manuscript held in J. Graham Parsons Papers, Lauinger Library, Georgetown University, p. 33.

58. Quoted in Takemae, *Inside GHQ*, p. 443.

59. 1954 report of US Armed Services Committee, House of Representatives, quoted in Alvah, *Unofficial Ambassadors*, p. 169.

60. US Civilian Administration of the Ryukyu Islands, APO 719; see also Headquarters, United States Civil Administration of the Ryukyu Islands,

Programs and Statistics Section, *Ryukyu Islands Economic Statistics*, 17 (March–May 1952), p. 11.

61. See Yamatani, *Okinawa no Harumoni*, p. 32. She was one of around six thousand foreigners who had to register under the Japanese alien registration system when Okinawa reverted to Japan. See Hōmushō Nyūkoku Kanrikyoku, *Shutsunyūkoku Kanri no Kaikō*, p. 305.

62. Hōmushō Nyūkoku Kanrikyoku, *Shutsunyūkoku Kanri no Kaikō*, p. 305.

63. Office of High Commissioner, APO San Francisco 96248, 6 September 1967, 'Control of Travel by Residents of the Ryukyu Islands', in Gekkan Okinawa Sha, *Law and Regulations*, Vol. II, p. 411.

64. 'Tokyo Trouble', *Pacific Stars and Stripes*, 10 October 1951.

65. 'Tokyo Airlift', *Pacific Stars and Stripes Far East Weekly Review*, 2 September 1950.

66. 'Home from Battle', *Pacific Stars and Stripes Far East Weekly Review*, 18 November 1950.

67. Their existence seldom appears in Japanese records except when they deserted and became 'illegal immigrants': one example is the case of a Korean serviceman who was brought to Japan in 1950 for special training at Yokosuka, deserted, was later arrested and interned in Ōmura Detention Centre and asked to be deported to North rather than South Korea (where he faced prosecution for desertion), but at the last moment changed his mind and was apparently deported to South Korea in 1962. See letter from Inoue Masutarō to Michel Testuz, 8 October 1962, in Archives of the International Committee of the Red Cross, Geneva (ICRC Archives), B AG 251 105–009.02, Correspondance reçu du 12 juin 1962 au 21 janvier 1966, 12.06.1962–21.01.1966.

68. 'Distaff Side of War'.

69. 'Welding together the UN Team', *Pacific Stars and Stripes*, 24 September 1951.

70. 'Mailmen of the Pacific', *Pacific Stars and Stripes*, 17 September 1951.

71. 'Information Please', *Pacific Stars and Stripes Far East Weekly Review*, 28 April 1951.

72. 'An Army Marches on Its Stomach', *Pacific Stars and Stripes Far East Weekly Review*, 27 January 1951.

73. Constitution of Japan, in Government Section, Supreme Commander for the Allied Powers, *Political Reorientation of Japan, September 1945 to September 1948* (Washington, DC: US Government Printing Office, 1949), pp. 670–7, quotation from p. 671.

74. Nishimura Shigeki, *Ōsaka de Tatakatta Chōsen Sensō: Fukita Maikata Jiken to Seishun Gunzō* (Tokyo: Iwanami Shoten, 2004), p. 117.

75. See 'No Compensation Given Father of Nippon Youth Killed in Korea', *Nippon Times*, 14 November 1952, copy held in National Archives of New Zealand, file W2619, 324/4/29 pt. 1, 'Individual Countries, Korea: Political Affairs, War in Korea: Use of Japanese Personnel'.

76. 'Foreign Ministry Requests US Forces Not to Take Japanese to Korea', article from *Mainichi Daily News*, 17 November 1952, copy held in ibid.
77. Ibid.
78. Nishimura, *Ōsaka de Tatakatta*, p. 117.
79. Delegations of the International Committee of the Red Cross to Korea, 'Allgemeiner Bericht – Febuar–März 1952', in ICRC Archives, B AG 225 056–001, Généralités. Rapport d'activités, extraits de rapports de visites, memorandum aux autorités, correspondance, comptes rendus d'entretiens, rapport d'activités de l'UNCACK en faveur des prisonniers civils.
80. Kim Chang-Jung, *Zainichi Giyūhei Kikan sezu: Chōsen Sensō Hisshi* (Tokyo: Iwanami Shoten, 2007).
81. Ibid, pp. 175–201.

CHAPTER 6

Worlds apart II

The liminal space of Ōmura

THE SQUARE HOUSE ON THE BAY

Of all the US military bases which linked Japan to the Asian continent, none was more crucial than Sasebo. Built on a large sheltered inlet on the west coast of the island of Kyushu, Sasebo lay directly across the waters from the Korean peninsula, and had been one of the Japanese Imperial Navy's most important ports. After Japan's defeat, US forces took over the naval base and also supervised the flow of people into and out of the neighbouring Hario repatriation centre. Then, with the outbreak of the Korean War, Sasebo became 'the main launching point for the United Nations and U.S. Forces. Millions of tons of ammunition, fuel, tanks, trucks, and supplies flowed through Sasebo on their way to U.N. Forces in Korea'.[1]

Early in 1951, at the time when Sasebo was at its busiest ferrying troops to and from Korea, a ship set out from the smaller port town of Ōmura, some thirty-five kilometres further south, also bound for Korea though on a very different mission. For if Sasebo formed part of a distinct space of movement which linked Japan to the surrounding region, Ōmura was a different sort of heterotopia – a place which (for many people) marked the radical postwar separation of Japan from its Asian neighbours.

Like Sasebo and the neighbouring city of Nagasaki, Ōmura itself had been transformed into a garrison town in the years leading up to the Asia–Pacific War. A large Japanese military base and naval airstrip were established, and a vast factory, employing (at its wartime peak) over 30,000 workers, was built on land reclaimed from the bay.[2] Although Ōmura was spared the atomic attack that destroyed Nagasaki, this military presence meant that the town experienced heavy conventional bombing in the final year of the Asia–Pacific War, and its economy suffered a drastic contraction during the years immediately following Japan's defeat. But unexpectedly, in the second half of 1950, a new source of employment began to offer a little relief from hardship for the people of Ōmura. Advertisements appeared around the town inviting local people to apply for training and recruitment to Japan's new migration control service. For Ōmura had been selected as the site for a new and permanent detention centre to replace Hario as a holding centre for illegal entrants, almost all of them from the Korean peninsula.

The 190 or so job applicants who passed the initial selection were instructed to gather at an inn known as the Square House (*Masugata Tei*) overlooking Ōmura Bay, where they were joined by ten senior officers brought in from other parts of Japan. These two hundred were to form the core of Japan's fledgling migration control service. Their main tasks in the early days would be escorting deportees from other parts of Japan to Ōmura, guarding them during their sojourn in a new detention centre (then being constructed amidst the ruins of Ōmura's bombed-out aircraft factory), and finally deporting them by ship to Korea. At this stage, SCAP was still responsible for issuing entry permits for travellers to Japan, so immigration officials posted to Japan's ports and airports had little to do but check names against the list of SCAP approvals. For the first years of the Immigration Agency's existence, then, guarding and deporting convoys of deportees (almost all of them Korean) was by far the most important of its duties: the Agency was, indeed, often casually referred to at the time as the 'Convoy Office' (Gosō Kanchō).[3]

The senior ranks of the Immigration Agency were staffed mainly by former Foreign Service Police who had worked in Japanese-occupied areas of China, and who presumably brought with them attitudes to the world moulded by their experience on the front line of Japan's imperial expansion into Asia.[4] In 1950, the Agency (later to become the Immigration Bureau) had barely begun to take shape, and everything was in short supply. Nakamura Masakichi, who was among the first group of immigration officers trained in Ōmura, recalls that his introduction to the skills of migration control was provided by local policemen, and consisted mainly of military-style drills. As time went on, however, the quality of training improved, and experts were seconded from Nagasaki University to provide lectures on immigration law and related subjects.[5] Meanwhile, other contingents of immigration officers were being trained in Fukuoka and elsewhere, bringing the total size of the service to over six hundred.[6]

The Ōmura trainee guards completed their course in December 1950, the month when over nine hundred detainees from Sasebo's Hario concentration camp were deported en masse to war-torn Korea (see p. 80) Hario was then closed, and the small number of detainees who had (for one reason or another) avoided deportation were moved from there to

Ōmura, where they were soon to be joined by others from all around the country. As Japan's new migration control network was established, twelve local immigration offices were set up in major cities across the country, from Sapporo in the north to Kagoshima in the south, each equipped with its own detention cells, where suspected illegal migrants were held while their circumstances were investigated.[7] Those who were identified for deportation would then be sent to Ōmura to await the ship that would remove them from Japan. On 4 January 1951, Ōmura Immigration Detention Centre celebrated its official opening, and on 2 March that year, the first consignment of 405 deportees from Ōmura were dispatched to Korea from the nearby docks.[8]

Almost sixty years later, as I write this chapter, the detention centre (now officially known as Ōmura Immigration Reception Centre) is still in existence. The buildings have been remodelled several times, and the centre has shifted across the road from the original site of the old aircraft factory. But Ōmura remained Japan's largest detention centre until February 2008, when it was equalled in size by the newly constructed Tokyo Regional Immigration Bureau in Shinagawa.[9] It is certainly Japan's best-known (or most notorious) detention centre, and must by now surely be one of the longest-lived migrant detention institutions in the world.

THE MODERN LIMBO

If the US bases in Japan were microcosms of the ambivalent US–Japanese relationship, Ōmura in the 1950s and 1960s was a heterotopia of a different sort – one in which three conflicts became concentrated and magnified: first, the conflict between the Japanese state and its Korean former colonial subjects; second, the conflict between Japan and the Republic of Korea (ROK – South Korea); and third, the conflict between the two sides of the divided Korean peninsula – North and South.

As a space apart, Ōmura also epitomized the phenomenon which Erving Goffman (writing in the late 1960s) termed the 'total institution'. Whereas everyday life in modern society is generally divided into distinct spheres – sleep, play and work – conducted in separate places, a total institution is a place isolated from the outside world, which breaks down the barriers separating these spheres of life:

First, all aspects of life are conducted in the same place and under the same single authority. Second, each phase of the member's daily activity is carried out in the immediate company of a large batch of others, all of whom are treated alike and required to do the same thing together. Third, all phases of the day's activities are tightly scheduled ... Finally, the various enforced activities are brought together into a single rational plan purportedly designed to fulfill the official aims of the institution.[10]

Total institutions also create a peculiarly bifurcated and authoritarian relationship between 'staff' and 'inmates'. However, the rituals of power governing this relationship vary, and their specific forms are often physically represented in the contrasting architecture of different institutions. In Ōmura, the architectural remodelling of the detention centre made visible the shifting relationship between guards and detainees, and this in turn reflected wider shifts in the relationship between the Japanese state and the migrant community.

Though Ōmura had already been in existence for more than fifteen years in the late 1960s, when Goffman published his analysis of total institutions, at that time migrant detention centres were far less ubiquitous and visible institutions than they are today, and it is not surprising that his book does not mention them. He subdivides total institutions into five categories, and this taxonomy is useful because it highlights the peculiar features of the migrant detention camp. According to Goffman, total institutions can be categorized as: institutions for 'persons felt to be both incapable and harmless' (e.g. orphanages and old people's homes); those for people seen as both helpless and 'a threat to the community, albeit an unintended one' (e.g. TB sanatoria); institutions 'to protect the community against what are felt to be intentional dangers to it' (e.g. prisons); places 'established the better to pursue some worklike task' (e.g. boarding schools and military barracks); and 'establishments designed as retreats from the world' (e.g. monasteries and convents).[11]

The modern migrant detention centre occupies an uneasy and unstable position in this categorization. Although the people detained there are confined because they are believed to have broken the law, the detention centre is not supposed to be a place of punishment or of moral reformation. In most modern democracies, undocumented entry, though it is against the law, is not seen as a major felony, and the normal punishment is deportation. In a formal legal sense, then, the detention centre is not a place of punishment but a place of waiting – a limbo.

The concepts of migration which have been embedded in national laws and international treaties from the mid-twentieth century onward draw a conceptual line between two categories – illegal migrants, who cross borders without proper documentation and, if caught, are to be deported; and asylum seekers, who often cross borders without documentation, but are driven to do so by a genuine fear of persecution which gives them a right to shelter in the receiving country. In theory, illegal migrants remain in the detention centre only until transport can be arranged to send them home, and genuine refugees remain only as long as it takes to check their credentials, confirm their right to asylum and release them into the community. The detention centre is therefore envisaged merely as a temporary shelter through which flows a steady stream of transients.

But in fact, these tidy categories were never wholly congruent with reality, and have become more and more incongruent as the decades have passed. Since the end of the Cold War in particular, migrant detention centres worldwide have found themselves host to growing populations of long-term inmates – indeed, to some groups of inmates whose confinement seems to have no foreseeable end. This problem arises because there are increasing numbers of people who do not qualify for asylum in the strict sense in which it is defined by national or international laws, but who cannot be deported, either because no country will accept them, or because their lives would be imperilled by sending them back to their place of origin.

The peculiar pain of their confinement lies not so much in the physical conditions of their detention (which may or may not be harsh), but in its indefinite and purposeless nature. It is detention with no aim other than to detain, and with no temporal horizon on which to pin one's hopes. The detained are deprived of the prisoner's ultimate consolation – crossing off the days on the calendar that marks the span of their sentence. They live in the temporal void vividly captured by novelist John Le Carré, whose fictional figure Salvo, after spending most of his life in Britain, finds himself stripped of his British nationality. The novel closes with Salvo gazing out at the world from behind the fence of a camp on the English south coast, where he is held in indefinite migrant detention:

Each morning my heart rises with the morning sun. Each evening it sinks. But if I bring my chair to the window, and there's a good moon shining, I can just make out a sliver of sea a mile beyond the wire. And that's where their England ends and my Africa begins.[12]

Ōmura Detention Centre is of interest above all because, long before the construction of France's Nanterre detention centre, Britain's Colnbrook or Australia's Villawood, it was a place where the emerging dilemma of such modern limbos became starkly visible.

MIGRANT DETENTION AND THE POLITICS OF
KOREA–JAPAN RELATIONS

The origins of Ōmura's problems lay in the failure of the Japanese government and the Allied occupation authorities to resolve fundamental problems of the decolonization of Korea.

Neither the Republic of Korea (ROK – South Korea) nor the Democratic People's Republic of Korea (DPRK – North Korea) was represented at the San Francisco Peace Conference, and the peace treaty which emerged from that conference therefore left unresolved major issues between former colonizer and former colony. Negotiations between Japan and South Korea were still continuing when the Allied occupation of Japan ended, and were to drag on acrimoniously for more than a decade, until a controversial settlement was reached in 1965. Key points of dispute included the questions of compensation for colonial exploitation, the payment of wages withheld from forced labourers, the repatriation of Korean art treasures removed to Japan in the colonial period, and the division of fishing rights in the East Sea/Sea of Japan.

A particularly intractable set of difficulties arose from the Japanese government's unilateral ruling that Koreans in Japan had lost their right to Japanese nationality on the day when the San Francisco Peace Treaty came into effect. As we saw in Chapter Four, this decision was not accompanied by any clear statement about the residence rights of Koreans in Japan. Instead, the government simply announced that Koreans who had been in Japan since colonial times would be allowed to remain there until some future agreement on their status was reached. The Japanese government's official position was that, even though they had been declared foreigners only *after* entering the country as Japanese, Koreans in Japan would now be treated like any other foreigners. In practice, though, the extent to which they applied the Immigration Control Law to *Zainichi* Koreans was discretionary and sometimes arbitrary.

For example, as we have seen (p. 114), the law stated that foreigners who had been found guilty of crimes with a sentence of more than one year's imprisonment were to serve their sentence in Japan and then be deported. After Koreans in Japan had been re-defined as foreigners, this ruling was applied to them, even if they had been Japanese nationals when they had committed the crime for which they were now being deported. However, not all Korean lawbreakers who were liable for deportation under the Immigration Control Law were in fact deported, but only those whom the Japanese authorities deemed to be particularly 'wicked criminals',[13] a category that in practice often seems to include those with undesirable political opinions. Predictably enough, this discretion provoked unease in South Korea, since it created the impression that Japan, having welcome (or forced) the arrival of immigrants when it needed their labour, was now dumping the 'undesirables' back on Korea.

The South Korean position on the issue was not without its own problems, though. These stemmed from the fact that the South Korean regime defined itself as the only legitimate government of the entire Korean peninsula, and therefore claimed all Koreans in Japan (whatever their place of origin or political preferences) as its nationals. However, it also argued that Koreans who had migrated to or been taken to Japan before the end of the Pacific War should not be subject to Japan's postwar Immigration Control Law, but had the right to special treatment, including permanent residence in Japan. While the Yi Seung-Man regime accepted Japan's right to deport Koreans who had entered Japan without official documentation since August 1945, it refused to accept Japan's right to deport colonial-era migrants who had been convicted of crimes in Japan.

Conflict over the deportation issue first came to a head in May 1952. By this time, Ōmura had been in existence for almost eighteen months, and during that period over 3,500 detainees had been loaded onto ships in nearby Ōmura Bay and deported to Busan in Korea. Meanwhile, normalization talks between Japan and South Korea had been dragging on desultorily, with no resolution in sight. And just two weeks earlier, on 28 April 1952, the San Francisco Peace Treaty had come into effect, and Koreans in Japan had been transformed into 'foreigners'. On 12 May, 410 detainees were marched out of the gates of Ōmura and onto the decks of the *Sansui*, the deportation ship which was to take them to Korea. Of these deportees, 285 had entered (or re-entered) Japan as undocumented migrants since the war, but the remaining 125 were colonial-period migrants who had been sentenced to imprisonment and deportation for crimes committed in Japan.

When the *Sansui* docked in the port of Busan, the accompanying guards found themselves facing a crisis. As far as the South Korean authorities were concerned, colonial-period migrants to Japan were the Japanese government's problem, and they adamantly refused to take back the 125 people who were being expelled from Japan after serving prison sentences. Eventually the Japanese authorities had no option but to ship these 125 people back to Japan.[14] When they disembarked at Ōmura, the 125 detainees sat down on the concrete expanse of the quay and refused to re-enter the detention centre, some insisting that they would rather die than go back behind the barbed wire of the camp. These were, after all, people who had served their sentences in prison. Now they found themselves again facing detention with no end to their incarceration in sight. Police were called in, but encountered stubborn resistance which lasted well into the night.[15] Eventually, hunger and exhaustion persuaded some of the older and weaker protestors to enter the detention centre, and the others were carried in bodily by the police. Some were to remain interned in Ōmura for years.[16]

Thus began an international stand-off in which the detainees found themselves inextricably entangled. South Korea refused to take them back; Japan refused to free them. Meanwhile, the number of people held in Ōmura with no clear prospect of release steadily increased. At the end of January 1952, there had been 118 inmates, of whom twenty were people who had completed sentences for crimes; by January 1954, there were 413, including 362 who had served prison sentences.[17] Among the 'illegal entrants' detained in Ōmura were a number of Korean War volunteers who lacked alien registrations, and had been arrested as they attempted to re-enter Japan on people-smuggling boats. A few eventually managed to prove that they had been registered as foreign residents in Japan, and were released. Most, however, were deported to South Korea: in the end, of the 641 Koreans in Japan who had volunteered for war service, only 265 were allowed back into Japan.[18]

As conditions in the camp worsened, in November 1952 detainees attempted a mass breakout, resulting in a riot lasting several days, which was ultimately put down by a force of over seven thousand police and fire brigade members.[19] Following the riot, new and more strongly fortified buildings were hastily erected in the Ōmura compound. Japan's network of detention centres was also expanding.

As a publication issued by the Immigration Control Bureau explains, with rather disconcerting candour, Ōmura's purpose throughout the first decades of its existence was 'interning Korean deportees', unlike a second institution in Yokohama which was 'set up to intern other (mostly European and Chinese) detainees'.[20] The Yokohama detention centre was created around the same time as Ōmura, mainly as a place of temporary detention for sailors who had come ashore in Japan and (for one reason or another) failed to reboard their ships. Unlike Ōmura, the Yokohama centre received regular visits from various consular representatives, who frequently complained about conditions there, and in 1956 it was relocated to a new and much more spacious purpose-built compound in the nearby town of Kawasaki. As numbers in Ōmura continued to swell, the

Image 6.1. Ōmura Detention Centre in the mid-1950s.

authorities also found it necessary to open overflow accommodation for Korean and some Chinese detainees in a disused section of a prison in the central Honshu town of Hamamatsu.[21]

By the end of 1954, the situation in Ōmura had deteriorated still further. In October of that year, the South Korean government began to suspect that the Japanese authorities were secretly including 'undesirable' colonial-period migrants among the contingents of 'illegal immigrants' whom they were deporting to Korea, and promptly stopped accepting any deportees from Ōmura at all. This led to a flurry of negotiations, which fleetingly appeared to produce a breakthrough. Japan agreed to release colonial-period migrants from Ōmura on parole, and Korea agreed to accept the deportation of over seven hundred illegal entrants.[22]

However, the compromise soon broke down amid a volley of mutual accusations of bad faith.[23] The Yi government reinstated its total ban on accepting deportees from Japan, and deportations from Ōmura once again came to a complete halt: a hiatus which was to last for more than two years. Between January 1954 and January 1957, the number of people detained in Ōmura rose from 413 to 1,383, with a further 243 interned in Hamamatsu.[24] In an effort to contain a potentially explosive situation, the Immigration Bureau began releasing some Ōmura detainees on parole, generally on the understanding that those released would arrange their own return to Korea on an individual basis.[25] This seems a humanitarian approach to the problem, but (as we shall see) release on parole also became entangled in the increasingly complex and murky politics of repatriation.

During the first half of the 1950s, the detention issue gradually evolved into a strange international game of diplomatic chess, in which the detainees themselves took on the role of pawns. Early in 1952, South Korean president Yi Seung-Man had claimed Korean fishing rights over the wide expanse of sea extending to the Peace Line/Rhee Line.[26] Japanese fishing boats which crossed this line were frequently captured by Korean coastguards, and their crews were interned in a detention camp on the outskirts of Busan. Until 1954, the fishermen had generally been sentenced to brief prison terms for violating Korean fishery laws, and then returned home. But in response to Japan's insistence on sending 'undesirable' long-term Korean residents to Ōmura to await deportation, South Korea began to retaliate by refusing to return Japanese fishermen who had completed their sentences for illegal fishing.[27] Busan detention camp thus became a mirror image of Ōmura, with the detainees in each camp entangled in the increasingly intractable knots of an international diplomatic dispute. The media on both sides of the frontier fanned the flames, each accusing the other side of unreasonably imprisoning their citizens.

Meanwhile, a further layer of complexity was added to the unhappy situation of the Ōmura detainees by that most explosive Northeast Asian political problem: the division of the Korean peninsula. As men, women and children remain incarcerated in the detention centre for months and then years, the 38th parallel between North and South Korea became a tangible reality, running through daily life within the narrow confines of the Ōmura compound itself.

LIFE BEHIND THE BARBED WIRE

Even former guards agree that, in the early days, life for detainees in Ōmura was grim. Initially, the accommodation consisted of a single large hall in one of the few surviving buildings of the heavily bombed aircraft factory. There, inmates of both sexes and all ages were crammed together, their only privacy being provided by makeshift screens or tents created by the detainees themselves out of sheets and blankets. In the crowded camp, where people were thrown together in involuntary intimacy, conditions were chaotic and sometimes violent. The guards themselves seem to have focused mainly on patrolling the camp perimeters, leaving the inmates as far as possible to govern themselves.

Former Ōmura guard Nakamura Masakichi recalls one incident from the early days of the camp: three detainees, a woman and two men, could not be found on the day when they were scheduled for deportation. The woman, as it turned out, had become pregnant by one of the two men, and she and her partner were desperate to remain in Japan. She was eventually discovered hiding in the roof of the camp, while the two men had concealed themselves in the latrine pits. 'The Immigration Bureau Guards couldn't go in to investigate', recalls Nakamura. 'At that time, they [the inmates] had such powerful solidarity that we didn't go into the place where they were interned.'[28]

After the attempted breakout of November 1952, new and more secure buildings were hastily constructed, and a 4.5-metre concrete wall topped with barbed wire was built around the compound, with watchtowers at each corner. The male detainees were moved into five new two-storey masonry buildings, while women and children aged under fourteen remained in the old hall (which was now subdivided into four large dormitories).

The physical conditions now became less squalid than before, but the atmosphere became increasingly prison-like, as guards sought (with varying degrees of success) to reimpose control over the daily lives of detainees. This change within the camp paralleled wider changes in Japanese society as, following the implementation of the San Francisco Peace Treaty, Japanese authorities sought to reimpose their power over Korean communities where groups such as the Korean League had once exercised control. Squads of police or excise officers were sent in to crack down on activities like illegal liquor production.[29] Within the walls of Ōmura, each of the new blocks was equipped with loudspeakers through which guards could issue orders to detainees from a central guardpost and, although internees continued to govern themselves to some degree, the anarchic conditions of the old camp were replaced by a system where each block elected its own representative to communicate with camp officials. Former convicts now were separated from illegal entrants, and, as part of the reconstruction of the camp, six sets of isolation cells for interning 'troublemakers' were built.[30] Between 1953 and 1970, 1,620 Ōmura inmates were to spend part of their detention in these isolation cells, some being kept in isolation for as long as 150 days.[31]

In the mid-1950s, the day of an internee in Ōmura began with the unlocking of cell doors at 7 a.m. Between 7 and 7.30 a.m. the detainees

Image 6.2. The women and children's section of Ōmura Detention Centre, mid-1950s.

washed and dressed, and at 8 they ate breakfast served from a central
kitchen, before gathering for morning roll call at 9 a.m.[32] The camp shop,
selling goods such as toothpaste, cigarettes, underwear and stationery,
opened at 10 a.m., and provided some relief from monotony for those
who had access to money. There were separate exercise yards for the men's
section and the women's and children's section, as well as some ping-
pong tables, playing cards and other forms of entertainment.[33] Lunch was
served at midday, and dinner at 5 p.m., followed by evening roll call at 6.[34]
Films were generally shown once a month, but the camp contained no
library, and there were no classes for children, nor any religious services.
Internees had neither an obligation nor an opportunity to do any work,
other than cleaning their rooms and the compound.[35]

Men slept ten to a room on *tatami* matting; women and children
shared the old hall. The men's section contained an infirmary, but health
conditions in the women's and children's section were said to be poor,
and infectious diseases often swept through their large dormitories.
The segregation of sexes meant that families were broken up, and married couples were allowed to meet for just two periods of thirty minutes
per month, during which they were instructed to communicate only in
Japanese.[36]

By now, many internees had been held in Ōmura for four years or more, and suicides were frequent. Camp guards attempted to address the problem by introducing regular exercise and organizing sport events; and after complaints from inmates and the Red Cross, education for children was started and health conditions gradually improved. But boredom, hopelessness and endless regimentation remained the common lot of Ōmura's inhabitants. A visitor to the camp in the late 1960s described how the walls were plastered with a mass of rules and regulations which governed everyday life: from prohibitions on gambling and the use of matches or lighters, to the instructions, 'do not make unnecessary requests and demands to the authorities' and 'unless you have received permission, it is forbidden to make contact, meet or have private conversations with inmates from other blocks'.[37]

Even in the 1970s, when physical conditions were very much better than they had been two decades earlier, boredom remained the curse of the detention centre. One man who spent three years there in the early 1970s recalls,

Time passed so slowly … At 4 p.m. we had dinner; 6 p.m. was cleaning time; at 9 p.m. the rooms were locked and we had to go to sleep. Just on the odd special occasion, if there was a film or the like, you could stay up until midnight. On New Year's Day we got white rice. Otherwise it was rice mixed with wheat. Everything was predetermined. You couldn't do anything about it – you just had to go along with the rules.[38]

Political discussion with fellow inmates was one way of passing the long hours, and in the atmosphere of the early Cold War years it was not surprising that Ōmura soon became a hotbed of political activity. The people who inhabited Ōmura during the years from mid-1955 to early 1958, when deportations recommenced, came from very diverse backgrounds. Many were spouses and children of Koreans living in Japan, who had been arrested while trying to be reunited with their families: in May 1956, Ōmura contained 140 children aged under fifteen, of whom thirty-one were unaccompanied by adult relatives.[39]

However dreary life was in Ōmura, some detainees viewed the prospect of ultimate deportation to South Korea as an even more appalling fate. These included people who had fled to Japan from South Korea to avoid conscription into the South Korean armed forces, or to escape the oppressive Yi Seung-Man regime. Among them was 'Lee Shin-Ok', who was eighteen years old in 1958. Both her parents had been executed on Jeju Island, and she had narrowly escaped with her life, and secretly entered Japan in an effort to reach her uncle, who lived in Kobe, only to find herself arrested as an illegal immigrant and detained to await deportation back to her homeland.[40] Koreans who had become involved in any form of left-wing politics in Japan saw deportation as a path to imprisonment in South Korea, and such fears were not idle. In 1962, for example, eleven deportees who had just arrived back in Korea following detention in Ōmura were arrested after a defector from North Korea informed the South Korean government that Ōmura detainees were conspiring to carry out communist subversion. The eleven were accused of spreading 'slanderous rumours' against the South Korean military regime, including a rumour that progressive politicians were going to do well in forthcoming elections.[41]

Within Ōmura, communication with the outside world was possible, though letters were censored. Some inmates even wrote articles for magazines or corresponded with literary groups – for the inhabitants of this total institution were far from being mere passive victims of Cold War politics. The former convicts included people who had served sentences for involvement in political demonstrations, and some were educated, highly articulate and possessed of strong ideological convictions. One Ōmura poet, Chung Hun-Sung, composed a detainees' anthem, 'The Song of Ōmura', which was put to music by a teacher from a Korean school in Aichi Prefecture. It went as follows:

> Comrades! Brethren! Citizens of Korea!
> Thick iron windows and strong walls;
> Let's fight, march on, and win,
> Honourable brethren subjected to humiliation!
> Don't forget, don't forget
> The Ōmura Detention Camp.
> Comrades! Brethren! Korean citizens in the Ōmura Camp!
> Let's march on to Pyongyang today
> To build our glorious motherland,
> Honourable brethren!
> Let's remember, let's remember
> The Ōmura Detention camp.[42]

NORTH VERSUS SOUTH IN ŌMURA

As Chung's anthem suggests, political refugees interned in Ōmura often found the image of Kim Il-Sung's Democratic People's Republic of Korea very much more appealing than that of Yi Seung-Man's Republic of Korea. At that time, of course, Japanese socialists and communists also held bright hopes for the future of North Korea, which appeared to be recovering rapidly from the devastating bombing and napalm attacks of the later phases of the Korean War. The Korean War had hardened the line between North and South and sharpened the political split within the Korean community throughout Japan. Within the walls of Ōmura, conflict between pro-North and pro-South detainees became common, with those who identified themselves with the DPRK complaining of discrimination from guards and physical violence from their more numerous pro-ROK fellow inmates. By the mid-1950s, the men's section of Ōmura had become segregated along political lines, with the pro-North Korean inmates housed separately from others on the ground floor of one of the centre's new blocks. Interestingly, this split does not seem to have extended to the women's section – women being assumed to be either less politically aware, or less likely to act out their ideological convictions through violent action.

Both South and North Korean governments sought to exert influence over Ōmura detainees. Politically minded detainees kept contact with the two major Korean community associations in Japan – the South Korean-affiliated Mindan and the North Korean-affiliated General Association of Korean Residents in Japan (Chongryun in Korean, Sōren in Japanese, founded in 1955), and each of these associations in turn was closely linked to its home government. From 1957 onward North Korea succeeded in creating a system for sending gifts of money to Ōmura detainees via the Red Cross. This money was distributed equally to all detainees (pro-South as well as pro-North), and camp officials sought to conceal the source of the funds,[43] but it is likely that the North Korean-affiliated detainees (who were in touch with the North Korean government via Chongryun) would have known where the money came from and broadcast the news as widely as possible in the camp. Most Ōmura inmates had little or no money to buy goods from the camp store, and this generosity by the North Korean government provided a powerful propaganda message – all the more potent because the ROK government had failed to do anything practical to improve the detainees' lot.

Gestures like this enhanced the positive image of the DPRK in the minds of many detainees, and encouraged a growing movement to demand deportation to the North rather than the South of their divided homeland. In November 1955, forty-seven Ōmura inmates who had decided that they wished to be deported to the DPRK rather than the ROK composed a petition written in blood, which was later presented to the North Korean government by a member of a visiting Red Cross delegation.[44] North Korea took up their cause, demanding that the

Image 6.3. ICRC representative Harry Angst distributes aid to Ōmura detainees, 1958.

Japanese government accept the right of detainees to choose their place of deportation, and offering to accept those who wished to be sent to the DPRK. Unbeknownst to the detainees themselves, however, from the very start their protest had become entangled in a covert policy on repatriation; and behind the scenes, moves were already under way which would eventually lead to a movement of people from Japan to North Korea on a much larger scale than they themselves could have imagined (see Chapter Eight).

Meanwhile, the Geneva-based International Committee of the Red Cross (ICRC) was becoming involved in efforts to resolve the stand-off between Japan and South Korea over the problems of Ōmura and the Rhee Line. On the very last day of 1957, the Committee succeeded in brokering a deal under which Japan would parole colonial-period former convicts held in Ōmura, while South Korea would accept other deportees from the camp and also release and return the Japanese fishermen who had served sentences in Busan. But, as had happened before, the agreement quickly collapsed into acrimony. On this occasion, the problem was the issue of pro-North Korea Ōmura detainees.

The Yi Seung-Man regime insisted that all postwar undocumented migrants who were held in Ōmura must be deported to South Korea. Its fear was that if people from South Korea travelled to Japan as undocumented migrants, and were then deported by Japan to North Korea, then this would create a back-door route for ROK citizens to defect to the Communist North: something which South Korea wished to avoid at all costs. By this time, however, more than a hundred detainees (including people like Lee Shin-Ok, whose story is outlined above) were insisting that they wanted to be deported to North Korea. In mid-1958, some seventy of them began a hunger strike to press their case, and in July of that year the Japanese government responded by quietly releasing twenty-five of them on parole.

The Japanese government, then headed by Prime Minister Kishi Nobusuke, repeatedly stated that it wished to avoid any conflict with South Korea, but at the same time that it was eager to respect deportees' personal choice of destination. This seems a reasonable and principled position, but below the surface things were more complex than they appeared. On the one hand, many people within the Japanese government were by now eager to see a mass departure of ethnic Koreans (including detainees) to North Korea, and they clearly hoped that pro-North Korea detainees released on parole would add their voices to a growing public movement in support of a mass migration of Koreans from Japan to the DPRK.[45] On the other hand, despite its public protestations, the Japanese government did not in fact necessarily respect the wishes of deportees. Indeed, in 1958 it 'began sending back to ROK some of the worst Ōmura camp trouble makers, particularly criminal types, who had been demanding return to North Korea'.[46]

Eventually, in the face of intense opposition from South Korea, the Japanese government agreed to authorize a mass resettlement of ethnic Koreans from Japan to the DPRK. This scheme was brokered by the Japanese and North Korean Red Cross Societies, and overseen by the International Committee of the Red Cross. The first ships carrying Koreans from Japan to North Korea left the port of Niigata on 14 December 1959 and (as we shall see in Chapter Eight) in the course of the next two years almost 80,000 people left Japan to start new lives in the Democratic People's Republic of Korea. Among them were 2,370 people who had been detained for violating the Immigration Control Law and had chosen deportation to North rather than to South Korea. Of these, most had been released on parole to allow them to prepare for their departure, but 421 were taken directly from Ōmura and escorted onto the waiting ships in Niigata.[47] Meanwhile, it seems that police and local officials in some parts of Japan at least had begun to implement a kind of amnesty, under which undocumented migrants who volunteered for relocation to North Korea would not be subject to the normal punishments for illegal entry, but would be let off with a token fine.[48] In 1960, the Yi Seung-Man regime was overthrown, and soon after deportations of undocumented migrants to South Korea were resumed on a regular basis.

LITERATURE, ACTIVISM AND MIGRANT DETENTION

When I visited Ōmura Detention Centre (now rebadged Ōmura Immigration Reception Centre) in 2005, the old buildings had all disappeared – mere hummocks under the grass of an open space awaiting construction. The illustrated brochure presented to us by the Immigration Control staff who guided me and my fellow visitors round the centre explained that 'in August 1996, the Ōmura Immigration Control Centre was reincarnated in wonderful new building which is acclaimed for its innovative and beautiful form which fits into the surrounding environment, and which might be taken for the research institute of some high tech industry'.[49] The sleek new Ōmura Detention Centre, with its tile and mirror-glass façade, its battery of computer-controlled security systems and its well-equipped clinics and barber's shop, is certainly a far cry from the chaos and overcrowding of the centre's first incarnation. The segregation of Japan's detention centres by nationality has long since ceased, and Ōmura today contains a mixture of nationalities.

The sleeping quarters, however, still follow the pattern established in 1952: ten-person dormitories where detainees sleep side by side on *tatami*-mat floors. The design of the new structure, in which exercise areas are all enclosed within the hollow core of the four-storey square building, deprives inmates of Salvo's vision: that fleeting glimpse of the sea beyond the wire. The new Ōmura contains nothing so aesthetically offensive as barbed wire, but, although the sea is just a stone's throw away, the only view from the exercise yards is of the grey ferro-concrete inner walls of the building.

The hummocks in the earth on the site of the old detention centre contain the relics of some of the darker aspects of Japan's postwar migration controls. Ōmura, as Hyun Moo-Am observes, was an immensely powerful symbol, whose very name, when spoken in *Zainichi* Korean circles, evoked the power of the Japanese state to intervene in their lives.[50] At the same time, Ōmura also revealed and symbolized the complex cross-border forces influencing Japan's postwar migration control system. The detention camp was not simply the product of rational border control policies or of internal political debate. Its genesis and development were shaped by the troubled confluences of Japan–South

Image 6.4. Ōmura Immigration Reception Centre, 2005.

Korea relations, of the politics of a divided Korea, and of the activities of international bodies (exemplified by the International Committee of the Red Cross).

But the history of Ōmura also sheds light on another aspect of Japanese history which is too often overlooked. The image of Japan as an inherently xenophobic society encourages a belief that all Japanese people are hostile to the presence of migrants in their midst. Certainly, postwar Japanese history is full of examples of popular and media prejudices against minorities. However, Ōmura reminds us, too, of the many occasions when groups of Japanese people have rallied to defend the rights of foreigners in Japan. Some of these human rights movements were organized by political activists closely associated with the Japanese Communist Party or the Japan Socialist Party, or with the new left-wing student movements of the 1960s. Others were simply spontaneous efforts by small groups of local people to protect some foreign friend or neighbour facing deportation. The people who participated in such movements may have been only a small fraction of the total Japanese population, but their actions constitute an important part of the history of social movements in East Asia.

One intriguing example of such action emerged between 1956 and 1958, as the crisis surrounding deportations from Ōmura was reaching its height. A group of North Korean-affiliated Ōmura detainees decided to establish a literary group within the camp, which they named the Ōmura Korean Literary Society (Ōmura Chōsen Bungakukai). They hoped to publish a magazine containing works by camp inmates, but, needless to say, acquiring the necessary paper, ink and printing facilities proved impossible. Eventually, they established contact by letter with a Japanese left-wing literary circle known as the Southern Districts Literary Group (Nambu Bungaku Shūdan), based in the central-southern area of Tokyo, and the circle's members agreed to print the Ōmura Korean Literary Society's journal and send the finished copies to the detention centre. The first two volumes of the journal, entitled *Ōmura Literature* (*Ōmura Bungaku*), were published by the Southern Districts Literary Group in 1956 and 1957, and later issues were produced by Chongryun and the Japan–Korea Association (Nitchō Kyōkai, a Japanese group which promoted improved relations between Japan and North Korea). Unfortunately *Ōmura Literature* was printed in very small numbers, and there seem to be no surviving publicly available copies. However, an attractively illustrated letter of thanks from the Ōmura creative writers to their Japanese comrades in Tokyo was printed in one of the Southern Districts Literary Group's magazines.[51]

From its very inception, Ōmura was a topic of debate in the Japanese Diet, and opposition members repeatedly took up the question of conditions within the camp. Delegations of parliamentarians, as well as Red Cross officials, were sometimes allowed to make visits of inspection to Ōmura.[52] With the rise of student and anti-Vietnam War protest movements in Japan, Ōmura also became a focus of protest for the Japanese New Left. The centre was seen by the Japanese left as representative both of human rights abuses by the Japanese state and of the neocolonial relationship between Japan and its Asian neighbours. From March 1969 onward, activists from the anti-Vietnam War movement Beheiren and the student movement Zengakuren staged a series of demonstrations outside the detention centre, culminating in August in an incursion into the compound by about fifty demonstrators.[53]

Among the inmates whose plight attracted attention in the 1960s were deserters from the South Korean army who had fled to Japan to escape being sent to fight in Vietnam: people like Kim Dong-Gi, who came from Jeju and had first entered Japan as a 'stowaway' in 1950 at the age of thirteen. Ten years later, Kim was arrested and deported, but in 1962 he again attempted to reach Japan, where his three elder brothers were living. Once again he was caught and sent back to South Korea, and this time he was drafted into the military contingent which the Republic of Korea was about to send to Vietnam to support the military action of US troops. In July 1965, Kim deserted from his unit and fled to Japan for a third time, only to be arrested and interned in Ōmura awaiting deportation. A number of Japanese activists and intellectuals rallied to his cause.

One of them, Hayashi Kōzō – a scholar of German literature who had also been active in supporting American military deserters – appealed to the consciences of fellow Japanese with an analogy drawn from wartime Germany. Many of those deported from Ōmura, he pointed out, were arrested and tortured in South Korea. To remain silent about their fate was to echo the silence of Germans who closed their ears and eyes to evidence of the existence of concentration camps. 'Today, on the western shores of Kyushu,' wrote Hayashi, 'there is an "East Asian version of the Nazi concentration camps" ... We should not be misled by the fact that it has no gas chambers.'[54] Although Japanese student activism declined sharply in the 1970s, movements to protect and improve the rights of those incarcerated in Ōmura and other migrant detention centres have been sustained by human rights and Christian welfare organizations in Japan, and are continued in the twenty-first century by groups such as the Solidarity Network with Migrants Japan (SNMJ) and the Japanese branch of Amnesty International.[55]

Meanwhile, human rights lawyers and local community groups also worked on behalf of individual detainees in their struggle to secure the one key that could release them from captivity and from the fear of deportation. This key was not political asylum, since Japan had no process for recognizing the rights of asylum seekers. Rather, it was special permission to stay in Japan, a status which could be granted only at the discretion of the minister of justice, but which came to play a surprisingly central role in Japan's postwar policy towards foreigners on its soil. Such campaigns on behalf of individual detainees had very mixed results; for, as we shall see in the next chapter, the path to special permission to stay was a labyrinthine and mysterious one. Like the story of Ōmura, the history of discretionary special permission to stay can only be understood if we see it in the context of Japan's evolving relations with neighbouring countries. But the system of special permission to stay must also be understood in the framework of the backdoor workings of the Japanese political system: an issue that is seldom discussed in official government publications on migration policy.

NOTES

1. Homepage of the Commander, Fleet Activities Sasebo, http://www.cfas. navy.mil/History/history.htm (accessed 7 June 2008).
2. Ōmura Shi Bunkazai Hogo Kyōkai, *'Rekishi' to natta Fūkei: Furushashin ni Miru Ōmura Seikatsushi* (Ōmura: Ōmura Shi Bunkazai Hogo Kyōkai, 1997), p. 52.
3. Hōmushō Nyūkoku Kanrikyoku, *Shutsunyūkoku Kanri no Kaikō to Tenbō: Nyūkan Hasoku 30-Shūnen o Kinen shite* (Tokyo: Hōmushō Nyūkoku Kanrikyoku, 1980), p. 346.
4. Ibid., p. 343.
5. Ibid., pp. 345–8.
6. Ibid., p. 342.
7. See Hōmushō Nyūkoku Kanrikyoku, *Shutsunyūkoku Kanri Hakusho, Shōwa 34-Nen* (Tokyo: Ōkurasho Insatsukyoku, 1959), p. 30.
8. Hōmushō Ōmura Nyūkokusha Shūyojo (ed.), *Ōmura Nyūkokusha Shūyojo 20-Nenshi* (Tokyo: Hōmushō, 1970), p. 5.
9. See C. Betros, 'New Tokyo Immigration Center Tries to Get It Right', *Japan Today*, 2 March 2008, http://www.japantoday.com/news/jp/e/tools/ print.asp?content=feature&id=421 (accessed 2 March 2008).
10. E. Goffman, *Asylums: Essays on the Social Situation of Mental Patients and Other Inmates* (Harmondsworth: Penguin Books, 1968), p. 17; I am indebted to Dr Christine Winter for drawing my attention to the relevance of Goffman's work.
11. Ibid., p. 16.
12. J. Le Carré, *The Mission Song* (London: Hodder and Stoughton, 2006), p. 337.
13. See, for example, letter from Shimazu Tadatsugu, president of the Japan Red Cross Society, to Leopold Boissier, president of the International Committee of the Red Cross, 10 January 1957, in archives of the International Committee of the Red Cross, Geneva (hereafter ICRC Archives), File B AG 232 105–002, Problème du rapatriement des Coréens du Japon, dossier I : généralités, 17.2.1953–11.10.1957.
14. Hōmushō Nyūkoku Kanrikyoku, *Shutsunyūkoku Kanri no Kaikō*, pp. 360–1; Hōmushō Ōmura Nyūkokusha Shūyojo, *Ōmura Nyūkokusha Shūyojo*.
15. Hōmushō Ōmura Nyūkokusha Shūyojo, *Ōmura Nyūkokusha Shūyojo*, p. 95; see also Hōmushō Nyūkoku Kanrikyoku, *Shutsunyūkoku Kanri no Kaiko*, pp. 360–1. Tanaka Tomizō, who was the officer in charge of Ōmura Detention Centre during this incident, recalls the number of people shipped out on 12 May as having been 'about 700', but the figure given in the detention centre's official history is 410.
16. Hōmushō Nyūkoku Kanrikyoku, *Shutsunyūkoku Kanri no Kaikō*, pp. 361–2.
17. Hōmushō Nyūkoku Kanrikyoku, *Shutsunyūkoku Kanri Hakusho, Shōwa 34-Nen*, p. 95.

18. Kim Chang-Jung, *Zainichi Giyūhei Kikan sezu: Chōsen Sensō Hisshi* (Tokyo: Iwanami Shoten, 2007), pp. 207–8.
19. Hōmushō Ōmura Nyūkokusha Shūyojo, *Ōmura Nyūkokusha Shūyojo*, p. 2.
20. Hōmushō Nyūkoku Kanrikyoku, *Shutsunyūkoku Kanri to sono Jittai – Shōwa 39-nen* (Tokyo: Ōkurashō Insatsukyoku, 1964), p. 109.
21. Hōmushō Nyūkoku Kanrikyoku, *Shutsunyūkoku Kanri no Kaikō*, p. 373.
22. Hōmushō Ōmura Nyūkokusha Shūyojo, *Ōmura Nyūkokusha Shūyojo*, p. 2; see also documents on Korea–Japan relations released by the Foreign Ministry of the Republic of Korea, 2006, File 723.1. JA, record no. 771, Vol. VII, *Buksong Kwangye Chamgo Jaryo* 1955–1960, pp. 337–8.
23. *Buksong Kwangye Chamgo Jaryo* 1955–1960, p. 338.
24. Hōmushō Nyūkoku Kanrikyoku, *Shutsunyūkoku Kanri Hakusho, Shōwa 34-Nen*, p. 95.
25. Hōmushō Nyūkoku Kanrikyoku, *Shutsunyūkoku Kanri to sono Jittai – Shōwa 39-nen* (Tokyo: Ōkurashō Insatsukyoku, 1964), p. 112.
26. See Chapter Two, p. 31.
27. Japan Korea Fishery Deliberation Committee, 'Appeal of Japanese Fishing People to the World Concerning the Question of the Rhee Line', Tokyo, Japan Korea Fishery Deliberation Committee, 1957, pamphlet held in ICRC Archives, File B AG 232 105–027, Documentation concernant le rapatriement des Coréens et les pêcheurs japonnais détenus à Pusan, 10/10/1956–04/02/1959.
28. Hōmushō Nyūkoku Kanrikyoku, *Shutsunyūkoku Kanri no Kaikō*, p. 364.
29. See Kang Sang-Jung, *Zainichi* (Tokyo: Kōdansha, 2004), pp. 25–7.
30. 'Omura Immigration Centre', report of a visit on 19 May 1956 by W. Michel, E. de Weck and H. Angst of the International Committee of the Red Cross, in ICRC Archives, File B AG 232 105–002.
31. Hōmushō Ōmura Nyūkokusha Shūyojo, *Ōmura Nyūkokusha Shūyojo*, p. 57; Itanuma Jirō, 'Ōmura Shūyōjo Teppai no tame ni', in Pak Seongkong (ed.), *Ōmura Shūyōjo* (Kyoto: Kyoto Daigaku Shuppankai, 1969), pp. 1–42, quotation from pp. 36–7.
32. 'Ōmura Shūyōsho Hishūyōsha Shintoku', document contained in Tōdai Hōkyōtō (ed.), *Nyūkan Taisei Shiryōshū* (Tokyo: Aki Shobō, 1971), p. 194.
33. 'Omura Immigration Centre' report.
34. Tōdai Hōkyōtō, *Nyūkan Taisei*, p. 194.
35. 'Omura Immigration Centre' report.
36. 'Omura Immigration Centre' report; Itanuma, 'Ōmura Shūyōjo Teppai', pp. 37–9.
37. Itanuma, 'Ōmura Shūyōjo Teppai', pp. 27–8.
38. Interview with Mr 'Heo', originally from Jeju Island, who was interned in Ōmura for three years in the 1970s; interview conducted 19 January 2005, Osaka.
39. 'Omura Immigration Centre' report.
40. Ibid., pp. 14–15.

41. *Japan Times*, 1 December 1962.

42. 'The Song of Ōmura', words by Chung Hun-Sung, music by Choe Yang-Su, translation in ICRC Archives, File B AG 232 105–002. I have slightly modified spelling and punctuation.

43. Inoue, 'Report: Visit to the Omura Detention Camp', p. 3.

44. Nihon Ōmura Shūyōsho Chōsen Minshushugi Jinmin Kyōwakoku Kikoku Kibōsha Ichidō 131-Mei 'Yōsesho' (Petition jointly presented by 131 people in the Ōmura Detention Centre, Japan, seeking to return to the Democratic People's Republic of Korea), 27 September 1957, in ICRC Archives, File B AG 232 105–002; see also Masutaro Inoue, *Report of the Phyongyang Conference held by Japanese and North Korean Red Cross Societies (January 27th–February 28th 1956)*, 17 March 1956, p. 3, in ICRC Archives, B AG 232 055–001, Ressortissants japonais en Corée du Nord, 22.01.1954–11.05.1956.

45. For further details of this movement, see Chapter Eight.

46. Telegram from Douglas MacArthur II (US Ambassador to Japan) to Secretary of State, Washington, DC, 30 November 1959, in National Archives and Records Administration, College Park, Maryland, decimal file 294.9522/11–3059.

47. Immigration Control Bureau, Justice Ministry, 'Monthly Report on Repatriation to North Korea', no. 59, 30 November 1964, in ICRC Archives, BAG 232 105–030.01, Monthly Reports on the Repatriation to North Korea, 31/03/1962–31/12/1964.

48. 'Koreans who have failed to register as aliens will also be permitted to repatriate. According to Mr. Sakata [head of the Foreign Affairs Section, Osaka Metropolitan Government], there are currently about 50,000 Koreans in the Osaka area who have not properly registered their presence. Arrangements are being made so that such persons may apply for the prerequisite alien registration and once they have this they can proceed to make the regular repatriation application. Mr. Sakata adds that these persons would of course be subject to legal penalties for failing to register as aliens but that, if they really wished to go, this was no serious obstacle since the penalty would probably be a token two or three thousand yen fine.' Dispatch from US Consulate General, Kobe-Osaka, to US Department of State, Washington, 1 September 1959, in NARA, College Park, 694.95B/9–1959.

49. Hōmushō, *Ōmura Nyūkoku Kanri Sentā*, n.d., p. 1.

50. Hyun Moo-Am, 'Mikkō, Ōmura Shūyōjo, Saishūtō: Ōsaka to Saishūtō o Musubu "Mikkō" no Nettowāku', *Gendai Shisō*, 35 (June 2007), pp. 158–73.

51. Michika Chikanobu, 'Shimomaruko Bunka Shūdan to sono Jidai: 50-nendai Tōkyō Sākuru Undō Kenkyū Josetsu', *Gendai Shisō*, 35, 17 (December 2007), pp. 38–101, quotation from pp. 82–6.

52. Hōmushō Nyūkoku Kanrikyoku, *Shutsunyūkoku Kanri no Kaikō*, p. 366.

53. Ibid., p. 298; Hōmushō Ōmura Nyūkokusha Shūyojo, *Ōmura Nyūkokusha Shūyojo*, p. 4.

54. Hayashi Kōzō, 'Kim Dong-Gi to Wareware', *Res Novare: Jōkyō to Bunseki*, 3 (May–June 1967), reproduced in *Hayashi Kōzō Kobunshū: 'Kako no Kokufuku' ni tsuite no Tekisuto o Chūshin ni* (Kyoto: privately printed, 2008), pp. 33–40, quotation from p. 33.
55. See the websites www.jca.apc.org/migrant-net/English/html and http://secure.amnesty.or.jp/index_e.html.

CHAPTER 7

Special permission to stay

'Hidden lives' in postwar Japan

A SECRET JOURNEY

Shin Chang-Seok was born in 1930, in the workers' quarters of a gravel quarry west of Tokyo. His grandfather was well educated, and owned his own farmland in the southern part of the Korean peninsula, but, after losing his land as a result of colonization, migrated to Japan, bringing with him Chang-Seok's father, who was then in his teens.[1] Chang-Seok was the eldest son in a large family of three boys and four girls, and his early life was an unsettled one, as his parents separated in 1934, and his father moved from one unstable job to another.

For part of his childhood Chang-Seok lived with his paternal grandparents, and remembers how his grandfather, who longed for Korea's liberation from colonial rule, refused to speak the colonizers' language even though he had lived in Japan for years. In an account of his life published in 2006, Shin Chang-Seok (writing in the third person) describes how his grandfather taught him Korean from an early age and recalls,

in his entire life, Grandfather never uttered a word of Japanese, and when he went to the market, he would use the young Chang-Seok as an interpreter to ask prices, and to bargain them down. And later [during the Pacific War], scattering ashes from his precious cigarettes as he walked along the road which passed in front of the tenement housing of the Kosaka Coalmines [in Akita Prefecture], Grandfather would see Australian prisoners of war with backs bent as they made their way to their workplace at the mine, and would pat them on the back and say in Korean, 'ah, how you are suffering! You will win in the end, for sure.'[2]

As the war in China expanded in the late 1930s, so too labour conscription from Korea intensified, and the Japanese authorities found themselves urgently needing Korean-speaking managers to oversee the tens of thousands of colonial workers whom they had shipped in to work in mines and construction sites all over the country. In 1940, Shin Chang-Seok's

172

father found work as a labour supervisor at a mine in north-eastern Japan run by the Dōwa Mining Company. By the final years of the Pacific War he was attending a junior high school in Akita Prefecture. Like almost all Koreans at that time, he used a Japanese name; it was only after the war ended that Chang-Seok realized that there were also four other Korean students at his school.[3]

In wartime Japan, schools fostered an intense and passionate nationalism. Teenage boys were encouraged to believe that it was their destiny to fight, and very probably to die, for the greater glory of the Japanese Empire, and Shin Chang-Seok was just as susceptible to the power of these Japanese nationalist emotions as any other schoolboy.[4] He joined the Naval Junior Reserve, where he was trained in skills such as Morse code and semaphore.

For Chang-Seok, then, the day of Korea's liberation, when a mass of forced labourers gathered in his family's home, partying deep into the night to celebrate the joy of freedom, was a deeply unsettling event. Soon, however, he too was swept up in enthusiasm for the vision of an independent Korea. He attended special study camps organized by the League of Korean Students in Japan (Zai-Nihon Chōsenjin Gakusei Dōmei, a youth group affiliated to the Korean League), and in 1948, when he graduated from school and entered Hokkaido University, he gave up the Japanese name which his family had used in colonial times – Shigemitsu – and resumed his Korean name.

The new-found excitement of Korean independence was quickly overshadowed by the dark realities of the Cold War. Far from being free, Korea was divided, with Soviet troops in the northern half and US troops in the south. When the Korean War broke out, and Japan became a major support base for US and other United Nations forces fighting on the southern side, it seemed to Shin Chang-Seok and his Korean fellow students as though all their worst fears were being realized. They were torn between the need to study and prepare for examinations, and the sense that 'we are being colonized again! We have to act!'[5]

Shin joined others protesting against the war. With two classmates, he took part in a demonstration at a US base in the northern Japanese city of Sendai, demanding the withdrawal of American troops from Korea, and in October 1950 he was arrested for distributing anti-war leaflets outside a factory belonging to the major Japanese ship-building company Ishkawajima Harima, which manufactured war matériel for use in Korea. However, with the support of a sympathetic Japanese lawyer, he was found innocent. The court's ruling may have saved him from an early death. As he recalls, 'I heard that the fellow activists who were arrested before and after me were forcibly deported [to South Korea] and then executed by firing squad under the Yi Seung-Man regime. I literally came within an inch of my life.'[6]

The experience, however, did not discourage him from political activism, and in April 1953 he was once again in trouble with the law, when he was accused of being involved in the 'Red Lamp Incident', a protest action during which opponents of US actions in the Korean War used a red lamp to stop a train carrying supplies for American forces in Korea, and absconded with the train's cargo of coal. After graduating from the Agriculture Faculty of Hokkaido University in 1955, Shin Chang-Seok continued his left-wing political activism, and the following year embarked on a venture which involved his first trip outside Japan.

People sympathetic to North Korea within the Korean community in Japan had decided to send reconstruction aid to the DPRK, then still struggling to recover from the devastating bombing raids to which it had been subjected in the latter stages of the war. There was, of course, no legal way to do this, since Japan had absolutely no political, trade or financial connections to North Korea. However, left-wing activists collected small-scale industrial equipment such as transceivers, sewing machines, fishing nets and so on worth more than 5 million yen, and Shin Chang-Seok was given the task of transporting these secretly to the DPRK.

At night, on 28 August 1956, he set out from a small port in Tottori Prefecture on the west coast of Japan in a thirty-ton fishing boat. After a difficult and dangerous journey Shin reached North Korea, where he remained for more than a month, returning by small boat to the port of Sakai Minato on 7 October. On subsequent visits to North Korea in the 1980s, Shin Chang-Seok was to become deeply disillusioned with the society created by Kim Il-Sung's brand of communism. But on this first visit, he felt admiration for the enthusiasm and courage with which North Koreans were rebuilding their country after the devastation of the Korean War.

Shin Chang-Seok and his left-wing Korean comrades had believed they were carrying out their mission in secret, but it seems that they had been under the surveillance of the Japanese police from the very start. In 1957 Shin was arrested. His unauthorized journey had transformed him into an illegal immigrant, not to mention a 'subversive' (as defined by the Immigration Control Law). He was to spend the next twenty years of his life fighting to avoid deportation from the land of this birth.

AT THE MINISTER'S DISCRETION

During the second half of the twentieth century many countries became host to large numbers of immigrants who lacked proper documentation, but whose mass deportation would have caused considerable social disruption and human suffering. One common response to this dilemma was to grant intermittent amnesties to undocumented migrants. For example, in 1981 and 1982 France granted an amnesty to some 130,000 undocumented migrants, mostly from Portugal and Algeria, while around 110,000 received amnesties in Italy between 1987 and 1988.[7]

Some countries, including the US, the UK, France, Germany and Australia, have also made increasing use of clauses in the law which allow the government to make discretionary decisions granting residence rights to undocumented migrants who, in normal circumstances, would have been deported. These 'special cases' are usually decided either on humanitarian grounds, or because the migrants concerned have lived and worked in the country for a long time, become integrated, and are seen as 'contributing to society'.[8] With the changing pattern of refugee flows since the end of the Cold War, these discretionary powers have been more and more widely used, and have become a source of growing controversy in many parts of the world. In the UK, for example, the 1971 Immigration Act gave the Home Secretary the discretionary right to grant migrants 'exceptional leave to remain' (ELR). This power was not widely used until the 1990s, but since then, ELR numbers have soared.[9]

In Japan (as we have seen) as far back as the Allied Occupation period, SCAP had begun to grant special reprieves on humanitarian grounds to people scheduled for deportation, one of the beneficiaries being 'Mr Koh', whose story we encountered in the first pages of this book. These discretionary powers were incorporated into the 1951 Migration Control Law, which gave far-reaching authority to the Japanese minister for justice (on the one hand) to deport those deemed a threat to national security, but also (on the other) to grant 'special permission to stay' (*zairyū tokubetsu kyoka*). The minister was empowered to cancel deportation orders and allow any individual to remain indefinitely in Japan where 'the circumstances warrant special permission to remain'; though the law made no attempt to elaborate what these circumstances were.

What is distinctive about Japanese policy is not the fact that such discretion exists, but the fact that from the middle of the twentieth century onward special permission to stay has consistently been used as a crucial policy tool for managing migration. Between 1952 and 1979, 44,890 foreigners were given such permission, an average of 1,603 a year.[10] The numbers were highest in the early years, and fell during the 1960s: in 1960 2,703 people (2,427 Koreans, 178 Chinese and ninety-eight others) were granted special permission to stay, but by 1970 the number had fallen to 618 (590 Koreans, eight Chinese and twenty others).[11] Recently, in Japan as elsewhere, discretionary ministerial decision has again become a major route through which foreigners obtain residence rights in Japan. Throughout the 1980s, grants of permission were running at around five hundred per year, but from the mid-1990s they rose rapidly, reaching 4,318 in 1999, 10,327 in 2004 and 13,239 in 2005.[12]

This recent growth in the use of special permission in part reflects the large number of long-term visa overstayers in Japan and particularly the growing numbers of marriages between Japanese and foreigners. Special Permission is often used to address the issue of foreign visa over-stayers who have married Japanese partners and established families in Japan.[13] As many observers have pointed out, however, the discretionary granting of residence rights is a two-edged sword.[14] On the one hand, it is often a genuinely humanitarian way of relieving the suffering and anxiety of those undocumented migrants for whom deportation would have particularly devastating consequences. On the other, discretionary acts of clemency by ministers lack transparency, raise serious questions of equity and at worst can become a source of structural corruption.

The official documents of the day provide a clear and confident statement of the path to be followed by those seeking special permission to stay in the 1950s and 1960s. When someone was suspected of violating the Immigration Control Law, a Immigration Guard officer (*Nyūkan Keibikan*) would first take out a detention order, and the suspect would be given forty-eight hours to provide documentation to support any appeal against detention. If the appeal was not accepted, the suspect would then be handed over to an Immigration Bureau investigation officer (*Nyūkan Shinsakan*), and could be questioned and then detained for a period of up to thirty days, which if necessary could be extended by a further thirty days. In some cases, detainees could be released on bail or on parole while their cases were being examined. When the investigation officer handed down his ruling, the suspect had three days in which to ask for an oral appeal hearing by a special investigation officer (*Tokubetsu Shinsakan*), at which a lawyer could be present. If this appeal failed, there was a further period of three days within which to appeal to the minister of justice. The minister had three options: to reject the appeal; to accept it on the grounds that the suspect had not violated the law; or to accept the appeal on the grounds that the suspect, although in violation of the Immigration Control Law, was affected by exceptional humanitarian or other circumstances which justified granting special permission to stay.[15]

As the reminiscences of Shin Chang-Seok show, however, the process in some cases became extremely long-drawn-out, and bore very little resemblance to the measures set out in the official guidelines.

FROM SUBVERSIVE ALIEN TO PERMANENT RESIDENT

Shin was arrested on 2 December 1957, five days before he was due to be married, and was charged over his unauthorized visit to North Korea. He was held in prison until July 1958, and was then detained for a further period by the immigration authorities. At his trial, he was given a suspended sentence of one year and five months with hard labour, with a further substantial fine. As part of the conditions of his release, he was also told to change his alien registration from *Chōsen seki* to *Kankoku seki*.[16] Since he had been found guilty of a crime with a sentence of more than one year, Shin was now liable to deportation, but appealed against this, claiming that he had only gone to North Korea out of curiosity, and that he wanted to remain in Japan. He stressed the fact that he been born and brought up in Japan and did not speak Korean (although in fact, as he himself points out, his Korean was reasonably fluent).[17] After his release on parole he married, and worked in a variety of jobs while fighting to obtain a reversal of the deportation order.

In the Japan of the 1950s and 1960s, foreigners were debarred from all public service positions and were in practice almost always excluded from permanent employment in large companies. Koreans and Chinese in Japan therefore tended to find work in small firms, particularly in restaurants, entertainment businesses and areas of industry where working conditions were harsh and pay was low. Probably the best known of all the areas of the economy associated in the public mind with the Korean community was the *pachinko* (pinball) parlour industry – an industry which boomed in the postwar years: by the start of the twenty-first century *pachinko* parlours had a turnover exceeding that of the steel industry.

Shin Chang-Seok, with his degree from a prestigious Japanese university, found work first in a *pachinko* business run by his father, and then helped to set up a chain of petrol stations, before moving to a job in a tourism company. In the course of his career, he developed friendships with a number of lawyers and politicians who helped to plead his case. Despite the fact that Shin himself was linked to pro-North Korean organizations, his business partners and supporters included a Liberal Democratic Party politician who made representations on his behalf to the senior LDP politician Fukuda Takeo and to the chair of the Justice Committee of the Lower House of Parliament, but without avail. He also obtained the services of a prominent and well-connected lawyer, who managed to gain access to the extensive file on Shin Chang-Seok held by Japan's intelligence bureau, the Public Security Agency (*Kōan Chōsa Chō*). It seems that the authorities incorrectly suspected him of being in league with a major North Korean spy.

Appeals and negotiations over Shin's case dragged on for months, and then years. Finally, in 1970, thirteen years after his original arrest, an arrangement was reached which was ultimately to remove the shadow of deportation from Shin Chang-Seok's life. According to Shin's understanding, the arrangement was that he would spend three months in Ōmura Detention Centre, but would not in fact be deported. For Shin, this deal created a serious dilemma. He was half afraid that it was a trap, and that once he entered Ōmura, he would find himself forcibly shipped to South Korea, where, under the dictatorship of Park Chung-Hee (which lasted from 1961 to 1979), he faced almost certain imprisonment, and possible execution as a North Korean spy. However, feeling that he had no other choice, Shin accepted the arrangement and entered Ōmura Detention Centre on 10 October 1970.

For Shin, with a visible time limit to his detention, life in Ōmura was less harsh than he had feared. As he writes in his third-person account of his experiences,

During the daytime he could go in and out of the cell, and could do things like playing volleyball, table-tennis, *hanafuda* (a Japanese card game) and cards as much as he wanted … Maybe this was a trick by the authorities to get him to reveal himself.[18]

In other words, he suspected that the authorities thought his ability to communicate freely with other detainees in Ōmura would lead him to reveal secrets which would be overheard by the guards or passed on by informers, enabling them to pick up pieces of information about the activities of the left-wing Korean groups with which he was associated.

From Shin's perspective, on the contrary, his time in Ōmura provided an opportunity to learn more about the backgrounds of his fellow inmates. Soon after his arrival, around fifty undocumented migrants from Jeju Island arrived at the detention centre, and in response to their request for help he began to teach them the Japanese language, using Korean as his medium of instruction, and in the process entirely forgetting that one of the grounds for his appeal against deportation had been the statement that he 'only spoke Japanese'. He also engaged in heated discussions with a young Korean undocumented migrant who had reached Japan from Jeju after serving with the Korean army in Vietnam. Unlike Kim Dong-Gi (see p. 166) and other Korean conscientious objectors who fled to Japan to avoid service in Vietnam, this Ōmura internee believed that his military service in Vietnam had been a justified action against dangerous communists. Shin felt moved to remind the young man of the disasters brought to his own home island of Jeju by military actions against those whom the government had defined as 'Reds'.

The immigration authorities detained Shin for longer than the anticipated three months, but although they may not have gained the information they hoped for during his incarceration, they did (to Shin's great relief) eventually release him on parole in April 1971, although he was still required to register with the immigration authorities just once each year. However, the lingering fear of deportation did not finally disappear until 1977. In that year, when he made his annual visit to his local immigration office, he was surprised to be informed that he was being given special permission to stay. 'You are now free', the immigration officer told him. 'Free' meant that at the age of forty-seven, for the first time in his life, he was able to travel overseas and then legally return to the country where he had been born and always lived.[19]

MIGRANTS AND POWER-BROKERS

Shin Chang-Seok's story is in many ways a very unusual one, but there is evidence to suggest that complex negotiations involving lawyers, bureaucrats (or former bureaucrats) and politicians were a common part of the special-permission process in the postwar decades. A more typical experience was probably that of 'Mr Heo', who had smuggled himself into Japan from Jeju at the age of nineteen, in 1962.

Like many Jeju migrants, Mr Heo settled in the Ikuno-ku district of Osaka, an area home to a mass of very small manufacturing firms producing metal, rubber and vinyl goods. The life-stories of people like Mr Heo vividly illustrate the role of foreign migrant labour in Japan's postwar economic miracle. Although the percentage of foreigners in Japan's workforce was low by comparison with other industrialized countries, there were certain corners of the economy where migrants from Korea came to play a central role. The tiny workshops of Ikuno-ku and surrounding districts constituted one of those corners. Mr Heo initially worked in a factory producing vinyl sheeting, and later in an industry which was largely pioneered by Korean migrant workers and entrepreneurs: the production of 'hep': slip-on sandals, very popular in the 1960s, which were modelled on those worn by Audrey Hepburn in the film *Roman Holiday* (hence the name 'hep').

According to a report published by the Immigration Bureau in 1975, most irregular migrants in Japan lived in the two major metropolitan areas: the Osaka–Kobe conurbation and the Tokyo–Yokohama conurbation: 'in particular, some 40% of them are believed to be living in Osaka'.[20] The main reason given for this concentration is the historical link between some Osaka districts and the Korean peninsula, more especially the link between Osaka and Jeju Island, which was a source of much irregular migration. This report estimates the number of undocumented migrants – people 'living hidden lives' (*senzai kyojūsha*) – in Japan in the mid-1970s at 'several tens of thousands'.[21] The precise figure, of course, was unknown, and until 1990 (when the Immigration Bureau began regularly publishing figures on visa overstayers) official publications rarely provided even estimated figures. In personal discussions with journalists or diplomats, however, government officials did sometimes attempt to put a number on the 'illegal-resident problem', though the numbers they came up with varied fairly widely.

In 1959, one national newspaper reported that immigration officials estimated the number of undocumented immigrants from Korea at around 50,000–60,000, while the police put the figure at about 200,000.[22] In the same year, the Japanese Ministry of Foreign Affairs also informed the US ambassador to Japan, Douglas MacArthur II, that the number of Korean illegal immigrants in Japan 'may now amount to as many as 200,000', while a senior local government official from Osaka suggested that the number of undocumented Korean migrants in his city was about 50,000 (suggesting a nationwide total of a little over 100,000).[23] It is likely that the figure fell somewhat in the early 1960s, as a considerable number of undocumented migrants probably chose to leave for North Korea under the resettlement scheme discussed in the following chapter. The precise number is unknown, but a letter from the head of Japan's Immigration Bureau to the Red Cross in 1962 makes it clear that by that date several thousand undocumented migrants from South Korea had already participated in this scheme with the knowledge and acquiescence of the Japanese government.[24]

The 1975 Immigration Bureau report notes that most undocumented migrants worked for low wages in firms with five employees or less, often in firms that were run by fellow Koreans. Their main areas of employment were the 'plastics, hep, machine, sheet metal and vinyl industries etc.' The instability of their situation was made worse by the fact that many were obliged to pay back loans which they had taken out in order to pay the people-smugglers who had brought them to Japan. Poverty, insecurity and concern for families back home persuaded many to hand themselves in to the immigration authorities: in the years from 1970 to 1974 over 40 per cent of those detained for illegal entry were people who had handed themselves in.[25]

But Mr Heo was not about to give up easily. Work, particularly in the vinyl factory, was very hard. 'The smell was terrible,' he says. 'In the hep factory where I work now it's bad enough, but in the vinyl factory it was even worse. The smell of the glue we use in hep making isn't so bad when you've got used to it, but to begin with I used to find it made me feel drunk, as though I'd been sniffing solvent.'[26] His working day began at eight in the morning and often did not finish until after midnight. Nevertheless, he was determined to make a success of his life in Japan. He married, had three children, and took out a loan to buy a house.

Meanwhile, an event had occurred which improved the situation of many Koreans in Japan, but made Mr Heo's situation more difficult than ever. In 1960 the Yi Seung-Man regime in South Korea was deposed by a popular uprising but, after a brief democratic interregnum, a military coup led by Park Chung-Hee ushered in a new dictatorship. Park was eager to improve relations with Japan and to gain an inflow of aid for his ambitious economic development plans. In 1965 Japan and the Republic of Korea finally signed a Treaty of Basic Relations. An agreement appended to the treaty gave colonial-period Korean migrants to Japan (and their descendants) special status as 'treaty permanent residents' (*Kyōtei Eijūsha*).[27] But, although this greatly improved their situation, the treaty also had many limitations. One of these was the fact that it did nothing to help the many Korean residents who had entered or re-entered Japan in the postwar period without official permission; indeed the agreement specified that the only people eligible to apply for treaty permanent residence were those who 'have lived in Japan permanently from before 15 August 1945 to the date of their application'.[28] As Heo recalls, irregular migrants like himself felt more insecure than ever once the accord had been concluded:

We knew we could be arrested at any moment. Particularly after the Japan–South Korea Treaty was signed, the Immigration Bureau became stricter than ever in cracking down on illegal migrants, because now they knew for sure that South Korea would accept the people they deported.[29]

His eldest child was still at kindergarten at the time when, after living in Japan for over twelve years, Heo was arrested one day on his way home from work, and charged with being an unregistered alien. After investigation and a brief court hearing, he was paroled, but despite his efforts to win the right to stay in Japan the deportation proceedings went ahead, and he was sent to Ōmura to await expulsion to Korea.

Meanwhile, Mr Heo's family and friends rallied to his cause. His father had lived in Japan before the war, and he had many relatives in Osaka, one of whom found a lawyer for him. Heo's wife visited the immigration office to plead his case, and members of the Ikuno-ku Korean community, as well as a local Japanese Christian pastor who assisted many people in similar situations, took up his case. They gathered letters of support from Mr Heo's workplace and his children's kindergarten, stressing that he was a law-abiding and hard-working man whose children had all been born in Japan, and whose family life would be torn apart if he were deported.

Mr Heo and his supporters also used a route commonly followed by people seeking special permission to stay in the 1960s and 1970s: they sought the assistance of a migration agent. Such agents were often former officials of the Immigration Bureau, and tended to set up their offices near local Immigration Bureau branches, often charging an 'introduction fee' of around one million yen (about US$2,800) to introduce the migrant to a politician who was willing to make representations on their behalf to the Ministry of Justice. The politicians might come either from the ruling Liberal Democratic Party or from opposition parties, though it seems that certain politicians with large numbers of foreign residents in their constituencies were particularly active in this process. In relatively long-drawn-out cases like Mr Heo's however, this initial payment to the agent might just be the beginning. Further fees were demanded as additional negotiations and meetings with politicians became necessary. After three years in Ōmura, Mr Heo was finally released, and not long after obtained permanent residence status in Japan. Now, for the first time, he was legally able to visit the family and friends he had left behind in Jeju. But the cost of this freedom had been high: he had lost his house in the process of finding money to pay the migration agent's fees.[30]

Even some immigration officials themselves raised concerns about the way the special permission system operated. Sakanaka Hidenori, who was then a middle-ranking official and was ultimately to become head of the Tokyo Immigration Bureau, noted that

for illegal migrants, whether they are deported to their own country or are able to remain in Japan is an issue which determines the entire course of their lives.

They therefore take desperate measures such as seeking to have influential power brokers [*yūryokusha*] take up their cases in order to obtain the special permission to stay from the Minister of Justice.[31]

The consequences were often very inequitable:

even though the period of their illegal entry and their family circumstances are almost identical, one foreigner may obtain special permission to stay because of lobbying by a member of parliament or other power broker, while another foreigner is forcibly deported. If such things take place, it is obvious to everyone that this must cause the foreigners concerned, and citizens in general, to experience an almost irreparable loss of confidence in the migration control system.[32]

UNDOCUMENTED MIGRANTS AND JAPANESE SUPPORT NETWORKS

Not all applicants for special permission to stay made use of migration agents and politicians. A further crucial element for those seeking residence rights in Japan (as evident also in the case of Mr Heo) was support from the local community. Researcher Koh Sun-Hui, in her studies of the Jeju islander community in Japan, has collected a mass of documents generated by the local groups formed in Osaka in the 1960s and 1970s to support the cause of undocumented migrants facing deportation.[33] In many cases, the migrants concerned had been in Japan for many years, and had stable jobs and children at local schools. The petitioners on their behalf included neighbours, employers, work colleagues, and members of the parents' and teachers' associations of schools attended by their children. Support groups sometimes organized rallies and petitions on behalf of those seeking special permission.

Typical of this support are letters addressed to the immigration authorities in 1984 by the neighbours and employer of a man who had been detained as an 'illegal migrant', and then temporarily released pending determination of his fate. The man had entered Japan as an undocumented migrant in 1969, and now lived in Osaka with his wife and young daughter. He had joined a very small printing works as one of its three employees in 1979. The firm's owner writes in his letter of testimony,

we start work at 8.30 a.m. and finish at 5.15 p.m., but X was always at work by 8.15 a.m., and did overtime every day until about 6.30 p.m. Moreover, in the five years he has worked here he never had a day's sick leave, and of course was never absent without reason … It came as bolt from the blue to hear that X had been detained. I want X to continue working for me, and have re-employed him since his release from detention.[34]

Such support could often be the decisive factor in determining the fate of the migrant, as suggested by 'Mr Jae's' memories of his struggle to remain in Japan. Mr Jae's family came from Jeju Island, but had migrated to Osaka in colonial times. His four older sisters were all born in Japan, and his mother was pregnant with her son when the family fled Osaka to escape wartime bombing raids, and returned to Jeju Island. Here they were overtaken by a particularly ironical tragedy. Because Jeju was home to many Japanese military bases during the war, Mr Jae's parents were concerned that the island itself would soon come under attack from US forces, so in the final months of the war his father decided to travel to the Korean mainland in search of a safer place for the family to live. On 7 May 1945, the ship on which he was travelling was hit by an Allied air raid, and Mr Jae's father, along with most of the other passengers, was killed. Japan's surrender came before US troops reached Korea, and Jeju Island in the end escaped wartime bombardment.[35]

For the Jae children, with no father, life was very harsh, and became even harder after their mother died at an early age, while her son was still in his mid-teens. The children of the family struggled to survive by farming their family's small plot of land, and the young Mr Jae became enthusiastically involved in the 4H movement, a rural improvement movement promoted in a number of Asian countries by US development agencies. He longed to study agriculture and work for rural development in Jeju. A few decades later, it might have been possible for a young man like Mr. Jae to win a scholarship to study abroad, but in the early 1960s such an idea was beyond the wildest dreams of a poor farm boy like Mr Jae.

In 1965, shortly before the signing of the treaty between Japan and South Korea, Jae decided to travel to Osaka, where he had relatives. By working there for a few years, he hoped to earn enough money to enrol in a Japanese agricultural college. Like others seeking places on people-smuggling boats to Japan, Mr Jae travelled to Busan, where he stayed near the port, while an acquaintance looked for a boat willing to take him to Japan.

As he recalls,

One morning this man who was helping me woke me up early.

'Get up quickly. You're leaving today,' he said. He took me by car to a café, where we had to wait for quite a long time. Then I was taken by car to the port. The man pointed to a boat and said, 'that's the boat you are going on.' Then he took me to a nearby restaurant and said 'wait here.'

I ate a meal, and waited and waited, but no one came. I was beginning to get anxious, and to think that maybe I had been tricked, but eventually I walked across to the boat and found the captain there waiting for me.

I had been warned not to pay until I got to the boat, otherwise I might be cheated. I was to pay half the money on boarding the boat, and another half when I arrived in Japan.

The captain gave me instructions. He warned that when we arrived, Japanese customs officers would come on board and try to trick any boat people who might be on board into giving themselves away. They would come on board and shout: 'It's safe, you can come out now.' The captain told me, 'don't say anything until I give you a signal.' Then he said, 'get into this space.'

I climbed into a cramped space in the very bottom of the boat. The boat was going to Japan to collect a cargo of shellfish, and I was the only *mikkōsha* on board. I had no idea what course the boat took. It left at about 8 p.m., and the sea was very rough. You know what the Genkai Sea is like [Here Mr Jae demonstrates the rise and fall of waves with his hand]. I was so seasick; I wanted to die, and thought 'I will *never never* do this again.'[36]

Although the captain had promised to take Jae all the way to Osaka, he was in fact unloaded at the port of Shimonoseki, and had to make his way alone to Osaka, where his relatives gave him a place to sleep and helped him to find work. He had hoped to find work on a Japanese farm, so that he could develop his agricultural skills, but soon discovered that this was impossible, and instead found himself working in a small steelworks. At first it was difficult to make friends, as he had to conceal the fact that he was an illegal immigrant, but after labouring on the family farm, he says, the work in the steel factory seemed 'really easy'. He adopted a Japanese name, 'Motoyama', and studied hard to become fluent in the language.

After several years in Osaka, Mr Jae moved to Tokyo, where he found work as an apprentice jeweller. He quickly learnt the skills of shaping precious metals, and was eventually able to set up his own small business making and selling rings. Soon after, he married and had a child. For Mr Jae, as for many other undocumented entrants to Japan, this was the point at which difficult decisions had to be made. In order to register the child's birth, it was necessary to fill in a form which included details of family registration or, for foreigners, a space for the parents' alien registration number. Jae, who had no alien registration card, decided that the only course was to leave this space on the form blank, thus providing the authorities with a clear signal that he was an illegal migrant.

For three months [Mr Jae recollects] nothing happened. Maybe the authorities were waiting for me to hand myself in. Then one day, I had come back late from

work and was eating dinner at about 10 o'clock in the evening when there was a
loud knock at the door. I went to the door and there was a group of men. One
asked, 'are you Mr Motoyama?'

I realized what was about to happen. 'We are from Immigration,' said the
man, showing his ID. There were four immigration officials and a driver. The
officials came into the house. The baby woke up and started screaming. My wife
was very anxious, and I tried to calm her. The men took me away in an ordinary
unmarked car to the old Shinagawa Immigration Office.[37]

He was detained for a week in the holding cells of the Shinagawa office,
sharing one of two *tatami*-matted rooms with about fifteen or twenty
other people, many of whom were Chinese from Southeast Asia (probably attempting to escape from anti-Chinese movements then sweeping
Indonesia and Malaysia). Since the cells were overcrowded, he was then
transferred to Kawasaki Detention Centre for two weeks, before returning to Shinagawa. The attitude of the immigration officials was initially
rather contemptuous (he recalls) but gradually became polite as his friends
began to lobby on his behalf.

Mr Jae tried to tell his story straightforwardly and truthfully to the
immigration officials, hoping that his steady job and family life would
help to win him clemency. The officials advised him against consulting a lawyer, warning that it would cost a large amount of money and
make the Immigration Bureau regard him with even greater suspicion.
He did, however, get outside support from another quarter. Before his
arrest Jae had been involved in voluntary work, helping day labourers in Tokyo. Through this work he had come to know a network of
Japanese social activists who now rallied to support him, drawing up a
petition on his behalf which was signed by Christian ministers, university professors and others. This support seems to have been a key factor
in securing his freedom. As soon as his supporters began to contact
the authorities, Jae recalls, the attitude of Immigration Bureau staff
changed from brusque officiousness to politeness. Some weeks after his
arrest, Jae was released on parole, but restricted from travelling outside
the Tokyo area; and the following year, some fourteen years after his
arrival in Japan, he received special permission to stay. Initially, this
took the form of a residence permit which had to be renewed every
three years, but eventually he was allowed to convert it to special permanent residence.

One of the best things about regularizing his position, Jae says, is
that he was able to take back his real name. 'Getting rid of the name
Motoyama,' he says, 'gave me a sense of freedom. While I was using it, I

always felt that I was concealing my true self, even from close friends, and I felt as though I could never really be myself.'

REFUGEES AND THE LAW

Migration agents, lawyers and lobbying by support groups all helped undocumented migrants to obtain discretionary permission to stay in Japan, but by the 1960s some unauthorized entrants were also starting to attempt another, much more difficult and uncertain, route to permanent residence: appeals to Japanese and international law. Japan did not ratify the Geneva Convention on the Status of Refugees until 1981, but (as we have seen) as early as the postwar occupation period some of those fleeing to Japan from the Asian continent had asked the Occupation authorities or the Japanese government for political asylum. During the 1960s, asylum seekers began to take a new approach, appealing to the Japanese courts to invalidate their deportation orders on the grounds that expulsion from Japan violated fundamental human rights.

The recourse to legal action was partly a response to political developments in Korea. After the brief wave of democratization which followed the fall of the Yi Seung-Man regime, the establishment of the Park Chung-Hee dictatorship in March 1961 brought with it a new wave of repression. In August of that year, a South Korean military court handed down death sentences on three journalists accused of subversion for having promoted closer ties between North and South Korea and advocated Korean reunification. The case created shockwaves throughout the region, and was one of the factors behind the establishment on 20 August 1962 of a Committee for Republic of Korea Political Refugees in Japan. The Committee was made up mainly of Koreans in Japan, but its secretary-general, Pak Duk-Man, noted that the problem of South Korean refugees had also been debated in the Japanese Diet, and that 'the Japanese public also has come round to show deep concern towards the issue'.[38] In fact, around the same time a group of Japanese lawyers and Socialist Party politicians including Inomata Kōzō and Eda Saburō formed a study group to examine the South Korean refugee problem.[39]

The manifesto of the Committee for Republic of Korea Political Refugees in Japan demanded that:

1. The Japanese government shall immediately suspend expatriation of South Korean refugees in Japan.

2. The Japanese government shall not use South Korean refugees in the negotiations such as the ROK–Japan normalization talks for the purpose of strengthening Japan's position in the negotiations.

3. The Japanese government shall offer proper treatment to all South Korean refugees in Japan based on the international convention; and also safeguard the rights and interests and promote improvement of living standards and status of ROK refugees in Japan.[40]

Pak Duk-Man suggested that, at the time of the Committee's creation, as many as 250 political refugees were trying to enter Japan from South Korea each month, 'about half of whom succeed in reaching Japan and smuggling themselves into this country. The other half are intercepted by the Japanese maritime forces and detained temporarily at Ōmura until repatriation to ROK'. Reporting on his discussions with Pak, ICRC representative in Tokyo Harry Angst noted,

These political refugees are obviously scared to death of the prospect of being forcibly repatriated to South Korea as long as the present military regime remains in power. Their wish is to be permitted to remain in Japan until such time as the administration of the country has reverted to truly democratic hands.[41]

While the plight of refugees from countries such as Hungary and China was receiving worldwide attention, Pak argued, South Korean refugees were ignored by governments and media alike.[42]

One of the main roles of the Committee for Republic of Korea Political Refugees in Japan was to support court cases brought by asylum seekers, the first of which was launched in the Tokyo District Court at the start of 1963 by Ōmura detainee Yoon Soo-Gil. Yoon had entered Japan in the late 1940s, and was a researcher at the University of Tokyo when, twelve years after arriving in the country, he was arrested for being an unregistered foreigner.[43] Like the three journalists executed the previous year, he was an outspoken advocate of the peaceful reunification of North and South Korea, and feared that, if deported, he would share their fate.

Yoon and his supporters, together with several others seeking asylum in Japan, also appealed to the Japan Red Cross Society (JRC), the International Committee of the Red Cross (ICRC) and the United Nations High Commissioner for Refugees (UNHCR) for support. The response, however, was cautious. The JRC asked the asylum seekers to present prima facie evidence that they faced persecution if they returned to Korea. This carefully documented evidence was then passed on to the Japanese government, which failed to respond.[44] The ICRC expressed sympathy and gathered useful information on the case, but argued that it was really a matter for the UNHCR. The UNHCR, meanwhile, pointed out that the Geneva Convention on the Status of Refugees only covered people displaced by events in Europe before 1951, so did not apply to Yoon Soo-Gil and his fellow asylum seekers. A UNHCR official did, however, offer to make informal representations to the Japanese government on their behalf, and the organization agreed to provide some funds for Yoon's legal team.[45]

Within Japan, the refugees gained the support of (amongst others) socialist parliamentarian Inomata Kōzō. With this backing, they launched a court case asking for Yoon's deportation order to be revoked on the grounds that it was a violation of the human rights enshrined both in the Japanese Constitution and in international law. The Japanese legal system, however, is notoriously slow-moving, and Yoon's court case proved painfully long-drawn-out. In March 1963 Yoon was released from Ōmura because of ill health, but more than three years later, after ten meetings between his lawyers and the judges hearing the case, his case had still not been decided. It was not until 1969 that the Tokyo District Court ruled in favour of Yoon. But, as often happens in Japan, the government then appealed, and the case went to the Tokyo High Court and ultimately to Japan's Supreme Court, both of which reversed the lower court decision. The final rejection of Yoon's appeal was handed down in 1976 – fifteen years after his arrest and twenty-seven years after his entry into Japan. Ultimately, however, he was not deported. Perhaps for humanitarian reasons or perhaps to avoid political controversy, the minister of justice used his discretionary power to grant Yoon Soo-Gil special permission to stay in Japan.[46]

Yoon was relatively lucky. Other asylum seekers received much shorter shrift. In 1962, for example, a Chinese interpreter named Zhou Hongjing came to Japan with a delegation from the People's Republic of China. While in Tokyo, he defected from the mission and asked to be sent to the Republic of China (Taiwan). In response, the Japanese government placed him in a Red Cross hospital under close surveillance. He remained there for several months, while both the PRC and Taiwanese governments lobbied Japan to hand him over. In January 1963, Zhou was escorted onto a ship under heavy guard, and returned to mainland China. Whether he had changed his mind about defecting, or whether Japan (which was then developing trade ties with the PRC) had bowed to political pressure remains unclear, as does the fate which Zhou encountered on his return home.[47]

The Zhou case, however, evidently did not represent any bias towards the People's Republic of China. Until 1972, Japan had diplomatic relations only with Chiang Kai-shek's Republic of China in Taiwan, and during the 1960s Japan also responded to requests from the Chiang Kai-shek regime by unceremoniously deporting several Taiwanese activists who had formed a Taiwan independence movement in Tokyo.[48] All in all, it is not surprising that those who sought refuge from persecution in Japan's relatively liberal society often chose to seek the discretionary residence rights offered by special permission to stay, rather than pursuing the long and perilous path of claiming asylum under international law.

Even today, refugee recognition continues to be a complex and contentious area. In 1981 Japan ratified the Geneva Convention on the Status of Refugees, and in 1982 a revised Immigration Control Law, now called the Immigration Control and Refugee Recognition Law, came into force (see Chapter Nine below). Yet still, more than quarter of a century after the ratification of the Geneva Convention, far more foreigners obtain residence rights through special permission than under the refugee recognition system: in 2006, a year when 9,360 people were granted special permission to stay, the number of people officially granted asylum was just 34.[49]

Amongst those who inhabit the shadowy world created by discretionary policies today are a growing number of refugees from North Korea. To date, while tens of thousands of refugees have crossed the border out of North Korea, fleeing hunger, poverty and political repression, not one North Korean refugee has been granted asylum under Japan's refugee recognition process. Yet, very quietly, the Japanese government has given discretionary residence rights to almost two hundred recent arrivals from North Korea. The number is likely to grow in coming years. To understand this curious 'backdoor' flow of refugees into Japan, it is necessary to understand its historical origins, which lie in the Cold War politics of the 1950s and 1960s, and are indeed entangled with the question of the South Korean refugees discussed in this chapter. Indeed, as we shall see, the repatriation plans of the Cold War era not only transformed the nature of Japan's foreigner population, but also had consequences which continue to haunt Japan's migration and border control policies into the twenty-first century.

NOTES

1. Shin Chang-Seok, 'Fuse Tatsuji Sensei no Omoide', in Fuji Shinji, *Shokuminchi Kankei Shiryōshū 2: Chōsen, Taiwan Hen* (Tokyo: Fuji Shinji Shiryō Kenkyū Junbikai, 2006), pp. 181–99, citation from pp. 184–5 (copy kindly provided by the author).

2. Ibid., p. 185.
3. Ibid., p. 187.
4. On the impact of nationalist education on young Koreans in wartime, see also Kim Shi-Jong, *Waga Sei to Shi* (Tokyo: Iwanami Shoten, 2004), pp. 5–17.
5. Shin, 'Fuse Tatsuji Sensei', p. 183.
6. Ibid., p. 184.
7. Inaba Nanako, 'Furansu ni okeru Hiseiki Taizaisha to Amunesti: "Sanpapie no Undō" to Shimin Shakai kara no Taiō', in Komai Hiroshi, Watado Ichirō and Yamawaki Keizō (eds.), *Chōka Taizai Gaikokujin to Zairyū Tokubetsu Kyoka: Kiro ni Tatsu nihon no Shutsunyūkoku Kanri Seisaku* (Tokyo: Akashi Shoten, 2000) pp. 36–43, citation from p. 37; Kondō Atsushi, 'Zairyū Tokubetsu Kyoka no Hōteki Konkyo: Kenpō, Kokusai Jinkenhō jō no Kenri to "Kokusai Kijun"', in Komai, Watado and Yamawaki, *Chōka Taizai Gaikokujin*, pp. 52–60, citation from p. 57.
8. Kondō, 'Zairyū Tokubetsu Kyoka', p. 58.
9. See Migration Watch UK, *A Review of Exceptional Leave to Remain and Humanitarian Protection*, briefing paper 9.4, 2003 www.migrationwatchuk.com/archive/migration_trends/exceptional_leave_to_remain.asp (accessed 7 July 2008).
10. Hōmushō Nyūkoku Kanrikyoku, *Shutsunyūkoku Kanri no Kaikō to Tenbō: Nyūkan Hasoku 30-Shūnen o Kinen shite* (Tokyo: Hōmushō Nyūkoku Kanrikyoku, 1980), p. 157.
11. Hōmushō Nyūkoku Kanrikyoku, *Shutsunyūkoku Kanri: Sono Genkyō to Kadai* (Tokyo: Ōkurashō Insatsukyoku, 1975), p. 135.
12. Watado Ichirō and Suzuki Eriko (eds.), *Zairyū Tokubetsu Kyoka to Nihon no Imin Seisaku: 'Imin Senbetsu' Jidai no Tōrai* (Tokyo: Akashi Shoten, 2007), p. 19.
13. Ibid., pp. 19–20.
14. See Watado and Suzuki, *Zairyū Tokubetsu Kyoka*; S. A. M. Shahed and Sekiguchi Chie, *Shinpan Zairyū Tokubetsu Kyoka: Ajia-kei Gaikokujin to no Ōbāsutei Kokusai Kekkon* (Tokyo: Akashi Shoten, 2002).
15. Hōmushō Nyūkoku Kanrikyoku, *Shutsunyūkoku Kanri to sono Jittai* (Tokyo: Ōkurashō Insatsukyoku, 1964), pp. 101–2; see also letter from Seishiro Ogawa, director, Immigration Bureau, Justice Ministry, to Masutaro Inoue, director, Foreign Affairs Department, Japan Red Cross Society, 'South Korean Political Refugees in Japan (Reply)' 2 November 1962 (English translation), in ICRC Archives, file B AG 234 056–003, *Réfugiés politiques sud-coréens au Japon*, 15.09.1962–26.06.1966.
16. For further details on *Chōsen seki* and *Kankoku seki*, see pp. 93–4.
17. Shin, 'Fuse Tatsuji Sensei', pp. 190–1.
18. Ibid, p. 193.
19. Ibid, pp. 193–4.
20. Hōmushō Nyūkoku Kanrikyoku, *Shutsunyūkoku Kanri: Sono Genkyō to Kadai* (Tokyo: Hōmushō Nyūkoku Kanrikyoku, 1975), p. 125.
21. Ibid., p. 121.

22. *Asahi Shinbun*, 16 June 1959. The Japanese Ministry of Foreign Affairs also informed US Ambassador Douglas MacArthur II in 1959 that the number of Korean illegal immigrants in Japan 'may now amount to as many as 200,000'.

23. Telegram from MacArthur, embassy, Tokyo, to Secretary of State, 30 November 1959, in NARA, College Park, decimal file 294.9522/11–3059; dispatch from US Consulate General, Kobe–Osaka, to US Department of State, Washington, 15 September 1959, in NARA, College Park, 694.95B/9–1959.

24. See letter from Seishiro Ogawa to Masutaro Inoue, 'South Korean Political Refugees in Japan (Reply)'.

25. Hōmushō Nyūkoku Kanrikyoku, *Shutsunyūkoku Kanri: Sono Genkyō to Kadai*, p. 126.

26. Interview with 'Heo Man-Sik', Osaka, 19 January 2005.

27. In 1991, 'treaty permanent residence' was replaced by the rather more comprehensive 'special permanent residence' status. See Kim Il-Hwa, 'Zainichi Chōsenjin no Hōteki Chii', in Pak Jeong-Myeong (ed.), *Zainichi Chōsenjin: Rekishi, Genjō, Tenbō* (Tokyo: Akashi Shoten, 1995), pp. 189–232, citation from p. 210.

28. Quoted in Yoshitome Roju, *Ōmura Chōsenjin Shūyōjo* (Tokyo: Nigatsusha, 1977), p. 38.

29. Interview with 'Mr Heo', Osaka, 19 January 2005.

30. Ibid.

31. Sakanaka Hidenori, *Kongo no Shutsunyūkoku Kanri Gyōsei no Arikata ni tsuite* (Tokyo: Nihon Kajo Shuppan, 1989), p. 137 (originally published in 1977).

32. Ibid.

33. Koh Sun-Hui, *Senzai Kyojūsha Shiryōshū*, unpublished appendix to Koh Sun-Hui, *20 Seiki no Tainichi Chejudōjin* (Tokyo: Akashi Shoten, 1998).

34. Letter reproduced in Koh Sun-Hui, *Senzai Kyojūsha Shiryōshū*, p. 113, quoted with kind permission of the author; See also Koh Sun-Hui, *20 Seiki no Tainichi Chejudōjin*, p. 210.

35. Interview with 'Mr Jae', Tokyo, 12 January 2007.

36. Ibid.

37. Ibid.

38. See letter from Pak Duk-Man to Léopold Boissier, International Committee of the Red Cross, 15 September 1962, and memo from H. Angst to J.-P. Maunoir, 'South Korean Political Refugees in Japan', 1 November 1962, both in ICRC Archives, B AG 234 056–003.

39. *Japan Times*, 2 December 1962.

40. 'Proclamation: Inaugurating Committee for ROK Political Refugees in Japan', 20 August 1962, in ICRC Archives, B AG 234 056–003.

41. Memo from H. C. Angst to J. P. Maunoir, 1 November 1962.

42. Letter from Pak Duk-Man to Léopold Boissier, 15 September 1962.

43. Osamu Arakaki, *Refugeee Law and Practice in Japan* (London: Ashgate, 2008), p. 13.

44. M. Testuz to ICRC Geneva, 4 October 1963, in ICRC Archives, B AG 234 056–003.
45. See minutes of meeting between Mr Jahn, UNHCR and J.-P. Maunoir, ICRC, 16 December 1963, in ICRC Archives, B AG 234 056–003.
46. Arakaki, *Refugeee Law and Practice in Japan*, p. 13.
47. See M. Testuz to J.-P. Maunoir, 11 November 1963, and M. Testuz to J.-P. Maunoir, 21 January 1964, both in ICRC Archives B AG 251 105–009.02, *Correspondance reçue du 12 juin 1962 au 21 janvier 1966*, 12.06.1962–21.01.1966.
48. One of those deported was placed on a plane to Taipei one day after being arrested as a visa overstayer, despite his pleas to be allowed to remain in Japan. The Tokyo District Court later ruled that his deportation had been in breach of the law, and ordered the government to pay compensation to the deportee's familty. See R. Mukae, *Japan's Refugee Policy: To Be of the World* (Fucecchio: European Press Academic Publishing, 2001), p. 101; also Yamazaki Shigeki, *Shutsunyūkoku Kanri: Gendai no 'Sakoku'* (Tokyo: Sanseidō, 1970), pp. 18–28.
49. See UNHCR, *Statistical Yearbook 2006* (Geneva, UNHCR, 2006), statistical annex, Table 6; Letter from Seishiro Ogawa, director, Immigration Bureau, Justice Ministry, to Masutaro Inoue, director, Foreign Affairs Department, Japan Red Cross Society. Nyūkoku Kanrikyoku, *Nyūkoku Kanri 2007*, www.moj.go.jp/NYUKAN/nyukan67–2.pdf.

CHAPTER 8

A point of no return

Repatriation to China and North Korea

GOING HOME

After the mass repatriations which immediately followed Japan's defeat in war, the flow of people across the seas from Japan to the Asian mainland subsided. The establishment of the People's Republic of China, the outbreak of the Korean War and the rise of Cold War tensions all made continued repatriation of former colonial subjects from Japan more difficult. Meanwhile, the South Korean government showed no enthusiasm for accepting a further return of Koreans from Japan. The ROK was struggling with poverty, high unemployment and the after-effects of the Korean War; besides, the Yi Seung-Man regime suspected the loyalty and ideological inclinations of Koreans in Japan. Ever since Prime Minister Yoshida's calls for mass deportations in 1950, however, there had been those in the Japanese government who were eager to reduce the number of foreigners in Japan, if not by deportation, then at least by encouraging voluntary repatriation, and in the late 1950s, as Japan tentatively began to open economic links to some of its communist neighbours, the issue of repatriation once again came to the surface.

The repatriation question wove together many of the themes that we have encountered in this book. Its defining context was the Cold War. Repatriation to China was a product of the internal politics of migration control, of Japan's changing relationship with its largest Asian neighbour, and of the growing role of international organizations, particularly the Red Cross, in East Asian cross-border migrations. The mass resettlement of *Zainichi* Koreans in North Korea was also profoundly influenced by Japan's relations with the Cold War superpowers. Though these departures did not, in the end, bring about the disappearance of the migrant communities in Japan, they did have consequences – some of them tragic – which cast a continued shadow over issues of migration in Japan today.

Throughout the twenty-five years following the end of the Asia–Pacific War, Japan's migration control policies focused mainly on the Korean community in Japan. But policies towards *Zainichi* Koreans were also closely interconnected with policies towards the smaller Chinese community in Japan, and these connections became particularly evident where the vexed questions of deportation and repatriation were concerned.

THE HAMAMATSU RIOT AND REPATRIATION TO CHINA

Hamamatsu Detention Centre was opened in December 1954 to house the overflow of Koreans from Ōmura and Chinese from Yokohama.[1] It was a converted prison consisting of wooden barracks, together with some workshops which had been turned into dormitories for women detainees. A contemporary account paints a somewhat gloomy picture of the Hamamatsu compound: 'a high wall of about 5 meters surrounds the buildings and the sun beams do not enter, consequently all the rooms are rather dark and damp and chilly always'.[2] By reducing overcrowding, however, it was hoped that the new centre would diminish the risk of unrest. But on the morning of 4 November 1955, a large-scale riot broke out at Hamamatsu as Chinese detainees fought with guards to prevent the deportation of five of their compatriots. Seventeen people were arrested, including several members of Chinese community associations who had been in contact with the detainees in the days leading up to the incident.

The Hamamatsu riot highlighted the impact of Cold War tensions on the movement of people between Japan and neighbouring countries. In 1952, Japan had a registered Chinese population of around 44,000 (though, as in the case of Koreans in Japan, this understated the real figure, since some Chinese residents were unregistered).[3] But China, like Korea, was divided by the Cold War. Almost half of the Chinese in Japan came from the former Japanese colony of Taiwan, to which nationalist leader Chiang Kai-shek had fled following the Communist revolution on the mainland, establishing the Republic of China (ROC). The remainder (including some who had been conscripted as forced labourers during the war) came from mainland China. There were, however, Chinese originating from Taiwan who identified with the mainland People's Republic of China (PRC) for political reasons, and vice versa.

Since Japan had political relations only with Chiang Kai-shek's ROC, this was the only place to which it could officially deport Chinese arrested for illegal entry or for other offences. But some of those awaiting deportation in Yokohama and Hamamatsu came from the mainland, and risked persecution and separation from their families if deported to Taiwan. In other words, the problems of the Cold War divide that beset the Korean community in Japan were replicated in the Chinese community. There was a significant difference between the two cases, though, for Japan's political relationship with the two Chinas was better than its relationship with the two Koreas. The Chiang Kai-shek regime was vulnerable and embattled, and needed the friendship and economic support of Japan. Many Japanese businesses, meanwhile, were very eager to re-establish relations with the vast market of mainland China, and although Japan did not officially recognize Mao Zedong's People's Republic of China, a range of informal economic and cultural ties had been created between the two countries.

The origins of improving relations between Japan and the PRC can be traced back to an agreement reached between the Red Cross Societies of China and Japan in 1953 to bring back to Japan some of the thousands of Japanese people (including prisoners of war) who had remained in mainland China after Japan's defeat in 1945. As part of this deal, the Chinese government also asked Japan to repatriate Chinese residents in Japan who wished to return to the PRC, and whose number was variously estimated at anywhere between seven hundred and two thousand.[4] The Japanese government readily agreed to this request since it offered a way of resolving the problem of pro-PRC Chinese detainees held in Yokohama and Hamamatsu detention centres. Early in 1955, an informal arrangement was made with ninety of these detainees, under which they would be released from detention on condition that they promised to board a Red Cross repatriation ship which was soon to leave for mainland China.

However, it quickly became clear that many detainees wanted above all to remain in Japan: when the day came for the repatriation ship to sail, only thirty-eight of the ninety released detainees turned up to board it, the rest having disappeared into the Japanese community.[5] Soon after, three of the missing detainees were picked up by police and returned to custody in Hamamatsu. This time, the authorities were determined to allow no chance of escape. Despite their place of origin and political views, the three were scheduled for forcible deportation to Taiwan. Chinese community associations became aware of the three men's plight, and began to lobby the authorities on their behalf, and it was on the day when the three were due to be deported that their fellow detainees in Hamamatsu rioted in protest.[6]

The riot produced shockwaves which were felt well beyond the walls of Hamamatsu Detention Centre. Amongst those arrested for complicity

in inciting the riot were four members of the Chinese community in
Japan who had themselves been planning to leave on a repatriation ship
in November 1955. They were detained by Japanese police at Nagoya railway station in the company of a fifth man, Hong Jinshan, who had been
sent by the Taiwanese government to Japan for police training, but had
decided that he wanted to defect to the PRC. When the news of the arrests
reached the wider Chinese community, they evoked a wave of protests.
The Chinese repatriates due to travel on the next repatriation ship for
China staged a sit-down strike in sympathy, refusing to board their ship
until their fellow travellers were released. It took much complex negotia-
tion to broker a solution to the stand-off. In the end all those arrested for
involvement in the Hamamatsu riots were released and allowed to return
to the PRC.[7]

THE PROBLEM OF REPATRIATION TO NORTH KOREA

The agreement reached with the Communist regime in mainland China
to 'exchange' returning Japanese for departing Chinese foreshadowed
and influenced a much larger, more complex and potentially politically
explosive scheme: a plan to send large numbers of Koreans from Japan to
Communist North Korea.

This project was intensely contentious for several reasons. First, as we
have seen, the great majority of Koreans in Japan originated from South
Korea, and even though a substantial number were politically sympathetic to North Korea, most had no roots or relatives there. Second, the
numbers involved were very uncertain, but some Japanese officials certainly had in mind a figure much greater than the number of returnees to
the People's Republic of China. The problem of numbers was highlighted
by sociologist Pak Jae-Il, himself a member of the *Zainichi* Korean community, in a study published in 1957.

As Pak pointed out, most Koreans in Japan in the 1950s hoped to
return to Korea at some point in the future. However, there was a large
gap between this somewhat abstract longing for home and any real
plan by *Zainichi* Koreans to uproot themselves from the lives they had
established in Japan and set off for an uncertain future in a still-divided
Korea.[8] By the mid-1950s there were at least several hundred, and perhaps
over a thousand, Koreans in Japan who expressed an active wish to be
repatriated to North Korea as soon as possible: in testimony given to a
committee of the Japanese parliament, officials of the pro-North Korean
General Association of Korean Residents in Japan cited the number at

the end of 1955 as 1,424, though the officials expected this number to rise considerably in the future, since they believed that many more would choose to 'return home' if travel between the two countries became easier.[9] It was very unclear, though, how many of the thousands more who felt vaguely sympathetic to the vision of a socialist Korea, and who sometimes voiced a longing to 'go home', were really expressing a concrete desire to leave Japan and live the rest of their lives in the communist DPRK.

A third element which turned the repatriation issue into a political minefield was the fact that the South Korean government claimed all Koreans in Japan as its citizens, and adamantly refused to countenance any repatriation to the DPRK. There were even fears that the South Korean navy might attack ships attempting to carry groups of repatriates to the DPRK.[10] The attitude of the North Korean regime was also uncertain. North Korea was still struggling to recover from the devastation of the Korean War, and although its government wanted to promote certain forms of cross-border movement, the North Korean and Japanese approaches to the problem of repatriation were significantly different.

In 1954 pro-North Korean activists in Japan, evidently with the blessing of the DPRK regime, embarked on a campaign to encourage Koreans in Japan who had specialized technical skills to volunteer for work on reconstruction projects in North Korea. Since there was no official means of travel between Japan and North Korea at that time, they also began to lobby the Japanese government to grant travel permits to the five hundred to a thousand technical experts whom they hoped to recruit. By 1955, the North Korean government – and particularly its foreign minister Nam Il – was taking a growing interest in the plight of Koreans in Japan, and at the end of that year Nam sent a long message to the Japanese government asking it to improve the welfare and educational conditions of *Zainichi* Koreans. In this message, he demanded that Japan should accede to the requests of all Ōmura detainees who wished to go to North Korea instead of being deported to the South.[11] This demand coincided rather well with the interests of the Japanese government. Sending some Ōmura detainees to North Korea, just as some had been sent to mainland China, would be a way of resolving the crisis in the overcrowded detention centre. The North Korean government also expressed its willingness to accept students who had graduated from pro-North Korean high schools in Japan and wanted to enter college or university in the DPRK.

But there was another group of Koreans whose departure for North Korea would be particularly welcome in the eyes of many members of the Japanese establishment: the poor, especially those Koreans who were both poor and left-wing. In the mid-1950s, as the Japanese economy moved from postwar recovery towards high growth, there were many Koreans in Japan who remained impoverished and were either unemployed or employed in marginal areas of the economy. Information compiled by the Japanese Red Cross in consultation with government ministries in 1956 emphasized the large number of Koreans who were either wholly jobless, working as day labourers or employed in areas such as illegal alcohol brewing, running pinball (*pachinko*) or garbage collecting.[12] The information also pointed out that relatively large numbers of Koreans received Livelihood Protection (*Seikatsu Hogo*) – the basic welfare payments made by the Japanese government to the destitute.[13]

The government's 1952 decision to define Koreans and Taiwanese in Japan as 'foreigners' had left them without a legal right to claim welfare, but Livelihood Protection continued to be provided on a discretionary basis, probably because the Japanese authorities feared that social disorder might erupt if these payments were cancelled altogether. There were, however, many in government circles who saw this as an imposition, and were eager to find ways of decreasing the scale of welfare payments to non-Japanese. In the discomfortingly blunt words of a Japan Red Cross study (produced in consultation with the relevant Japanese government ministries),

Frankly speaking, it is for the interest of the Japanese government to get rid of these troublesome Koreans. The Japanese government is spending about 2.4 billion yen to support their livelihood. No country is obliged to keep a foreigner at the expense of the national treasury. A foreigner unable to earn his living is usually deported.[14]

The report argued that the ideal solution would be for the Japanese government to 'deport all the Koreans residing in Japan to Korea … just as the Polish government deported all Germans to East Prussia', since this would 'eliminate the seeds of eventual disputes that might cause a trouble between Japan and Korea in future', as well as helping to solve problems of Japanese overpopulation.[15]

But the report's author, Japan Red Cross Director of Foreign Affairs Inoue Masutarō, went on to acknowledge that since Japan was a democratic country, it was not in fact possible to deport all Koreans against their will. His comments make it clear, though, that it would be a source of considerable satisfaction in official circles if impoverished Koreans could be persuaded to leave of their own accord.

The same point was made very clear a couple of years later, at the height of the repatriation debate, by Japanese Foreign Minister Fujiyama

Aiichirō in a confidential conversation with US ambassador to Tokyo Douglas MacArthur II. As MacArthur reported the conversation in a telegram to Washington, Fujiyama explained that the

prospect of ridding country of Korean minority is highly popular in view of their high crime rate, their political agitation and their pressure on the labour market. One of principle factors favouring repatriation has been that of internal security, Fujiyama said. With increasing agitation from pro-Communist Koreans in Japan, problem of controlling demonstrations and preventing riots has been special concern of public safety authorities and Justice Ministry ...

Other factors concern both expense and legality of policy Japan has followed since end of war. Burden of destitute Koreans on Japanese govt. institutions at all levels totals 2.5 billion yen annually.[16]

But would they volunteer to go? And even if they did, where would they go to? South Korea refused to take them back unless Japan paid substantial compensation for colonization, and in the mid-1950s there was no indication from the North Korean side of any enthusiasm to accept a mass of Koreans from Japan either.

A PLAN FOR RESOLVING THE PROBLEM

It was in this context that the Japanese government began to explore ways of implementing a mass repatriation of Koreans from Japan to North Korea. As newly declassified Japanese documents reveal, the first moves can be traced as far back as September 1953.

In that month Li Chang-Yeon, a central figure in a left-wing and pro-North Korean organization called the *Zainichi* Korean Unified Democratic Front (Zainichi Chōsenjin Tōitsu Minshu Sensen, generally known as Minsen for short), approached the Japanese government with a request for a travel permit which would enable him to attend a conference in China. Japanese intelligence, however, discovered that Li was really planning to travel via China to North Korea, where he intended to hold talks with government officials about the situation of Koreans in Japan. Armed with this information, the Immigration Bureau, in consultation with the Foreign Ministry, police and National Security Bureau, took a most unusual step. It entered into a secret agreement with Li, under which he would be given a travel permit on the understanding that he would try to persuade the North Korean government to accept a mass repatriation of Koreans from Japan. It was essential, though, that this agreement remain strictly confidential, for fear of a fierce backlash from South Korea. To the great dismay of the Japanese authorities, just before his departure, Li gave a press conference at which he revealed crucial parts of his mission. The agreement with Li was hastily abandoned, and his travel permit was revoked.[17]

This, however, was merely the beginning the story. In 1955, Minsen was dissolved and succeeded by a new pro-North Korean organization, the General Association of Korean Residents in Japan (Chongryun in Korean, Sōren in Japanese). Unlike Minsen, which had sought to promote revolution within Japan, Chongryun officially avoided involvement in Japanese politics, and encouraged its members to identify themselves as citizens of the Democratic People's Republic of Korea. However, even more than Minsen, the new association developed inseparable links with the North Korean government, and over time came to operate in effect as a branch of the Kim Il-Sung regime in Japan. For that reason it was, and still is, regarded with profound suspicion by many in Japan, who see it as the instrument of an alien and hostile communist state.

Some six months after the founding of Chongryun, the Fifth Section of the Asia Bureau of Japan's Ministry of Foreign Affairs produced a secret 'Plan for Dealing with the Sending to North Korea of Those Who Wish to Be Repatriated' (Hokusen e no Kikan Kibōsha no Sōkan Shori Hōshin[18]). This is particularly fascinating because of the emphasis it places on cooperation between, on the one side, the Japanese government and Japan Red Cross Society and, on the other, Chongryun. The plan aimed to establish a repatriation agreement between Japan and North Korea, similar to the one signed between Japan and the People's Republic of China. As in the Chinese case, the agreement was to be signed not between governments, but between the Red Cross Societies of both countries. Part of the Foreign Ministry document, apparently giving some details of the people to be sent to North Korea, still remains secret more than half a century after the event: it has been blacked out in the publicly released version. However, the declassified sections (despite their quintessentially bureaucratic prose) make absorbing reading.[19]

The plan sets out 'Outline Sending Procedures (Proposed)', according to which the Japanese government would pay the costs of transporting departing Koreans to their port of embarkation, while the North Korean Red Cross would be responsible for providing ships to convey them to Korea. The proposed procedures also spelled out the large part in the repatriation which the ministry envisaged for the newly established Chongryun. The ministry explicitly recognized the advantages of using this body as a key partner in the repatriation.

The exodus was to be carried out (in the words of the Foreign Ministry plan) 'on the basis of a register of volunteers for repatriation drawn up by Chōsen Sōren [Chongryun]'. Only those on Chongryun's register would be allowed to leave for the DPRK. The association was also to issue its own 'repatriation certificates' (*kikan shōmeisho*), which would be imprinted with an exit stamp by the Immigration Bureau as each departing Korean left. The Japan Red Cross Society, meanwhile, was instructed to 'use Chōsen Sōren as its partner, and request the organization's cooperation in the above matters. The two organizations will exchange documents to confirm the correct conduct of each item of business.'[20] The plan also specified that 'those to be repatriated will be impoverished people [*seikatsu konkyūsha*] only'.

It is unclear whether (as the Ministry of Foreign Affairs proposed) the Japan Red Cross Society and Chongryun did in fact enter into a written agreement on repatriation. However, in a letter written the following month, Inoue Masutarō (who had recently joined the Japan Red Cross Society after a career in the Ministry of Foreign Affairs) confirmed that his organization was planning to pursue the repatriation by seeking a 'mutual understanding' with Chongryun. He also pointed out that the ruling Japanese Liberal Democratic Party had recently taken a decision to 'start a movement to support the repatriation of the Koreans [to North Korea]'.[21]

By this time, however, another aspect of the scheme had become evident. It was clear that South Korean antagonism was going to be the major barrier to any repatriation agreement with the North, and some Japanese officials were expressing concerns that the plan might fatally damage efforts to establish diplomatic relations with South Korea. In the background, a further important actor, the USA, cast its shadow across the scheme. The United States was the major ally of both Japan and South Korea, and as the leader of the anti-communist 'free world', was certain to look with some concern on any large-scale migration of people from a non-communist to a communist country. In order to overcome such concerns, and to prevent the US and other countries from siding with South Korea in opposition to the repatriation, it was essential that the scheme be presented to the world as a purely apolitical and humanitarian project to relieve the sufferings of Koreans in Japan.

Influential figures in the Japanese establishment came to the conclusion that the best way of doing this was to secure the services of the Geneva-based International Committee of the Red Cross (ICRC). During the Korean War, the United States and its allies had strongly insisted that

North Korean and Chinese prisoners of war should not automatically be repatriated to the places that they came from, but should be allowed to choose their destinations. POWs were 'screened' – those from Korea were asked whether they wished to be returned to North Korea or remain in the 'free world', and those from China were asked whether they wished to be repatriated to mainland China or Taiwan. In practice, this screening proved a very troubled exercise, with (sometimes violent) propaganda campaigns being waged by both sides within the camps in order to persuade POWs one way or the other.[22] In order to demonstrate the fairness of the process, however, the United Nations Command for Korea called in the ICRC, whose representatives were asked to adjudicate on contentious cases, confirming that the wishes of the POW in question were truly being respected.[23] Japanese politicians believed that similar ICRC intervention would satisfy US concerns and hold the key to carrying out a mass repatriation of Koreans from Japan to North Korea despite objections from the South.

According to the recently declassified documents, the Ministry of Foreign Affairs and the other governmental departments therefore soon had second thoughts about the December 1955 'Plan for Dealing with the Sending to North Korea of Those Who Wish to Be Repatriated'. Senior Japanese Red Cross officials argued forcefully that the ICRC should be brought into the process and become a central participant in the repatriation.[24] In most other respects, however, the December 1955 plan proved to be a surprisingly accurate prediction of the repatriation process actually put into practice four years later.

THE PLAN IN ACTION

Elsewhere I have described the complex negotiations and lobbying which led to the repatriation accord of August 1959 and the departure of the first repatriation ship from Japan to North Korea in December of that year.[25] Here I shall simply outline the most important features of the process, before going on to consider its historical meaning and consequences.

In January 1956, the month after the Ministry of Foreign Affairs produced its plan, a Japan Red Cross Society mission travelled to Pyongyang for negotiations with the North Korean Red Cross. The ostensible purpose of the mission was to secure the return of Japanese nationals who had remained in North Korea since colonial times. However, during secret talks immediately before the formal Red Cross conference, Inoue Masutarō, who was a member of the Japanese mission, tried to persuade the North Koreans to accept a large-scale resettlement of Koreans (particularly of impoverished Koreans) from Japan.[26] One member of the Japanese delegation also brought back to Japan a North Korean film about the reconstruction of the DPRK, which was shown both to Japanese government officials and 'to various groups of self-proclaimed North Koreans in Japan for propaganda purposes'. The aim was evidently to recruit volunteers for repatriation, but this part of the project appears to have backfired: 'not only did this film not attain its objective, it seems on the contrary to have discouraged a number of candidates for repatriation from undertaking their journey'.[27]

Other factors within Japan itself, however, were making the prospect of repatriation to North Korea seem more appealing. Around the time when the Ministry of Foreign Affairs composed its repatriation plan, Japan's Ministry of Health and Welfare launched a crackdown on the payment of Livelihood Protection to Koreans. This involved sending squads of police into the homes of Korean welfare recipients to check for any signs of fraud or concealed prosperity. Using the evidence gathered, the ministry either stopped or substantially reduced payments to around 55 per cent of Korean recipients: a total of some 77,000 people.[28]

Meanwhile, the Japanese Red Cross entered into intense negotiations with its North Korean counterpart and with the ICRC to secure the repatriation of a first group of forty-seven would-be repatriates. This group, which included undocumented entrants and detainees released on parole from Ōmura, was viewed as a 'test case' for a larger repatriation.[29] Indeed, Inoue reported that in March 1956 the governing council of the Japan Red Cross Society – among whose members were politicians from both sides of Japanese politics – had unanimously agreed that it was 'indispensable to repatriate at least 60,000 Koreans within this year'.[30] The figure of 60,000 was repeatedly mentioned by the Japanese Red Cross as a target for repatriation, and also appears in the statements of Japanese government officials. It is unclear how this figure was calculated, but it may have represented an estimate of the number of Koreans who were both welfare recipients and deemed to be 'pro-North Korean'.

Attempts to repatriate the first forty-seven volunteers, however, proved fraught with problems. The South Korean government quickly learnt of the scheme and expressed outrage, threatening not only to break off normalization talks with Japan but also to use the Japanese fishermen detained in Busan as leverage to prevent the repatriation. The Yi Seung-Man regime also put pressure on shipping companies to prevent them from providing ships to carry Koreans travelling from Japan to North

Korea. At this point, despite the increasing difficulties of their life in Japan, there was still little sign of an upsurge in demand for repatriation to North Korea from *Zainichi* Koreans.

HUMANITARIANISM, FREE WILL AND REPATRIATION

The initial small band of volunteers for repatriation was eventually sent to North Korea in two groups in 1956 and early 1957, but the difficulties encountered along the way made the Japanese government and Red Cross more cautious about the repatriation project. It became clearer than ever that a truly large-scale repatriation to North Korea would only be possible if it were carried out under the name of the ICRC, preferably using Red Cross ships. Throughout 1957 and 1958, Japan continued to request ICRC commitment to the project.

Meanwhile, however, an event occurred which transformed the situation. In mid-1958, the North Korean government embarked on a new policy on repatriation. Until that time, it had expressed a willingness only to accept a relatively small number of repatriates from Japan (people belonging to specific categories such as pro-North Korean Ōmura detainees and graduates from Korean high schools). But in September 1958, North Korean leader Kim Il-Sung very publicly changed position on the repatriation issue and announced his country's decision to welcome all Koreans from Japan who wished to 'return to the bosom of the fatherland'.[31] Other announcements by the North Korean government offered repatriates from Japan jobs, free housing, welfare, education and so on.

Although Japan had been quietly requesting North Korea for more than two years to adopt just such a policy, there is no evidence that the North Korean decision was a direct response to requests from Japan. Rather, it seems to have been motivated by North Korean calculations of self-interest: the DPRK needed labour for its ambitious economic development plans, and the Kim Il-Sung regime also wished to disrupt moves towards the normalization of relations between Japan and South Korea. Another likely motive was the fact that the US and Japan were engaged in highly sensitive negotiations to renew their Security Treaty. The North Korean government believed that the US would oppose a mass repatriation of Koreans to the DPRK, and evidently hoped that this would damage Japan–US relations at a crucial moment in their evolution.[32]

The shift in the DPRK's policy towards repatriation was accompanied by a mass movement within Japan to encourage Koreans to volunteer for repatriation to North Korea. This was orchestrated by Chongryun, but also strongly supported by some Japanese groups, most notably the *Zainichi* Korean Repatriation Cooperation Society (Zainichi Chōsenjin Kikoku Kyōroku Kai), established in November 1958 by prominent figures including politicians from all sides of Japanese politics and headed by former Liberal Democractic Party prime minister Hatoyama Ichirō. Most of the Japanese media also expressed strong support for a large-scale departure of Koreans to the DPRK. In this new environment, the number of people volunteering for immediate repatriation to North Korea soared. The rosy promises of a better life propagated by North Korea were doubtless the key element in this phenomenon, but another factor was the bleak prospect for improvements in the rights of Koreans in Japan at that stage. Not only were thousands of families struggling to make a living after their Livelihood Protection had been cut, but the Japanese government was also in the process of introducing new National Pension and National Insurance schemes which (unlike the limited measures existing from pre-war years) explicitly excluded foreign residents in Japan.

Following a decision by the Japanese Cabinet in February 1959, the Japanese and North Korean Red Cross societies entered into negotiations in Geneva, and in June agreed to an accord on a mass repatriation. In the course of these negotiations, however, an important obstacle became evident. The United States was prepared to countenance the repatriation only if it took place under the auspices of the International Committee of the Red Cross, and included a 'confirmation of free will' of repatriates conducted by the ICRC along the lines of the screening of POWs which had occurred during the Korean War.[33] The North Koreans, on the other hand, wanted the project to be run by Japan and North Korea without international involvement, and flatly refused to accept any process of ICRC screening.[34] The International Committee itself was uneasy about the unfolding process, and afraid of being drawn into a project which it was unable to control, and whose humanitarian aspects were outweighed by political considerations.

To overcome these hurdles, the Japanese Red Cross and government undertook an almost frenzied round of negotiations with the ICRC and governments around the world in an attempt to find a compromise formula for ICRC involvement. Inoue Masutarō personally visited all twenty-five members of the International Committee individually to persuade them of the merits of the project.[35] Repeated discussions took place between senior Japanese government politicians and the US ambassador to Japan, during which the Americans were warned that a failure to conclude a repatriation agreement would jeopardize the future of the Kishi government, on whose strong support the US relied for concluding a revised Mutual Security Treaty with Japan.[36] In London, the Japanese Embassy gave the British government a report by Inoue Masutarō on the 'humanitarian' value of the repatriation, and urged Britain not to 'make any protest or otherwise criticize the repatriation'.[37] In Canberra, the Japanese ambassador insisted to the Australian government that 'it was a sound objective for the Japanese government to send North Koreans [*sic*] to North Korea and to send South Koreans to South Korea'.[38] An even more interesting encounter took place in the Vatican, where Japanese prime minister Kishi met Pope John XXIII during a 1959 visit to Europe. Kishi used the opportunity to lobby the Vatican to exert its influence in helping to secure ICRC involvement in the repatriation to North Korea. The Vatican, which was 'very desirous of establishing cordial relations with Japan', duly passed on its message of support for the scheme to ICRC president Léopold Boissier.[39]

THE CALCUTTA ACCORD AND BEYOND

Ultimately, the ICRC decided to give its agreement to an Accord only after seeking and receiving several promises from the Japanese government about the way in which the repatriation was to be conducted. Not all these promises were kept. For example, the Japanese government assured the ICRC that it would take responsibility for protecting Koreans from propaganda about the repatriation, by keeping people other than the repatriates and their families away from registration and embarkation centres. But, in response to demands from Chongryun, the association's activists were in fact allowed to play key roles in every stage of the repatriation. The International Red Cross also believed that it had secured a commitment from the Japanese government that the legal and social position of the Koreans who remained in Japan would be made more secure. But despite demands from South Korea for such improvements, nothing was done, and instead the new Japanese welfare system put in place in 1959 excluded Koreans and other foreigners.

To satisfy the concerns of the ICRC and of the US government, a 'Guide Book' for returnees was created, setting out their rights and options, and explaining the process for repatriation to North Korea. However, after pressure from the DPRK, the Japanese government and Red Cross agreed to a substantial watering-down of the safeguards embodied in the Guide Book, and in the end it seems that very few returnees ever saw the document. Central to the entire process was the 'confirmation of free will', during which (the ICRC had been led to believe) its delegates were going to be able to 'verify, by questioning without witness each individual concerned, that this ultimate decision [to leave for North Korea] is the expression of his own free will'.[40] How this worked out in practice will become clear from the discussion that follows.

The ICRC had sufficient faith in the commitments given by the Japanese government to endorse the repatriation accord, which was then officially signed in the Indian city of Calcutta on 13 August 1959. The first repatriation ship left the Japanese port of Niigata for Cheongjin in North Korea four months later, and between then and the termination of repatriation in 1984, 93,340 people left Japan to start new lives in North Korea. Of them, 86,603 were Korean, 6,731 Japanese (spouses and dependents of Koreans) and six Chinese. The vast majority left within the first three years of the repatriation scheme. By the end of 1962, 78,276 had departed. Much smaller numbers left during the following five years, when the Calcutta accord was repeatedly extended. In 1967 the Accord lapsed, but between 1971 and 1984 a further 4,729 people were repatriated under an agreement between the Japanese and North Korean Red Cross societies in which the ICRC did not participate.[41]

How did the repatriation project launched in 1959 compare to the Japanese Foreign Ministry's original plan of December 1955? There were two important differences: the 1955 plan had not envisaged a major role for the International Committee of the Red Cross, and it had been designed exclusively to repatriate members of the *Zainichi* Korean community who were dependent on welfare. The project actually put into practice four years later was overseen by the ICRC, and was not confined to welfare recipients. The tens of thousands of Koreans who left Japan came from every section of the social spectrum, and although they certainly included many very poor people, they also included wealthy entrepreneurs and successful professionals.

However, just as the 1955 Foreign Ministry plan had envisaged, the repatriation project was jointly operated by the Japan Red Cross Society and Chongryun. Since the Red Cross Society was a pillar of the Japanese establishment, with very close links both to the conservative government and to the imperial family, the two organizations made strange bedfellows. The collaboration between the Red Cross and Chongryun indeed gave the scheme a curiously Janus-faced character. In its 'public' incarnation, the repatriation was a strictly Red Cross project. Those volunteering for a new life in North Korea went to specially created local 'Red Cross Windows' to register (although these windows were in fact staffed by local government officials rather than Red Cross workers). They travelled in train carriages marked with Red Cross signs to the port of Niigata, where they were accommodated in a Red Cross centre, and their free wish to leave for North Korea was confirmed by officials of the International Committee of the Red Cross. The ships on which they left Japan forever were also prominently painted with the Red Cross insignia: this use of the famous symbol indeed provoked some debate, since the ships were actually Soviet vessels on loan to North Korea.

But, as many of those directly involved in the process were well aware, there was another 'unofficial' face to the proceedings. This was a parallel system of registration run by Chongryun, in close collaboration with the North Korean government. Before registering at the Red Cross Windows, it was in practice necessary to register with the General Association of Korean Residents in Japan, which acted as a de facto consular service, deciding which repatriates were and which were not desirable from North Korea's point of view. Chongryun sent its officials to the houses of those they wished to recruit for repatriation to encourage them to 'return to the Fatherland', and refused repatriation clearance to 'undesirables'. It briefed repatriates on the registration process. Its officials often accompanied repatriates to the Red Cross Windows, and were on hand in Niigata to sort out last-minute problems. One person who signed up for repatriation told an ICRC representative that 'the great majority of Koreans are convinced that it is Sōren [Chongryun] alone that is organizing the repatriation'.[42] Finally, the association handed over to the North Korean government a file of information on all returnees which reportedly included intelligence on the political reliability of everyone leaving Japan for the DPRK.

Yet the shadowy role played by the Chongryun was never a *clandestine* role. It was thoroughly understood by the Japanese government, who had indeed first proposed just such a central role for the North Korean-affiliated body as early as 1955. As the repatriation unfolded, moreover, the government carefully monitored the unofficial part of the repatriation with the help of its police and intelligence agents, who operated under cover within Chongryun. On the basis of this intelligence, the police were able to pass on to the Japanese Red Cross detailed information on the debates about the repatriation issue which took place at various Chongryun meetings around the country.[43]

THE SPECIAL ROOMS

As they arrived in Niigata by special train from every corner of the country, departing Koreans were taken to the Niigata Red Cross Centre, where they spent the last few days of their lives in Japan.[44] The Red Cross Centre was a converted air force base which had until recently been occupied by the US military.[45] Somewhat ironically, it had been used as an aircraft control and early-warning centre for operations against North Korea during the Korean War. These military origins were visible in the row of uniform barracks which were converted into dormitories and a refectory for the repatriates, and (at least when the camp was handed over to the Red Cross) in surrounding barbed-wire entanglement which, as ICRC delegate Marcel Junod observed, gave the centre a rather prison-like appearance.[46]

If Ōmura Detention Centre was a point at which the contradictions and complexities of Japan's relations with the two Koreas became visible, the Niigata Red Cross Centre was a place which came to embody all the paradoxical politics of the repatriation. Close to the main gates of the camp, with their guard post and small waiting room for visitors, stood a row of cubicles which were converted into spaces officially termed 'rooms for the confirmation of free will', but more commonly known as the 'special rooms' (*tokubetsushitsu*). These were the chosen sites (as Marcel Junod put it) for the 'final questioning which would show that freedom of choice has been respected and that everything can still be changed'.[47]

Each special room contained a functional set of tables and chairs, a Red Cross flag, a basket of lollies for the children and posters in Japanese and Korean setting out the three options (supposedly) open to Koreans in Japan – to remain in Japan, or to leave for either North or South Korea. At the request of the General Association of Korean Residents in Japan, which opposed the whole process, the doors of the cubicles had been carefully removed and replaced with a moveable metal and cotton-fabric screen of the sort often found in doctors' consulting rooms, making conversations within the special rooms audible to anyone standing in the corridor outside.[48]

In Chapter One, I compared the ballot box with the border post, and suggested that for many migrants, it is the latter that has the greater impact on their lives and on their interaction with the nation state. For those who left Japan for North Korea, the special rooms played a central and symbolic role in their destiny, yet it was a role of which the returnees themselves were often unaware. This, too, was a place of fateful choice, but the ritual that took place within the special rooms reveals the narrow bounds of freedom within which this choice was enacted.

On paper, the scene played out again and again, hour after hour, in the special rooms appeared to have an impeccable logic: those leaving for

Image 8.1. Inside the Red Cross Centre, Niigata: returnees to North Korea
prepare their luggage for the journey.

North Korea were either going of their own free will, or they had been
bribed or coerced by outside forces (most likely the North Korean government and its agent, Chongryun). At the private meeting in the special room with a representative of that impartial, humanitarian body the
International Committee of the Red Cross, all returnees would have the
opportunity to report any coercion, and, if they wished, to annul their
application for repatriation. Only those who assured the ICRC representative that they really wanted to leave Japan for North Korea would board
the repatriation ships. Those who changed their minds and decided to
stay, it was envisaged, would

pass to the left of this barrack, where all the windows are covered with wire-
netting, and where there is a private exit which will thus allow the exit of the
objectors without their having to have any further contact with the repatriates.[49]

This procedure would guarantee that the repatriation was a truly voluntary, humanitarian project.

On the ground, however, things worked out quite differently. The
ICRC had no delegates who spoke fluent Japanese or Korean, so their
questions had to be posed by Japanese Red Cross staff with the ICRC
representatives looking on. Acceding to demands from the North Korean
side, the Japanese government had agreed that only a small range of

simple questions could be posed in the special rooms.[50] The ICRC had also been persuaded that East Asian culture required a family-based process, so instead of encountering each returnee individually as originally planned, they interviewed them by family group, with the head of the family often answering on behalf of a large extended household.[51]

The information that repatriates received before they arrived in Niigata was woefully inadequate and extremely one-sided. Despite pleas from various quarters, the Japanese government had done nothing to clarify the status of Koreans in Japan, or to make that status more secure. This left Koreans in Japan all the more susceptible to the 'high-pressure tactics' used by Chongryun: tactics which, as one ICRC delegate discovered, ranged from house-to-house canvassing to offering to settle the debts of Koreans willing to volunteer for repatriation.[52] Many of those leaving for North Korea had never heard of the International Committee of the Red Cross; a substantial number apparently thought that the foreigners they fleetingly encountered in the special room were either Russians or Americans.[53] In any case, by the time they reached Niigata, the repatriates had already left their homes and jobs (if they had any), sold or packed their possessions and cancelled their foreigner registration in Japan (if they were registered). The Japanese Ministry of Health and Welfare had laid on free transport to take them into the Niigata Red Cross Centre; the only free outbound transport on offer was a berth on a ship to North Korea.

There are, in other words, many degrees of freedom, determined by the range of options facing each individual, the available information about those options, and the social and economic pressures that are brought to bear upon that individual's choice. For most repatriates, the decision confirmed in the special room was technically a 'free choice': when the Japan Red Cross official in the special room, under the eyes of the ICRC delegate, asked them to confirm their decision, they could indeed say 'No'. But this was a profoundly depleted, poor-quality freedom. Everything about the physical and social environment of the special rooms militated against the answer 'No'.

Despite the fact that they knew virtually nothing about the negotiations which had led up to their repatriation, some of the potential repatriates were obscurely conscious of the constraints surrounding their freedom of choice, and made valiant efforts to confront the problem. One man from Tokyo, whom I shall call 'Mr Han', pleaded with the ICRC delegate in Niigata to give him more reliable information about what the real situation in North Korea was, because he had heard 'conflicting news' about conditions there. He also explained that his family was originally from South Korea and were 'undecided where to go, though by preference, to South Korea, eventually'. Mr Han was told that none of the ICRC delegates had ever visited North Korea, and therefore it was

impossible to answer his question, nor would it be possible to do so by the strictly observed neutrality of the ICRC whose delegates at Niigata are pledged to restrict their duty to ascertain that all Koreans going to North Korea do so upon their own free will.

The next day, the day when he was scheduled to leave for North Korea, Mr Han called once more on the ICRC delegate, with the help of the Japanese Red Cross Centre chief, Mr. Takahashi, and again begged for some reliable information on the situation in North Korea. 'He was answered in the same way and left a few hours later for North Korea.'[54]

An ICRC delegate based in Hiroshima reported a prolonged conversation with a determined and articulate twenty-year-old woman whom I shall call 'Miss Lim', who also raised profound concerns about the repatriation process. Miss Lim had been persuaded by her parents to register for repatriation to North Korea with the rest of the family, but she did not want to go. She had lived all her life in Japan and graduated from a Japanese high school. She was evidently an admirer of the dissident Soviet writer Boris Pasternak, for she cited the repression of Pasternak's writings in the USSR to illustrate her concerns about the situation that returnees from Japan would face in Communist North Korea. Miss Lim then

described the situation of other young men and women of her age, who, she said, find themselves torn between their desire to stay in Japan and separation from their parents, or between expressing their own opinion and coming into conflict with their families. It is very difficult to escape the sphere of influence of the family. She cited the case of a friend who had been mistreated by her father because she dared express her opposition to repatriation. She said she knew young men and women who had left [Japan] against their will, out of fear of their parents and fear for the future that awaited them in a society which did not provide them with any means of existence. She referred to the case of one of her friends who had claimed to be Japanese in order to get a job. It did not take long for the company who hired this friend to discover the deception, and she was dismissed on the spot.[55]

In the end, Miss Lim made the difficult decision to stay in Japan, at the cost of separation from her family which (if they are still alive) presumably continues to the present day.

The reports written by ICRC delegates in Japan are repeatedly interspersed with similar disquieting anecdotes: cases of people who arrived in Niigata for 'voluntary repatriation' directly from mental hospitals,[56] the case of a woman who had been arrested as an accomplice to theft but was released apparently on condition that she 'volunteer' to leave for North Korea,[57] stories of people who complained of pressure from Chongryun within the Niigata Red Cross Centre.[58] Then there was the man who had lived in Japan for twenty-seven years, married and had a family, but become an 'illegal immigrant' because he had worked as a sailor and had disembarked from his ship in Korea. He was scheduled for deportation to South Korea, leaving his wife and children in Japan. He told the ICRC representatives that he wanted to go to North Korea simply because it was 'the only country where they could be together'.[59] Or the case of an asylum seeker from South Korea who had spent three years in Ōmura Detention Centre, and begged the Red Cross to help him either stay in Japan or leave for another country such as Argentina. This last returnee, a young man in his twenties, was described as being 'visibly in a state of confusion, in fear and tears', but later calmed down sufficiently for his decision to leave for North Korea to be deemed a 'free choice'.[60]

But by the time they had passed through the multiple filters that separated them from the realm of global politics, these haunting voices had become almost entirely inaudible. ICRC Chief Delegate André Durand, reviewing the overall progress of the repatriation up to mid-1960, faintly echoed their unease. He gave a rather frank description of the mass propaganda campaign, the central organizational role of Chongryun, and the pressures of life as aliens in Japanese society. Having so publicly committed itself to its role in the repatriation, however, it would have been an enormous embarrassment to the ICRC to admit officially that all was not well. Durand's conclusions put the best face on the situation, while still amounting to something less than a resounding endorsement of the voluntary nature of the project:

The repatriates, who are placed in a quite unfavourable moral and material position in Japan and currently lack the means to go to South Korea, are primarily guided by their hope to improve their situation in at least two areas: employment and education. The decisions [to repatriate] seem to be made freely and individually, if we take into account the fact that in requesting to go to a communist democracy, they have agreed to submit to certain decisions and collective orders.[61]

But when this information was converted into a form designed for public consumption, the subtle qualifications and nuances were lost. A short documentary on the repatriation, made by the International Committee of the Red Cross for the new mass medium of television and completed

Image 8.2. The smiling face of repatriation: commemorative stamp issued
by the DPRK in 1960 to celebrate the return of the Korean compatriots from Japan.

just one day after Durand signed his report, concludes with a shot of
bus-loads of freshly arrived repatriates heading down the wide boulevard
in front of Pyongyang railway station, as the narrator, accompanied by a
background of triumphal music, proclaims, 'so they board the long line
of buses and set off amidst the cheering crowd on the road to a future
which the Red Cross has enabled them to choose in total freedom'.[62]

NO PARTY IN THE RECEPTION ROOM OF HEAVEN

The quality of freedom matters because, as it turned out, the life at the
end of that road was one of great suffering for many of the migrants.
The first boatloads of people to be repatriated were mostly sent to live
in the North Korean capital, Pyongyang, and initial reports suggested
satisfaction with the welcome which they found waiting for them. The
longer-term fates of the repatriates after their arrival in the DPRK, like
the lives they left behind them in Japan, were very varied. Some Koreans
from Japan developed successful careers in the DPRK in areas such as
academia, medicine and the arts. One married future North Korean
leader Kim Jong-Il. Because the majority of survivors of the scheme still
live in North Korea, they are unable to speak openly, and it is impossible
to gain a truly balanced picture of their experiences. There is no doubt,

however, that many of the repatriates suffered extreme poverty and political repression. From about the mid-1960s onward, the North Korean government became concerned that returnees from Japan were failing to adapt appropriately to life in socialist society, and were importing 'undesirable' values into the DPRK.[63] They became the subject of close control and surveillance and thousands disappeared into labour camps. Since the 1990s, as some former 'returnees' have begun to leave North Korea as refugees, accounts of their sufferings have begun to be published in Japan and elsewhere. One particularly chilling account, published under a pseudonym by a man who was born in Japan, 'returned' to North Korea under the repatriation scheme and escaped back to Japan in 2004, describes the hunger, poverty, political repression and death which awaited his fellow 'returnees' in the DPRK.[64] The families they left behind in Japan also suffered separation from their relatives. Half a century after the start of the repatriation, many were still struggling to help their repatriated family members survive by sending them money and goods.

It is, of course, risky to project the wisdom of hindsight back onto the 1950s and early 1960s. At that time, life in North Korea for most people was no harder than life in South Korea, and for some it was probably easier. Many people – left-wing Japanese as well as Koreans in Japan – genuinely believed that the DPRK's socialist system would produce future prosperity (though the ruling-party politicians and bureaucrats who so energetically promoted the repatriation were unlikely to have shared such optimism). A particularly troubling aspect of the repatriation story, however, is the fact that both Japanese and North Korean authorities were already aware within months of the departure of the first repatriation ship that many newly arrived migrants from Japan were suffering distress and hardship in the DPRK. During the first years of the project's operation, news leaking out of North Korea suggested that a disturbing number of repatriates were expressing regret at having left Japan. Nevertheless, despite this knowledge, both sides continued to press energetically for the scheme to be continued, and did nothing to address the concerns raised by the repatriates' distress.

For example, in January 1961, a meeting between Japan Red Cross and government officials was told that 'according to letters received by those who have repatriated already, it seems that life in the North is really quite hard';[65] nine months later, any uncertainties had disappeared, and an ICRC delegate in Japan could write of the 'undeniable truth in reports about hard life of returnees in North Korea'.[66] By this time, indeed, the Japanese government was actually quoting letters from repatriates in its intelligence assessments in order to illustrate the dire economic situation in North Korea. One of these letters commented that 'rural communities are suffering from the acute shortage of commodities including food'. Others noted that 'only the inhabitants of large cities live on rice, while people in rural districts eat barley, wheat or soy beans for staple food', and that 'in front of every shop there is a long queue ... There is not even a scrubbing brush or a wooden spoon. Products of light industry are very scarce'.[67] This information was passed on in secret to Japan's allies as part of intelligence-sharing operations, but does not seem to have prompted any active concern for the plight of those who had left, and were still leaving, on the repatriation ships to North Korea.

Michel Testuz, who was in charge of the ICRC repatriation operation in Japan from 1962 on, had no illusions about the situation either. As he wrote to Geneva in January 1962, 'many Koreans who leave Japan to go to North Korea are disappointed with what they find on their arrival; contrary to what they are told, life over there is not a pleasant party in the reception room of heaven'.[68] Yet his awareness of the problems does not seem to have produced any action, nor even any serious signs of concern. On the contrary, Testuz continued to send messages to Geneva urging them to support further extensions of the repatriation accord: as he noted in March 1964, 'I believe the Japanese government wishes the repatriation to continue, for it is undeniable that the presence of a foreign community like the Korean one – quite numerous, well-organized and composed of quite violent and turbulent elements – represents a grave problem.'[69] Testuz shared this vision of Koreans in Japan as a 'problem', reducing the *Zainichi* Koreans whose rights and freedom he had been sent to protect down to an emblematic being – 'the Korean' – whom he described in astonishingly discriminatory terms as being characterized by 'his terrible character', which is 'almost savage', 'violent and quick tempered, quarrelsome and combative, disingenuous and lying', 'lacking a sense of honour and dignity', and a great deal more in the same vein.[70]

In 1966, Testuz had a meeting with Oh Gi-Wan, a North Korean official who had defected to South Korea. Oh had been an assistant to the DPRK's minister of agriculture, and as such had been a member of the committee set up by the North Korean government to receive repatriates from Japan. The broad outlines of the story which Oh gave to Testuz are confirmed by information that has since become available from hundreds of former repatriates who have left North Korea as refugees, and from the families of repatriates who have maintained contact with relatives in the DPRK. It was not until the 1990s that the information which Oh had privately given to the authorities some twenty-five years earlier became publicly available in Japan.[71]

Oh told Testuz that the political data on returnees sent by Chongryun to Pyongyang was used by the North Korean government to grade repatriates into three groups: reliable and active communists (about 3 to 5 per cent of the total, who were sent to live in Pyongyang); those who were seen as having potential to become good communists (about 20 to 25 per cent, often people with professional training, who were sent to live in regional cities); and the rest, who were sent to manual jobs in rural areas. After their arrival, returnees spent some time in special reception centres. While in these centres, they were relatively free to express their own views, but their behaviour was rigorously monitored by the authorities. 'The first reaction of the repatriates,' said Oh, 'is generally disillusionment.' The standard of living was low, and the cost of consumer goods other than food very high. For example, the average worker's salary was thirty won per month, while a man's suit cost 250 won to buy.

It is painful to witness the disillusionment of the returnees. It is accompanied by rage and words of insult towards the Red Cross and towards the 'humanitarianism' of which it always speaks, and which does nothing but send them down the slope to a miserable country and a miserable situation.

Oh also pointed out that returnees' letters to their families in Japan were censored by the authorities, and that the returnees often developed codes to try to circumvent the censorship. For example, if a letter was written in pen this would mean 'you can believe what I have written here', but if it was written in pencil, that would mean 'do not believe what you are reading'. The North Korean authorities were aware of these codes and tried to crack them.[72]

The information, however, does not seem to have affected Testuz's willingness to urge the continuation of the repatriation. For (unlike other ICRC representatives involved in the project, some of whom showed real sensitivity and sympathy towards the situation of the returnees) Testuz's approach to his mission was riven with simple stereotypes about 'the orient'. In one letter dated January 1963, after reporting stories of the disillusionment of Korean repatriates, he went on to discount the significance of such reports, remarking,

As you know very well, in Asia the truth is not something absolute. The Cartesian principle of non-contradiction does not exist in oriental logic: a thing may be at once black and white, true and false … There 'to be or not to be' is never the question, because one can be and not be at the same time.[73]

Unfortunately for *Zainichi* Koreans, the choice between remaining in Japan or leaving for North Korea was a very Cartesian one. They faced two mutually exclusive options. They could not be in both places at the same time, and once they had left Japan, however much they might regret their decision, they could not return.

The bilingual posters in the Niigata special room offered not two but three options – the third choice being repatriation to South Korea. In practice, ever since the creation of the Republic of Korea in 1948, the South Korean regime had shown no real interest in accepting a return flow of Koreans from Japan. However, for a brief moment in late 1959 and early 1960, it seemed as though that position was about to change. Angered and embarrassed by the outflow of Koreans from Japan to North Korea, the Yi Seung-Man regime entered into serious negotiations about a mass repatriation to South Korea. If this had been carried out, the whole future of the Korean community in Japan would (for better or worse) have been very different.

The first serious moves towards a mass repatriation to South Korea were taken by senior officials of the ROK Foreign Ministry around the end of June 1959, when the negotiations over the repatriation agreement between Japan and North Korea were still at their most intense.[74] The proposal was taken up enthusiastically by the United States, who saw the mass return to the North as a disquieting propaganda victory for communism. A mass repatriation to the South as well would, they hoped, offset some of that propaganda advantage, and also smooth the troubled relationship between Japan and the ROK.

The idea of repatriation to South Korea appealed to some influential people in Japan, too. In November 1959 the Japan Red Cross Society sent a message to the Japanese government urging it to give its support to the scheme, so that the return of Koreans to the South could be carried out alongside, and in exactly the same way as, their 'return' to the North. The Red Cross message noted that,

If the repatriation to South Korea can be carried out simultaneously with the repatriation to North Korea, it would certainly make a good impression on the general public, despite some technical difficulties.

The face of the ROK side will be saved. The intervention of the ICRC will be more easily justified ... Moreover, questions of the Omura and Pusan [Busan] camps would be solved, which has great significance.[75]

By now, the South Korean government had actually produced a draft joint communiqué on the subject, which it hoped would be signed by the ROK and Japan. The communiqué promised that the South Korean government would 'accept the repatriation of Korean residents in Japan regardless of their political affiliations during their stay in Japan'. But it also required Japan to pay a 'certain amount of fund, which will be used for the repatriation of Korean residents in Japan to and their resettlement in the Republic of Korea'.[76] The sum which the Korean side had in mind was US$1,500 for each family returning from Japan, and this proved to be a sticking point.[77] Just as it firmly refused to pay compensation for its colonization of Korea, the Japanese government also firmly refused to contribute to the costs of resettling returnees in Korea. As ruling-party politician Funada Naka explained to the US ambassador in Tokyo, if the Japanese government 'agreed to compensation for Koreans returning to ROK they would have to do [the] same for those returning to North [Korea] and this was impossible'.[78] What the Japanese government was prepared to do was to pay some form of development aid to South Korea, so long as this was not specifically identified either as compensation for past wrongs or as assistance to repatriates. Lengthy negotiations ensued, as both sides attempted to work out a compromise, but meanwhile other factors were also reducing the prospect of a mass repatriation to South Korea.

One problem apparent from the start was that the number of people likely to volunteer for repatriation to the South was uncertain. The South Korean-affiliated organization in Japan, Mindan, had not been conducting any active campaign to promote an exodus to the South. Meanwhile, the political situation in South Korea was in a state of confusion and uncertainty. In April 1960, after widespread allegations of electoral fraud, mass student demonstrations finally succeeded in unseating the ageing dictator Yi Seung-Man, who fled into exile in Hawaii, where he died in 1965. The prospect of a new democratic South Korea encouraged some Koreans in Japan to think again of returning to the South. But the democracy proved an unstable and short-lived one, dominated by factional rivalries as relatively weak and divided liberal and conservative parties jostled for power. Huh Chung, who became foreign minister and later prime minister in the new administration, insisted that Japan must stop the repatriation to North Korea before he would negotiate on other matters. He was also deeply suspicious of the US attitude to the repatriation saga, accusing the State Department of having taken Japan's side and allowed repatriation to North Korea to proceed in return for a favourable revision of the US–Japan Security Treaty.[79]

Huh was willing to open South Korea's doors to a mass return of Koreans from Japan, but at the same time he emphasized that a large proportion of Koreans in Japan were now second-generation residents and were more likely to want to remain in Japan than to return to Korea, North or South. The most important step, he argued, was to remove the forms of discrimination which made their life in Japan insecure.[80] The Japanese government, though, was doing nothing to address the discrimination issue, and was also taking a tough line on the funding issue, apparently because it recognized that politics in Korea were in a state of flux and wanted to wait and see how events unfolded, in the hope of gaining greater concessions from a future regime.[81]

In May 1961 their hopes were realized when right-wing members of the South Korean military staged a coup d'état, and installed in power Colonel (later General) Park Chung-Hee, who was to remain president of the Republic of Korea until his assassination in 1979. Park had served in the Japanese Imperial Army in Manchuria during the Asia–Pacific War, had good relations with some senior Japanese politicians, and was willing to take a relatively flexible approach to negotiations with Japan – most significantly by abandoning demands for reparations in favour of requests for development aid. This (in the words of political scientist Samuel Kim) helped to 'reinvigorate' the Japan–South Korea normalization process, and (after considerable prompting from the US) led to the signing of the Treaty of Basic Relations between Japan and the Republic of Korea in 1965.[82] By now, however, the issue of repatriation was no longer high on the agenda. The flood of repatriation to North Korea had declined to a trickle, and the South Korean government no longer felt impelled to compete for returnees with its northern neighbour.

Indeed, as more and more evidence of the hardships endured by repatriates in the North emerged, the hostile South Korean attitude to the issue underwent a fundamental change. When a new Japan–North Korea repatriation agreement was signed in Moscow in 1971, Prime Minister Kim Jong-Pil, Park Chung-Hee's chief political confidante, observed that the Koreans from Japan

had presented considerable problems to the authorities in North Korea. After living in the free society of Japan they had found it extremely difficult to settle down in a regimented society and therefore complaints had been made to the authorities. In some cases, some of these returnees had been sent to the coalmines in north Korea. Prime Minister Kim felt that it was in the interests of south Korea and the free world not to discourage the continued repatriation of these residents as their influence in north Korea could have a significant impact on the peoples of north Korea.[83]

From the Japanese point of view, by the mid-1960s the figure of 60,000 returnees (originally envisaged as a suitable target for repatriation to North Korea) had been exceeded. Many of the poorest and most disaffected Koreans had left Japan already, and Japan itself was now in the middle of the most phenomenal period of economic growth in its history. The agreement signed by Japan and the ROK in 1965 therefore said nothing about encouraging Koreans to return from Japan to South Korea. Instead, the issue now was to determine the social status and the futures of over 600,000 Koreans who had chosen to remain in Japan.

NOTES

1. Hōmushō Ōmura Nyūkokusha Shūyojo (ed.), *Ōmura Nyūkokusha Shūyojo 20-Nenshi* (Tokyo: Hōmushō, 1970), p. 2.
2. 'Observations on the Hamamatsu Detention Camp submitted to Mr. Uchida, Director of the Immigration Bureau of the Ministry of Justice by Mr. Masutaro Inoue, Director, Foreign Affairs Department, Japan Red Cross Society (G-498)', in ICRC Archives, B AG 229 105–003, Copies pour information transmises par la Croix-Rouge japonais, 14.12.1955–13.12.1962.
3. A. Vasishth, 'A Model Minority: The Chinese Community in Japan', in Michael Weiner (ed.), *Japan's Minorities: The Illusion of Homogeneity* (London and New York: Routledge, 1997), pp. 108–39, quotation from p. 133.
4. See letters from Shimazu Tadatsugu, president of the Japan Red Cross Society, to Paul Ruegger, president of the International Committee of the Red Cross, 6 May 1953 and 26 July 1953, both in ICRC Archives, B AG 232 105–001, Chinois au Japon, 06.05.1953–24.05.1956.
5. See note annexed to letter from Shimazu to Léopold Boissier, 28 November 1955, in ICRC Archives B AG 232 105–001. Boissier had replaced Ruegger as president of the ICRC in 1955.
6. Ibid.
7. *Nippon Times*, 9 June 1956.
8. Pak Jae-Il, *Zainichi Chōsenjin ni kansuru Sōgō Chōsa Kenkyū* (Tokyo: Shin-Kigen Sha, 1957), p. 155.
9. Testimony given to the Lower House Foreign Affairs Committee Meeting of 14 February 1956, see Shūgiin Gaimu Iinkai, 14 February 1956. See *Kokkai Gijiroku,* available at http://kokkai.ndl.go.jp .
10. As the repatriation got under way in December 1959, Japanese and US intelligence not only warned that the ROK military had been put on a semi-war footing, but also reported a rumour (which proved incorrect) that 'President Syngman Rhee will order invasion of North Korea when second shipment of Koreans to North Korea passes Takeshima Island': see CIA message from Tokyo to Secretary of State, Washington, 18 December 1959, in NARA, College Park, decimal file no. 294.9522/11–1859.

11. See telegram from Li Byung-Nam to Shimazu Tadatsugu, 31 December 1955, in ICRC Archives, File no. B AG 232 105–002, Problème du rapatriement des Coréens du Japon, dossier I: généralités, 17.2.1953–11.10.1957.
12. Japan Red Cross Society, *Fundamental Conditions of Livelihood of Certain Koreans Residing in Japan* (Tokyo: Japan Red Cross Society, 1956), pp. 21–5.
13. Ibid., pp. 32–4.
14. Japan Red Cross Society, *The Repatriation Problem of Certain Koreans Residing in Japan*, (Tokyo: Japan Red Cross Society, 1956), pp. 17–18, report held in ICRC Archives, B AG 232 105–027, Documentation concernant le rapatriement des Coréens et les pêcheurs japonais détenus à Pusan, 10.10.1956–04.03.1959.
15. Ibid., p. 18.
16. Telegram from US ambassador MacArthur to Secretary of State, Washington, 7 February 1959, in NARA, decimal file no. 694.95B/759, parts 1 and 2.
17. Details of the negotiations with Li are contained in 'Nikkan Kokkō Seijōka Kōshō no Kiroku Sōsetsu Vol. 6 – Zainichi Chōsenjin no Kikan Mondai to Kikan Kyōtei no Teiketsu', document 126 of the third release of official material pertaining to Japan–ROK relations, released 16 November 2007, pp. 14–35, available at www7b.biglobe.ne.jp/~nikkan/nihonkokai/3ji-kokai/2006–00588–17/ 2006–00588–0126–01–01-IMG.xdw (accessed 23 December 2007). I am very grateful to Yi Yang-Soo for drawing my attention to this document.
18. The term *Hokusen* is a derogatory abbreviation of the full name of North Korea.
19. The Plan is reproduced in Nikkan Kokkō Seijōka Kōshō no Kiroku Sōsetsu, pp. 44–53.
20. Ibid., pp. 49–50.
21. Letter from Inoue to Boissier, 19 January 1956, ICRC Archives, B AG 232 105–002.
22. C. Rey-Schyrr, *De Yalta à Dien Bien Phu: Histoire du Comité internationale de la Coix-Rouge 1945–1955* (Geneva: International Committee of the Red Cross, 2007), pp. 552–3.
23. Ibid., p. 553.
24. *Nikkan Kokkō Seijōka Kōshō no Kiroku Sōsetsu*, p. 52.
25. T. Morris-Suzuki, *Exodus to North Korea: Shadows from Japan's Cold War* (Lanham, MD and New York: Rowman and Littlefield, 2007).
26. Masutaro Inoue, 'Report of the Phyongyang Conference Held by Japanese and North Korean Red Cross Societies (January 27th–February 28th 1956)', 17 March 1956, p. 3, in ICRC Archives, B AG 232 055–001, Ressortissants japonais en Corée du Nord, 22.01.1954–11.05.1956.
27. W. Michel, 'Mission Extrême-Orient, MM. Michel et de Weck (mars–juin 1956)', in ICRC Archives B AG 251 075–002, Mission de William H. Michel et d'Eugène de Weck, du 27 mars au 2 juillet 1956, 01.03.1956–06.08.1956.

28. *Tokyo Shimbun* (evening edition), 24 April 1956. Translation held in ICRC Archives B AG 232 105–002. The newspaper reports that some 140,000 Koreans were receiving Livelihood Protection, and that the government had decided to cancel payments in 24 per cent of cases and reduce them in over 30 per cent of cases.

29. See letter from Shimazu Tadatsugu to Li Byung-Nam, 6 June 1956, in ICRC Archives, B AG 232 105–004, Problème du rapatriement des Coréens du Japon, dossier III: rapatriement de 48 Coréens en Corée-du-Nord, 28.05.1956–03.12.1957.

30. Letter from Inoue to Boissier, 31 March 1956, in ICRC Archives, file no. B AG 232 105–002.

31. 'An Extract from Premier Kim Il Sung's Speech Made on the 10th Anniversary of the Founding of the People's Democratic Republic of Korea', 8 September 1958, in *On the Question of 600,000 Koreans in Japan* (Pyongyang: Foreign Languages Publishing House, 1959), contained in South Korean Declassified Documents on Korea–Japan Negotiations, 723.1 JA, file number 177, p. 422.

32. An insight into these varied motives can be obtained from 'Zapis' Beseda s Tovarishchem Kim Ir-Syenom', 14 and 15 July 1958', in Dnevnik V. I. Pelishenko, 23 July 1958, Foreign Policy Archives of the Russian Federation, Archive 0102, Collection 14, File 8, Folder 95.

33. 'Note de dossier' by R. Gallopin, 12 June 1959, in ICRC Archives, B AG 232 105–009.

34. See official diary of the Soviet ambassador to the Democratic People's Republic of Korea, A. M. Puzanov, 13 March 1959 and 17 July 1959, Dnevnik posla SSSR v KNDR A. M. Puzanova (hereafter Puzanov diaries), in Russian archival material held by the *Jungang Ilbo*, Seoul, (*Jungang* Russian archive, hereafter JRA) file no RU-secret 1959–2–2 and 1959–2–4.

35. Inoue Masutarō, 'Rapatriement des Coréens résidant au Japon', French translation of an article first published in the journal *Kokusai Jihyō*, copy held in ICRC Archives B AG 232 105–035, Problème du rapatriement de Coréens du Japon, dossier XXI, 12.01.1965–24.11.1967.

36. For example, telegram from MacArthur, US Embassy, Tokyo, to Secretary of State, 29 June 1959, in National Archives and Records Administration, College Park, File 294.9522/6–2959.

37. Masutaro Inoue, 'Repatriation of Koreans', 5 February 1959, report held in UK Foreign Office files, with handwritten annotation 'communicated by the Japanese Embassy'; draft letter from Dalton, Foreign Office, to A. L. Mayall, Tokyo, 18 February 1959; both documents held in British National Archives, File FO 371, 141540.

38. Notes of Conversation with H.E. the Japanese Ambassador, 'Repatriation of Koreans from Japan; Relations between Japan and the Republic of Korea', 30 June 1959, in Australian National Archives, Canberra, 3103/11/90, Japan – Relations with Korea, Part 2.

39. Minutes of meeting between Léopold Boissier and Mgr. Ferrofino, secretary of the apostolic nuncio, Berne, 4 August 1959, in ICRC Archives, B AG 232 105–010; see also confidential telegram from John Villard, US Consul-General Geneva to Secretary of State, Washington, 4 August 1959, in National Archives and Records Administration, College Park, decimal file ref. 294.9522/8–459.

40. 'Memorandum', attached to letter from R. Gallopin to M. Inoue, 24 July 1959; also 'English translation of the cable received from President Shimadzu addressed to President Boissier, ICRC, on July 27th 1959', both in ICRC Archives, B AG 232 105–011.03, Aide-mémoire du 24 juillet 1959 transmis à la Coix-Rouge japonais et projets de communication, réponses, 03.07.1959–12.08.1959.

41. Kim Yeong-Dal and Takayanagi Toshio, *Kita Chōsen Kikoku Jigyō Kankei Shiryōshū* (Tokyo: Shinkansha, 1995), p. 341.

42. Memo from Michel Giroud to ICRC, 'Compte-rendue de l'entretien du délégué sous-signé et Mademoiselle … [name withheld for reasons of privacy]', 1 March 1960, ICRC Archives, B AG 251 105–005.02 Correspondance reçue du 29 août 1959 au 28 avril 1960, 26.08.1959–28.04.1960.

43. See for example 'Conversation with Mr. Masutaro Inoue, International Relations Director, JRCS, on Saturday October 24th at 9.30am and MM Lehner, Hoffman and Borsinger', 31 October 1959, in ICRC Archives B AG 232 105–013, Problème du rapatriement des Coréens du Japon, dossier XI: Généralités pour la période septembre–décembre 1959, deuxième partie, 11.10.1959–29.12.1959.

44. The centre was in existence from late 1959 to 1967. After 1971, returnees to North Korea were generally housed in guesthouses in Niigata while they waited to board their ships.

45. 'Mission Junod Japon – Rapport no. 2', 3 September 1959, p. 1, in ICRC Archives, B AG 232 105–014, Problème du rapatriement des Coréens du Japon, dossier XII: Rapports du Dr. Marcel Junod, délégué, et annexes, 28.08.1959–06.10.1959.

46. See *Asahi Shinbun*, 28 August 1959; it is unclear whether or not the barbed wire was later removed.

47. 'Mission Junod Japon – Rapport no. 2', p. 1.

48. 'Supplementary Explanations on Certain Aspects of Actual Operation of Repatriation Work', in ICRC Archives, B AG 232 105–013; see also letter from Borsinger to ICRC, 31 October 1959, in ICRC Archives, B AG 232 105–013.

49. 'Mission Junod Japon – Rapport no. 2', p. 1.

50. 'Supplementary Explanations on Certain Aspects of Actual Operation of Repatriation Work'.

51. Ibid.

52. Max Zeller, 'Report on Osaka Prefecture', 26 October 1961, in ICRC Archives, B AG 232 105–031.01, Première partie, 1961, 03.01.1961–26.12.1961.

53. André Durand, 'Note no. 98 au CICR', 14 March 1960, in ICRC Archives B AG 232 105–016, Problème du rapatriement des Coréens du Japon, dossier XIV: Généralités concernant l'année 1960, première partie, 05.01.1960–08.04.1960.
54. 'Note nr. 197 to the ICRC in Geneva', 11 July 1960, in ICRC Archives B AG 232 105–018.01, Rapport sur les convois, 11.01.1960–20.12.1960.
55. Memo from Michel Giroud to ICRC, 1 March 1960.
56. See, for example, 'Note no. 66 to ICRC Geneva', 1 February 1960, held in ICRC Archives, B AG 232 105–018, Rapports sur les Convois, 11/01/1960–20/12/1960.
57. 'Report Concerning Operation 12, of the 34th Ship', ICRC Archives, B AG 232 105–018.01, Rapports sur les Convois, 11.01.1960–20.12.1960.
58. For example, 'Note no. 412 to the ICRC', 19 July 1961, in ICRC Archives, B AG 232 105–028.02, Rapports sur les convois, 17.01.1961–28.12.1964; also A. Dunant to ICRC, 26 January 1960, ICRC Archives, BAG 232–016, Problème du rapatriement des Coréens du Japon, dossier XIV: Generalités concernant l'année 1960, première partie, 05.01.1950–08.04.1960; these involve claims of pressure both to volunteer for repatriation and (in other cases) to annul applications for repatriation.
59. 'Note 724 au CICR à Genève', 15 August 1963, in ICRC Archives B AG 232 105–028.02.
60. Special Room No. 5, special case op. no. 135, 21 June 1961, in ICRC Archives, B AG 232 105–028.02.
61. André Durand, 'Aide-mémoire: Rapatriement des Coréens de Japon', 23 June 1960, p. 18, in ICRC Archives, B AG 232 105–019.03, Aide-mémoire sur le rapatriement des Coréens de Japon par André Durand, 23.06.1960–02.08.1960.
62. *Le Rapatriement de Coréens de Japon en République Democratique Populaire de Corée*, documentary film made by the International Committee of the Red Cross, 1960, and subsequently broadcast on Télévision Suisse, Zurich.
63. See, for example, B. Szalontai, *Kim Il Sung in the Khrushchev Era: Soviet–DPRK Relations and the Roots of North Korean Despotism* (Washington, DC: Woodrow Wilson Center Press, 2005), p. 153.
64. Han Sok-Gyu, *Nihon kara 'Kita' ni Kaetta Hito no Monogatari* (Tokyo: Shinkansha, 2007).
65. Memo of meeting, 27 January 1961, ICRC Archives, B AG 232 105–031, Problème du rapatriement des Coréens du Japon, dossier XIX: Generalités pour la periode 1961–1964, 03.01.1961–14.12.1964.
66. Max Zeller, 'Report on Osaka Prefecture'.
67. 'Information for Judgment of North Korean Situation', English translation of report by the Japanese Ministry of Foreign Affairs, sent to the British Foreign Office by British Embassy, Tokyo, 2 August 1961, in British National Archives, file no. FO 371, 158554. It is not clear how the Japanese government obtained copies of these letters.

68. Memo from Testuz to Maunoir, ICRC, 18 January 1963, in B AG 215 105–009.02, Correspondence reçue du 12 juin 1962 au 21 janvier 1966, 12.06.1962–21.01.1966.

69. Memo from Testuz to Maunoir, ICRC, 27 March 1964, in ICRC Archives, B AG 215 105–009.02.

70. Michel Testuz, 'Rapport sur l'activité de la mission speciale au Japon', ICRC Archives, B AG 232 105–031.03, Troisième partie, 1963–1964, 04.01.1963–14.12.1964.

71. In March 1992, the journal *Gekkan Asahi* published an interview with Oh which repeated much of the information he had given to Testuz in 1996. See Satō Hisashi, 'Kikokusha no sono ato', in Takasaki Sōji and Pak Chongjin (eds.), *Kikoku Jigyō to wa Nan data no ka: Fuin sareta Nicchō Kankeishi* (Tokyo, Heibonsha, 2005), pp. 93–120, quotation from p. 100.

72. Letter from Testuz to Maunoir, ICRC, 4 August 1966, in ICRC Archives, B AG 232 105–035.

73. Testuz to Maunoir, ICRC, 18 January 1963.

74. See 'Synopsis of State and Intelligence Material Reported to the President, July 1–6, 1959', Thompson Gale Declassified Documents Reference Service, document number CK3100317878.

75. Appendix to memo from André Durand to ICRC, 9 February 1960, in ICRC Archives, B AG 232 105–016.

76. Telegram from MacArthur, US Embassy Tokyo, to Department of State, Washington, 18 November 1959, in NARA, College Park, decimal file no. 294.9522/11–1859.

77. Telegram from MacArthur, US Embassy Tokyo, to State Department, Washington, 25 November 1959, in NARA, College Park, decimal file no. 294.9522/11–2559.

78. Telegram from MacArthur, US Embassy Tokyo, to State Department, Washington, 12 November 1959, in NARA, College Park, decimal file no. 294.9522/11–1259.

79. 'Lane (Korean Affairs) told us on 10 May that State Department had been surprised and puzzled by Acting President Huh Chung's public criticism of the US attitude regarding the repatriation of Koreans from Japan to North Korea. Lane commented that while many Koreans felt that the USA had adopted a "compromising" stand so that the US/Japan Security Treaty would not be jeopardized, it was not clear why Chung was making a public issue of the matter at this time.' Telegram from Australian Embassy, Washington to External Affairs, Canberra, 10 May 1960, Australian National Archives, Series no. A3092, control symbol 221/12/5/5/2, Part 1, Japan South Korea Relations.

80. See memorandum of conversation between Acting President Huh Chung and US ambassador Walter P. McConaughy, Seoul, 26 May 1960, in NARA, College Park, decimal file no. 694.95B/6–360.

81. See for example telegram from McConaughy, US Embassy, Seoul, to State Department, Washington, 2 June 1960, in NARA, College Park, decimal file no. 694.95B/6–260.

82. S. S. Kim, *The Two Koreas and the Great Powers* (Cambridge: Cambridge University Press, 2006), p. 69.
83. Letter from G. C. Allen, Australian chargé d'affairs, Seoul, to secretary, Department of Foreign Affairs, Canberra, 1 October 1971, in Australian National Archives, control symbol 3125/11/87, North Korea: Relations with Japan.

CHAPTER 9

Beyond the postwar system

What changed; what stayed the same

STAYING ON

In 1975, Japan's migration control service celebrated its twenty-fifth birthday. To commemorate the occasion, the Immigration Bureau ran a competition in which its officers were invited to write essays describing their vision for the future. The winner of the competition was Sakanaka Hidenori, a young immigration officer who had joined the service five years earlier, and who represented the new breed of official: a cohort very different from the ex-imperial policemen who had formed the core of the old Immigration Agency. A graduate from a prestigious private university, Sakanaka had entered the public service on graduation, choosing the Justice Ministry's Immigration Bureau (in his own words) 'for no particular reason'.[1] The early years of his service with the Bureau had been spent in Osaka, where he came into close contact with that city's large Korean community, and it was this experience that inspired the content of his winning essay.[2]

Although the senior immigration bureaucrats who devised and judged the competition were doubtless unaware of the fact, the events of 1975 were indeed to produce an important turning-point in Japan's migration controls, and Sakanaka Hidenori's vision of the future was to grow from a small essay into a grand design for Japanese society: a design being intensely debated by Japanese politicians and media more than thirty years later, as I write these pages.

By the mid-1970s, more than 12 per cent of the Korean population in Japan, including many of those whom the Japanese government had viewed with the greatest alarm, had departed for North Korea. Coinciding as it did with the start of Japan's 'economic miracle', this mass exodus had transformed the landscape of *Zainichi* Korean communities. As some Koreans left for North Korea and others moved out of impoverished ghetto-like areas in search of new job opportunities, many of the most readily visible 'Korean districts' gradually disappeared – swept up in the urban redevelopment plans of the 1960s to become new housing schemes and shopping arcades.

The majority of Koreans in Japan in the mid-1960s had been born and brought up there and, as enthusiasm for migration to North Korea waned, it became increasingly clear that most would remain permanently. Tight border controls had prevented them travelling back and forth between Japan and their ancestral homes. Most of the second generation were still 'aliens', yet Japanese was their first language, and only those who attended ethnic schools (*minzoku gakkō* – most of which were pro-North Korean) – could speak fluent Korean. For this generation, the cross-currents of nationality and identity would pose particularly perplexing problems.

The Treaty of Basic Relations signed with South Korea in 1965 included an accord on the status of Koreans in Japan, which came into force on 17 January 1966. Under this, Koreans in Japan acquired permanent residence rights, provided that they were registered as nationals of the ROK and had migrated to Japan before 15 August 1945, or were children of pre-war and wartime migrants born between 15 August 1945 and 22 June 1965 (the day when the accord was signed). The treaty, however, was bitterly opposed by many Koreans in Japan, as well as by large sections of the Japanese left. It tied Japan into a close relationship with the Park Chung-Hee dictatorship in South Korea, and involved the renunciation of Korean claims to compensation for colonial wrongs, in return for a mass injection of funds into the Park regime's ambitious industrial development projects.

The agreement on the status of Koreans in Japan also left many issues unresolved. The long-term problem of resolving the residence rights of third-generation Koreans in Japan was postponed for twenty-five years (until 1991). The agreement also excluded Koreans who did not register as nationals of the Republic of Korea, as well as those who had arrived in Japan after the end of the Pacific War. Even those who had lived in Japan since colonial times were excluded if they had been discovered making unauthorized postwar return trips to Korea.³ For those who did obtain 'treaty permanent residence' under the agreement, Livelihood Protection continued to be available only on a discretionary basis, and they still had no voting rights, no right to any form of national or local government employment, and no access to public housing. It remained extremely difficult to obtain loans from private banks or employment in large private firms.⁴

The employment issue was highlighted just five years after the signing of the treaty, when a young man named Pak Jeong-Sok took and passed an entrance test for employment in the manufacturing giant Hitachi. Like the vast majority of Koreans in Japan, Pak had both a Korean real name (*honmyō*) and a Japanese 'public name' (*tsūmei*), which he used in school and when applying for his job with Hitachi. When asked to produce a copy of his family registration document, he explained that he had no such document, because he was Korean. At that point, the Hitachi management promptly informed Pak that the company was withdrawing its job offer, since it did not employ foreigners in its regular workforce. Pak took Hitachi to court, claiming ethnic discrimination.[5]

The judgement in the case, handed down four years later by the Yokohama District Court, was a resounding victory for Pak Jeong-Sok. However, the case also highlighted many problems. Pak's struggle for justice was essentially an individual one, conducted outside the framework of the two big community associations – Chongryun and Mindan. In fact, the two associations were generally unsympathetic to Pak's struggle, which they tended to view as an individually motivated effort to be accepted by mainstream Japanese society.[6]

Meanwhile, Pak's success in the courts was far from marking the end of employment discrimination. Quiet and unofficial discrimination persisted in some private firms, and indeed continues to do so to the present day. In the 1970s, however, the exclusion of foreigners from employment in the public sector had particularly far-reaching implications for Korean and Taiwanese residents. It still closed the door not simply to jobs as government officials, but also to positions as teachers in state schools and colleges or as workers in a large number of state-owned enterprises such as the national railways and the public telecommunications sector. It was only gradually, and after prolonged grass-roots campaigns throughout the 1970s and early 1980s, that some local governments and public corporations began partially to relax these bans.

THE SAKANAKA ESSAY AND THE MANY THIRD WAYS

Recently recruited migration official Sakanaka Hidenori had come into contact with many young *Zainichi* Koreans during his time in Osaka. He realized that, for almost all of them, Japan was the only home they had ever known. He was particularly shocked to hear stories of young Koreans who had grown up using a Japanese name and believing themselves to be Japanese, only to be suddenly told on their fourteenth birthday that they were foreigners and had to apply for an alien registration card.[7] The future image of Japan's migration controls which he painted in his prize-winning essay therefore focused on the plight of these young people.

His essay pointed out that Koreans in Japan had three options: they could return to the 'fatherland', they could stay in Japan and become Japanese citizens, or they could remain as a permanent foreign community within Japan. By 1975, however, it was clear that most of those who wanted (or could be encouraged) to leave Japan had already departed. Meanwhile, although some Koreans and Taiwanese in Japan had become naturalized Japanese citizens, this was a cumbersome and (for many people) an unattractive choice.

Japan's nationality law made it possible for foreigners to apply for naturalization provided that they were over twenty years old, had lived in Japan for at least five years, were 'of good conduct' and had the skills or assets needed to maintain their own livelihood.[8] In practice, though, naturalization, like the granting of special permission to stay, was a discretionary gift of the minister of justice, and could be withheld if officials judged the applicant to be 'undesirable' or insufficiently 'Japanese' in lifestyle. As a result, the naturalization process often involved intrusive checks of the applicant's finances, family, friends and personal life. Until 1986, the guidelines given to officers who handled applications for naturalization advised that anyone becoming a Japanese citizen should 'as far as possible' take a 'Japanese-style name'.[9] All of this was discouraging, particularly to Koreans who had unhappy memories of having been forced to adopt Japanese names during the colonial period. Between 1952 and 1975 some 78,000 *Zainichi* Koreans had become naturalized Japanese, but over half a million remained foreigners.[10]

Sakanaka's 1975 vision for the future of Japanese migration control proclaimed that the best course, both for *Zainichi* Koreans themselves and for the nation as a whole, was for them to be treated as a permanent part of the community and encouraged to become Japanese nationals. To promote this gradual process of absorption into mainstream Japanese society, the naturalization process should be made easier, and education, employment and welfare should be made more accessible to *Zainichi* Koreans:

If Japanese society secures social equality for *Zainichi* Koreans in education and employment, and creates a level playing field where they can compete freely, *Zainichi* Koreans will start aspiring to live in Japanese society, and some members of the *Zainichi* Korean community will begin to be highly socially valued for their 'ability' and 'professional work'. In that case, Japanese people's view of

Koreans will spontaneously change, and a positive consensus in favour of acquiring Japanese nationality will be formed within *Zainichi* Korean society.[11]

These sentiments won high praise from Sakanaka's superiors in the Immigration Bureau, but when a revised section of his essay was published two years later, it provoked a major controversy. Some commentators welcomed his liberal emphasis on removing discrimination and encouraging Japanese acceptance of the permanent place of the Koreans in their midst. But the essay also attracted a good deal of criticism from members of the Korean community itself. Korean critics clearly felt uncomfortable at the spectacle of a Japanese immigration official presuming to dictate the terms of their present and future identity. Besides, not all Koreans in Japan agreed with Sakanaka's negative view of their foreign status. Retaining Korean nationality and identity (whether *Kankoku Seki* or *Chōsen Seki*), it was argued, allowed members of the minority to sustain proud links to their origins, while also giving them a separate space – a 'third way' – from which to take a critical perspective on Japanese society. As one commentator argued, it was possible to seek ways to 'continue living for the long term in Japan without naturalizing, but as ethnic Koreans with a sense of ethnic consciousness and pride'.[12]

The debate about the third way, indeed, was just part of a complex series of controversies surrounding nationality and identity which generated much heat throughout the 1980s, and (in subtly changing forms) continues to the present day. These debates are a reminder of the diversity that exists within the Korean community. Identity is a profoundly personal thing, and individuals' sense of their ethnicity, nationality and place in society are influenced by many factors, including age, generation, gender, class and ideology. Those who have attended Korean schools and those who have grown up in the mainstream Japanese educational system view the problem from slightly differing angles, and there are further differences between those who live in large Korean communities (like those of Osaka and Yokohama) and people who live in areas where they have little everyday contact with their fellow ethnic Koreans.

The debates of the 1970s and 1980s were complex, and in fact defied reduction to the simple image of 'three ways'. For example, some who chose naturalization still sought to maintain and emphasize their Korean cultural identity, while for others naturalization meant assimilation. Besides, those who accepted the need for a distinctive *Zainichi* Korean third way did not necessarily agree where that way was leading. They might share a common sense of being 'foreign denizens' (*teijū gaikokujin*) in Japan, but still vary in the extent to which they put the emphasis on the word 'foreign' or the emphasis on the word 'denizen'.[13] For some, the third way meant a commitment to fight for greater ethnic equality within Japanese society; for others, it required the maintenance of a distinctive culture and sense of history; for others again, it involved cross-border links to the struggle for democratization which, throughout the 1970s and 1980s, was being fought out in South Korea.[14]

These debates were not simply abstract arguments about the definition of ethnic or national identity; they were also enacted within multiple currents of political and social action – some converging, some conflicting – which flowed through and around the Korean community in Japan during the 1970s and 1980s. The most visible and probably the most influential of the new political movements was the anti-fingerprinting campaign which emerged from 1980 onward.

Ever since it had been introduced in 1955, the practice of fingerprinting foreigners as part of the alien registration process had been profoundly resented by Korean and Taiwanese residents in Japan. By the 1980s, when most of those being fingerprinted had been born in Japan, and when many held 'treaty permanent residence', the practice seemed more inappropriate and discriminatory than ever. In 1980 a man named Han Jong-Seok, who had moved from Osaka to Tokyo's Shinjuku District, went to renew his alien registration card at the local immigration office. When asked to provide his fingerprints for the new card, he refused, pointing out that he had already been fingerprinted eight times – once on each of the five-yearly occasions when he renewed his card – and that his fingerprints had not changed since his last registration. This act of resistance, which Han defined as his personal protest against a 'system designed to oppress human rights', evoked widespread support from local sympathizers and sparked a nationwide campaign of fingerprint refusals.[15] By November 1985, more than seven thousand foreign residents throughout Japan (most of them *Zainichi* Koreans) were refusing to be fingerprinted.[16]

The anti-fingerprint movement marked a new stage in the development of those coalitions between *Zainichi* Koreans and grass-roots Japanese activists which had begun to coalesce around campaigns for special permission to stay in the 1960s and 1970s. Another interesting aspect of the movement was the fact that, almost for the first time, it also built links between *Zainichi* Korean activists and other groups of foreigners in Japan – those who participated in the fingerprinting boycott included, amongst others, Catholic missionaries from Europe and a British woman married to a Japanese husband.[17] Foreigners who refused to give their fingerprints for more than a year were threatened with imprisonment, and some of the campaigners did in fact serve prison terms before the movement finally bore fruit. In 1991, the Japanese and South Korean governments issued a new joint statement which made the residence rights of special permanent residents inheritable by third- and fourth-generation *Zainichi* Koreans, and promised an abolition of fingerprinting for special permanent residents: a promise which was put into effect the following year in a revised Alien Registration Law.

While the anti-fingerprinting campaign created new forms of collaboration between *Zainichi* Koreans and the Japanese human rights movement, the prolonged and fierce struggle for democracy in South Korea renewed links between *Zainichi* Koreans and their ancestral homeland. As we saw in Chapter Seven, by the late 1960s, growing numbers of South Korean dissidents were seeking political refuge in Japan. During the following decades, events in both halves of the Korean peninsula continued to reverberate through the *Zainichi* Korean community, not least because these events affected the ability of the community's members to move back and forth between their country of residence and their country of nationality. In some cases, indeed, political conflicts in South Korea had important ramifications for the Japanese state and the wider international community. In 1973, South Korean opposition leader in exile Kim Dae-Jung was kidnapped from a Tokyo hotel by agents of the South Korean government, and taken to Seoul, where he was held under house arrest and later put on trial. (There is evidence to suggest that the South Korean Central Intelligence Agency had in fact planned to kill Kim and dump his body at sea, but were prevented from doing so by US and Japanese intervention.[18])

Many Koreans in Japan, even if they had never lived in Korea itself, felt a deep sense of connection to the political dramas unfolding in their homeland. *Zainichi* Koreans participated in protests against the kidnapping of Kim Dae-Jung and the arrest of other political dissidents. Some became even more closely involved in events within the Republic of Korea: the arrest, imprisonment and torture of two *Zainichi* Korean brothers studying in Seoul – Suh Sung and Suh Joon-Shik – provoked widespread protests in Japan and internationally during the 1970s,[19] and in 1974 the 'Moon Se-Gwang incident' sent further shockwaves through the Korean community in Japan. Moon Se-Gwang was a young ethnic Korean from Osaka who embarked on a crusade to assassinate South Korean ruler Park Chung-Hee, and although his attempt to shoot Park during a National Day celebration on 15 August went astray, his bullets killed the president's wife. Moon was arrested and executed; Park himself was to be felled by another assassin's bullet five years later.

THE NEW BOAT PEOPLE AND THEIR IMPACT

Zainichi Korean identity, then, was not simply a matter of the relationship between foreign minority and Japanese majority, nor of the relationship between foreigners and the Japanese state. For these relationships in turn existed within a wider international framework, and the changing nature of the regional and global order repeatedly shifted the parameters of identity debates in Japan. The international context also profoundly affected the Japanese government's response to migration and the legal status of foreign residents. Just as the Cold War had set the scene for the creation of Japan's postwar migration control system, so the gradual shift towards a 'new world order' during the 1980s set the scene for some important reforms of the system.

In the year when the Immigration Bureau celebrated its anniversary and Sakanaka Hidenori wrote his prizewinning essay, another event occurred which was to have an even more profound effect on the future of foreigners in Japan. After decades of war, the South Vietnamese government and its US and other allies were defeated, and Vietnam was united under a Communist government. The collapse of the South Vietnamese regime caused a mass exodus of refugees, and a further wave followed in 1979 when the Pol Pot regime in Cambodia collapsed and Vietnam and China fought a brief but fierce border war. By that year, the number of Indochinese refugees living in camps scattered across East and Southeast Asia had reached an estimated 390,000.[20]

As in the case of the Korean War, Japan was not a combatant, but US bases on Japanese soil played a vital role in the fighting. In Okinawa (which had been returned to Japanese control in 1972), US bases became the staging points for bombing raids on North Vietnam in the final stages of the war. However, this time the US and Japanese response to the refugee problem was very different from their response during the early 1950s. By the end of the 1970s, Japan was one of the richest countries in the world, and as America struggled to deal with the aftermath of its defeat in Vietnam, the US government increasingly called on its Japanese ally to share the 'burden', both of security in East Asia and of the human aftermath of the war. Japan itself was meanwhile trying to establish a new and more active global role in the United Nations and other international forums. This background helps to explain the far-reaching impact that the Indochinese refugee crisis had on Japan's migration policy.

The first Vietnamese boat people began to appear on Japan's southern shores in the late 1970s, and the flow continued and swelled throughout the 1980s. Many had made long and tortuous journeys through the South China Sea. As their rickety and overcrowded boats attempted to make landfall along the shores of Kyushu and Shikoku, the events of the late 1940s and early 1950s seemed to be repeating themselves. Yet an article in the *New York Times*, reporting the arrival of some 2,600 Indochinese boat people on Japan's shores between January and August 1989, reflected the historical amnesia that besets migration debates in Japan: 'never before', the article informed its readers, 'have large numbers of boat people come to Japanese shores directly'.[21]

Faced with a worsening humanitarian crisis, the Japanese government reacted to domestic, US and international pressure in 1978 by accepting some refugees for resettlement. Initially, strict conditions kept the numbers very low.[22] Gradually, however, the programme was expanded, and in 1985 Japan made a formal commitment to accept 10,000 refugees from Indochina.[23] Equally importantly, in response to the humanitarian crisis, the government on 3 October 1981 finally ratified the 1951 Geneva Convention on the Status of Refugees, and in January of the following year also ratified the 1967 Protocol. The effects of this new openness to international law were felt far beyond the bounds of the refugee community. Articles 23 and 24 of the Geneva Convention require that refugees accepted for resettlement be given equality with nationals of the host country in terms of public assistance, social security and other forms of welfare.[24] However, giving these rights to newly arrived refugees, while continuing to deny them to Koreans and Taiwanese who had been in Japan since colonial times, would have been manifestly inequitable and might have caused a public uproar.

After some debate, the solution chosen by the Japanese government was to remove the nationality clauses restricting access to public housing, national pensions, national insurance, state housing loans and child support, making these available to all permanent residents. On 1 January 1982, a revised migration control law, now renamed the Migration Control and Refugee Recognition Act, also came into force. This created a new category of 'special permanent residence' (*tokurei eijū*) which, for the first time, extended permanent residence rights to colonial-period Taiwanese immigrants and their descendants, and to those *Zainichi* Koreans who held *Chōsen Seki*.[25]

The response of the Japanese government to Indochinese refugees was, indeed, in some ways a generous one, and marked a major departure from previous approaches to issues of asylum and migration. Though the numbers accepted by Japan were relatively small (far lower than the numbers accepted by countries such as the USA, Canada and Australia), the authorities planned the reception of the refugees with care. Two reception centres were set up, one in the western Japanese city of Himeji and one in Tokyo, where arriving refugees could stay for several months on arrival in Japan (though some chose instead to stay with friends or relatives). Within the centres, the new arrivals were given intensive Japanese language training and courses in the 'survival skills' necessary to navigate their way around a very unfamiliar society. Employment training was also provided, and the government worked with employers – mostly small firms in industries like mechanical engineering and garment making – to find jobs for the refugees.[26]

The new refugee policy and the revised migration control law were just two examples of the growing power of international law and international organizations to influence Japanese policy during the latter stages of the Cold War. Another important example was the impact of the UN International Decade of Women (1976–85) on Japanese nationality law. In the final year of that decade the pressure of international opinion, combined with the internal lobbying from women's rights groups and several court cases on nationality issues, persuaded the Japanese government to remove the most obviously patriarchal features from the postwar Nationality Law. Until 1985, children of Japanese fathers had an automatic right to inherit Japanese nationality whatever the nationality of their mother, but children of Japanese mothers and foreign fathers did not.

The reformed law, while retaining the 'bloodline' (*ius sanguinis*) approach to nationality, gave all children of mothers with Japanese nationality the right to inherit that nationality.[27] This had particularly large implications for the *Zainichi* Korean community. More than 70 per cent of *Zainichi* Koreans who married in 1985 chose a Japanese partner, and by 1995 the figure had risen to over 80 per cent.[28] All the children of these marriages now have a right to choose Japanese nationality when they reach adulthood, and it is likely that, having spent all their lives in Japan, most will make that choice. The descendants of colonial migrants born since 1985 will therefore predominantly be Japanese citizens – though what that means for their long-term definitions of identity remains to be seen.

THE FICTION OF A NEW BEGINNING

Changing official visions of migration control reduced some of the barriers to the entry of foreigners into Japan, while also making certain aspects of the foreign presence more visible than before. As we have seen, the flow of 'unauthorized arrivals' onto Japanese shores had continued unbroken since the late 1940s, but in the 1960s and early 1970s the numbers arriving were relatively small. From 1975 on, however, arrivals began to increase again. Not all of these were boat people. By now, most of those who became undocumented migrant workers in Japan were arriving by plane on tourist visas, and staying on to work in restaurants, bars, small factories and so on. The immigration authorities continued to treat these newcomers with the discretionary approach which they had earlier applied to undocumented migrants from Korea. By the late 1970s, labour shortage was becoming a serious problem in many sectors of the Japanese economy, and the authorities were generally relatively relaxed about enforcing the law as long as the irregular migrants were seen as fulfilling an important economic role and not causing visible social problems. However, discretion was also used to remove those identified as 'undesirable', or from time to time to make examples of those who breached the law.

As labour shortage encouraged the search for a new vision of Japan's future migration policy, one important change did occur: undocumented migrants in Japan became more visible than before, subjects of popular and official scrutiny and discourse. During the 1980s, there were growing numbers of media reports on the 'migrant worker problem' and the presence of undocumented migrants in Japan, and from 1990 the Immigration Bureau began regularly publishing statistics of estimated numbers of visa overstayers in Japan. This 'discovery' of foreigners in Japan helped to frame the widespread sense of the 'foreign worker problem' as something entirely new and unconnected to Japan's earlier history. As Wolfgang Herbert notes, this was similar to the situation in Germany, where 'despite Germany having a history of more than one hundred years of employing "alien workers" (*Fremdarbeiter*), and despite its having channelled millions of forced labourers into the (armaments) industry during World War II', the debates about 'guest workers' from the 1960s onward 'commenced with the ahistorical fiction of a "new beginning"'.[29]

In Japan, the fiction of a new beginning was all the more readily sustained, not only because the numbers of foreigners in Japan were increasing, but also because many of those arriving after 1975 were visibly different from earlier waves of migrants. Between 1985 and 2004 the total number of registered foreigners in Japan more than doubled, from 850,612 to 1,973,747, with the largest increases being in the number of foreign residents from China, Brazil, Peru and parts of Southeast Asia (including Vietnam, the Philippines, Thailand and Indonesia). In 1985, 80 per cent of registered foreigners in Japan had been Korean; by 2004, the proportion had fallen to 30 per cent.[30] Meanwhile, Chinese as a percentage of all registered foreigners in Japan had increased from 9 per cent in 1985 to 25 per cent in 2004, Brazilians from 0.2 per cent to 14 per cent and Filipinos/Filipinas from 1 per cent to 10 per cent.[31] The newcomers included people who had arrived with work permits, people on training schemes, a large and growing number of college students (some of whom combined study with part-time work) and foreign spouses of Japanese people.

This visibility evoked waves of concern. During the 1970s, the annual White Papers produced by Japan's Police Agency regularly included sections on the alarming phenomenon of foreigner crime, particularly crimes committed by 'ordinary aliens' (*ippan gaikokujin*) – a category which was defined as 'aliens not including Chinese, South and North Koreans and Americans':

As we face an age of internationalization, we are set on a course by which the number of foreigners entering our country rises year by year, and in 1978 the number of arriving aliens reached 1,017,149 (34,080 more than the year before). In line with this trend, we can assume that the cases of international professional criminals mixing with ordinary travellers and entering our country to commit crimes will increase.[32]

This alarming scenario was illustrated by selected cases of crimes committed by foreigners. In the 1980s and 1990s, Southeast Asians figured prominently in these illustrative examples. But although the targets of concern were new, the rhetoric was oddly familiar. Stereotypes of criminality, in which undocumented migrants were associated with lawlessness and disorder, proved both enduring and versatile, and could be applied as easily to Filipinos, Iranians and Chinese newcomers in the late twentieth century as they had been to Koreans and Taiwanese in the days of the postwar occupation. Indeed, right-wing Tokyo governor Ishihara Shintarō was to make this lineage of ideas explicit in the year 2000, when he spoke of a possible need, in case of emergency, to use Japan's Self Defence Force to put down 'vicious crimes' committed by foreigners in Japan. The term he used for foreigners was *sangokujin* ('third-country people'), a term unfamiliar to many younger Japanese, since it was originally used during the occupation to describe people in Japan who were neither Japanese nor Allied occupiers – i.e. former colonial subjects.[33]

'OLDCOMERS' AND 'NEWCOMERS', VISIBLE AND NOT SO VISIBLE

Yet alarm at the new faces in the population was also accompanied by a growing recognition that, as the Japanese economy confronted the labour shortages of the 1980s, some loosening of restraints on entry was necessary. After much debate between those who favoured a more open migration policy and those who wished to maintain tight controls on entry, at the start of the 1990s the government brought in a series of further cautious reforms to the Immigration Control and Refugee Recognition Law. While the core features of the old system were retained – including the generally restrictive approach to labour migration and wide-ranging discretionary powers for the minister of justice to define 'special cases' – a series of 'loopholes' were created to allow a greater flow of migrant workers into Japan. The most important of these loopholes were, first, an expanded 'Worker Training Programme', which allowed workers (mostly from other Asian countries) to enter Japan for on-the-job training, and to work for a period of up to two years after finishing their training; and, second, a provision allowing Latin Americans of Japanese descent (*Nikkeijin*) and their immediate family to work in Japan for up to three years.[34]

The *Nikkeijin* were descendants of some quarter of a million Japanese who had emigrated to Brazil, Peru and other Latin American countries, mostly during the pre-war decades. The assumption behind the new policy was that, as ethnic Japanese, they would be easily assimilable, and would expand Japan's workforce without seriously upsetting the official image of Japan as a highly homogeneous society.[35] They were also viewed as *dekasegi* workers – people who would come to Japan for a few years to earn the high wages on offer in Japanese firms, and then return home. Neither of these expectations proved realistic. Once they arrived, many of the migrants found that the high cost of living in Japan made it more difficult to save than they had expected. Like the hopes of their ancestors who had made the same journey in the opposite direction decades earlier, their dreams of returning home with new-found wealth after a few years were, in many cases, repeatedly postponed. Meanwhile, as they established roots and connections in Japan, a growing number became 'circular migrants', moving repeatedly back and forth between Japan and Latin America.[36]

The great majority of the *Nikkeijin*, moreover, were second- or third-generation emigrants, and most did not speak fluent Japanese. Ironically but perhaps predictably, many, having been strongly conscious of their 'Japaneseness' when they were in Latin America, became more sharply aware of their *difference* from other Japanese once they were in Japan. As one wrote in a community newspaper,

I was brought up as a weird Brazilian ... in a world where there were *us* [the *Nikkei*] and the *Gaijin* ['foreigners', i.e. other Brazilians] ... I was a Brazilian eating beans (Brazilian dish) with *misoshiru* (Japanese soup) ... We, the *Nikkeijin*, arrive in Japan and we face a reality that confuses us even more: we are Brazilians ... To be *dekasegi* is to know how to cope with the stereotype of being Japanese ... and not to have to apologize for not being able to behave like Japanese.[37]

Their presence, in other words, has helped to destabilize widely accepted but simplistic notions of the equivalence of ethnic ancestry, culture and identity.

At the same time, though, official statistics and systems of classification continue to reinforce stereotypes – particularly the assumption that the category 'Japanese' is both a legal and an ethno-cultural one.[38] Official figures show that the number of registered Koreans in Japan (both *Kankoku seki* and *Chōsen seki*) has fallen slightly, from 683,313 in 1985 to 607,419 in 2004. They also suggest the presence of around 50,000 South Korean visa overstayers in Japan in 2004.[39] These figures are very widely interpreted as meaning that the size of the Korean community in Japan is not growing, and that it stands at around 700,000.[40] But the fall in the number of Koreans registered as foreign residents, despite ongoing migration from South Korea, reflects the fact that people of Korean or half-Korean ancestry are disappearing from the statistics for 'foreigners' as they acquire Japanese nationality either through naturalization or by birth under the 1985 amendment to the Nationality Law.

From 1986 onwards, the government relaxed its insistence that applicants for naturalization had to take 'Japanese-style' names and, although the naturalization process continued to depend heavily on the discretion of individual Immigration Bureau officers, the hurdles to becoming Japanese were gradually lowered.[41] These reforms encouraged a steady rise in the number of naturalizations: by the year 2000, a total of 333,429 people had acquired Japanese nationality since the end of the occupation, of whom 243,762 were Koreans.[42] As a result, scholars such as Fukuoka Yasunori estimated the number of people of Korean descent in Japan by the mid-1990s was around 1.2 million.[43]

Since there are no public figures on population by ethnicity in Japan, the half a million or so people of Korean descent who have Japanese nationality, whatever they may feel about their own identity, become statistically invisible, and are also regularly written out of general statements about 'Japanese nationals', whether made by the Japanese government or its critics. Though the term 'Korean-Japanese' has begun to be more widely used both by the media and by some 'Korean-Japanese' themselves, this term (it seems) has not yet acquired the power to decouple the assumed equivalence of ethnicity, identity and nationality that underlies political discourse in Japan today. The same invisibility even more effectively shrouds the presence of Taiwanese in Japanese society. The normalization of Japan's relations with the People's Republic of China in 1972, following US president Richard Nixon's unexpected visit to China, caused concern and confusion in Japan's Taiwanese community, and persuaded many *Zainichi* Taiwanese in Japan to become Japanese citizens. Throughout the 1960s, the figures for naturalizations by 'Chinese' (which included Taiwanese) had been running at less that four hundred a year, but in the three years from 1972 this jumped to an annual average of almost four thousand.[44]

In early November 1973, while the North Korean repatriation ships were still making their way to and fro between Niigata and Cheongjin and when the repercussions of the Kim Dae-Jung kidnapping were still reverberating through Japanese society, I sat on a flight from Hong Kong to Tokyo's Haneda Airport, looking down at the lights of the city spread out in the darkness below, and wondering what experiences awaited me on the ground. In my luggage was a guidebook, a paperback edition of *Teach Yourself Japanese* and an eighteenth-month contract with a private English conversation school. Looking back, I realize that I too was part of the wave of newcomers – lured by Japan's high wages and the prospect of travelling a long way from home.

The young Americans, Britons, Australians and others who lived and worked in Japan in large numbers from the late 1960s onwards do not often figure in the debate on 'migrants' or 'foreign workers' in Japan. Like the people of the American bases (for whom we were often mistaken), we were at once very visible and blessed with a curious form of invisibility. The emerging media debate about visa overstayers, for example, focused on Chinese, Filipinos, Iranians and others, but no one seemed to notice how many Americans and Europeans came to Japan on tourist visas and stayed on to work, renewing their visas on three-monthly trips to South Korea or Hong Kong, in cheerful and generally unpunished breach of the Immigration Control Law. And rising concern at the presence of the *'Japayuki san'* – Southeast Asian women who came to Japan to work in bars and nightclubs – rarely extended to the middle-class women from developed nations who supplemented their incomes from English language teaching by moonlighting as models or bar hostesses. (The wages were much better than in teaching, though the working conditions were worse.) Like other newcomer migrants, we too were seen as *dekasegi* employees, who would head home after a year or two in Japan – and many did. But others put down roots, became permanent residents, or (like me) became cross-border people, living mostly outside Japan but with Japanese spouses, half-Japanese children and a permanent link to a society of which we both are and are not part.

The newcomer phenomenon, then, was a complex and multifaceted one. Southeast Asians, and later South Asians and Africans, attracted attention because their presence was noticeably new. But the new wave of Americans and other rich-nation English speakers who arrived in Japan from the 1970s slipped readily into the spaces left by the diminishing numbers of US military. In the 1990s, they were followed by other waves of young professionals – bankers, stock-market traders, software designers and others – each new wave gravitating in turn to the metropolitan areas like Roppongi and Harajuku which had once provided housing and entertainment to US troops.

COEXISTENCE AND CONTROL

Sakanaka Hidenori's success in the 1975 essay competition was the first step on a rapid rise through the ranks which would see him, by the early years of the twenty-first century, occupying the position of director of the Tokyo Immigration Bureau. Throughout his career he retained his penchant (unusual in a Japanese bureaucrat) of making public statements on his visions for the future, and after his retirement in 2005 he published his *Migration Control War Diary*, a battle-cry for a radical overhaul of Japan's migration system to allow a mass inflow of millions of foreign workers[45] (see Chapter One, p. 9). At a time of growing alarm about Japan's shrinking population, and about the rising might of other populous Asian nations such as China and India, Sakanaka's ideas have become the focus of a great deal of political attention. In 2005, the ruling Liberal Democratic Party (LDP) set up a 'Diet Members' League for Promoting Exchanges of Foreign Human Resources' (Gaikoku Jinzai Kōryū Suishin Giin Renmei), whose interim proposals, published in July 2008, proclaimed that 'accepting foreign immigrants is the only remedy for saving Japan from population crisis'.[46]

The Diet Members' League's practical suggestions echo much of Sakanaka's vision. Though they cut his target for Japan's foreign population in the mid-twenty-first century from an ambitious 20 million to a somewhat more modest 10 million, their practical policy suggestions are far-reaching. Japan, they propose, should actively seek out and recruit highly skilled and business migrants, while retaining restrictions on large-scale inflows of the unskilled. To turn Japan into an appealing magnet for skilled workers and entrepreneurs from around the world, and into a country based on multiethnic 'coexistence' (*kyōsei*), the current immigration control policies should be replaced by a new 'immigration law' and Japan's nationality policy should be transformed into one based on *ius soli*, giving those born in Japan the automatic right to acquire Japanese citizenship.[47]

Predictably, though, this vision has met with resistance from other parts of the Liberal Democractic Party, including then Economics Minister Yosano Kaoru, who argues that the plan would take jobs away from Japanese.[48] Meanwhile, sections of the main LDP's opponents, the Democratic Party, have been debating a proposal to give local-government voting rights to permanent foreign residents in Japan: a scheme which Sakanaka opposes, since he sees naturalization – the full transfer of loyalties to Japan – as the essential prerequisite for participation in Japanese political life.[49]

These are important debates. They suggest major shifts in thinking within the world of Japanese politics, and may result in far-reaching reforms. Both a *ius soli* nationality law and voting rights for foreigners would make the life of migrants in Japan more secure, and enhance the ability of foreigners to participate actively in Japanese society. At the same time, though, several points need to be made about grand plans for Japan as a 'multiethnic coexistence state' (*taminzoku kyōsei kokka*). First, in emphasizing the urgent need for radical change, Sakanaka Hidenori and the politicians of the Diet Members' League are also implicitly acknowledging that many things have *not* changed over the past decades. In other words, their calls for reform implicitly highlight the fact that, despite incremental changes, Japan still has a migration control and nationality system whose core elements were created at the start of the Cold War. The nationality law is still based on bloodline; the immigration control system still focuses on keeping people out rather than encouraging the smooth settlement of immigrants, and still relies heavily on the discretionary measures which Nick Collaer insisted were essential to save Japan from Cold War communist subversion.

Second, the calls for a new opening of Japan are being debated against a background of a tightening of some border controls in the context of the 'global war on terror'. Having abolished the fingerprinting of permanent residents in 1992, and of all other foreign residents in 2000, in November 2007 the Japanese government reintroduced the fingerprinting of foreigners as they enter Japan.[50] The new measures differ from the old in that fingerprinting is now conducted at airport immigration booths, rather than as part of the alien registration process, and in that special permanent residents are exempt. However, the return of the fingerprint – now collected in high-tech format and accompanied by digital photographs – is an indication of the way in which, in Japan as elsewhere, increased cross-border movement is being accompanied by increasingly intrusive personal surveillance. The reintroduction of fingerprinting was, of course, part of an international push to tighten border controls: a push led by the United States in the wake of the 9/11 attacks and the invasion of Iraq. In Japan, high-tech and high-profile anti-terrorist border checks have been brought in despite the fact that the only terrorist acts carried out in the country in the past two decades have been by home-grown terrorists, and most indeed have been carried out by members of right-wing nationalist organizations.[51]

The international context of tightened border security is a reminder of a third and most important point about contemporary Japanese debates on immigration: such debates, although they are all about globalization and cross-border movement, are conducted in a quintessentially national, and sometimes nationalistic, framework. This, it must be said, is not distinctively a Japanese problem. Around the world, debates about border controls and migration follow the same pattern. The focus is on the relationship between migrants and the nation state. Will migrants save the nation from the perils of population decline, or will they take our jobs? Which migrants are good for the nation, and which are bad? How can the good be attracted and the bad kept out? Behind these questions stand the assumptions that the state actually possesses the power to control the flow of people across its boundaries, and that migration policy is therefore a strictly national matter.

The history traced in this book challenges those assumptions. Certainly, national policies influence the cross-border flow of people and the fate that awaits migrants on their arrival. But this influence is always constrained by the wider regional and global order. Immigration services may open the door to some migrants and strive to keep out others, but they have little or no power to determine which waves of migrants arrive on the doorstep. These waves are shaped by complex global forces – international wealth gaps, transport links and information flows, wars and revolutions.

Besides, as they devise migration controls, governments seldom work in isolation. As we have seen throughout this book, national policies towards border crossers are moulded by the global geopolitical order, by political conflicts and compromises with neighbouring countries, and by unequal security relationships which (as in the US bases in Japan) may even lead states to surrender the right to control the entry of certain foreigners to their territory.

In the twenty-first century, it seems reasonable to conclude that the time has come for these inherently international dimensions of cross-border movement to be openly acknowledged. In other words, the future of Japan's migration policy is not, and never has been, something that the Japanese state can determine on its own. The framework of debate needs to be expanded. Future visions should involve dialogue between migrant-sending and migrant-receiving countries, and between the local governments of migrant-sending and migrant-receiving regions (between Jeju and Osaka, for example, and between São Paulo and the manufacturing cities of Aichi Prefecture where many *Nikkei* Brazilians live and work). To envisage Japan's future, we will need to listen not just to the voices of the Diet Members' League for Promoting Exchanges of Foreign Human Resources, but also to the voices of those who queue for visas outside Japanese consular offices in Manila and Shenyang, and those who campaign for special permission to stay from within the walls of Ōmura, Shinagawa and other detention centres.

As the economic and political order in Northeast Asia is transformed, new paths of human movement will be opened up across the region, creating waves of movement over which individual governments will have only limited control. Just and sustainable responses to these movements will require international collaboration, rather than merely national initiatives. Visions of future migration, whether national or international, also need to keep a careful eye on the past, for both the trajectories of migration and the structures of migration control are products of history.

One of the greatest migration challenges for Northeast Asia, for example, is the outflow of undocumented migrants from North Korea. As I write, some 50,000 undocumented border crossers from North Korea are believed to be living in China, often in conditions of great hardship, and the threat of famine is likely to make this number rise. Amongst these unauthorized emigrants are former 'returnees' from Japan, now attempting to make their way back to the place from which they were 'repatriated' decades ago. The Japanese government has, as yet, no official policy for accepting them, and although some two hundred have been quietly

allowed back into Japan, once there, they rely on the support of a hand-
ful of non-governmental organizations (one of which was established by
Sakanaka Hidenori on his retirement from the Immigration Bureau in
2005). Unlike the response to the Indochinese refugee crisis of the 1970s,
the response to the North Korean crisis has been marked by an almost
total absence of international cooperation. But such cooperation is essential if the painful journeys of the past are not to be endlessly repeated in
the coming decades.

In 2005, when I visited Ōmura, in the company of former detainees
and others, we found the migrant detention centre thinly populated.
Designed to hold eight hundred people, in the autumn of 2005 it had only
about 130 inmates, a figure which had changed little over the previous five
years, and has fallen further since. The vast and technologically sophis-
ticated complex seemed an expensive operation to maintain for such a
small number of people. A video which we were shown on arrival by the
Immigration Centre staff highlighted the new face of multiethnic Japan –
the determination to create a migration control system which welcomes
law-abiding foreigners while keeping out the undesirable. Ōmura itself
has certainly been physically transformed since its early squalid and overcrowded days. But when asked about the cost of maintaining an institution which is less than one-quarter full, the officials explained that they,
too, are thinking of the future. Who knows what crises may be just round
the corner? More than half a century after the establishment of Ōmura
at the height of the Korean War, they were keeping the detention centre
open, just in case.

NOTES

1. Sakanaka Hidenori, *Nyūkan Senki: 'Zainichi' Sabetsu, 'Nikkeijin' Mondai,
   Gaikokujin Sabetsu to Nihon no Kinmirai* (Tokyo: Kōdansha, 2005), p. 146.
2. Ibid., pp. 150–1.
3. Ibid., p. 14.
4. Kim Jeol-Un, 'Zainichi Chōsenjin no Keizai Mondai', in Pak Jeong-Myeong
   (ed.), *Zainichi Chōsenjin: Rekishi, Genjō, Tenbō* (Tokyo: Akashi Shoten, 1995),
   pp. 103–42, quotation from pp. 115–16.
5. See *Mindan Shimbun*, 16 April 2008.
6. See Pak Il, 'Sangoku no Hazama ni Ichi suru "Zainichi"', *Kan*, 11 (Autumn
   2002), pp. 62–9, reference to p. 64–5.
7. Sakanaka, *Nyūkan Senki*, pp. 146–8.
8. S. Hirowatari, 'Foreigners and the "Foreigner Question" under Japanese
   Law', *Annals of the Institute of Social Science*, 35 (1993), pp. 91–122, quotation
   from p. 96.

9. Quoted in M. Sugihara, 'The Right to Use Ethnic Names in Japan', *Journal of Intercultural Studies*, 14, 2 (1993), pp. 13–33, quotation from p. 22.

10. Asakawa Akihiro, *Zainichi Gaikokujin to Kika Seido* (Tokyo: Shinkansha, 2003), p. 14; interestingly enough, during the same period, there were over 40,000 cases of applicants (of all nationalities) being *refused* naturalization.

11. Quoted in Sakanaka Hidenori, '"Sakanaka Ronbun" no Haikei to Tōji no Hankyō', 8 January 2008, http://blog.livedoor.jp/sakanakacolumn/archives/525818.html; for a discussion of the debates surrounding the Sakanaka essay, see 'Sangoku no Hazama', pp. 67–8.

12. See Iinuma Jirō and Kim Dong-Myeong, 'Zainichi Chōsenjin no "Daisan no Michi"', in Iinuma Jirō (ed.), *Zainichi Kankoku Chōsenjin: Sono Nihon Shakai ni okeru Sonzai Kachi* (Osaka: Kaifūsha, 1988), quotation from p. 68 (original published in the journal *Chōsenjin*).

13. Kang Sang-Jung, 'Hōhō toshite no "Zainichi": Yang To-Ho Shi no Hanron ni Kotaeru', in Iinuma, *Zainichi Kankoku Chōsenjin*, pp. 275–87, quotation from p. 276.

14. For varying perspectives on the 'third way', see the essays in Iinuma, *Zainichi Kankoku Chōsenjin*; also Ueda Masaaki, Sugihara Tōru, Kang Sang-Jung and Pak Il, 'Rekishi no naka no "Zainichi"', *Kan*, 11 (Autumn 2002), pp. 46–95.

15. See Han Jong-Seok, 'Gaitōhō no Genjitsu to Jinken', in Mullei no Kai (ed.), *Shimon Ōnatsu Seido to Zainichi Kankoku-Chōsenjin* (Tokyo: Mullei no Kai, 1985), pp. 19–29.

16. *Asahi Shinbun*, 9 November 1985.

17. Ibid.

18. See 'S. Korean Spies Admit 1973 Snatch', *BBC News*, 24 October 2007, available at http://news.bbc.co.uk/2/hi/asia-pacific/7059648.stm (accessed 30 August 2008).

19. On the story of Suh Sung and Suh Joon-Shik, see Suh Sung (trans. Jean Inglis), *Unbroken Spirits: Nineteen Years in South Korea's Gulag* (Lanham, MD: Rowman and Littlefield, 2001).

20. Ministry of Foreign Affairs, Japan 'Refugees' (website), available at www.mofa.go.jp/policy/refugee/japan.html (accessed 2 July 2008).

21. 'Wave of Vietnamese Refugees Straining Japan', *New York Times*, 31 August 1989.

22. Under the 1978 policy, the refugees had to be 'either (a) a spouse, child or parent of a Japanese citizen or a lawful resident foreigner with a stable livelihood in Japan; (b) a person who has a secure guarantor in Japan; (c) a spouse, child or parent of a person who meets the requirement spelled out in category (b)'. See R. Mukae, *Japan's Refugee Policy: To Be of the World* (Fucecchio: European Press Academic Publishing, 2001), p. 107.

23. Ibid.; see also K. Koizumi, 'Resettlement of Indochinese Refugees in Japan (1975–1989): An Analysis and Model for Future Services', *Journal of Refugee Studies*, 4, 2 (1991), pp. 182–99.

24. Geneva Convention on the Status of Refugees, Articles 23 and 24; see website of the United Nations High Commission for Refugees, available at www.unhchr.ch/html/menu3/b/0_c_ref.htm (accessed 30 August 2008).

25. Mukae, *Japan's Refugee Policy*, pp. 147–8. Mukae here echoes a common misperception by describing those with *Chōsen Seki* as being 'of North Korean descent' or 'resident foreigners originally from North Korea'. A further revision to the Immigration Control Law in 1992 combined the various residence statuses of colonial-period migrants (Taiwanese, *Kankoku Seki* and *Chōsen Seki*) and their descendants into a single category of special permanent residents (*tokubetsu eijūsha*); see Yasunori Fukuoka, *Lives of Young Koreans in Japan* (Melbourne: Trans Pacific Press, 2000), p. 19.

26. Koizumi, 'Resettlement of Indochinese Refugees'.

27. S. Murphy-Shigematsu, 'Identities of Multiethnic People in Japan', in M. Douglass and G. A. Roberts (ed.), *Japan and Global Migration: Foreign Workers and the Advent of Multicultural Society* (Honolulu: University of Hawaii Press, 2000), pp. 196–216, see particularly p. 205.

28. Fukuoka, *Lives of Young Koreans in Japan*, p. 35.

29. W. Herbert, *Foreign Workers and Law Enforcement in Japan* (London: Kegan Paul International, 1996), p. 22.

30. Immigration Bureau, Ministry of Justice, Japan, *Immigration Control 2005* (Tokyo: Ministry of Justice), p. 30; see www.moj.go.jp/NYUKAN/nyukan46.html (accessed 15 August 2008).

31. Ibid., p. 30.

32. Keisatsu Chō, *Keisatsu Hakusho 1979* (Tokyo: Ōkurasho Insatsukyoku, 1979), pp. 145–6.

33. For further discussion, see T. Morris-Suzuki, 'Packaging Prejudice for the Global Marketplace', *Japan in the World*, 2 May 2001, available at www.iwanami.co.jp/jpworld/text/packaging01.html.

34. See Y. Sellek, '*Nikkeijin*: The Phenomenon of Return Migration', in M. Weiner (ed.), *Japan's Minorities: The Illusion of Homogeneity* (London: Routledge, 1997), pp. 178–210, see particularly pp. 183–5.

35. See B. Brody, *Opening the Door: Immigration, Ethnicity and Globalization in Japan* (New York and London: Routledge 2002); D. de Carvalho, *Migrants and Identity in Japan and Brazil* (London and New York: Routledge Curzon, 2002).

36. Sellek, '*Nikkeijin*', p. 200.

37. Quoted in de Carvalho, *Migrants and Identity*, p. 140; see also T. Tsuda, 'Crossing Ethnic Boundaries: The Challenge of Brazilian *Nikkeijin* Return Migrants to Japan', in N. Adachi (ed.), *Japanese Diasporas: Unsung Pasts, Conflicting Presents and Uncertain Futures* (London and New York: Routledge, 2006), pp. 202–16.

38. For a discussion of this problem, see John Lie, *Multiethnic Japan* (Cambridge, MA: Harvard University Press, 2001), pp. 142–69.

39. Immigration Bureau, Ministry of Justice, Japan, *Immigration Control 2005*, pp. 30 and 44.

40. To give just a few examples, 'Today, there are approximately 700,000 Korean residents in Japan, concentrated primarily in the Osaka and Kyoto areas': Brody, *Opening the Door*, p. 96; 'there are about 700,000 ethnic Koreans in Japan, with many of them living in the region around Kobe and Osaka': Pradyumna P. Karan, *Japan in the 21st Century: Environment, Economy, and Society* (Lexington: University Press of Kentucky, 2005), p. 37; 'the nearly 700,000 Koreans now residing in Japan, mostly descendents of conscripted laborers like Son's forbears, live at the periphery of Japanese society, angry and unassimilated': John Nathan, *Japan Unbound* (New York: Houghton Mifflin, 2004), p. 102.

41. Sugihara, 'The Right to Use Ethnic Names', pp. 22–3.

42. Asakawa, *Zainichi Gaikokujin*, p. 15.

43. Yasunori Fukuoka, 'Koreans in Japan: Past and Present', *Saitama University Review*, 31, 1 (1996), available at www.han.org/a/fukuoka96a.html (accessed 10 August 2008).

44. Asakawa, *Zainichi Gaikokujin*, p. 14.

45. Sakanaka Hidenori, *Nyūkan Senki*.

46. *Tōkyō Shinbun*, 5 August 2008.

47. Ogawa Naoki, 'Jimintō Giren no Teigen Sōan no Pointo: "Taminzoku Kyōsei Kokka" Nippon e no Michisuji', *Shūkan Ekonomisuto*, 17 June 2008, pp. 74–5; see also Akashi Jun'ichi and Ogawa Naoki, 'Imin 1000-mannin "iminzoku kokka" e: Tabū ni chōsen suru Jimintō Giren', *Shūkan Ekonomisuto*, 17 June 2008, pp. 68–72.

48. *Tokyo Shinbun*, 10 July 2008.

49. *Sankei Shinbun*, 9 May 2008; see also Sakanaka, *Nyūkan Senki*, p. 143.

50. See 'Japan Fingerprints Foreigners as Anti-terror Move', *Reuters*, 20 November 2007, available at www.reuters.com/article/worldNews/idUST23858020071120 (accessed 20 July 2007).

51. See T. Morris-Suzuki, 'When Is a Terrorist Not a Terrorist?', *Japan Focus*, 10 October 2003. Available at www.japanfocus.org/products/search/1838.

References

ARCHIVES CONSULTED

Archives of the International Committee of the Red Cross (ICRC), Geneva,
 Switzerland
Australian National Archives, Canberra
Australian War Memorial, Canberra
British National Archives, Kew, UKJ.
Graham Parsons Papers, Lauinger Library, Georgetown University,
 Washington, DC
Jungang Ilbo newspaper, Seoul, database of Soviet archives related to Korea
Korean National Library database of GHQ/SCAP documents related to Korea
Modern Japanese Political History Material Room (*Kensei Shiryōshitsu*), National
 Diet Library (*Kokkai Toshokan*), Tokyo, Japan
National Archives and Records Administration (NARA), College Park,
 Maryland, USA
New Zealand National Archives, Wellington
Thompson Gale Declassified Documents Reference Service

NEWSPAPERS AND NEWS BULLETINS

Asahi Shinbun
Japan Times (known between 1942 and 1956 as the *Nippon Times*)
Mainichi Shinbun
New York Times
Pacific Stars and Stripes
Pacific Stars and Stripes Far East Weekly Review
Reuters
Sankei Shinbun
Tokyo Shinbun
Tsushima Shinbun
Yomiuri Shinbun

SECONDARY SOURCES

21-Seiki Nihon no Kōsō Kondankai. 2000. *Nihon no Furontia wa Nihon no
 Naka ni aru.* Tokyo: '21-Seiki Nihon no Kōsō' Kondankai. www.kantei.
 go.jp/jp/21century/houkokusyo/1s.html (accessed 1 September 2001).

Abe, Kohki. 2006. 'Are You a Good Refugee or a Bad Refugee? Security Concerns and Dehumanization of Immigration Policies in Japan', *AsiaRights*, 6.

Ahn, Hyung-Ju. 2002. *Between Two Adversaries: Korean Interpreters at Japanese Alien Enemy Detention Centers During World War II*. Fullerton: California State University Oral History Program.

Akashi, Jun'ichi and Ogawa Naoki. 2008. 'Imin 1000-mannin "iminzoku kokka" e: Tabū ni chōsen suru Jimintō Giren', *Shūkan Ekonomisuto*, 17 June.

Alvah, Donna. 2007. *Unofficial Ambassadors: American Military Families Overseas and the Cold War, 1946–1965*. New York and London: New York University Press.

Anderson, Malcolm. 1996. *Frontiers: Territory and State Formation in the Modern World*. Cambridge: Polity Press.

Anderson, Malcolm and Bort, Eberhardt (eds.). 1998. *The Frontiers of Europe*. London: Pinter.

Anthias, Floya and Yuval-Davis, Nira. 1992. *Racialized Boundaries: Race, Nations, Gender, Colour and Class and the Anti-racist Struggle*. London: Routledge.

Appadurai, Arjun. 1990. 'Disjuncture and Difference in the Global Cultural Economy', in M. Featherstone (ed.), *Global Culture: Nationalism, Globalization and Modernity*. London: Sage, 295–310.

Arakaki, Osamu. 2008. *Refugeee Law and Practice in Japan*. London: Ashgate.

Asakawa, Akihiro. 2003. *Zainichi Gaikokujin to Kika Seido*. Tokyo: Shinkansha.

Balibar, Etienne and Wallerstein, Immanuel. 1991. *Race, Nation, Class: Ambiguous Identities*. London: Routledge.

Bennett, Marion T. 1963. *American Immigration Policies: A History*. Washington, DC: Public Affairs Press.

Betros, Chris. 2008. 'New Tokyo Immigration Center Tries to Get It Right', *Japan Today*, 2 March. www.japantoday.com/news/jp/e/tools/print. asp?content=feature&id=421 (accessed 2 March 2008).

Brimelow, Peter. 1995. *Alien Nation: Common Sense about America's Immigration Disaster*. New York: Random House.

Brocklebank, Laurie. 1997. *Jayforce: New Zealand and the Military Occupation of Japan 1945–1948*. Auckland: Oxford University Press.

Brody, Betsy. 2002. *Opening the Door: Immigration, Ethnicity and Globalization in Japan*. New York and London: Routledge.

Buck-Morss, Susan. 2000. *Dreamworld and Catastrophe: The Passing of Mass Utopias in East and West*. Cambridge, MA: MIT Press.

Calder, Kent. 2007. *Embattled Garrisons: Comparative Base Politics and American Globalism*. Princeton and Oxford: Princeton University Press.

Caprio, Mark E. 2008. 'The Forging of Alien Status of Koreans in American Occupied Japan', *Japan Focus*, January. www.japanfocus.org/products/ topdf/2624 (accessed 10 March 2008).

Carrington, Kerry. 2003. 'Ministerial Discretion in Migration Matters: Contemporary Policy Issues in Historical Context'. Canberra: Parliament of Australia

Parliamentary Library Current Issues Brief no. 3. www.aph.gov.au/Library/
Pubs/CIB/2003–04/04cib03.htm (accessed 5 May 2008).

Castles, Stephen and Miller, Michael J. 1998. *The Age of Migration: International
Population Movements in the Modern World*. Basingstoke: Macmillan.

Cheong, Sung-Hwa. 1991. *The Politics of Anti-Japanese Sentiment in
Korea: Japanese–South Korean Relations under American Occupation, 1945–
1952*. New York and Westport, CT: Greenwood Press.

Choi, Deok-Hyo. 2003. 'Wartime Mobilization and Zainichi Koreans: Focussing
on the "Experiences" Surrounding the Volunteer Soldier Recruitment
Movement'. Paper presented at the Experiences of the Korean War workshop, September, Tokyo University of Foreign Studies.

Clifton, Allan S. 1950. *Time of Fallen Blossoms*. London: Cassell.

Commission on Wartime Relocation and Internment of Civilians. 1997.
*Personal Justice Denied: Report of the Commission on Wartime Relocation and
Internment of Civilians*. Washington, DC and Seattle: Civil Liberties Public
Education Fund, University of Washington Press.

Culley, John Joel. 1996. 'A Troublesome Presence: World War II Internment of
German Sailors in New Mexico', *Prologue*, 28, 4 (Winter), 279–95.

Cummings, Bruce. 1997. *Korea's Place in the Sun: A Modern History*. New York
and London: W. W. Norton and Co.

Davis, George. 2001. *The Occupation of Japan: The Rhetoric and Reality of Anglo-
Australian Relations, 1939–1952*. Brisbane: University of Queensland Press.

De Carvalho, Daniela. 2002. *Migrants and Identity in Japan and Brazil*. London
and New York: Routledge Curzon.

Denoon, Donald, Hudson, Mark, McCormack, Gavan and Morris-Suzuki,
Tessa (eds.). 1996. *Multicultural Japan: Palaeolothic to Postmodern*.
Cambridge: Cambridge University Press.

Dō, Khiem and Kim Sung-Soo, 'Crimes, Concealment and South Korea's Truth
and Reconciliation Commission', *Japan Focus*, August 2008, www.japanfo-
cus.org/ (accessed 8 August 2008).

do Soto, Hernando. 2000. *The Mystery of Capital: Why Capitalism Triumphs in
the West and Fails Everywhere Else*. London: Black Swan Books.

Douglass, Michael and Roberts, Glenda A. (eds.). 2000. *Japan and Global
Migration: Foreign Workers and the Advent of Multicultural Society*.
Honolulu: University of Hawaii Press.

2000. 'Japan in an Age of Global Migration', in Douglass, Michael and
Roberts, Glenda A. (eds.), *Japan and Global Migration: Foreign Workers and
the Advent of Multicultural Society*. Honolulu: University of Hawaii Press,
3–37.

Dower, John. 1999. *Embracing Defeat: Japan in the Wake of World War II*. New
York: W. W. Norton.

Duus, Peter. 1995. *The Abacus and the Sword: The Japanese Penetration of Korea
1895–1910*. Berkeley: University of California Press.

Eltis, David (ed.). 2002. *Coerced and Free Migration: Global Perspectives*.
Stanford: Stanford University Press.

Evans, Humphrey. 1960. *Thimayya of India: A Soldier's Life*. New York: Harcourt, Brace and Co.

Fiset, Louis. 2001. 'Return to Sender: US Censorship of Enemy Alien Mail in World War II', *Prologue*, 33, 1, 21–35.

Foucault, Michel. 1967. 'Des Espaces autres'. Trans. Jay Miskowiec. http:// foucault.info/documents/heteroTopia/foucault.heteroTopia.en.html (accessed 10 February 2008).

Fukuoka, Yasunori. 1996. 'Koreans in Japan: Past and Present', *Saitama University Review*, 31, 1. www.han.org/a/fukuoka96a.html (accessed 10 August 2008).

——— 2000. *Lives of Young Koreans in Japan*. Melbourne: Trans Pacific Press.

Gardiner, C. Harvey. 1981. *Pawns in a Triangle of Hate: The Peruvian-Japanese and the United States*. Seattle: University of Washington Press.

Gekkan Okinawa Sha (ed.). n.d. *Laws and Regulations during the US Administration of Okinawa 1945–1972*, vol. I. Naha: Ikemiya Shōkai, 2–207.

——— n.d. *Laws and Regulations during the US Administration of Okinawa 1945–1972*, Vol II. Naha: Ikemiya Shōkai.

Gillem, Mark L. 2007. *America Town: Building the Outposts of Empire*. Minneapolis and London: University of Minnesota Press.

Goffman, Erving. 1968. *Asylums: Essays on the Social Situation of Mental Patients and Other Inmates*. Harmondsworth: Penguin Books.

Government Section, Supreme Commander for the Allied Powers. 1949. *Political Reorientation of Japan, September 1945 to September 1948*. Washington, DC: US Government Printing Office.

——— 1990. *History of the Non-military Activities of the Occupation of Japan, 1945 through 1950*, Vol. XIV, *Natural Resources*, Part B (facsimile reprint). Tokyo: Nihon Tosho Sentā.

Graham, Euan. 2005. *Japan's Sea Lane Security 1940–2004: A Matter of Life and Death?* London: Routledge.

Haenyo Museum (ed.). 2007. *Mothers of the Sea: The Jeju Haenyo*. Jeju City: Jeju Communication.

Hage, Ghassan. 1998. *White Nation*. Sydney: Pluto Press.

Han, Jong-Seok. 1985. 'Gaitōhō no Genjitsu to Jinken', in Mullei no Kai (ed.), *Shimon Ōnatsu Seido to Zainichi Kankoku-Chōsenjin*. Tokyo: Mullei no Kai.

Han Sok-Gyu. 2007. *Nihon kara 'Kita' ni Kaetta Hito no Monogatari*. Tokyo: Shinkansha.

Hara Kimie, 2006. 'Cold War Frontiers in the Asia–Pacific: The Troubling Legacy of the San Francisco Treaty'. *Japan Focus*, 4 September. http:// japanfocus.org/ (accessed 10 June 2007).

Hatsusei, Ryūhei. 1996. 'Nihon no Kokusaika to Tabunkashugi', in Hatsusei Ryūhei (ed.), *Eshunishiti to Tabunkashugi*. Tokyo: Dōbunkan, 205–30.

Hayashi Kōzō. 2008. 'Kim Dong-Gi to Wareware', *Res Novare: Jōkyō to Bunseki*, no. 3, May–June 1967, reproduced in *Hayashi Kōzō Kobunshū: 'Kako no Kokufuku' ni tsuite no Tekisuto o Chūshin ni*. Kyoto: privately printed.

Head, Timothy E. and Daws, Gavan. 1968. 'The Bonins – Isles of Contention', *American Heritage*, 29, 2 (February), 58–74.

Headquarters, Far East Command. 1953. *Information for Dependents Coming to Japan*. www.militarybrat.com/yokohama.cfm (accessed 14 April 2008).

Headquarters, United States Civil Administration of the Ryukyu Islands, Programs, and Statistics Section. 1952. *Ryukyu Islands Economic Statistics*, no. 17 (March–May), 11.

Henshall, Kenneth G. 1999. *Dimensions of Japanese Society: Gender, Margins and Mainstream*. London: Macmillan.

Heo Yeong-Seon. 2006. *Cheju Yonsan*. Seoul: Minjuhwa Undong Ginyeom Saobhoe.

Herbert, Wolfgang. 1996. *Foreign Workers and Law Enforcement in Japan*. London: Kegan Paul International.

Hernandez, Kelly Lytle. 2002. 'Distant Origins: The Mexican Roots of US Border Control Practice and American Racism, 1924–1954'. Paper presented at the UCLA Second Annual Interdisciplinary Conference on Race, Ethnicity and Migration, 28 May, in Los Angeles.

Hirowatari, Seigo. 1993. 'Foreigners and the "Foreigner Question" under Japanese Law', *Annals of the Institute of Social Science*, 35, 91–122.

Homepage of the Commander Fleet Activities Sasebo. http://www.cfas.navy.mil/History/history.htm (accessed 7 June 2008).

Hōmushō Nyūkoku Kanrikyoku. 1959. *Shutsunyūkoku Kanri Hakusho, Shōwa 34-Nen*. Tokyo: Ōkurasho Insatsukyoku.

———. 1964. *Shutsunyūkoku Kanri to sono Jittai – Shōwa 39-nen*. Tokyo: Ōkurashō Insatsukyoku.

———. 1975. *Shutsunyūkoku Kanri: Sono Genkyō to Kadai*. Tokyo: Ōkurashō Insatsukyoku.

———. 1980. *Shutsunūkoku Kanri no Kaikō to Tenbō: Nyūkan Hasoku 30–Shūnen o Kinen shite*. Tokyo: Hōmushō Nyūkoku Kanrikyoku.

———. *Nyūkoku Kanri 2007*. Tokyo: Hōmushō Nyūkoku Kanrikyoku. www.moj.go.jp/NYUKAN/nyukan67-2.pdf (accessed 15 August 2008).

Hōmushō Ōmura Nyūkokusha Shūyojo (ed.). 1970. *Ōmura Nyūkokusha Shūyojo 20-Nenshi*. Tokyo: Hōmushō.

Hyun, Moo-Am. 2007. 'Mikkō, Ōmura Shūyōjo, Saishūtō: Ōsaka to Saishūtō o Musubu "Mikkō" no Nettowāku', *Gendai Shisō*, 35 (June): 158–73.

Iinuma Jirō and Kim Dong-Myeong. 1988. 'Zainichi Chōsenjin no "Daisan no Michi"', in Iinuma Jirō (ed.), *Zainichi Kankoku Chōsenjin: Sono Nihon Shakai ni okeru Sonzai Kachi*. Osaka: Kaifūsha.

Immigration Bureau, Ministry of Justice, Japan. 2000. *Basic Plan for Immigration Control*, 2nd edition. Tokyo: Ministry of Justice. www.moj.go.jp/ENGLISH/information/bpic2nd-01.html (accessed 30 November 2007).

Immigration Control 2005. Tokyo: Ministry of Justice. www.moj.go.jp/NYUKAN/nyukan46.html (accessed 15 August 2008).

———. 2005. *Basic Plan for Immigration Control*, 3rd edition. Tokyo: Ministry of Justice. www.moj.go.jp/ENGLISH/information/bpic3rd-03.html#3-1 (accessed 30 November 2007).

2006. *Immigration Control Report 2006, Part 1: Immigration Control in Recent Years*. Tokyo: Ministry of Justice. www.moj.go.jp/NYUKAN/nyukan54-2. pdf (accessed 20 November 2007).

Inaba, Nanako. 2000. 'Furansu ni okeru Hiseiki Taizaisha to Amunesti: "Sanpapie no Undō" to Shimin Shakai kara no Taiō', in Komai Hiroshi, Watado Ichirō and Yamawaki Keizō (ed.), *Chōka Taizai Gaikokujin to Zairyū Tokubetsu Kyoka: Kiro ni Tatsu nihon no Shutsunyūkoku Kanri Seisaku*. Tokyo: Akashi Shoten, 36–43.

Inokuchi, Hiromitsu. 2000. 'Korean Ethnic Schools in Occupied Japan, 1945–1952', in Sonia Ryang (ed.), *Koreans in Japan: Critical Voices from the Margin*. London: Routledge, 140–56.

Itanuma, Jirō. 1969. 'Ōmura Shūyōjo Teppai no tame ni', in Pak Seongkong (ed.), *Ōmura Shūyōjo*. Kyoto: Kyoto Daigaku Shuppankai, 1–42.

Itoh, Mayumi. 1998. *Globalization of Japan: Japanese Sakoku Mentality and US Efforts to Open Japan*. New York: St. Martin's Press.

Iyotani, Toshio. 2005. 'Migration as Method', in T. Iyotani Toshio and M. Ishii, *Motion in Place/Place in Motion: 21st Century Migration*. Osaka: Japan Center for Area Studies/National Museum of Ethnography, 3–16.

Iyotani, Toshio and Kajita, Toshimichi (eds.). 1992. *Gaikokujin Rōdōsha Ron: Genjō kara Riron e*. Tokyo: Kōbundō.

Izumi Seiichi. 1966. *Saishūtō*. Tokyo: Tōkyō Daigaku Shuppankai.

Japan Red Cross Society. 1956. *Fundamental Conditions of Livelihood of Certain Koreans Residing in Japan*. Tokyo: Japan Red Cross Society.

Kane, Tim. 2004. *Global US Troop Deployments, 1950–2003*. Washington, DC: Heritage Foundation. www.heritage.org/research/nationalsecurity/cda04-11.cfm (accessed 15 March 2008).

Kang, Sang-Jung. 1988. 'Hōhō toshite no "Zainichi": Yang To-Ho Shi no Hanron ni Kotaeru', in Iinuma Jirō (ed.), *Zainichi Kankoku Chōsenjin: Sono Nihon Shakai ni okeru Sonzai Kachi*. Osaka: Kaifūsha, 275–87.

2003. *Nicchō Kankei no Kokufuku*. Tokyo: Shūeisha Shinsho.

2004. *Zainichi*. Tokyo: Kōdansha.

2006 'Memories of a *Zainichi* Korean Childhood'. Trans. Robin Fletcher. *Japanese Studies*, 26, 3 (December), 269–70.

Karan, Pradyumna P. 2005. *Japan in the 21st Century: Environment, Economy, and Society*. Lexington: University Press of Kentucky.

Keisatsu Chō. 1979. *Keisatsu Hakusho 1979*. Tokyo: Ōkurasho Insatsukyoku.

Kichi Mondai Chōsa Iinkai (ed.). 1954. *Gunkichi no Jittai to Bunseki*. Tokyo: San-Ichi Shobō

Kim, Chang-Jung. 2007. *Zainichi Giyūhei Kikan sezu: Chōsen Sensō Hisshi*. Tokyo: Iwanami Shoten.

Kim, Il-Hwa. 1995. 'Zainichi Chōsenjin no Hōteki Chii', in Pak Jeong-Myeong (ed.), *Zainichi Chōsenjin: Rekishi, Genjō, Tenbō*. Tokyo: Akashi Shoten, 189–232.

Kim, Jeol-Un. 1995. 'Zainichi Chōsenjin no Keizai Mondai', in Pak Jeong-Myeong (ed.), *Zainichi Chōsenjin: Rekishi, Genjō, Tenbō*. Tokyo: Akashi Shoten, 103–42.

Kim, Samuel S. 2006. *The Two Koreas and the Great Powers*. Cambridge: Cambridge University Press.

Kim, Seok-Beom. 2005. 'Mangetsu', in Kim Seok-Beom, *Kim Seok-Beom Sakuhinshū*, Vol. II. Tokyo: Heibonsha.

Kim, Seok-Beom and Kim Shi-Jong. 2001. *Naze Kakitsuzukete Kita ka, Naze Chinmoku shite Kita ka: Saishūtō 4.3 Jiken no Kioku to Bungaku*. Tokyo: Heibonsha.

Kim Shi-Jong. 2004. *Waga Sei to Shi*, Tokyo: Iwanami Shoten.

Kim, Tae-Gi. 1997. *Sengo Nihon Seiji to Zainichi Chōsenjin Mondai*. Tokyo: Keisō Shobō.

Kim, Yeong and Yang Jungja. 1988. *Umi o Watatta Chōsenjin Ama*. Tokyo: Shinjuku Shobō.

Kim, Yeong-Dal and Takayanagi, Toshio. 1995. *Kita Chōsen Kikoku Jigyō Kankei Shiryōshū*. Tokyo: Shinkansha.

Koh, Sun-Hui, 1998. 'Seikatsushi no Shiryō 3: 1946-nen ikō Rainichi' (recorded interview), unpublished appendix to Koh Sun-Hui, *20 Seiki no Tainichi Chejudōjin: Sono Seikatsu Katei to Ishiki*. Tokyo: Akashi Shoten.

      1998. *Senzai Kyojūsha Shiryōshū, 20 Seiki no Tainichi Chejudōjin*. Tokyo: Akashi Shoten.

      1998. *20 Seiki no Tainichi Chejudōjin: Sono Seikatsu Katei to Ishiki*. Tokyo: Akashi Shoten.

Koizumi, Koichi. 1991. 'Resettlement of Indochinese Refugees in Japan (1975–1989): An Analysis and Model for Future Services', *Journal of Refugee Studies*, 4, 2, 182–99.

Komai, Hiroshi (ed). 1996. *Nihon no Esunikku Shakai*. Tokyo: Akashi Shoten.

Komai, Hiroshi. 2001. *Foreign Migrants in Contemporary Japan*. Trans. Jens Wilkinson. Melbourne: Trans Pacific Press.

Komai, Hiroshi, Watado Ichirō and Yamawaki Keizō (eds.). 2000. *Chōka Taizai Gaikokujin to Zairyū Tokubetsu Kyoka: Kiro ni Tatsu Nihon no Shutsunyūkoku Kanri Seisaku*. Tokyo: Akashi Shoten.

Kondō Atsushi. 2000. 'Zairyū Tokubetsu Kyoka no Hōteki Konkyo: Kenpō, Kokusai Jinkenhō jō no Kenri to "Kokusai Kijun"', in Komai Hiroshi, Watado Ichirō and Yamawaki Keizō (eds.), *Chōka Taizai Gaikokujin to Zairyū Tokubetsu Kyoka: Kiro ni Tatsu Nihon no Shutsunyūkoku Kanri Seisaku*. Tokyo: Akashi Shoten, 52–60.

Kōseishō Hikiage Engo Chō, 2000. *Hikiage Engo no Kiroku*, Vol. 1 (reprint). Tokyo: Kusersu Shuppan.

Kurihara, Akira (ed.). 1997. *Kyōsei no Kanata e*, Tokyo: Kōbundō.

Kuwahara, Yasu. 1998. 'Japan's Dilemma: Can International Migration be Controlled?', in M. Weiner and T. Hanami (eds.), *Temporary Workers or Future Citizens? Japanese and US Migration Policies*. New York: New York University Press, 355–83.

Le Carré, John. 2006. *The Mission Song*. London: Hodder and Stoughton.

Lie, John. 2001. *Multiethnic Japan*. Cambridge, MA: Harvard University Press.

MacKellar, Landin, Ermolieva, Tatiana, Horlacher, David and Mayhew, Leslie. 2004. *The Economic Impacts of Population Ageing in Japan*. Cheltenham: Edward Elgar.

Maeda, Tetsuo. 2000. *Zainichi Beigun Kichi no Shushi Kessan*. Tokyo: Chikuma Shinsho.

Matsumoto Kunihiko (ed.). 1996. *GHQ Nihon Senryōshi 16 – Gaikokujin no Toriatsukai*. Tokyo: Nihon Tosho Sentā.

Michika, Chikanobu. 2007. 'Shimomaruko Bunka Shūdan to sono Jidai: 50-nendai Tōkyō Sākuru Undō Kenkyū Josetsu', *Gendai Shisō*, 35, 17 (December), 38–101.

Migration Watch UK. 2003. 'A Review of Exceptional Leave to Remain and Humanitarian Protection'. Briefing paper 9.4 London: Migration Watch UK. www.migrationwatchuk.com/archive/migration_trends/exceptional_leave_to_remain.asp (accessed 7 July 2008).

Miles, Jack. 1995. 'The Coming Immigration Debate', *Atlantic Monthly (Online Edition)*, April. www.theatlantic.com/politics/immigrat/miles2f.htm (accessed 3 May 2008).

Miles, Robert. 1999. 'Analysing the Political Economy of Migration: The Airport as an "Effective" Institution of Control', in A. Brah, M.J. Hickman and M. Mac an Ghaill (eds.), *Global Futures: Migration, Environment and Globalization*. London: Macmillan, 161–84.

Ministry of Foreign Affairs, Japan, website. 'Refugees'. www.mofa.go.jp/policy/refugee/japan.html (accessed 2 July 2008).

Mitchell, Richard Hanks. 1963. 'The Korean Minority in Japan 1910–1963', unpublished Ph.D. thesis, University of Wisconsin.

Miyazaki, Shigeki. 1986. *Gaikokujin Tōroku Hō to Shimon Ōnatsu*. Tokyo: 'Chōsen Mondai' Konwakai.

Monna, Naoki. 1996. *Amerika Senryō Jidai Okinawa Genron Tōseishi: Genron no Jiyū e no Toi*. Tokyo: Yūzankaku.

Moon, Gyeong-Su. 2005. *Chejudō Gendaishi*. Tokyo: Shinkansha.

2008. *Saishūtō 4.3 Jiken: 'Tamna no Kuni' no Shi to Saisei no Monogatari*. Tokyo: Heibonsha.

Morris-Suzuki, Tessa. 2001. 'Packaging Prejudice for the Global Marketplace', *Japan in the World*. 2 May. www.iwanami.co.jp/jpworld/text/packaging01.html.

2003. 'When Is a Terrorist Not a Terrorist?', *Japan Focus*, 10 October. www.japanfocus.org/products/search/1838.

2004. 'An Act Prejudicial to the Occupation Forces: Migration Controls and Korean Residents in Post-surrender Japan', *Japanese Studies*, 24, 1, 4–28.

2007. *Exodus to North Korea: Shadows from Japan's Cold War*. Lanham, MD and New York: Rowman and Littlefield.

Mukae, Ryuji. 2001. *Japan's Refugee Policy: To Be of the World*. Fucecchio: European Press Academic Publishing.

Murphy-Shigematsu, Stephen. 2000. 'Identities of Multiethnic People in Japan', in Michael Douglass and Glenda A. Roberts (eds.), *Japan and Global Migration: Foreign Workers and the Advent of Multicultural Society*. Honolulu: University of Hawaii Press, 196–216.

Musil, Donna. 'Brats: A Journey Home'. www.bratsjourneyhome.com (accessed 8 May 2008).

Naimushō, Keibōkyoku. 1979. *Gaiji keisatsu reiki shū* (facsimile). Tokyo: Ryūkei Shosha.

Nakamura, Masanori. 1995. *Sengo Nihon: Senryō to Sengo Kaikaku*. Tokyo: Iwanami Shoten.

Nakano, Toshio (ed.). 2006. *Okinawa no Senryō to Nihon no Fukkō: Shokuminchishugi wa ika ni Keizokushita ka*. Tokyo: Seikyūsha.

Nathan, John. 2004. *Japan Unbound*. New York: Houghton Mifflin.

Nemeth, David J. 1987. *The Architecture of Ideology: Neo-Confucian Imprinting on Cheju Island, Korea*. Berkeley and Los Angeles: University of California Press.

Neumann, Klaus. 2004. *Refuge Australia: Australia's Humanitarian Record*, Sydney: University of New South Wales Press.

Niki, Fumiko. 1993. *Saigaika no Chūgokujin gyakusatsu: Chugokujin rōdōsha to wa naze gyakusatsu sareta ka*. Tokyo: Aoki Shoten.

Nishimura, Shigeki. 2004. *Ōsaka de Tatakatta Chōsen Sensō: Fukita Maikata Jiken to Seishun Gunzō*. Tokyo: Iwanami Shoten.

Ogawa, Naoki. 2008. 'Jimintō Giren no Teigen Sōan no Pointo: "Iminzoku Kyōsei Kokka" Nippon e no Michisuji', *Shūkan Ekokomisuto*. 17 June, 74–5.

Oguma, Eiji. 1995. *Tan'itsu Minzoku Shinwa no Kigen*. Tokyo: Shinyōsha.

Oguma, Eiji and Kang Sang-Jung (eds.). 2008. *Zainichi Issei no Kioku*. Tokyo Shūeisha Shinsho.

Oh, Bonnie B.C. (ed.). 2002. *Korea under the American Military Government, 1945–1948*. Westport and London: Praeger.

Okonogi Masao (ed.). 2004. *Zainichi Chōsenjin wa naze Kikoku shita no ka?* Tokyo: Gendai Jinbunsha.

Ōmura Shi Bunkazai Hogo Kyōkai. 1997. *'Rekishi' to natta Fūkei: Furushashin ni Miru Ōmura Seikatsushi*. Ōmura: Ōmura Shi Bunkazai Hogo Kyōkai.

Pak, Il. 2002. 'Sangoku no Hazama ni Ichi suru "Zainichi"', *Kan*, 11 (Autumn), 62–9.

Pak, Jae-Il. 1957. *Zainichi Chōsenjin ni kansuru Sōgō Chōsa Kenkyū*. Tokyo: Shin-Kigen Sha.

Pratt, Keith. 2007. *Everlasting Flower: A History of Korea*. London: Reaktion Books.

Rebich, Marcus and Takenaka, Ayumi. 2006. 'Introduction: The Changing Japanese Family', in M. Rebich and A. Takenaka (eds.), *The Changing Japanese Family*. London: Routledge, 3–16.

Rey-Schyrr, Catherine. 2007. *De Yalta à Dien Bien Phu: Histoire du Comité internationale de la Croix-Rouge 1945–1955*. Geneva: International Committee of the Red Cross.

Ryang, Sonia. 1997. *North Koreans in Japan: Language, Ideology and Identity*. Boulder, CO: Westview Press.

—— 2000. 'The North Korean Homeland of Koreans in Japan', in Sonia Ryang (ed.), *Koreans in Japan: Critical Voices from the Margin*. London: Routledge, 32–54.

—— (ed.). 2000. *Koreans in Japan: Critical Voices from the Margin*. London: Routledge.

Sakanaka, Hidenori. 1989. *Kongo no Shutsunyūkoku Kanri Gyōsei no Arikata ni tsuite*. Tokyo: Nihon Kajo Shuppan (originally published in 1977).

—— 2005. *Nyūkan Senki: 'Zainichi' Sabetsu, 'Nikkeijin' Mondai, Gaikokujin Sabetsu to Nihon no Kinmirai*. Tokyo: Kōdansha.

—— 2008. '"Sakanaka Ronbun" no Haikei to Tōji no Hankyō'. 8 January http://blog.livedoor.jp/sakanakacolumn/archives/525818.html (accessed 25 August 2008).

Satake, Kyōko. 2003. *Gunseika Amami no Mikkō, Mitsu Bōeki*. Tokyo: Nampō Shinsha.

Satō, Hisashi. 2005. 'Kikokusha no sono ato', in Takasaki Sōji and Pak Chongjin (eds.),*Kikoku Jigyō to wa Nan data no ka: Fuin sareta Nicchō Kankeishi*. Tokyo: Heibonsha, 93–120.

Satō Katsumi. 1971. *Zainichi Chōsenjin no Shomondai*. Tokyo: Dōseidō.

Schmitt, Carl. 1988. *The Crisis of Parliamentary Democracy*. Trans. E. Kennedy. Cambridge, MA: MIT Press.

Scott, James. 1999. 'The State and People Who Move Around: How Valleys Make the Hills in Southeast Asia' (IIAS Annual Lecture 1998), *IIAS Newsletter*, 19. www.iias.nl/iiasn/19/general/1.html (accessed 15 January 2008).

Sellek, Yoko. 1997. 'Nikkeijin: The Phenomenon of Return Migration', in Michael Weiner (ed.), *Japan's Minorities: The Illusion of Homogeneity*. London: Routledge, 178–210.

Shahed, S. A.M. and Sekiguchi, Chie. 2002 *Shinpan Zairyū Tokubetsu Kyoka:Ajia-kei Gaikokujin to no Ōbāsutei Kokusai Kekkon*. Tokyo: Akashi Shoten.

Shephardson, Mary. 1977. 'Pawns of Power: The Bonin Islanders', in Raymond D. Fogelson and Richard N. Adams (eds.), *The Anthropology of Power: Ethnographic Studies from Asia, Oceania, and the New World*. New York: Academic Press, 99–114.

Shin Chang-Seok. 2006. 'Fuse Tatsuji Sensei no Omoide', in Fuji Shinji (ed.), *Shokuminchi Kankei Shiryōshū 2: Chōsen, Taiwan Hen*. Tokyo: Fuji Shinji Shiryō Kenkyū Junbikai, 181–99.

Shin, Gi-Wook. 1996. *Peasant Protest and Social Change in Colonial Korea*. Seattle and London: University of Washington Press.

Siddle, Richard. 1996. *Race, Resistance and the Ainu of Japan*. London: Routledge.

Spencer, Stephen A. 1992. 'Illegal Migrant Labourers in Japan', *International Migration Review*, 26, 3, 754–86.

Sugihara, Mitsushi. 1993. 'The Right to Use Ethnic Names in Japan', *Journal of Intercultural Studies*, 14, 2, 13–33.

Sugihara, Tōru. 1998. *Ekkyō suru Tami: Kindai Ōsaka no Chōsenjinshi Kenkyū.* Tokyo: Shinkansha.

——— 2002. *Chūgokujin Kyōsei Renkō.* Tokyo: Iwanami Shoten.

Suh, Sung. 2001. *Unbroken Spirits: Nineteen Years in South Korea's Gulag.* Trans. Jean Inglis. Lanham, MD: Rowman and Littlefield.

Szalontai, Balász. 2005. *Kim Il Sung in the Khrushchev Era: Soviet–DPRK Relations and the Roots of North Korean Despotism.* Washington, DC: Woodrow Wilson Center Press.

Takaki, Robert. 1989. *Strangers from a Different Shore: A History of Asian Americans.* New York: Penguin Books.

Takasaki Sōji and Pak Jeong-Jin (eds.). 2005. *Kikoku Undō to ha Nan data no ka.* Tokyo: Heibonsha.

Takayanagi, Toshio. 2004. 'Tonichi Shoki no Yoon Hak-Joon – Mikkō, Hōsei Daigaku, Kikoku Jigyō', *Ibunka*, 5 (April), 1–35.

Takemae, Eiji. 2002. *Inside GHQ: The Allied Occupation of Japan and Its Legacy.* Trans. Robert Ricketts and Sebastian Swann. London: Continuum.

Tanaka, Hiroshi. 1984. 'Shokuminchi tōchi o sasaeta kokuseki', in Doi Takako (ed.), *'Kokuseki' o kangaeru.* Tokyo: Jiji Tsūshinsha, 155–76.

Tarr, David W. 1966. 'The Military Abroad', *Annals of the American Academy of Political and Social Science*, 368 (November), 31–40.

Tashirō, Aritsugu. 1974. *Kosekihō chikujō kaisetsu.* Tokyo: Yuzankaku.

Tōdai Hōkyōtō (ed.). 1971. *Nyūkan Taisei Shiryōshū.* Tokyo: Aki Shobō.

Tokyo Fu. 1929. *Ogasawarato Sōran.* Tokyo: Tokyo Fu.

Torpey, John. 2000. *The Invention of the Passport: Surveillance, Citizenship and the State.* Cambridge: Cambridge University Press.

Tsuboe, Senji. 1965. *Zai-Nihon Chōsenjin no Gaikyo.* Tokyo: Gannandō Shoten (original report composed in 1953).

Tsubouchi, Hirokiyo. 1998. *'Bōshū' to iu na no kyōsei renkō: Kikikaki aru Zainichi issei no shōgen.* Tokyo: Sairyūsha.

Tsuda, Takeyuki. 2006. 'Crossing Ethnic Boundaries: The Challenge of Brazilian *Nikkeijin* Return Migrants to Japan', in Nobuko Adachi (ed.), *Japanese Diasporas: Unsung Pasts, Conflicting Presents and Uncertain Futures.* London and New York: Routledge, 202–16.

Ueda Masaaki, Sugihara Tōru, Kang Sang-Jung and Pak Il. 2002. 'Rekishi no naka no "Zainichi"', *Kan*, 11 (Autumn), 46–95.

Umebayashi, Hiromichi. 2002. *Zainichi Beigun.* Tokyo: Iwanami Shinsho.

Underwood, William. 2006. 'Names, Bones and Unpaid Wages (1): Reparations for Korean Forced Labor in Japan', *Japan Focus,* September. www.japanfocus.org/products/topdf/2219 (accessed 10 September 2007).

UNHCR. 2006. *Statistical Yearbook 2006.* Geneva: UNHCR. United Nations High Commission for Refugees. www.unhcr.ch/html/menu3/b/o_c_ref. htm (accessed 30 August 2008).

United States Census of Population. 1970. 'Dependents of Armed Forces Personnel 1970', *United States Census of Population.* www2.census.gov/prod2/decennial/documents/42053794v2p10a10bch1.pdf (accessed 30 May 2008).

US Forces Japan. 'Welcome to US Forces Japan', *US Forces Japan.* www.usfj.mil/ (accessed 10 May 2008).

Utsumi, Aiko. 2006. 'Teikoku no Naka no Rōmu Dōin', in Kurasawa Aiko, Sugihara Tōru, Narita Ryūichi, Tessa Morris-Suzuki, Yui Daizaburō and Yoshida Yutaka (eds.), *Iwanami Kōza Taiheiyō Sensō 4: Teikoku no Sensō Keiken.* Tokyo: Iwanami Shoten, 91–118.

Vasishth, Andrea. 1997. 'A Model Minority: The Chinese Community in Japan', in Michael Weiner (ed.), *Japan's Minorities: The Illusion of Homogeneity.* London: Routledge, 108–39.

Watado, Ichirō, and Suzuki Eriko (eds.). 2007. *Zairyū Tokubetsu Kyoka to Nihon no Imin Seisaku: 'Imin Senbetsu' Jidai no Tōra.* Tokyo: Akashi Shoten.

Weiner, Michael. 1994. *Race and Migration in Imperial Japan.* London and New York: Routledge.

    (ed.). 1997. *Japan's Minorities: The Illusion of Homogeneity.* London and New York: Routledge.

    2000. 'Japan in the Age of Migration', in Michael Douglass and Glenda A. Roberts (eds.), *Japan and Global Migration: Foreign Workers and the Advent of Multicultural Society.* Honolulu: University of Hawaii Press, 52–69.

Willis, David Blake and Murphy-Shigematsu, Stephen (eds.). 2008. *Transcultural Japan: At the Boundaries of Race, Gender, and Identity.* London: Routledge.

Wyman, Mark. 1989. *DP: Europe's Displaced Persons, 1945–1951.* Philadelphia: Balch Institute Press.

Yakabi, Osamu. 2003. ' "Kokkyō" no Kengen: Okinawa Yonaguni no Mitsubōeki Shūsoku no Haikei', *Gendai Shisō* (September), 186–201.

Yamatani, Tetsuo (ed.). 1979. *Okinawa no Harumoni.* Tokyo: Banseisha.

Yamawaki, Keizo. 2000. 'Foreign Workers in Japan: A Historical Perspective', in Michael Douglass and Glenda A. Roberts (eds.), *Japan and Global Migration: Foreign Workers and the Advent of Multicultural Society.* Honolulu: University of Hawaii Press, 38–51.

Yamazaki Shigeki. 1970. *Shutsunyūkoku Kanri: Gendai no 'Sakoku'.* Tokyo: Sanseidō.

Yang, Hang-Won. 1988. ' "Saishūtō Yon-San Jiken" no Hakei ni Kansuru Kenkyū', in Saishūtō Yonsan Jiken Yonjisshū nen Tsuitō Kinen Kōenshū Kankō Iinkai (eds.), *Saishūtō 'Yon-San Jiken' to wa Nani ka.* Tokyo: Shinkansha.

Yi, Hoe-Seong. 1994. *Hyakunen no Tabibitotachi.* Tokyo: Shinchō Bunko.

Yoon, Hak-Jun, 1979. 'Waga Mikkōki', *Chōsen Kenkyū,* 190 (June), 4–15.

Yoshimi, Shunya. 2007. *Shinbei to Hanbei: Sengo Nihon no Seijiteki Muishiki,* Tokyo: Iwanami Shinsho.

Yoshimi, Yoshiaki. 2000. *Comfort Women: Sexual Slavery in the Japanese Military during World War II.* New York: Columbia University Press.

Yoshitome, Roju. 1977. *Ōmura Chōsenjin Shūyōjo.* Tokyo: Nigatsusha.

Yun, Ki-Hwang. 1983. *Die Rolle der Friedeslinie (Rhee Line) im Normalisierungs-prozess der Beziehungen zwischen Korea und Japan in der Nachkriegsära.* Frankfurt-am-Main and Bern: Peter Lang.

Index

alien registration cards, 1, 15, 90–4, 91
  fingerprints, 92–3, 234
  Korean nationality, 93
  Korean War volunteers, 141
  photographs, 91, 92
Alien Registration Law, 1, 114, 137
  exemptions, 123
  fingerprints, 114
  revision of 1992, 235
  see also Alien Registration Ordinance 1947
Alien Registration Ordinance 1947 90–1
  Koreans, 91, 93–4
  revision of, 114
  Taiwanese, 91
Allied military forces, 14–15
  New Zealand troops, 58
  see also US military bases; US military forces
Allied occupation, 14, 28, 46–7
  border control, 96
  former colonials, 60–2, 63–5
  liberty ships, 53
  nationality policy, 112
  Okinawa, 46, 136
  policies, 94
  South Korea, 46
  status of non-Japanese, 59
  see also General Headquarters of the
    Supreme Commander for the Allied
    Powers; US military bases Japan; US
    military forces Japan
Alvah, Donna, 131
Amami Islands, 31
amnesty for returnees to North Korea, 163
  for undocumented migrants, 175
Ampo see US–Japan Security Treaty
Anderson, Malcom, 7
Angst, Harry, 188
Appleton, Richard, 105
asylum seekers, 18
  from DPRK, 190

former colonials, 77
illegal migrants, 151
and Japanese courts, 187
political support, 189
from PRC, 189
from ROK, 188

base towns, 15, 128
Beheiren, 166
Bladin, Air Vice-Marshall Francis, 90
border controls, 3, 4, 6, 7, 17
  documentation, 21
  and the historian, 21
  international dimensions, 6–7
  Keibōdan, 95
  and terrorism, 246
border crossers, categories of, 17, 20,
  21
border politics see border controls
border post, 5
British Commonwealth Forces, Korea (BCFK),
  125
British Commonwealth Occupation Force
  (BCOF), 54, 64, 125
  and mikkōsha, 69
Brown, Margery Finn, 131
Buck-Morss, Susan, 115
Burns, C. R., 58
Busan detention camp, 156

Calcutta Accord see repatriation agreement,
  Japan and DPRK
Cambodia, refugees from, 236
Caprio, Mark, 64
censorship of letters from DPRK, 218
  Ōmura, 160
Chang, Myun, 80
Chiang Kai-shek, 190
China, People's Republic of, 189, 196
  repatriation to, 194

China, Republic of (Taiwan), 190, 195, 196
  deportation to, 195
Chinese in Japan
  employment, 177
  population, 195
Chinese labour migration, 44
Chinese Nationalist government, 61
Chitose, 132
Cho, Rin-Sik, 66, 67, 68
Choi, Deok-Hyo, 101
cholera, 68
  and border controls, 70
  at Senzaki, 56–8
Chongryun see General Association of Korean
  Residents in Japan
Chōsen seki, 94
Chung, Hun-Sung, 160
citizenship, and migration, 111
Civil Defence Force (Keibōdan), 94–5
Clark Line *see* United Nations Sea Defence
  Line
Clifton, Alan, 62–3
coastguard, 96
  see also Maritime Safety Agency
Cold War, 45, 173, 190
  and border controls, 14, 97–8
  and Chinese in Japan, 196
  cross-border movement, 195
  and nationality policy, 113
  repatriation, 194
  and US bases, 124
Collaer, Nicholas D., 97, 105–7, 111, 112
  background, 103–4
  on deportation, 106, 110
  'excluded aliens', 108, 120
  guide to migration law, 107–8
  on subversives, 106
colonization, Korea, 32
'comfort women', 135
Commission on Immigration and
  Naturalization (US), 99
Committee for Republic of Korea Political
  Refugees in Japan, 187
Committee on Counter-Measures against
  Communism in the Far East, 105
Conde, David, 65
Congressional debates, migration (US), 98–100
conscientious objectors, 179
conscription ordinance 1944, 39
Constitution of Japan, Article, 3, 96
Cottrell, Nickolas, 106, 107, 111
Crystal City, Texas, 105

Dadaepo, 81
death sentences, journalists in ROK, 187

dekasegi workers, 241, 244
deportation, of Koreans, 80, 100, 102–3
  appeals against, 110
  choice of destination, 163
  of deserters, 166
  to DPRK, 161
  in Migration Control Ordinance, 109–10
  from Ōmura, 149, 153–6, 155
  of people with criminal convictions,
    152–3
  protests against, 102
  to ROC, 195
  to ROK, 160, 162
  SCAP, 103
  Shin Chang-Seok case, 177
  see also repatriation, postwar, of Koreans in
    Japan
detention and fishing rights, 156
  Shin Chang-Seok, 179
  see also Ōmura Migrant Detention Centre
Diet Members' League for Promoting
    Exchanges of Foreign Human Resources,
    244
Directive No. 42, 1899, 44
disarmament, 96
discretionary decisions, 175–7
'displaced persons', 33
Dokdo [Takeshima], 29, 31
Douglass, Mike, 13
Dower, John, 11, 53
Durand, André, 214

East Sea, 33–4
  see also Sea of Japan
emigration, from Japan, 17, 33
ethnic minorities in Japan, 12
exceptional leave to remain (ELR), 175
extraterritoriality and statistics, 127
  US military forces, 127

family registration, 42–3
  in colonies, 43
Far Eastern Commission, 59, 61
fingerprinting, 90, 92, 114–5
  campaign against, 233–5
  and grassroots activists, 234
  reintroduction of, 246
Finn, R. B., 113
fishing rights, and detention, 156
fishing zone, 28, 29, 31
foreign residents, 177
  1975 onwards, 239
  Allied military forces, 14, 15
  employment, 177
  local voting rights, 195

foreign residents (*cont.*)
  'ordinary aliens', 240
  passports, 44
  permitted occupations, 44
  registration of, 45
  reports of crimes by, 240
Fort Stanton, Texas, 104
Foucault, Michel, 128
4H movement, 184
franchise, female vote, 60
  foreigners in local government, 245
frontiers, internal, 6
Fujiyama, Aiichirō, 199
Fukuda, Takeo, 178

General Association of Korean Residents in
    Japan (*Chongryun, Sōren*), 197, 201, 210,
    231
  and JRC, 208–9
  and Ōmura, 161, 166
  and 'repatriation project', 201–2, 205, 207,
    212
General Headquarters of the Supreme
    Commander for the Allied Powers (GHQ
    SCAP), 46, 59, 60
  on asylum seekers, 78
  deportation of Koreans, 103, 105
  disarmament, 94, 96
  immigration service, 97
  Imperial Ordinance No. 311, 68
  Korean War refugees, 78–81
  Migration Control Law, 97, 108–9
  nationality policy, 60, 112, 113
  see also Allied Occupation
Geneva Conference, 77
Geneva Convention on the Status of Refugees
    (1951), 76, 77, 187, 190, 237
  1967 Protocol, 237
  Koreans in Japan, 189
Gilbert M. Hitchcock (ship), 52, 53, 56, 57
Gillem, Mark, 128
Goffman, Erving, 149, 150
Great Kantō Earthquake 1923, 43

Hamamatsu Detention Centre, 155, 156, 195
  1955 riot, 195
Han, Jong-Seok, 234
Hario repatriation camp, 6, 57, 58, 67, 68, 78,
    147
  deportations from, 80, 148
Hatoyama, Ichirō, 206
Hayashi, Kōzō, 167
'Heo, Mr', 179–80, 181–2
'hep', 180
Herbert, Wolfgang, 239

heterotopia, 128
Hiratsuka, Shigeki, 140
Hitachi, ethnic discrimination case, 231
homogeneity, Japan, 10
Howard government (Australia), 4
Huh, Chung, 220–1
Hyun, Moo-Am, 128, 164

illegal immigrants and asylum seekers, 150
  parole, 178
  see also undocumented migrants
imin (migrant), 13
Immigration Agency, 105, 148
  local offices, 149
  and Ōmura, 148
  see also Immigration Bureau
Immigration and Nationality Act (US), 111
Immigration and Naturalization Law 1952
    (US) (McCarran-Walter Law), 98, 99–100
Immigration and Naturalization Service (US),
    104–5
Immigration Bureau, 109, 229
Immigration Control Agency *see* Immigration
    Bureau
Immigration Control and Refugee Recognition
    Law, 190, 237
  reforms in 1990s, 241
  'Work Training Program', 241
  see also Immigration Control Law
Immigration Control Law, 97, 109–11, 152,
    154, 175
  Collaer proposal, 108
  criminals, 152–3
  discretion of state, 110
  permanent residence, 113
  'sabotage', 110
  'subversives', 109
Immigration Control Ordinance 1951, 97, 108,
    176
  deportation, 109–10
  and former colonials, 114
  see also Immigration Control Law 1952
immigration policies, 4
  in 1980s, 18
  Cold War, 98
  and global events, 246
  of US, 98, 99
Immigration Service Division, 96
  see also Migration Agency
Imperial Ordinance No. 311, 68
Imperial Ordinance No. 352, 42, 43
  implementation of, 44
Incheon Landing, 141
Inomata, Kōzō, 189
Inoue, Masutarō, 199, 202, 203, 206

International Committee of the Red Cross
  (ICRC), 163, 165, 188
  and Ōmura, 162
  and 'repatriation project', 202, 204, 205, 207
  repatriation screening, 206, 211, 213
  review of repatriation, 214–5, 217
International Convention on the Status of
  Refugees, 18
interview data, 23
Ishihara, Shintarō, 240
Ishikawajima Harima, 173
Iyotani, Toshio, 4

'Jae, Mr', 184–7
Japan Red Cross Society (JRC), 188
  and *Chongryun*, 208–9
  negotiations with ICRC, 206
  repatriation from China, 196
  and 'repatriation project', 201, 202, 203, 204
  repatriation to ROK, 219
  welfare study, 199
Japan–Korea Association, 166
Japanese Maritime Security Agency, 81
Japayuki-san, 243
jazz, 133
Jeju Island, 29, 34, 71, 74, 178, 184
  1 March rising, 72
  4.3 Incident (Sa-Sam Sageon), 73,
    74–5, 95
  divers, 36
  labour recruitment, 38
  links with Osaka, 180
  migrants to Japan, 34, 179
  refugees from, 79
  tax protests, 36
Junod, Michel, 210

Kang, Sang-Jung, 100
Kaur, Amarjit, 3
Kawasaki Detention Centre, 154, 186
Kim, Dae-Jung, kidnapping of , 235
Kim, Dong-Gi, 166, 179
Kim, Il-Sung, 174, 205
Kim, Jong-Pil, 221
Kim, Seok-Beom, 13, 75
Kim, Shi-Jong, 75
Kimigayo II (ship), 34
Kishi, Nobusuke , 207
Kobe school demonstrations, 101
  SCAP perspective, 101
'Koh, Mr', 1–3, 79
Koh, Sun-Hui, 183
Komai, Hiroshi, 13
Korea, decolonization, 152
  as Japanese colony, 32, 33, 36

Korea, Democratic People's Republic of
  (DPRK), 160, 174, 198
  aid to, 174
  and *Chongryun*, 209
  and Ōmura, 161
  reception centres, 218
  refugees in Japan, 190
  repatriates' lives, 215
  repatriation to, 163, 194, 197–8,
    203, 205, 206, 218
Korea, Republic of (ROK), 93, 94
  asylum seekers, 235
  on deportation, 153
  and Jeju, 74
  and Ōmura detainees, 161, 162
  postwar negotiations with Japan, 152
  repatriation to, 194, 198, 219–21
'Korean-Japanese', 243
Korean League (*Chōren*), 100, 101, 173
  conflict with SCAP, 101
Korean peninsula 1945–8, 31
  38th parallel, 31
Korean Residents Union in Japan (*Mindan*),
    101, 220, 231
  Korean War, 141
  Ōmura, 161
Korean War, 19, 76, 173
  civilian executions, 76
  civilian movement, 139
  coordination from Japan, 139–40
  effect on youth, 174
  Japanese volunteers, 140–1
  Korean volunteers from Japan, 141, 154
  Okinawa, 136
  Ōmura, 161
  protests, 173, 174
  refugees in Japan, 78–81
  Tokyo Airlift, 139
  troops in Japan, 139
  and US bases in Japan, 125–6
Koreans and Chinese, under occupation, 59,
    60, 61, 63–5
Koreans in Japan (*Zainichi* Koreans), 100, 175,
    178–9, 229
  activism against ROK government, 235
  as 'aliens', 114–5
  associations, 100
  and asylum seekers, 235
  criminals, 152
  deportation of, 100
  diversity among, 233–5
  employment, 177, 231
  entrepreneurs, 179–80
  former colonials, 61, 111
  Korean War volunteers, 141

Koreans in Japan (*Zainichi* Koreans) (*cont.*)
  nationality, 93, 113
  Normalization Treaty, 230
  in Okinawa, 135
  options for youth, 232–3
  population, 34, 242
  poverty among, 199
  repatriate re-entry, 69
  repatriation to DPRK, 197, 198
  residence status, 114, 152, 235
  revised Nationality Law, 238
  second generation, 230
  stereotypes of, 217
  surveillance of, 174
  Third Way, 233
koseki system *see* family registration
Kuwabara, Yasuo, 12
kyōsei renkō (forced recruitment), 37, 39
  see also labour conscription
Kyushu, 31

labour conscription, 38–40
  implementation, 39
  of Koreans, 39, 41, 172
  numbers, 39–40
  of skilled migrants, 245
  stages of, 38
  of women, 39, *see also teishintai*
labour shortage, and migration policy, 241
  and undocumented migrants, 239
Le Carré, John, 151
League of Korean Residents in Japan, 62
'Lee, Shin-Ok', 159
Li, Chang-Yeon, 200–1
'liberated people', 59
liberty ships, 52, 53
'Lim, Miss', 213
Livelihood Protection, 199, 224
  crackdown on, 204
  under Normalization Treaty, 230

MacArthur, General Douglas, 3, 28, 61, 80
MacArthur Line, 28–31, 30
Maizuru, 68
Maritime Safety Agency, 96
Maritime Safety Board, 96
  see also Maritime Safety Agency
massacres, Jeju Island, 64
McCarran, Senator Pat, 99, 108
McCarran-Walter Law *see* Immigration and
  Naturalization Law 1952
Merritt, Marian, 131
migrant detention centres, long-term inmates,
  151
  as total institutions, 150

in US, 104, 105
migrant labour, 179–81
  Anglo-American and European, 243
migration, colonial, 34–7
  Chinese labour, 44
  employment, 37
  forced recruitment, 37, 38 *see also* labour
    conscription
  Koreans, 40
migration, to Japan, 6, 8, 9
  history, 9–11, 12–13
  terminology, 13–14
Migration Agency, 96
migration agents, 182
Migration Control Agency, 82
migration control system, 6, 7
  1920s and 1930s, 43
  Collaer report, 106
  foreign migration, 43
  Koreans and Chinese in Japan, 195
  history of, 41–5
  Ōmura, 148–9
  postwar, 11
mikkōsha (stowaways), 20, 55, 67, 95
  alien registration, 92
  coastal watch, 95
  from Jeju, 73
  Koreans, 69
  patrols against, 68, 69
  see also refugees; undocumented migrants
Miles, Robert, 5
'military brats', 127
Military Government of the Ryukyu
  Islands , 46
Mindan see Korean Residents Union in Japan
Ministry of Foreign Affairs (Japan), 96, 109,
  200, 201–3, 208–9
Ministry of Health and Welfare (Japan), 78,
  204, 212
Ministry of Justice (Japan), 78, 80, 108, 109,
  113, 182, 200
Minsen see Zainichi Korean Unified
  Democratic Front
Misawa, 134
Moon Se-Gwang Incident, 235

naisen ittai (integrating Japan and Korea), 10
Nakamura, Masakichi, 148, 157
Nam, Il, 198
National Labour Mobilization Law 1939, 38
Nationalism, immigration debates, 246
  in schools, 173
nationality in colonial period, 42, 43
  of former colonials, 60, 111
  Koreans in Japan, 113

Nationality Law 1899 (Kokuseki Hō), 42
Nationality Law 1950, 112
    revised 1985, 238
nationality laws, 41
    reforms, 246
naturalization of foreigners in Japan, 232
    Koreans, 232
    rise in numbers, 242
    Taiwanese, 243
Naval Junior Reserve, 173
New Left, and Ōmura, 166
New Zealand troops, Senzaki, 58
Niigata Red Cross Centre, 6, 209–10, 211
    Special Rooms, 210–12
Nikkeijin, 241–2
Normalization Treaty *see* Treaty of Basic
    Relations between Japan and the Republic
    of Korea 1965
North Korea *see* Korea, Democratic People's
    Republic of
North Korean Red Cross, 203, 204
North-West League, 73

occupation *see* Allied occupation
'occupation personnel', Okinawa, 136
Ogasawara archipelago, 134, 135
    reversion, 138
Oguma, Eiji, 10
Oh, Gi-Wan, 217
Okazaki, Katsuo, 108
Okinawa *see* Ryukyu archipelago
Okinawans, as former colonials, 61
Ōmura Korean Literary Society, 166
Ōmura Literature, 166
    see also Ōmura Korean Literary Society
Ōmura Migrant Detention Centre, 6, 17, 20,
    105, 147, 155, 158, 162, 165, 178
    accommodation, 156, 157
    communication with outside, 160
    control of life, 157, 159
    daily life, 156
    debate in Diet, 166
    deportation from, 153–6, 155, 163
    health conditions, 158
    as heterotopia, 149
    indefinite internment, 154
    isolation cells, 157
    Korean War, 161–4
    literary output, 166
    mass breakout, 154
    Nazi analogy, 167
    official opening, 149
    political activity, 159, 160–1
    purpose of, 154
    recent years, 164, 248

repatriation to DPRK, 198
    and social movements, 165–7
    suicides, 159
    as symbol, 164
Osaka, 34
    Ikuno-ku, 179
    Korean migrants, 36, 179
    links with Jeju, 180
    migrant population, 180
Oshitani, Tomizō, 102

pachinko, 177
Pacific Stars and Stripes, 126, 131
Pak, Heon-Yeong, 174
Pak, Jae-Il, 197
Pak, Jeong-Sok, 230
'Pak, Young-Sik', 19
Park, Chung-Hee, 178, 181, 187, 221, 230
    assasination plot, 235
    and repatriation, 221
passports, 44
Peace Line *see* Rhee Line
people smuggling, 55, 81, 181, 184–5
    see also mikkōsha
permanent residence, 113
Peruvians, of Japanese descent, 104
'Plan for Arranging the Sending to North
    Korea of those who wish to be
    Repatriated', 201–2, 203
police, Japanese, in occupation, 64
population crisis, and migrants, 244
population, Japan, 8
Potsdam Declaration, 28
prisoners of war, British, 3
    camps, 63
    Korean War, 103
    North Korean and Chinese, 203
    screening, 203
Pu, Song-Gyu, 40–1
Public Security Agency, 178

racial exclusion laws, 99
racial segregation, on US bases, 133
Recreation and Amusement
    Association, 132
Red Lamp Incident, 174
refugees, 151
    1978 policy, 6
    Cold War, 98
    from Indochina, 236, 237
    Jeju Island, 79
    Korean War, 78–81
    political, from ROK, 187
    reception centres, 238
    recognition, 190

refugees (*cont.*)
    see also asylum seekers; *mikkōsha*;
        undocumented migrants
relocation, Latin America to US, 104
    of Koreans in Japan *see* repatriation,
        postwar, of Koreans in Japan
repatriation, postwar, of Chinese in Japan, 55
    to PRC, 196
repatriation, postwar, of Japanese, 54, 196
repatriation, postwar, of Koreans in Japan, 17,
        156, 199
    Japan to Jeju, 71
    to ROK, 194, 219–21, 220
    Senzaki, 54
    targets, 204
    voluntary, 205–6
    see also deportation
repatriation, postwar SCAP program, 65, 66,
        67
    Cold War, 194
    voluntary, 194
'repatriation project', Japan and DPRK, 162,
        163–4, 197–8, 200, 204–5
    Calcutta Accord, 201, 203, 206
    Chongryun and JRC, 208
    concerns of youth, 213
    economic hardship, 216
    extensions, 217
    Guide Book, 207
    and ICRC, 202, 213, 214–5
    Japanese government role, 206–7
    and JRC, 219
    lack of information, 212
    life after arrival, 215–6, 218
    numbers to DPRK, 208
    and ROK, 202, 204
    screening, 207
    and US, 202
    versus original plan, 208
Rhee Line, 31, 30, 156
Roberts, Glenda, 13
Roosevelt, Franklin D., 32
Russo-Japanese War 1904–5, 33
Ryukyu Archipelago, 31, 61, 134, 135–8
    border control, postwar, 135
    cross-border movement, 136
    nationality issues, 137
    penal code, 136
    separation policy, 137
    US bases, 137

Sakanaka, Hidenori, 8, 182, 229, 231, 244
    essay, 232
sakoku (closed country), 10
San Francisco Peace Negotiations 1951, 61

San Francisco Peace Treaty, Korea, 152
    nationality of former colonials, 113
sangokujin ('third-country people'), 100, 240
Sansui (ship), 153
Sasebo, 147 *see also* Hario
SCAP *see* General Headquarters of the
        Supreme Commander for the Allied
        Powers
SCAP Directive, 47, 163
Schmitt, Carl, 18
schools, and nationalism, 173
Sea of Japan, migration across, 33–4
    see also East Sea
Senzaki repatriation camp, 6, 53–9, 56, 65, 68
    cholera, 56–8
    New Zealand troops, 58
servants, US bases, 130
Shaw, Patrick, 65, 77
Shephard, Mary, 135
Shin, Chang-Seok, 172, 173
    journey to DPRK, 174
    in Ōmura, 178–9
    presenting case, 177
    sentence of, 177
Shinagawa Immigration Office, 186
Sino-Japanese War 1894–5, 33
social movements, and Ōmura, 165–7
'Song of Ōmura', 160
South Korea *see* Korea, Republic of
South Korean Workers Party (Nam Joseon
        Nodongdang), 71, 72, 73
Special Investigations Division, Ministry of
        Justice, 108
special permanent residence (*tokurei eijū*), 235,
        237
special permission to stay (*zairyū tokubetsu
        kyoka*), 111, 167, 175, 176, 179,
        182, 190
    1950s–1960s, 176
    community support, 183, 186
    limitations of, 182
    marriages, 176
    migration agents, 182
    as policy tool, 175–7
    process of, 179
    role of politicians, 178, 179
    Shin Chang-Seok, 179
'Special Rooms', Niigata Red Cross Centre,
        210–2
Spencer, Stephen, 12
state, and the individual, 5
Status of Forces Agreement (SOFA),
        126, 127
    NATO, 126
stereotypes, 'Japanese', 242

in occupation, 64

Taikan Minkoku *see* Korea, Republic of
Taiwan, 195
  Nationality Law, 1899, 42
  see also China, Republic of
Taiwanese former colonials, 61, 111
  naturalization of, 243
  occupation attitude to, 63–4
  residence status, 114
Takahashi, Masaaki, murder of, 123
Takeshima *see* Dokdo
taxes, on colonies, 36
teishintai system, 39
  see also 'comfort women'
terrorism, and border controls, 246
Testuz, Michel, 217, 218
'Third Way', 233–4
thirty-eighth parallel, 31, 32
Tinian Island, 41
total institutions, 149–50
  categories, 150
Traitors' Punishment Law, 77
Treaty of Basic Relations between Japan and
  the Republic of Korea 1965, 181, 221
  status of Koreans in Japan, 230
treaty permanent residents (*kyōtei eijūsha*),
  181, 230
  fingerprinting, 234
Truman, President Harry S., 99
Tsushima, 29, 37

Ujina, 62
Ulleungdo, 29
undocumented migrants, 16, 18, 180
  1975 onwards, 239
  community support, 183, 186
  discretionary decisions, 175–7
  employment, 180
  legal appeals, 187–90
  letters, 22
  marriage, 185
  motivation of, 20
  population, 180
  stereotypes of criminality, 240
  see also refugees; asylum seekers
United Nations Convention on the Status of
  Refugees *see* Geneva Convention 1951
United Nations High Commissioner for
  Refugees (UNHCR), 188
United Nations International Decade of
  Women, and nationality law, 238
United Nations Sea Defence Line, 30, 31
United Nations Universal Declaration of
  Human Rights, 112

United States of America Military Government
  in Korea (USAMGIK), 46
US Internal Security Law (McCarran Law), 98
US military bases, Japan, 6, 47, 124, 126
  civilians on, 126
  connections between, 138–9
  economic impact of, 132
  education, 130–1
  as employers, 132
  food, 130
  as heterotopias, 128, 138
  housing, 128
  hygiene, 130
  influence of, 13, 124, 132
  Korean War, 139
  location of, 128
  'occupation personnel', 136
  Okinawa, 137
  protests against, 134
  racial segregation, 133
  Sasebo, 147
  servants, 130, 132
  size of, 131
  as towns, 125, 128–31
  Vietnam War, 236
  wives, 130, 131
US military forces, Japan, 123, 126
  AWOL personnel, 123
  dependents and civilians, 125, 126, 128
  extraterritoriality, 127
  see also Allied military forces; US military
  bases, Japan
US–Japan Security Treaty, 126, 127
  and DPRK repatriation, 205
  and Okinawa, 138
  protests against, 134

Vietnam, refugees from, 236
Vietnam War, 179, 236
  protests against, 166–7

Walter, Congressman Francis E., 99
War Relocation Authority (US), 104
Washington Heights, 133
welfare, to Koreans in Japan, 199, 206
welfare system 1959, 207
White Australia policy, 44

xenophobia, 10

Yakabi, Osamu, 136
Yamaguchi Prefecture, Keibōdan, 95
Yamawaki, Keizō, 13, 34
'Yang, Mr', 71, 73, 75
Yi Dynasty, 33

Index

Yi, Seung-man, 31, 173
  fall of, 181, 220
Yi, Hoe-Seong , 13
Yokohama Detention Centre, 154
Yonaguni, and Taiwan, 136
Yoon, Hak-Joon, 81–2, 92–3
Yoon, Soo-Gil, 188–9
Yoshida, Shigeru, 102, 109
Yoshikawa, Mitsusada, 108

Yoshimi, Shunya, 132

Zainichi Korean Repatriation Cooperation
  Society, 206
Zainichi Korean Unified Democratic Front
  (Minsen), 200, 201
Zainichi Koreans *see* Koreans in Japan
Zengakuren, 166
Zhou, Hongjing, 189

Made in the USA
Middletown, DE
06 January 2020